HOLT | SPANISH 1A

¡Exprésate!®

Nancy Humbach

Sylvia Madrigal Velasco

Ana Beatriz Chiquito

Stuart Smith

John McMinn

HOLT, RINEHART AND WINSTON

A Harcourt Education Company

Orlando • Austin • New York • San Diego • London

Holt Teacher Advisory Panel

As members of the **Holt World Languages Advisory Panel,** the following teachers made a unique and invaluable contribution to the *¡Exprésate!* Spanish program. They generously shared their experience and expertise in a collaborative group setting and helped refine early materials into the program design represented in this book. We wish to thank them for the many hours of work they put into the development of this program and for the many ideas they shared.

¡Muchísimas gracias a todos!

Erick Ekker
Bob Miller Middle School
Henderson, NV

Dulce Goldenberg
Miami Senior High School
Miami, FL

Beckie Gurnish
Ellet High School
Akron, OH

Bill Heller
Perry High School
Perry, NY

MilyBett Llanos
Westwood High School
Austin, TX

Rosanna Perez
Communications Arts
High School
San Antonio, TX

Jo Schuler
Central Bucks High School East
Doylestown, PA

Leticia Schweigert
Science Academy
Mercedes, TX

Claudia Sloan
Lake Park High School
Roselle, IL

Judy Smock
Gilbert High School
Gilbert, AZ

Catriona Stavropoulos
West Springfield High School
Springfield, VA

Nina Wilson
Burnet Middle School
Austin, TX

Janet Wohlers
Weston Middle School
Weston, MA

ISBN-13: 978-0-03-045133-1
ISBN-10:   0-03-045133-7
1 2 3 4 5 6 7 8 048 09 08 07 06

Authors

Nancy Humbach

Nancy Humbach is Associate Professor and Coordinator of Languages Education at Miami University, Oxford, Ohio. She has authored or co-authored over a dozen textbooks in Spanish. A former Fulbright-Hayes Scholar, she has lived and studied in Colombia and Mexico and has traveled and conducted research throughout the Spanish-speaking world. She is a recipient of many honors, including the Florence Steiner Award for Leadership in the Foreign Language Profession and the Nelson Brooks Award for the Teaching of Culture.

Sylvia Madrigal Velasco

Sylvia Madrigal Velasco was born in San Benito, Texas. The youngest of four siblings, she grew up in the Rio Grande Valley, between two cultures and languages. Her lifelong fascination with Spanish has led her to travel in many Spanish-speaking countries. She graduated from Yale University in 1979 and has worked for over 20 years as a textbook editor and author at various publishing companies. She has written bilingual materials, video scripts, workbooks, CD-ROMs, and readers.

Ana Beatriz Chiquito

Professor Ana Beatriz Chiquito is a native of Colombia. She teaches Spanish linguistics and Latin American culture at the University of Bergen, Norway, and conducts research and develops applications for language learning at the Center for Educational Computing Initiatives at the Massachusetts Institute of Technology. She has taught Spanish for more than thirty years and has authored numerous textbooks, CD-ROMs, videos, and on-line materials for college and high school students of Spanish.

Stuart Smith

Stuart Smith began her teaching career at the University of Texas at Austin from where she received her degrees. She has been a professor of foreign languages at Austin Community College, Austin, Texas, for over 20 years and has been writing textbook and teaching materials for almost as long. She has given presentations on language teaching methodology at ACTFL, SWCOLT, and TCCTA.

John McMinn

John McMinn is Professor of Spanish and French at Austin Community College, where he has taught since 1986. After completing his M.A. in Romance Linguistics at the University of Texas at Austin, he also taught Spanish and French at the secondary level and was a Senior Editor of World Languages at Holt, Rinehart and Winston. He is co-author of both Spanish and French textbooks at the college level.

Reviewers

These educators reviewed one or more chapters of the Student Edition.

Elizabeth Baird
Independence High School
Independence, OH

Paula Camardella Twomey
Ithaca High School
Ithaca, NY

Ana Carlsgaard
Zionsville High School
Zionsville, IN

Johnnie Eng
Alamo 7 High School
San Antonio, TX

Howard Furnas
Spain Park High School
Hoover, AL

Patricia Gander
Berkeley High School
Moncks Corner, SC

Laura Grable
Riverhead Central High School
District
Riverhead, NY

Lisa Greene
Southside High School
Greenville, SC

Mani Hernández
Presentation High School
San Jose, CA

Yoscelina Hernández
Montwood High School
El Paso, TX

Cathy Teal Johnson
Mountain Brook High School
Birmingham, AL

Jorge Muñoz
St. Stephen's Episcopal School
Austin, TX

Kathy Sherman
Hamilton Southeastern High
School
Fishers, IN

Jessica Shrader
Riverview High School
Sarasota, FL

Jeannette L. Sipp
Parkway South High School
Ballwin, MO

Sharlene Soto
D.C. Everest Jr. and Sr. High
Schools
Wausau, WI

Pamela Valdés
Emmerich Manual High School
Indianapolis, IN

Gail Valdez
Gadsden High School
Gadsden, AL

Nancy Walker de Llanas
George C. Marshall High School
Falls Church, VA

Jackie Weaver
Eastside High School
Taylors, SC

Dee Webster
North Central High School
Indianapolis, IN

Thomasina I. White
Lead Academic Coach
World Language Education
Philadelphia, PA

Shanna Yown
Mauldin High School
Mauldin, SC

Field Test Participants

We thank the teachers and students who participated in the field test of *¡Exprésate!*

Tim Burel
West Middle School
Rockford, IL

Liliana Camarena
Gueillen Middle School
El Paso, TX

Mariluz Julio
Clover Junior High School
Clover, SC

Patrice Kahn
Noel Grisham Middle School
Austin, TX

Rebekeh Lindsey
Campbell Middle School
Daytona Beach, FL

Estela Morel
Corlears Middle School 56
New York, NY

Linda Schell
Landmark Middle School
Jacksonville, FL

Sarah Taylor
Richland Middle School
Richmond, VA

Rebecca Taylor-Norton
Beechwood Middle School
Cleveland, OH

Amanda York
George Washington
Carver Academy
Waco, TX

Contenido en breve

España

Capítulo 1 ¡Empecemos! 4

Geocultura

Molinos de viento, España

En video

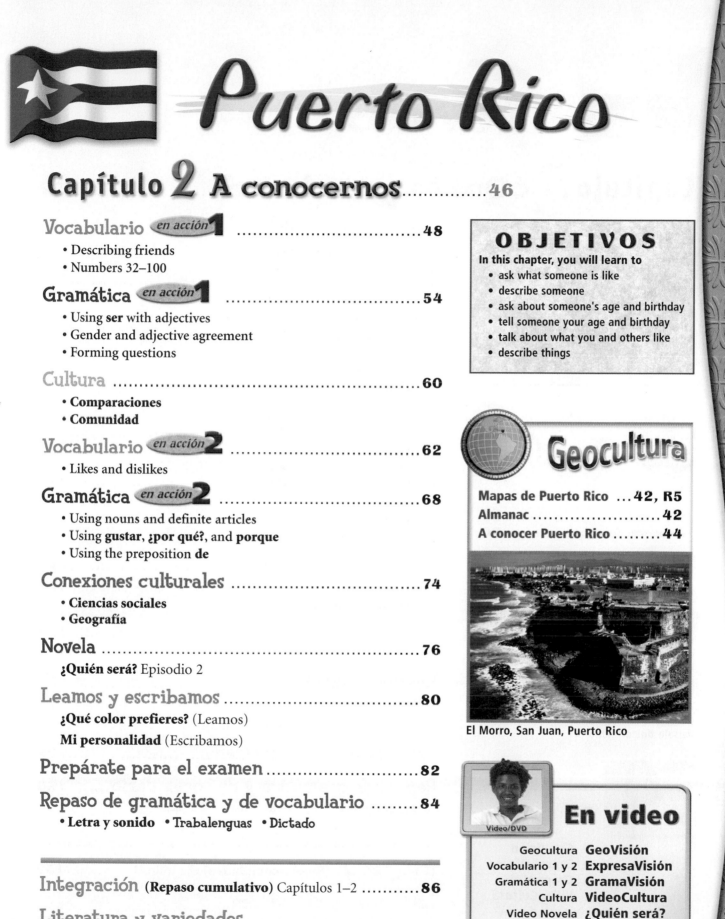

Puerto Rico

OBJETIVOS

In this chapter, you will learn to
- ask what someone is like
- describe someone
- ask about someone's age and birthday
- tell someone your age and birthday
- talk about what you and others like
- describe things

Geocultura

El Morro, San Juan, Puerto Rico

En video

Geocultura **GeoVisión**
Vocabulario 1 y 2 **ExpresaVisión**
Gramática 1 y 2 **GramaVisión**
Cultura **VideoCultura**
Video Novela **¿Quién será?**

Variedades

Texas

Capítulo 3 ¿Qué te gusta hacer? 92

Costa Rica

Capítulo 4 La vida escolar 138

OBJETIVOS

In this chapter, you will learn to
- say what you have and what you need
- talk about school supplies and school subjects
- talk about plans and give invitations
- talk about school events and places

Geocultura

El volcán Arenal, Costa Rica

Video/DVD

En video

Geocultura **GeoVisión**
Vocabulario 1 y 2 **ExpresaVisión**
Gramática 1 y 2 **GramaVisión**
Cultura **VideoCultura**
Video Novela **¿Quién será?**

Variedades

Chile

Capítulo 5 En casa con la familia 184

Páginas de referencia

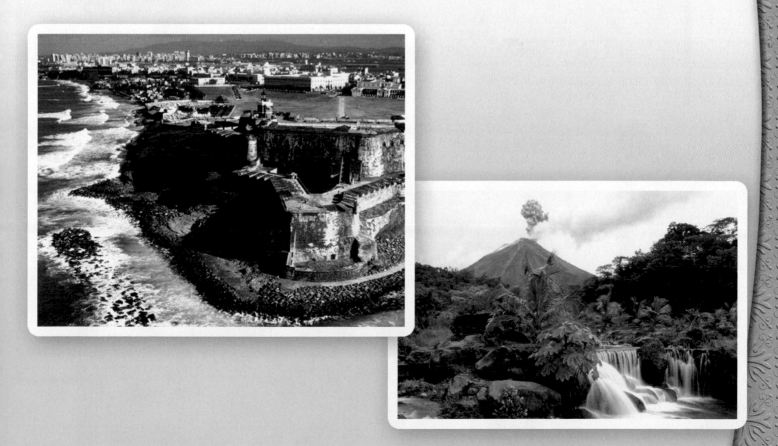

El español, ¿por qué?
Why Study Spanish?

Por lo mundial *Because it's worldwide*

Spanish is the fourth most commonly spoken language in the world. You can visit any one of 21 countries in the world that speak Spanish and feel at home. Even in the United States, knowing Spanish can open doors to you.

So whether you're in Europe, North, Central, or South America, or even Africa, as a Spanish speaker you won't have to rely on someone else to watch television or read a newspaper. You'll learn things on your own. You'll truly be a citizen of the world.

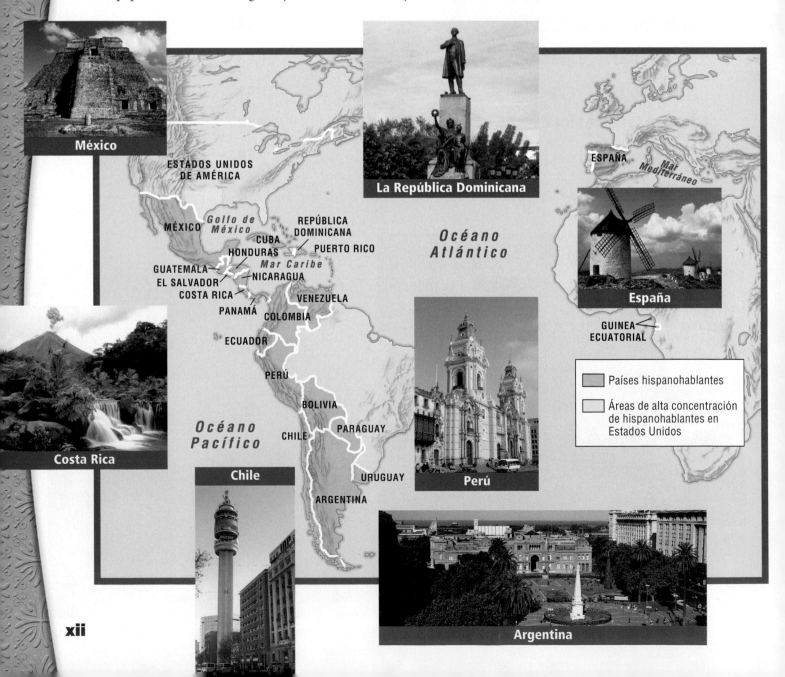

México

La República Dominicana

España

Costa Rica

Chile

Perú

Argentina

ESTADOS UNIDOS DE AMÉRICA

MÉXICO
Golfo de México
REPÚBLICA DOMINICANA
CUBA
HONDURAS
PUERTO RICO
GUATEMALA
Mar Caribe
EL SALVADOR
NICARAGUA
COSTA RICA
VENEZUELA
PANAMÁ
COLOMBIA
ECUADOR
PERÚ
BOLIVIA
PARAGUAY
CHILE
URUGUAY
ARGENTINA

Océano Atlántico
Océano Pacífico

ESPAÑA
Mar Mediterráneo
GUINEA ECUATORIAL

Países hispanohablantes

Áreas de alta concentración de hispanohablantes en Estados Unidos

Por lo bello *Because it's beautiful*

You'll be amazed to discover how rich the Spanish-speaking world is in works of music, literature, science, religion, and art. The novels of Miguel de Cervantes or Isabel Allende, the paintings of Fernando Botero or Frida Kahlo, the poetry of Gabriela Mistral or Pablo Neruda: all these treasures and many more await you as you explore the Spanish-speaking world.

Ceramic tiles form this mural by Dominican artist Said Musa.

Traditional painted carts in Costa Rica are a part of El Festival de las Carretas.

The fountain of Cibeles, named after the goddess Cybele, is one of Madrid's best-known landmarks.

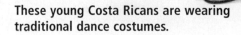

These young Costa Ricans are wearing traditional dance costumes.

Por lo práctico *Because it's practical*

You're living in the country with the fifth-largest Hispanic population in the world, more than 33 million people. And whether they're originally from Mexico, Puerto Rico, or Cuba—or from any other part of Latin America or Spain—almost nine out of ten are Spanish speakers.

Businesses, government agencies, educational institutions, and other employers will be looking for more bilingual employees every year. Give yourself an edge in the job market with Spanish!

Bilingual doctors, nurses, and others in the field of medicine provide care for Spanish-speaking patients.

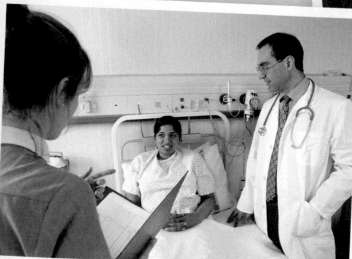

Patricia Janiot is a popular anchor at the Spanish language news department of CNN En Español.

Miami is an international center and a multicultural hub for Latin American trade.

¡Porque puedes! *Because you can do it!*

Applying your learning skills to a new language will be challenging at first. But you have the tools you need to do the job. And you're lucky to be living at a time when there are almost no limits to your opportunities to practice Spanish. You can interact with Spanish speakers not just in your community but all over the world, via pen pal organizations, at the library, or through a multitude of resources and online networks.

Bicyclists stop at a spot overlooking the historic city of Toledo, Spain.

En fin, porque sí *Finally, just because...*

The best reason of all to study Spanish is because you want to! You know better than anyone what motivated you to enroll for Spanish class. It might be one of the reasons given here, such as getting a job, learning about world issues, or enjoying works of art. Or it might be something more personal, like wanting to communicate with Spanish-speaking friends and family, or travel. So pat yourself on the back and **¡Exprésate!**

En la clase de espanol
In Spanish Class

Here are some phrases you'll probably hear in your classroom, along with some responses.

Phrases:

Tengo una pregunta.
I have a question.

¿Cómo se dice...?
How do you say . . .?

¿Cómo se escribe...?
How do you spell . . .?

No entiendo. ¿Puede repetir?
I don't understand. Could you repeat that?

Más despacio, por favor.
More slowly, please.

¿Sabes qué significa (quiere decir)...?
Do you know what . . . means?

Gracias.
Thank you.

Perdón.
I'm sorry.

Responses:

¿Sí? Dime.
Yes? What is it?

Se dice...
You say . . .

Se escribe...
It's spelled . . .

Claro que sí.
Yes, of course.

No, no sé.
No, I don't know.

Sí, significa (quiere decir)...
Yes, it means . . .

De nada.
You're welcome.

Está bien.
It's okay.

Here are some things your teacher might ask you to do.

Levanten la mano.
Raise your hand.

Escuchen.
Listen.

¡Su atención, por favor!
Attention, please.

Silencio, por favor.
Silence, please.

Abran sus libros en la página...
Open your books to page . . .

Cierren los libros.
Close your books.

Estamos en la página...
We're on page . . .

Miren la pizarra (la transparencia).
Look at the board (transparency).

Saquen una hoja de papel.
Take out a sheet of paper.

Pasen la tarea (los papeles) al frente.
Pass the homework (the papers) to the front.

Levántense, por favor.
Stand up, please.

Siéntense, por favor.
Sit down, please.

Repitan después de mí.
Repeat after me.

Nombres comunes
Common Names

Here are some common names from Spanish-speaking countries.

Nombres de muchachas

Ana	Inés	Patricia
Bárbara	Irene	Pilar
Beatriz	Isabel	Rosalía
Cecilia	Josefina	Rosario
Cristina	Lourdes	Sonia
Dolores	María	Susana
Elena	Maribel	Tamara
Elisa	Marisol	Teresa
Emilia	Nuria	Vanesa
Fátima	Olga	Yolanda

Nombres de muchachos

Alfredo	Francisco	Óscar
Antonio	Gilberto	Pablo
Arturo	Héctor	Pedro
Bruno	Javier	Rafael
Carlos	Julio	Ramón
Daniel	Lorenzo	Roberto
Eduardo	Luis	Sergio
Enrique	Manuel	Tomás
Esteban	Marcos	Vicente
Fernando	Miguel	Víctor

Instrucciones
Directions

Throughout the book, many activities will have directions in Spanish. Here are some of the directions you'll see, along with their English translations.

Completa... con una palabra del cuadro.
Complete . . . with a word from the box.

Completa el párrafo con...
Complete the paragraph with . . .

Completa las oraciones con la forma correcta del verbo.
Complete the sentences with the correct form of the verb.

Con base en..., contesta cierto o falso. Corrige las oraciones falsas.
Based on . . ., respond with true or false. Correct the false sentences.

Con un(a) compañero(a), dramatiza...
With a classmate, act out . . .

Contesta las preguntas usando...
Answer the questions using . . .

Contesta (Completa) las siguientes preguntas (oraciones)...
Answer (Complete) the following questions (sentences) . . .

En parejas (grupos de tres), dramaticen...
In pairs (groups of three), act out . . .

Escoge el dibujo (la respuesta) que corresponde (mejor completa)...
Choose the drawing (the answer) that goes with (best completes) . . .

Escribe..., usando el vocabulario de la página...
Write . . ., using the vocabulary on page . . .

Escucha las conversaciones.
Decide qué conversación (diálogo)
corresponde a cada dibujo (foto).
Listen to the conversations. Decide which conversation
(dialog) corresponds to each drawing (photo).

Mira las fotos (los dibujos) y decide
(di, indica)...
Look at the photos (drawings) and decide
(say, indicate) . . .

Pon en orden...
Put . . . in order.

Pregúntale a tu compañero(a)
Ask your partner

Sigue el modelo.
Follow the model.

Túrnense para...
Take turns . . .

Usa el vocabulario de... para completar...
Use the vocabulary from . . . to complete . . .

Usa una palabra o expresión
de cada columna para escribir...
Use one word or expression
from each column to write . . .

Usa los dibujos para decir lo que pasa.
Use the drawings to say what is happening.

Sugerencias para aprender el español
Tips for learning Spanish

Listen

Listen carefully in class and ask questions if you don't understand. You won't be able to understand everything you hear at first, but don't feel frustrated. You are actually absorbing a lot even when you don't realize it.

Visualize

It may help you to visualize the words you are learning. Associate each new word, sentence, or phrase with a mental picture. For example, if you're learning words for foods, picture the food in your mind and think about the colors, smells, and tastes associated with it. If you are learning about the weather, picture yourself standing in the rain, or fighting a strong wind— something that will help you associate an image with the word or phrase you are learning.

Practice

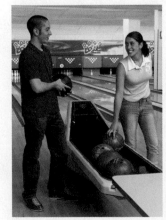

Short, daily practice sessions are more effective than long, once-a-week sessions. Also, try to practice with a friend or a classmate. After all, language is about communication, and it takes two to communicate.

Speak

Practice speaking Spanish aloud every day. Don't be afraid to experiment. Your mistakes will help identify problems, and they will show you important differences in the way English and Spanish work as languages.

Explore

Increase your contact with Spanish outside class in every way you can. Maybe someone living near you speaks Spanish. It's easy to find Spanish-language programs on TV, on the radio, or at the video store, and many magazines and newspapers in Spanish are published or sold in the United States and are on the Internet. Don't be afraid to read, watch, or listen, even if you don't understand every word.

Connect

Making connections between what you learn in other subject areas and what you are learning in your Spanish class will increase your understanding of the new material, help you retain it longer, and enrich your learning experience.

Have fun!

Above all, remember to have fun! Learn as much as you can, because the more you know, the easier it will be for you to relax—and that will make your learning easier and more effective.

¡Buena suerte! (Good luck!)

Ven a conocer más del mundo hispanohablante y...

¡Exprésate!

Video/DVD

GeoVisión

Picos de Europa

Galicia

Geocultura
España

▶ **La Mancha** is a region of Spain made famous in the book *Don Quijote de La Mancha* by Miguel de Cervantes. In the story, the hero sees these windmills as giants.

P O R T U G A L

Salamanca

Almanac

Population
40,341,462

Capital
Madrid

Government
parliamentary monarchy

Languages
Castilian, Catalan, Galician, Basque

Currency euro

Internet Code
www.[ ].es

OCÉANO ATLÁNTICO

▼ **Sevilla** The city of Seville celebrates its annual **Feria de abril** with parades, flowers, and brightly-colored traditional clothing.

Extrem

Río Guadiana

Sevilla

¿Sabías que...?
Did you know that you can see the north coast of Africa from the southernmost point in Spain?

ISLAS CANARIAS

◄ Los Pirineos The Pyrenees mountain range forms a natural border between Spain and France.

► Tossa de Mar is a beach that attracts sunbathers from around the world.

FRANCIA

ANDORRA

Santillana

Bilbao

País Vasco

Los Pirineos

Cataluña

Tossa de Mar

COSTA BRAVA

Barcelona

Castilla y León

Río Ebro

Río Duero

Segovia

Aragón

MAR MEDITERRÁNEO

Sierra de Guadarrama

Ávila

★ MADRID

Sierra de Gredos

Río Tajo

Toledo

Valencia

ESPAÑA

ISLAS BALEARES

dura

Castilla-La Mancha

Alicante

COSTA BLANCA

Córdoba

Murcia

Río Guadalquivir

Granada

Sierra Nevada

Andalucía

Málaga

▲ Madrid This monument to the author Miguel de Cervantes is found in Madrid's **Plaza de España.** The monument includes two of his characters from *Don Quijote de La Mancha,* Don Quijote and Sancho Panza.

▼ Andalucía is a region of Spain that exports olive oil worldwide.

Gibraltar (RU)

Ceuta (ESP)

¿Qué tanto sabes?
Which countries share a border with Spain? What bodies of water surround Spain?

MARRUECOS

A conocer España

Las celebraciones

▲ **Barcelona** The city of Barcelona is known for the **sardana,** a type of dance. Here people are dancing the **sardana** in the plaza in front of the cathedral.

▲ **Las castañuelas**
Castanets are rhythm instruments used in traditional Spanish music.

▲ **Galicia** The region of Galicia in far northwest Spain was settled by Celtic peoples. These Celtic roots are reflected in the musical instruments and festivals of this Spanish province.

La comida

◄ **La paella** Paella is a well-known Spanish dish made of rice, vegetables, seafood, chicken, and sausage.

▲ **La tortilla española** In Spain, a **tortilla** is an omelet made with eggs, onions, and potatoes. It is eaten cold as an appetizer.

La arquitectura

▲ **El Museo de Guggenheim** The Guggenheim Museum in Bilbao is famous for its ultramodern architecture.

El arte

¿Sabías que...?
Did you know that there are five Guggenheim Museums? They are in Bilbao, New York, Las Vegas, Venice, and Berlin. How would you compare the architecture of the Bilbao museum with the city wall of Avila?

▲ **Ávila** The city of Ávila is surrounded by medieval walls that have stood for almost 1000 years.

◀ **Las cuevas de Altamira** The Altamira Caves are famous for the colorful prehistoric art found on their walls. Which colors do you see in this cave painting?

◀ **Personnages Oiseaux** *(Bird People)* The Spanish artist **Joan Miró** lived from 1893 to 1983. Miró used bright, vivid colors in many of his paintings. Which colors does he use in this painting?

▲ **Joan Miró**

rojo · azul · anaranjado · morado · café

verde · amarillo · gris · blanco · negro

¡Empecemos!

Objetivos

In Part 1 you will learn to:
- ask someone's name and give your name
- ask and say who someone is
- ask how someone is and say how you are
- introduce people and say where they are from
- use subjects and verbs in sentences
- use subject pronouns

In Part 2 you will learn to:
- ask for and give phone numbers
- say the time, the date, the day, and the season
- ask how words are spelled and give e-mail addresses
- use the verb **ser** in the present tense
- write Spanish punctuation marks and written accents

¿Qué ves en la foto?

- How are these teenagers greeting each other?

- Based on the photo, what do you think Madrid is like?

PALACIO REAL

Amigos en el parque frente al Palacio Real, Madrid

Objetivos

- Asking someone's name
- Asking how someone is
- Introducing others
- Saying where you and others are from

Vocabulario en acción 1

En Madrid

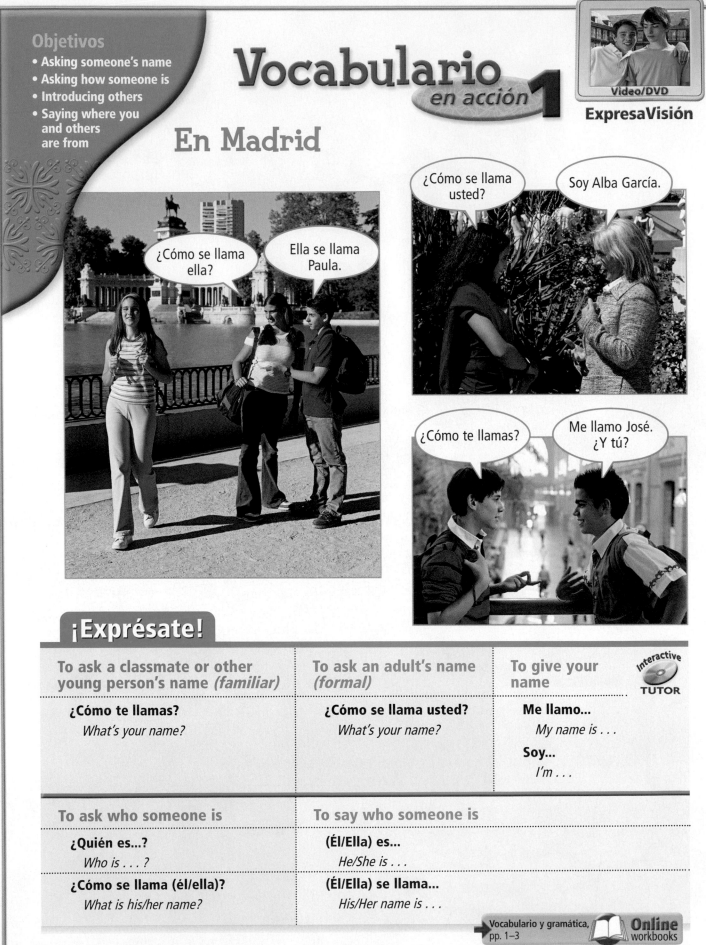

¿Cómo se llama ella?

Ella se llama Paula.

¿Cómo se llama usted?

Soy Alba García.

¿Cómo te llamas?

Me llamo José. ¿Y tú?

¡Exprésate!

Interactive TUTOR

To ask a classmate or other young person's name *(familiar)*	To ask an adult's name *(formal)*	To give your name
¿Cómo te llamas? *What's your name?*	**¿Cómo se llama usted?** *What's your name?*	**Me llamo...** *My name is . . .* **Soy...** *I'm . . .*

To ask who someone is	To say who someone is
¿Quién es...? *Who is . . . ?*	**(Él/Ella) es...** *He/She is . . .*
¿Cómo se llama (él/ella)? *What is his/her name?*	**(Él/Ella) se llama...** *His/Her name is . . .*

Vocabulario y gramática, pp. 1–3

Online workbooks

▶ For **nombres comunes,** see page xvii.

1 ¿Qué hacen?

Escuchemos As you listen, decide whether the people speaking are **a)** asking someone's name or **b)** giving a name.

Visit Holt Online

go.hrw.com
KEYWORD: EXP1A CH1

Vocabulario 1 practice

2 ¿Cómo te llamas?

Leamos Decide if you would say these phrases in scene **a, b, c,** or **d.**

1. ¿Cómo te llamas?
2. Me llamo Margarita.
3. ¿Cómo se llama usted?
4. ¿Cómo se llama él?

Nota cultural

Family members, friends, and teachers may add an ending such as **-ito** or **-ita** to a child's or friend's name to show affection. Rosa becomes **Rosita,** Teresa, **Teresita,** Juan becomes **Juanito,** and Miguel becomes **Miguelito.** How does your name change, adding **-ito** or **-ita** to the end? There are nicknames, **apodos,** associated with names that may be an abbreviation or part of a name. For example, Pilar, a very common girl's name in Spain, becomes **Pili,** and Santiago, a boy's name, becomes **Santi.**

Do we have similar nicknames in English?

3 Pareo

Leamos Match each question to the correct response. There may be more than one correct answer.

1. ¿Cómo se llama él?
2. ¿Cómo se llama ella?
3. ¿Cómo se llama usted?
4. ¿Cómo te llamas?

a. Me llamo Gustavo.
b. Se llama Pablo.
c. Soy Elena Rodríguez.
d. Se llama Josefina.

Comunicación

HOLT **SoundBooth**
ONLINE RECORDING

4 Nombres y más nombres

Hablemos Get together with three classmates and ask them their names in Spanish. Then report their names to the class.

España

siete **7**

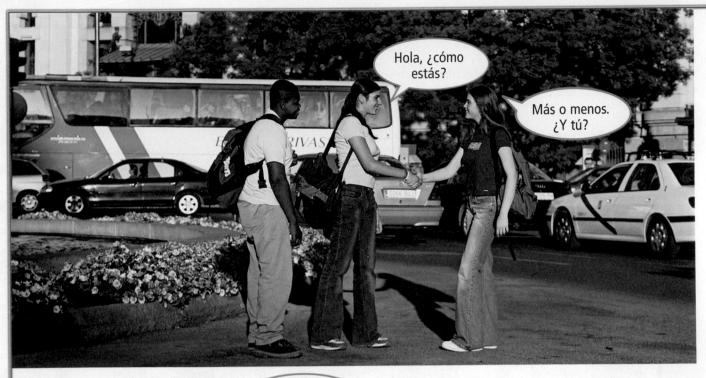

Hola, ¿cómo estás?

Más o menos. ¿Y tú?

Buenos días, Paco. ¿Cómo estás?

Estoy bien, gracias. ¿Y usted?

Más vocabulario...

Greetings and Goodbyes

Buenos días, señor.	*Good morning, sir.*
Buenas tardes, señorita.	*Good afternoon, miss.*
Buenas noches, señora.	*Good evening, ma'am.*
Adiós.	*Goodbye.*
Buenas noches.	*Good night.*
Hasta luego.	*See you later.*
Hasta mañana.	*See you tomorrow.*
Hasta pronto.	*See you soon.*
Nos vemos.	*See you.*
Tengo que irme.	*I have to go.*

¡Exprésate!

To ask how a friend is	To ask how an adult is	To respond	
Hola, ¿cómo estás? *Hi, how are you?*	**¿Cómo está usted?** *How are you?*	**Estoy bien/regular/mal.** *I'm fine/all right/not so good.*	**Interactive TUTOR**
¿Qué tal? *How's it going?*		**Más o menos.** *So-so.*	

➤ Vocabulario y gramática, pp. 1–3

Online workbooks

Capítulo 1 • ¡Empecemos!

5 ¿Qué dicen?

Escuchemos Are the people you hear
a) greeting each other or
b) asking each other how they are?

6 ¡Adiós!

Hablemos How would you say goodbye to someone . . .

MODELO you will see tomorrow?
Hasta mañana.

1. you will see again soon?
2. you will see again tomorrow in class?
3. when you don't know when you will see them next?
4. you will see in a few days?
5. wishing them a good night?
6. when you have to go?

Comunicación

HOLT **SoundBooth**
ONLINE RECORDING

7 Estoy bien, gracias.

Hablemos Work with a partner. Take turns deciding how you would greet these people and ask how they are. How would they respond? Base your answers on the pictures and times.

MODELO —Buenos días, Señor Garza. ¿Cómo está usted?
—Estoy bien, gracias.

8:00 A.M.
el señor Garza

11:00 A.M.
Teresa

2:00 P.M.
Santi

9:00 P.M.
Maribel

8 Conversación

Hablemos Create a conversation with a classmate. Greet each other, find out each other's name, ask how it's going, and say goodbye.

¡Exprésate!

To introduce someone	To respond	To say that you are also pleased to meet someone
Éste es Juan. (Él) es un compañero de clase. *This is Juan. He is a classmate.*	**Encantado(a).** **Mucho gusto.** *Pleased/Nice to meet you.*	**Igualmente.** *Likewise.*
Éste es el señor Vega. (Él) es mi profesor de español. *This is Mr. Vega. He is my Spanish teacher.*		
Ésta es Rosa. (Ella) es una compañera de clase. *This is Rosa. She is a classmate.*		
Ésta es la señora (la señorita) Talavera. (Ella) es mi profesora de ciencias. *This is Mrs. (Miss) Talavera. She is my science teacher.*		

Interactive TUTOR

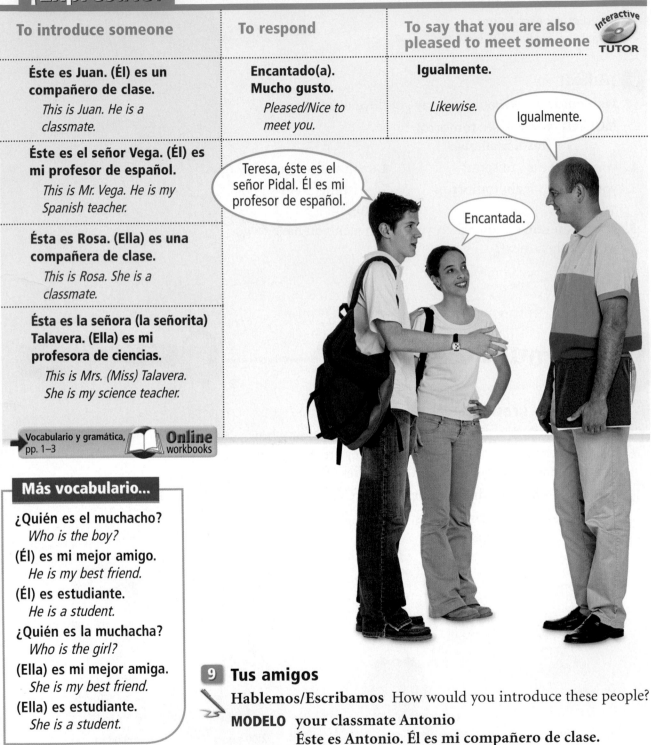

> Teresa, éste es el señor Pidal. Él es mi profesor de español.

> Encantada.

> Igualmente.

Vocabulario y gramática, pp. 1–3 Online workbooks

Más vocabulario...

¿Quién es el muchacho?
Who is the boy?

(Él) es mi mejor amigo.
He is my best friend.

(Él) es estudiante.
He is a student.

¿Quién es la muchacha?
Who is the girl?

(Ella) es mi mejor amiga.
She is my best friend.

(Ella) es estudiante.
She is a student.

9 Tus amigos

Hablemos/Escribamos How would you introduce these people?

MODELO your classmate Antonio
Éste es Antonio. Él es mi compañero de clase.

1. your best friend Ana
2. your best friend Juan
3. your classmate Enrique
4. your classmate Luisa
5. your Spanish teacher
6. yourself

¡Exprésate!

To ask where someone is from	To say where you and others are from
¿De dónde eres? *Where are you from? (familiar)*	**Soy de Estados Unidos.** *I'm from the United States.*
¿De dónde es usted? *Where are you from? (formal)*	**Soy de España.** *I'm from Spain.*
¿De dónde es...? *Where is . . . from?*	**Es de Cuba.** *He (She) is from Cuba.*

➤ Vocabulario y gramática, pp. 1–3

Online workbooks

10 ¿De dónde son?

Escuchemos As you listen, match the name of the person with the place he or she is from.

1. Javier
2. Angélica
3. la profesora Gutiérrez
4. Rafael
5. Fernando

a. Es de Cuba.
b. Es de México.
c. Es de España.
d. Es de Estados Unidos.
e. Es de Puerto Rico.

11 Es de...

Hablemos Using the photos, introduce these people and tell where they are from.

Carolina, España

MODELO Ésta es mi amiga Carolina. Ella es de España.

1. Juan José, la República Dominicana
2. María, Cuba
3. Blas, Puerto Rico
4. Irma, México
5. Alberto, Estados Unidos

 Comunicación  HOLT SoundBooth ONLINE RECORDING

12 El club de español

Hablemos Imagine you and your partner have joined the Spanish Club. Greet each other, ask each other's name and where each other is from. Then introduce each other to a classmate.

España

once **11**

Video/DVD
GramaVisión

Gramática en acción 1

Interactive TUTOR

Subjects and verbs in sentences

1 In English, sentences have a **subject** and a **verb**. The **subject** is the noun (person or thing) that is doing something or being described. The **verb** is the action word like **run** or **sing**, or a word like **am**, **is**, or **are** that links the subject to a description.

subject **Mrs. Pérez is** my teacher. *verb*
She is from Madrid.

2 In Spanish, sentences also have a **subject** and a **verb**.

subject **La señora Pérez es** mi profesora. *verb*
Ella es de Madrid.

3 Both English and Spanish use nouns as subjects. Nouns can be replaced with **pronouns**. Some examples of Spanish **pronouns** you have seen are **él**, **ella**, **tú** and **usted**.

Él stands for Juan.

Juan es un compañero de clase.   **Él es** mi mejor amigo.
Juan is a classmate.   *He is my best friend.*

4 English sentences always have a subject. But in Spanish the **subject** or the **subject pronoun** can be left out if everyone knows who you're talking about.

Maria is my friend.   **María es** mi amiga.
She is from Spain.   **Es** de España.   *Ella can be left out.*

Vocabulario y gramática, pp. 4–6
Actividades, pp. 1–4
Online workbooks

Plaza de Zocodover en Toledo

13 Mis amigos de Toledo

Leamos Identify the subjects and verbs. If there is no subject or subject pronoun, state who you think the subject is.

1. Luisa is my friend.
2. She is from Spain.
3. Mrs. García is my teacher.
4. She is from Toledo.

5. Luisa es mi amiga.
6. Es de España.
7. La señora García es mi profesora.
8. Es de Toledo.

14 **¿Quién más?**

Leamos Identify the subject and the verb in the following sentences.

1. Susana es de Perú.
2. Pablo es estudiante.
3. Ella es mi mejor amiga.
4. El muchacho es de México.

15 **¿Quién es quién?**

Leamos Identify the subjects and verbs in the following sentences. Then say whether you would use **él** or **ella** in place of each subject.

1. Laura es de Madrid. Es una compañera de clase.
2. Juan es mi mejor amigo. Es estudiante.
3. La señora Ayala es mi profesora de ciencias. Es de Perú.
4. El señor Garza es mi profesor de español. Es de España.
5. El muchacho es un compañero de clase. Es mi amigo.

Comunicación

HOLT **SoundBooth** ONLINE RECORDING

16 **¿De quién hablas?**

Escribamos/Hablemos Use at least three sentences from the word box to write a description of one of the people pictured below. Read your description aloud to your partner. He or she will guess which person you have just described. Then switch roles.

Éste es el señor Madero.	Ella es mi profesora de español.
Él es mi mejor amigo.	Es de Estados Unidos.
Es de España.	Ella es mi mejor amiga.
Ésta es Rosaura.	Él es un compañero de clase.
Éste es Mario.	Ella es una compañera de clase.
Él es mi profesor de ciencias.	Ésta es la señora Matute.

Gramática 1

Subject pronouns

1 These are the **subject pronouns** in Spanish.

yo	*I*	**nosotros**	*we*
		nosotras	*we (all female)*
tú	*you*	**vosotros**	*you*
		vosotras	*you (all female)*
usted	*you*	**ustedes**	*you*
él	*he*	**ellos**	*they*
ella	*she*	**ellas**	*they (all female)*

En inglés

In English, the subject pronoun *you* is used with anyone, no matter their age or relationship to you.

In Spanish, the choice of the pronoun **tú** or **usted** is based on your relationship to the person.

In English, is *you* used to talk to one person, more than one person, or both? How does this compare with Spanish usage of **usted** and **ustedes**?

2 The subject pronouns **tú** and **usted** both mean *you* when you're talking to one person. However, they are used in different situations.

friend
relative
someone your age
} **Familiar**
tú

Formal
usted {
teacher
adult you've just met
someone you show respect to

Although subject pronouns are often left out, the pronoun **usted** is commonly stated when addressing someone to show respect.

¿Cómo está **usted**?   *How are you?*

3 The subject pronouns **ustedes** and **vosotros** mean *you* when talking to more than one person. They are also used in different situations.

friends
relatives
people your age
} **Familiar (in Spain)**
vosotros

Formal and Familiar
ustedes { *any group*

4 The pronouns **nosotros**, **vosotros**, and **ellos** have feminine forms.

	Masculine	Feminine	
group of all males	nosotros	nosotras	
group of males and females	vosotros (Spain)	vosotras (Spain)	group of all females
	ellos	ellas	

> Vocabulario y gramática, pp. 4–6
> Actividades, pp. 1–3

17 **¿Cómo le(s) dices para hablarles?**

Hablemos What pronouns would you use to speak to these people?

1. two or more teachers
2. a group of female students (in Spain)
3. your best friend
4. a school principal
5. two or more males
6. a group of male and female students (in Spain)

Plaza de Cibeles, Madrid

18 ¿Con quién habla Javier?

Escuchemos Listen as Javier, a teenager from Spain, talks to his friends and teachers. Match each statement with the correct picture. Remember that Javier uses **vosotros** and **vosotras.**

19 Nuevos amigos

Leamos/Escribamos Complete this conversation using the correct subject pronouns.

—Hola. __1__ (I) soy Rosalinda Chávez. Y __2__ (he) es mi amigo Juan. ¿Cómo te llamas __3__ (you)?

— __4__ (I) me llamo Antonia. Y __5__ (she) es mi amiga Talía. __6__ (We–Talía and I) somos de Estados Unidos. Juan y tú, ¿de dónde son __7__ (you, plural)?

Comunicación

HOLT SoundBooth
ONLINE RECORDING

20 Eres reportero(a)

Hablemos Imagine that you are a reporter interviewing new students and teachers for the school paper. With a partner, role-play one interview with a student and one with a teacher. Use the cues below.

1. Greet the person you are interviewing.
2. Ask what his or her name is.
3. Ask where he or she is from.
4. Say goodbye.

Cultura

Comparaciones

Buenos amigos, Madrid

¿Cómo saludas a tus amigos, familiares y profesores?

Spanish speakers usually greet each other with a handshake or a kiss depending on the situation. Here, you will see several people greet each other in different situations. See if you can find any similarities to the greetings and goodbyes you use with your friends, family, and teachers.

 ### Saludos informales

In Spain, friends and family members may greet each other with two kisses, one on each cheek. In Latin America, friends and family members kiss each other on only one cheek. Men and boys greet each other with a hug, a pat on the back, or a handshake. In some Latin American countries, men who have not seen each other in a long time greet with a handshake, followed by a hug, followed by a second handshake.

—Hola, madrina, ¿cómo estás?

—¡Hola amigo! ¡Tanto tiempo!

—¿Cómo estás?

☀ Saludos formales

In professional or school settings, or when meeting someone for the first time, the usual greeting in Spain and Latin America is a handshake.

—Mucho gusto.
—Igualmente.

—Es un compañero de clase.
—Encantado.

Cultura

Para comprender

1. How would a young girl greet her grandparents in Spain?
2. How would a young girl greet her grandparents in Latin America?
3. How would a businessman and a businesswoman greet each other in Spain or Latin America?
4. In Latin America, how might a boy greet his uncle if they haven't seen each other in a long time?

Para pensar y hablar

Among family and close friends, hugs and kisses are common greetings throughout the Spanish-speaking world. Do family and close friends in your community greet each other with hugs, kisses, or handshakes? With a partner, model how two people might greet each other with a handshake.

Comunidad

What's in a name?

Use a local telephone book to familiarize yourself with common Hispanic last names. Work with a partner.

◆ Choose a letter (or letters) of the alphabet to work with.
◆ Make a list of the Hispanic family names in that section.
◆ Write down the number of entries for each name.
◆ Share your list with the rest of the class and determine which three names occur the most times.
◆ Practice Spanish pronunciation of the names with your teacher.

A family-owned store

Objetivos
- Giving phone numbers, the time, the date, and the day
- Spelling words and giving e-mail addresses

Vocabulario en acción 2

Video/DVD
ExpresaVisión

Los números

0	**1**	**2**	**3**	**4**
cero	uno	dos	tres	cuatro
5	**6**	**7**	**8**	**9**	**10**
cinco	seis	siete	ocho	nueve	diez

Más vocabulario...

11	once
12	doce
13	trece
14	catorce
15	quince
16	dieciséis
17	diecisiete
18	dieciocho
19	diecinueve
20	veinte
21	veintiuno
22	veintidós
23	veintitrés
24	veinticuatro
25	veinticinco
26	veintiséis
27	veintisiete
28	veintiocho
29	veintinueve
30	treinta
31	treinta y uno

21 Contando

Hablemos What numbers do you think of for the following things? Say the number in Spanish.

1. hours in a day
2. a rectangle
3. the English alphabet
4. a volleyball team
5. an octopus
6. a quarter
7. a driver's license
8. a carton of eggs
9. a trio
10. days in a week

22 ¿Qué números faltan?

Escribamos/Hablemos Complete these series of numbers logically. Then read them aloud.

1. 1, 3, =====, 7, 9, =====, 13, 15
2. 2, 4, =====, 8, =====, 12, =====
3. 16, 17, =====, 19, =====, =====
4. 31, 25, =====, =====, =====, 1
5. 19, 18, =====, 16, 15, =====, 13, 12
6. 20, 22, =====, 26, =====, 30
7. 3, 6, =====, 12, =====, =====
8. 5, 10, =====, 20, =====, =====

¡Exprésate!

To ask for phone numbers	To give phone numbers
¿Cuál es tu teléfono? *What's your telephone number?*	**Es tres-dos-cinco-uno-dos-tres-uno.** *It's 3-2-5-1-2-3-1.*
¿Cuál es el teléfono de Rosita? *What's Rosita's telephone number?*	**Es seis-uno-nueve-uno-cinco-dos-ocho.** *It's 6-1-9-1-5-2-8.*

Interactive TUTOR

Vocabulario y gramática, pp. 7–9

Online workbooks

Vocabulario 2

23 Números de teléfono

Escuchemos You and your friend Elena are double-checking phone numbers for some of the students in your class. Listen to what Elena says and fill in the missing numbers.

1. Beatriz   3-▬▬-▬▬-1-9-▬▬-▬▬
2. Jorge   2-▬▬-▬▬-▬▬-▬▬-2-8
3. Rosaura   ▬▬-1-3-▬▬-▬▬-3-1
4. Ángel   7-1-8-▬▬-▬▬-▬▬-▬▬
5. Gladys   ▬▬-2-8-1-5-▬▬-▬▬

Comunicación

HOLT **SoundBooth** ONLINE RECORDING

24 Directorio telefónico

Leamos/Hablemos Pick a person from the school directory and ask a classmate if you have the right number for him or her. When you give the number, get one number wrong. Your partner should correct the number.

MODELO —¿El teléfono de Teresa Benavides es uno-catorce-diecinueve-veintidós?
—No, es uno-catorce-dieciocho-veintidós.

	28
BENAVIDES, Teresa Núñez de Cáceres 11	1-14-18-22
GÓMEZ, Emilia Santo Tomás de Aquino 27	2-13-25-17
GONZÁLEZ, Rocío Avenida Juárez 18	6-15-29-17
MARTÍNEZ, Elena Camino Real 25	4-11-16-28
ORTEGA, Jaime Avenida Mella 31	3-31-13-27
RODRÍGUEZ, Alberto Calle Constitución 12	6-27-19-12
TORRES, Federico Carretera Simón Bolívar 13	9-21-15-10

25 Número secreto

Hablemos Try to guess the secret number between 0 and 31 that your partner has written down. If you are wrong, your partner will point up or down to indicate a higher or lower number. Keep trying until you guess right. Then switch roles and play again.

¿Qué hora es?

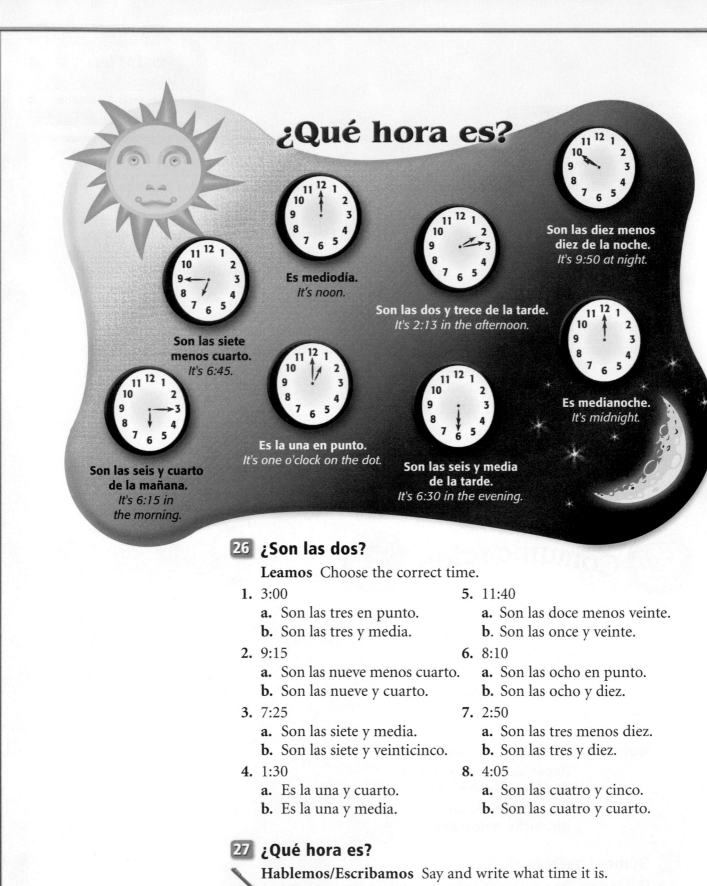

Es mediodía.
It's noon.

Son las diez menos diez de la noche.
It's 9:50 at night.

Son las siete menos cuarto.
It's 6:45.

Son las dos y trece de la tarde.
It's 2:13 in the afternoon.

Son las seis y cuarto de la mañana.
It's 6:15 in the morning.

Es la una en punto.
It's one o'clock on the dot.

Son las seis y media de la tarde.
It's 6:30 in the evening.

Es medianoche.
It's midnight.

26 ¿Son las dos?

Leamos Choose the correct time.

1. 3:00
   a. Son las tres en punto.
   b. Son las tres y media.

2. 9:15
   a. Son las nueve menos cuarto.
   b. Son las nueve y cuarto.

3. 7:25
   a. Son las siete y media.
   b. Son las siete y veinticinco.

4. 1:30
   a. Es la una y cuarto.
   b. Es la una y media.

5. 11:40
   a. Son las doce menos veinte.
   b. Son las once y veinte.

6. 8:10
   a. Son las ocho en punto.
   b. Son las ocho y diez.

7. 2:50
   a. Son las tres menos diez.
   b. Son las tres y diez.

8. 4:05
   a. Son las cuatro y cinco.
   b. Son las cuatro y cuarto.

27 ¿Qué hora es?

Hablemos/Escribamos Say and write what time it is.

1. 4:00 P.M.   3. 4:45 A.M.   5. 6:10 A.M.
2. 12:00 P.M.   4. 1:15 P.M.   6. 9:05 A.M

¡Exprésate!

To ask someone the date and day of the week	To respond
¿Qué fecha es hoy? *What's today's date?*	**Es el primero (dos, tres...) de enero.** *It's the first (second, third . . .) of January.*
¿Qué día es hoy? *What day is today?*	**Hoy es lunes.** *Today is Monday.*

Interactive
TUTOR

Vocabulario y gramática, pp. 7–9

Online workbooks

Los días de la semana

Los meses del año

lunes	martes	miércoles	jueves	viernes	sábado	domingo
14	15	16	17	18	19	20

l m m j v s d
1 2 3
4 5 6 7 8 9 10
11 12 13 14 15 16 17
18 19 20 21 22 23 24
25 26 27 28 29 30 31

enero
febrero
marzo
abril
mayo
junio
julio
agosto
septiembre
octubre
noviembre
diciembre

Las estaciones

la primavera	*spring*	el otoño	*fall*
el verano	*summer*	el invierno	*winter*

28 ¿Sabes?

Escribamos/Hablemos Complete the following series logically.

1. lunes, ════, miércoles, ════
2. viernes, ════, ════, lunes
3. enero, ════, marzo, ════
4. mayo, junio, ════, ════
5. primavera, ════, otoño, ════
6. invierno, ════, ════, otoño

Comunicación

HOLT SoundBooth
ONLINE RECORDING

29 ¿Cuándo es tu cumpleaños?

Hablemos Work in groups of three to guess one another's birthday. Guide your classmates by saying **antes** *(before)* or **después** *(after)* until they guess correctly. Guess the month first, then try for the date.

a *(a)*
árbol

b *(be)*
bebé

c *(ce)*
ciclismo

d *(de)*
dinosaurio

e *(e)*
elefante

f *(efe)*
flores

g *(ge)*
geografía

h *(hache)*
hipopótamo

i *(i)*
iguana

j *(jota)*
jirafa

k *(ka)*
karate

l *(ele)*
león

m *(eme)*
manzana

n *(ene)*
nido

ñ *(eñe)*
piñata

o *(o)*
oso

p *(pe)*
pez

q *(cu)*
queso

r *(ere)*
pera

s *(ese)*
salvavidas

t *(te)*
tortuga

u *(u)*
uvas

v *(ve or uve)*
violín

w *(uve doble)**
Wilfredo

x *(equis)*
examen

y *(i griega)*
yoyo

z *(zeta)*
zanahorias

Dos letras, un sonido

ch *(che)*
chimpancé

ll *(elle)*
llama

rr *(erre)*
burro

*Another way to say *W* in Spanish is **doble ve**.

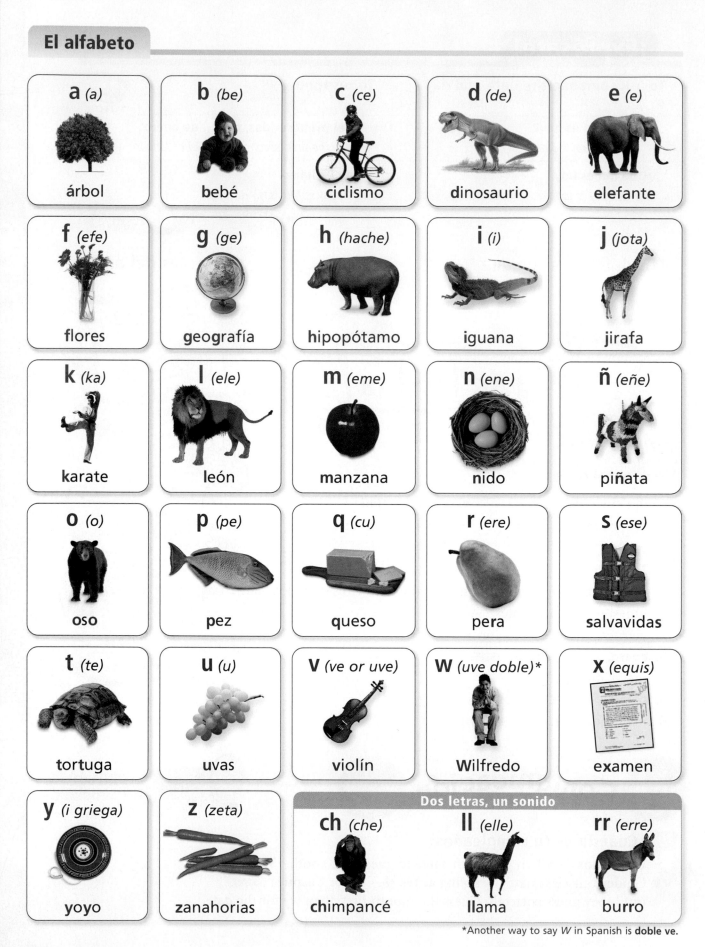

¡Exprésate!

To ask how words are spelled and give e-mail addresses	To respond
¿Cómo se escribe...? *How do you spell . . . ?*	**Se escribe...** *It's spelled . . .*
¿Cuál es el correo electrónico de Marisa? *What is Marisa's e-mail address?*	**Es eme punto ge-o-ene-zeta-a-ele-o arroba ere-e-de punto hache-ere-uve doble punto a-ere.** *It's m.gonzalo@red.hrw.ar.*
¿Cuál es tu correo electrónico? *What's your e-mail address?*	**Es...** *It's . . .*

Interactive TUTOR

➤ Vocabulario y gramática, pp. 7–9

Online workbooks

30 Dictado

Escuchemos/Escribamos Listen as several speakers say and spell out the Spanish words for some animals. On a separate sheet of paper, write the words in Spanish as you hear them.

Comunicación

HOLT SoundBooth ONLINE RECORDING

31 ¿Cómo se escribe...?

Hablemos/Escribamos Spell each item below aloud in Spanish while your classmates write it out.

MODELO eme-e-ere-ce-e-de-e-ese (Mercedes)

1. your name
2. your e-mail address
3. the city or town where you were born
4. your best friend's full name
5. your best friend's e-mail address
6. your favorite actor's name

Juan Carlos Cabello

Dirección:
Calle Aldama 28

Teléfono:
2-16-28-22

Correo electrónico:
jcc@amigos.hrw.com

Cumpleaños:
15 abril

Clara 7-13-25-29
Lorena 7-24-11-31
Pepe 7-10-29-22
Daniel 7-05-22-11
Paula 7-03-29-30

32 El proyecto

Hablemos You and several classmates have to finish a project outside of class. Work with three partners to create a conversation in which you ask one another's names (spell them out if you need to), phone numbers, and e-mail addresses.

Objetivos
- The verb **ser**
- Punctuation marks and written accents

Gramática en acción 2

Video/DVD
GramaVisión

The verb ser

Interactive TUTOR

1 In Spanish, a verb has different forms to tell you who the subject is. Changing a verb form so that it matches its subject is called **conjugating.** This is the conjugation of the verb **ser** *(to be).*

yo	**soy**	*I am*	nosotros(as)	**somos**	*we are*
tú	**eres**	*you are*	vosotros(as)	**sois**	*you are*
usted	**es**	*you are*	ustedes	**son**	*you are*
él	**es**	*he is*	ellos	**son**	*they are*
ella	**es**	*she is*	ellas	**son**	*they are*

With nouns and names of people, use the same form of the verb as for **él/ella** or **ellos/ellas.**

Mi profesora es de Cuba.
My teacher is from Cuba.

Juan y Carlos son de España.
Juan and Carlos are from Spain.

2 To make a sentence negative, place **no** in front of the verb.

Hoy **no es** martes, **es** jueves.
Today isn't Tuesday, it's Thursday.

Vocabulario y gramática, pp. 10–12
Actividades, pp. 5–7

Online workbooks

¿Te acuerdas?

You've used forms of the verb **ser** to say who someone is or where you or others are from, to give your telephone number, and to say the date, the day, and the time.

Éste **es** un compañero de clase.
Yo **soy** de Perú.
Mi teléfono **es** 555-5555.
Hoy **es** el diez de febrero.
Hoy **es** jueves.
Son las tres de la tarde.

33 Presentaciones

Leamos What is Maribel saying? Complete her statements by matching elements from the two columns.

1. Hola. Yo
2. Y ella
3. Nosotras
4. Y tú, ¿de dónde
5. Juan y tú, ¿de dónde
6. Jorge y Carlos
7. Juan, ¿cuál
8. Carla, ¿qué hora
9. No, Carla, no es la una,
10. Juan, ¿qué día
11. Y la señora Tan, ¿de dónde

a. son de Cuba.
b. somos de México.
c. eres?
d. son ustedes?
e. es mi amiga Carla.
f. soy Maribel Gómez.
g. es?
h. es hoy?
i. es tu teléfono?
j. es ella?
k. son las dos y media.

34 Nuestro club

Leamos/Escribamos Miguel has written a description of the International Spanish Club. Complete the paragraph with the correct forms of the verb **ser**.

Nosotros __1__ estudiantes y profesores del club internacional de español. Yo __2__ de Puerto Rico. Juan Emilio __3__ de la República Dominicana. Lisa y Rebeca __4__ de Estados Unidos. El teléfono del club __5__ 5-24-11-21. El correo electrónico del club __6__ club.internacional.deespañol@school.hrw.org. Nosotros __7__ el club internacional. ¡Hasta pronto!

Comunicación

HOLT **SoundBooth**
ONLINE RECORDING

35 Charla

Escribamos/Hablemos Work with two classmates to write out the following conversation in Spanish. Then take turns playing the roles.

Hi, where are you from?

I'm from the United States.

This is Juana, she's a classmate.

Pleased to meet you, Juana. Where are you from?

Likewise. I'm from Mexico. What time is it?

It's three thirty. See you tomorrow!

36 No es correcto

Hablemos Take turns with a partner giving information about the people in the pictures, but include at least one detail that is not correct. Your partner should then say **no** to disagree, and provide the correct information.

MODELO —Ana es de Guatemala. El teléfono de Ana es 3-20-16-04.
—No, el teléfono de Ana no es 3-20-16-04. Es 3-29-16-04.

Ana, Guatemala
3-29-16-04

Juan, Puerto Rico
5-14-07-21

Lupe, México
7-20-11-05

Ricardo, España
2-23-01-16

Gramática 2

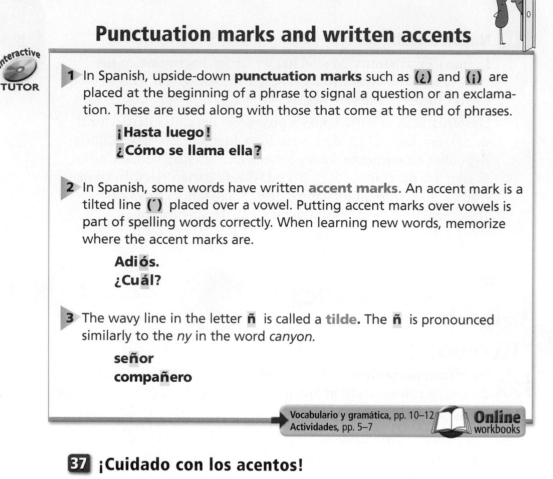

Punctuation marks and written accents

1 In Spanish, upside-down **punctuation marks** such as (¿) and (¡) are placed at the beginning of a phrase to signal a question or an exclamation. These are used along with those that come at the end of phrases.

> **¡Hasta luego!**
> **¿Cómo se llama ella?**

2 In Spanish, some words have written **accent marks**. An accent mark is a tilted line (´) placed over a vowel. Putting accent marks over vowels is part of spelling words correctly. When learning new words, memorize where the accent marks are.

> **Adiós.**
> **¿Cuál?**

3 The wavy line in the letter **ñ** is called a **tilde**. The **ñ** is pronounced similarly to the *ny* in the word *canyon*.

> **señor**
> **compañero**

Vocabulario y gramática, pp. 10–12
Actividades, pp. 5–7

Online workbooks

37 ¡Cuidado con los acentos!

Leamos/Escribamos On a separate sheet of paper, rewrite each sentence, placing accents and punctuation marks where needed.

1. Buenos dias senorita
2. Como esta usted senor
3. Que tal
4. Mucho gusto
5. Que hora es
6. De donde eres
7. Cual es tu telefono
8. Me llamo Pedro
9. Hola Como te llamas
10. El es un companero de clase
11. Quien es la profesora de ciencias
12. Como estas
13. Que fecha es hoy
14. Estoy bien gracias

Una carnicería *(butcher shop)* en Segovia, España

38 En contacto

Leamos/Escribamos When people write e-mails in Spanish, they sometimes leave out punctuation or written accents. On a separate piece of paper rewrite these two messages including the missing accent marks, tildes, and punctuation.

Hola, Beatriz!

Como estas Me llamo Gabriela Soy de Cuba De donde eres Quien es tu profesora Mi telefono es 9-14-32-03 Cual es tu telefono

Hasta luego
Gabi

Hola, Gabi!

Estoy bien Soy de Espana Mi profesora de espanol es la senora Gómez Quien es tu mejor amiga Mi telefono es 5-23-18-01 Tengo que irme

Adios
Beatriz

Comunicación

39 En la clase

Hablemos Today is the first day of school. With a partner, create brief conversations for each picture below. Choose the best conversation to perform for the class. Your classmates will guess which scene you role-played.

Gramática 2

Conexiones culturales

Conexión | Ciencias sociales

LOS CALENDARIOS Most of the words for days of the week in Spanish come from Latin. Look at the chart to see the roots of the Spanish words. Then answer the questions that follow.

lunes	martes	miércoles	jueves	viernes	sábado	domingo
Latin: *lunae*	Latin: *Martis*	Latin: *Mercurii*	Latin: *Jovis*	Latin: *Veneris*	Hebrew: *shabbat*	Latin: *dominus*
moon	Mars: Roman god of war	Mercury: Roman messenger of the gods	Jupiter: Roman king of the gods	Venus: Roman goddess of love	sabbath	Lord's day

1 Los planetas

What planet corresponds to each day of the week?

1. viernes
2. miércoles
3. jueves
4. martes

a. Júpiter
b. Venus
c. Mercurio
d. Marte

2 El calendario azteca

The Aztec Sun Calendar, the **xihuitl** (shee-wee-TAL) or "count of the years," is similar to ours. Both are 365 days long, the number of days it takes the earth to orbit the sun. The **xihuitl**, however, has 18 months of 20 days each, with extra "unlucky days" at the end of the year.

1. Can you find the ring on the Sun Calendar that represents the twenty days?

2. Since 18 months of 20 days each do not add up to 365 days, what is the Spanish word for the number of "unlucky days" at the end of the year?

Conexión Matemáticas

| 3:00 | 8:30 | 12:00 | 19:30 | 23:00 |

HOW THE 24-HOUR SYSTEM WORKS: Many countries around the world use schedules based on a 24-hour clock. Travelers can look at schedules and know the difference between 9:00 A.M. and 9:00 P.M. For example, using a 24-hour clock for a train schedule, a morning train would leave at 9:00 and a night train would leave at 21:00.

3 Convertir a 24 horas

Write the following times using the 24-hour system. For P.M. hours, add 12:00 to the hour. For A.M. hours, write the same hour but without using the abbreviation "A.M."

1:05 P.M.
+ 12:00
13:05

MODELO 2:35 A.M. 2:35

1. 7:20 A.M.   3. 9:25 P.M.   5. 11:00 A.M.
2. 3:15 P.M.   4. 4:30 P.M.   6. 8:15 P.M.

4 Convertir de 24 horas

Rewrite these times using A.M. and P.M. For times before 12:00, add A.M. to the end. For times after 12:59, subtract 12:00 from the hour and add P.M. at the end of the result.

13:05
− 12:00
1:05 P.M.

MODELO 2:35 2:35 A.M.

1. 23:40   3. 1:15   5. 20:39
2. 17:55   4. 15:25   6. 5:42

5 Horario de aviones

Answer the following questions using the 12-hour system (A.M. and P.M.).

1. What time does flight AO 444 to Madrid leave?
2. If you got to the airport at 2:00 P.M., would you have enough time to catch the flight to Barcelona? Why or why not?

VUELO FLIGHT	SALIDAS DESTINO TO	HORA TIME
IB 346	MADRID	1250
AO 444	MADRID	1310
IB 834	BARCELONA	1405
AO 452	P.MALLORCA	1445
AAN106	P.MALLORCA	1450
IB 387	MELILLA	1500
IB 397	MELILLA	1615

¿Quién será?

Episodio 1

ESTRATEGIA

Making connections Sometimes, as a story unfolds on screen, things happen in different parts of the world at the same time. Although the connection between those events may not be immediately obvious, as an experienced viewer, you know that one probably exists. In this episode, you will see things going on at the same time in Spain, Mexico, and Puerto Rico. Look for clues that help explain the connection among the events in all three locations.

En España

In Madrid, Spain, la profesora is studying the files of a Mexican student and a Puerto Rican student. She calls her assistant, Marcos, and makes an appointment to meet with him.

Francia

Portugal ★ Madrid
ESPAÑA

Mar
Mediterráneo

Marruecos   Argelia

1

La profesora Y tú, Sofía Corona Ramírez, eres de México, ¿no es así?

Hmmm... Nicolás Ortega García, el artista puertorriqueño.

2

La profesora Sí, Marcos. Necesito hablar contigo. Sí, pronto. Es urgente. A ver, mañana es domingo. Bien, el lunes, en mi casa. Sí, a las diez de la mañana.

Oye, ¿cuál es tu e-mail? Te quiero enviar unos documentos. Bien. Nos vemos el lunes.

En México

In Mexico City, Mexico, a girl named Sofía is having breakfast before going to school. Both her father and her little brother interrupt her.

3

Sr. Corona Buenos días, Sofía. Hola, Sofía, buenos días.

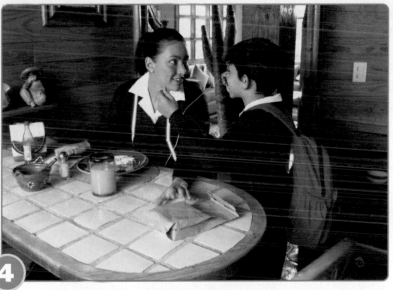

4

Quique Sofía, Sofía, ¡cara de tortilla!

A. CONTESTA

What is happening in the **Novela**? Check your understanding by answering these questions in English. Don't be afraid to guess!

1. Who are the people in the **Novela**? Make a list of their names and where they are from.

2. What do you know about Sofía and her family?

Novela en video

En Puerto Rico

In San Juan, Puerto Rico, a boy named Nicolás is in a rush on his way home from school. He bumps into some people.

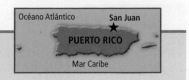

Océano Atlántico · San Juan

★

PUERTO RICO

Mar Caribe

5

Sra. Ortiz ¡Buenas tardes, Nico!

Nicolás ¡Buenas tardes, Señora Ortiz!

6

Nicolás ¡Uy, perdone, don Pablo! ¿Cómo está usted?

Don Pablo Estoy bien, gracias, Nico. ¿Y tú? ¿Cómo estás tú?

B. CONTESTA

1. Who are the people Nicolás is talking to?

2. Where do you think Nicolás is going in such a hurry?

Capítulo 1 • ¡Empecemos!

Actividades

1 Expresiones de cortesía

Match the English phrases to the Spanish phrases used by some characters in the **Novela.**

1. Hello.
2. Goodbye.
3. My name is . . .
4. How are you? (to an adult)
5. How are you? (to a young person)
6. I'm fine, thanks.

a. Me llamo...
b. ¿Cómo estás tú?
c. Estoy bien, gracias.
d. Hola.
e. Adiós.
f. ¿Cómo está usted?

2 ¿Cierto o falso?

Tell whether each statement is **cierto** *(true)* or **falso** *(false),* based on **la profesora's** phone call to her assistant.

1. She urgently needs to talk with him.
2. They will meet on Sunday.
3. The meeting will be at her house at 10 A.M.
4. She asks him for his mailing address.

3 ¿Comprendes la Novela?

Check your understanding of the events in the story by answering these questions.

1. What do you learn in Frame 3 on page 31 about Sofía and things she likes?
2. What do you think Nicolás is carrying under his arm? What does this tell you about him? Is there anything else to support your conclusion?
3. Who do you think Marcos is?
4. Why do you think **la profesora** is looking at photos of students?

> **Próximo episodio**
> *Marcos goes to visit la profesora. Can you predict what she might ask him to do?*
> PÁGINAS 76–79 ▸

Leamos y escribamos

ESTRATEGIA

para leer Recognizing cognates
Cognates are words that look alike and have similar meanings in two languages. Recognizing these words will help you get a general idea of what a reading passage is about.

A **Antes de leer**

Look at the homepage for one school's Spanish Club. To get an idea of what the club has to offer, write all the cognates you can find on a separate sheet of paper. Compare your list with a classmate's and try to guess what each word means. If you are not sure, look the word up in a dictionary.

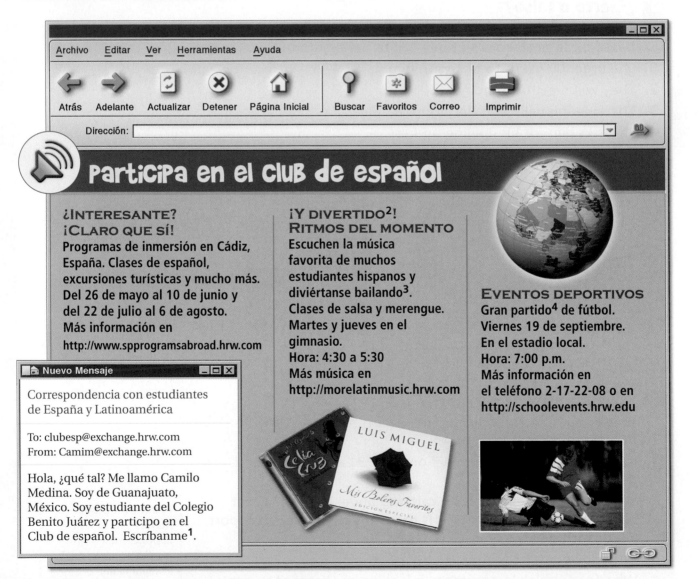

Archivo   Editar   Ver   Herramientas   Ayuda

Atrás   Adelante   Actualizar   Detener   Página Inicial   Buscar   Favoritos   Correo   Imprimir

Dirección:

participa en el club de español

¿INTERESANTE?
¡CLARO QUE SÍ!
Programas de inmersión en Cádiz, España. Clases de español, excursiones turísticas y mucho más. Del 26 de mayo al 10 de junio y del 22 de julio al 6 de agosto. Más información en http://www.spprogramsabroad.hrw.com

¡Y DIVERTIDO[2]!
RITMOS DEL MOMENTO
Escuchen la música favorita de muchos estudiantes hispanos y diviértanse bailando[3]. Clases de salsa y merengue. Martes y jueves en el gimnasio.
Hora: 4:30 a 5:30
Más música en
http://morelatinmusic.hrw.com

EVENTOS DEPORTIVOS
Gran partido[4] de fútbol. Viernes 19 de septiembre. En el estadio local.
Hora: 7:00 p.m.
Más información en el teléfono 2-17-22-08 o en http://schoolevents.hrw.edu

Nuevo Mensaje

Correspondencia con estudiantes de España y Latinoamérica

To: clubesp@exchange.hrw.com
From: Camim@exchange.hrw.com

Hola, ¿qué tal? Me llamo Camilo Medina. Soy de Guanajuato, México. Soy estudiante del Colegio Benito Juárez y participo en el Club de español. Escríbanme[1].

LUIS MIGUEL
Mis Boleros Favoritos
EDICIÓN ESPECIAL

1. write to me   2. fun   3. have fun dancing   4. game

B Comprensión

Based on the reading, say if the following statements are true (**cierto**) or false (**falso**). Correct the false statements.

1. The Spanish Club offers a variety of fun and interesting activities.

2. The club sponsors summer trips to Spanish-speaking countries.

3. If you join the club, you will be able to correspond with students from Asia.

4. The club offers **salsa** and **merengue** classes on Fridays.

5. The club homepage provides you with links to other sites.

C Después de leer

Would you like to become a member of this club? Why or why not? Which activity seems the most interesting to you? What other activities would you suggest if you were a member?

Taller del escritor

Nombre
Número de teléfono
Correo electrónico
Soy de ...

ESTRATEGIA

para escribir Jot down a list of ideas to include in your writing before starting to write sentences. List all your ideas even if you don't know how to say something in Spanish. Get help later from the dictionary if you need to find a specific word or phrase.

La página Web del club de español

Imagine you have joined the Spanish Club. Write a short paragraph about yourself to be posted on the club's Web site. In your paragraph, include

- your name
- where you are from
- your e-mail address

1 Antes de escribir

Make a list of the information you will need for the Web site. You may use English or Spanish for this step.

2 Escribir y revisar

Write your information in complete sentences in Spanish. Read your sentences at least twice. Make sure you have included all the information you want to post on the site. Then check your spelling and punctuation.

3 Publicar

Post your completed paragraph on the bulletin board or your class Web site.

Prepárate para el examen

1 Pretend you are introducing the following people to a classmate. Greet your classmate and ask how he or she is, then introduce each person, and say where he or she is from.

1. Beatriz, México

2. el señor Huang, Estados Unidos

3. Antonio, España

2 For each pair of sentences, identify the subject and verb in the first sentence. Then choose the correct subject pronoun in the second sentence.

1. Rosa es mi mejor amiga. (Ella/Él) es de Segovia, España.

2. La señora Cortez es mi profesora de español. (Ellos/Ella) es de Estados Unidos.

3. El muchacho es de México. (Él/Ustedes) es un compañero de clase.

4. El profesor Muñoz es de la República Dominicana. (Nosotros/Él) es mi profesor de ciencias.

3 Choose the correct subject pronoun to complete the following short conversations.

1. —Alicia y Laura, ¿de dónde son ═══ *(you, plural)*?
   —═══ *(We)* somos de Costa Rica.

2. —Hola, Señor Martínez. ¿Cómo está ═══ *(you, formal)*?
   —Bien, gracias, Jorge. ¿Y ═══ *(you, familiar)*?

3. —¿De dónde son Juan y Susana?
   —═══ *(They)* son de Bolivia.

4 Answer the following questions.

1. ¿Cuál es tu correo electrónico?
2. ¿Cuál es tu teléfono?
3. ¿Cómo se escribe tu nombre?
4. ¿Qué hora es?
5. ¿Qué día es hoy?
6. ¿Qué fecha es hoy?

5 On a separate piece of paper, copy the following conversation. Use the correct form of **ser** and add the correct punctuation and accent marks.

—Me llamo Pilar (Yo) ===== tu companera de clase

—De donde ===== (tu) Pilar

—(Yo) ===== de Espana Y tu, ===== de Miami

—Si, (yo) ===== de Miami Que hora =====

— ===== las cuatro en punto

6 Answer the following questions.

1. In Spanish, how do people change their friends' names to show affection for them? Give at least two examples.

2. Name four ways that a teacher might be addressed in a Spanish-speaking country.

7 Listen to the following conversations. For each one, decide whether the speakers are a) telling time, b) greeting each other, c) introducing someone, or d) exchanging phone numbers.

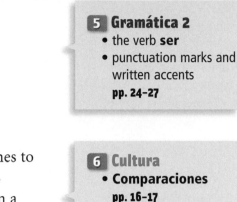

Visit Holt Online

go.hrw.com
KEYWORD: EXP1A CH1

Chapter Self-test

5 Gramática 2
• the verb **ser**
• punctuation marks and written accents
pp. 24–27

6 Cultura
• **Comparaciones**
  pp. 16–17
• **Notas culturales**
  pp. 7, 12
• **Geocultura**
  pp. xxii–3

Conversación

HOLT **SoundBooth**
ONLINE RECORDING

8 Role play the following conversation with a partner. Partner A is president of the Spanish Club and Partner B is a new student.

PARTNER A: Greet your partner and introduce yourself. Ask his or her name.

PARTNER B: Tell your partner you're pleased to meet him or her and say your name.

PARTNER A: Ask where your partner is from.

PARTNER B: Respond, then ask where your partner is from.

PARTNER A: Respond, then ask for your partner's e-mail address and phone number.

PARTNER B: Answer your partner's questions.

PARTNER A: Say you have to go. Say goodbye.

PARTNER B: Say goodbye. Say you'll see him or her tomorrow.

Gramática 1
- subjects and verbs in sentences
  pp. 12–13
- subject pronouns
  pp. 14–15
- **tú, usted** and **ustedes**
  pp. 14–15

Repaso de Gramática 1

Every sentence has a **subject** and a **verb.** The verb tells what the **subject** does or links the **subject** to a description.

La señora Pérez es mi profesora.

The **subject pronouns** in Spanish are

yo	nosotros(as)
tú	vosotros(as)
usted/él/ella	ustedes/ellos/ellas

The subject pronouns **tú** and **usted** both mean *you.* Use **tú** when you're talking to a friend. Use **usted** to show respect towards elders and teachers. When talking to a group of people, use **ustedes** to say *you.* In Spain only, use **vosotros(as)** to say *you* to a group of friends, family members, or children.

¿De dónde es usted? ¿De dónde eres tú?

Gramática 2
- the verb **ser**
  pp. 24–25
- punctuation marks and written accents
  pp. 26–27

Repaso de Gramática 2

This is the conjugation of ser *(to be).*

yo soy	*I am*	nosotros(as) somos	*we are*
tú eres	*you are*	vosotros(as) sois	*you are*
Ud./él/ella es	*you are/he/she is*	Uds./ellos/ellas son	*you/they are*

Question marks	Exclamation points	Accent marks
¿ ... ?	¡ ... !	á, é, í, ó, ú, ñ
¿Cuál es tu teléfono?	¡Hola!	cuál, qué, sí, cómo, tú, mañana

Letra y sonido   a e i o u

Las vocales *(The Vowels)*
The five vowels in Spanish are always pronounced clearly and fully no matter where they are in a word.
- **a:** between the *a* of *cat* and *father:* **a**migo, hol**a**
- **e:** as in *they,* but shorter: **e**nero, corr**e**o
- **i:** as in *police,* but shorter: **i**gualmente, abr**i**l
- **o:** as in *low,* but shorter: **o**nce, cóm**o**
- **u:** as in *sue,* but shorter: **u**no, est**u**diante

Trabalenguas
La a, la e, la i—son fáciles para mí.
La a, la e, la i—las puedo hacer así.
A, e, i, o, u—aprende a hacerlas tú.

Dictado
Escribe las oraciones de la grabación.

Repaso de Vocabulario 1

Asking someone's name and saying yours

¿Cómo se llama él (ella)?	What's his (her) name?
¿Cómo se llama usted?	What's your name? (formal)
¿Cómo te llamas?	What's your name? (familiar)
Él (Ella) es...	He (She) is . . .
Él (Ella) se llama...	His (Her) name is . . .
Me llamo...	My name is . . .
¿Quién es...?	Who is . . .?
Soy...	I'm . . .
¿Y tú?	And you? (familiar)

Asking and saying how you are

Adiós.	Goodbye.
Buenas noches.	Good evening, good night.
Buenas tardes.	Good afternoon.
Buenos días.	Good morning.
¿Cómo está usted?	How are you?
Estoy bien, gracias.	I'm fine, thanks.
Estoy regular/mal.	I'm all right/not so good.
Hasta luego.	See you later.
Hasta mañana.	See you tomorrow.
Hasta pronto.	See you soon.
Hola, ¿cómo estás?	Hi, how are you?
Más o menos.	So-so.
Nos vemos.	See you.
¿Qué tal?	How's it going?
señor	sir, Mr.
señora	ma'am, Mrs.
señorita	Miss

| Tengo que irme. | I have to go. |
| ¿Y usted? | And you? (formal) |

Introducing others

Encantado(a).	Pleased/Nice to meet you.
Ésta es Rosa/la señora...	This is Rosa/Mrs. . . .
Éste es Juan/el señor...	This is Juan/Mr. . . .
el/la estudiante	student (male or female)
Igualmente.	Likewise.
mi mejor amiga	my best friend (female)
mi mejor amigo	my best friend (male)
mi profesora	my teacher (female)
mi profesor	my teacher (male)
...de ciencias	science . . .
...de español	Spanish . . .
la muchacha	the girl
el muchacho	the boy
Mucho gusto.	Pleased/Nice to meet you.
una compañera de clase	a (female) classmate
un compañero de clase	a (male) classmate

Saying where you and others are from

¿De dónde eres?	Where are you from? (familiar)
¿De dónde es...?	Where is . . . from?
¿De dónde es usted?	Where are you from? (formal)
Es de...	He (She) is from . . .
ser	to be
Soy de...	I'm from . . .

Repaso de Vocabulario 2

Exchanging phone numbers

| ¿Cuál es el teléfono de...? | What's . . . telephone number? |
| ¿Cuál es tu teléfono? | What's your telephone number? |

Los números 0–31 . . . . See p. 18.

Telling time

de la mañana	in the morning, A.M.
de la noche	at night, P.M.
de la tarde	in the afternoon, P.M.
en punto	on the dot
Es la una.	It's one o'clock.
medianoche	midnight
mediodía	midday, noon
menos cuarto	a quarter to
¿Qué hora es?	What time is it?

Son las...	It's . . . o'clock.
y cuarto	a quarter past
y media	half past

Giving the date and the day

Es el primero (dos, tres) de...	It's the first (second, third) of . . .
Hoy es lunes.	Today is Monday.
¿Qué día es hoy?	What day is today?
¿Qué fecha es hoy?	What's today's date?

Los días de la semana . . . . See p. 21.
Los meses y las estaciones del año . . . . . . See p. 21.
El alfabeto . . . . See p. 22.

**Spelling words and giving
e-mail addresses** . . . . See p. 23.

Prepárate para el examen

Integración

capítulo 1

 1 Listen to each conversation and match it with the appropriate picture.

2 Read the following conversation between Marisa and Sonia and decide if the statements are **cierto** or **falso**.

MARISA	Hola Sonia. ¿Cómo estás?
SONIA	Bien. ¿Y tú?
MARISA	Más o menos. Dime, ¿cuál es el correo electrónico de Pilar, Alicia y Jorge?
SONIA	No sé el correo electrónico de Pilar. El correo electrónico de Alicia es a-ele-i arroba be-ese-te punto hache-ere-uve doble punto ce-o-eme y el correo electrónico de Jorge es jota-uno-tres-seis arroba a-te-ene punto hache-ere-uve doble punto ce-o-eme.
MARISA	Gracias. ¿Cuál es el teléfono de Pilar?
SONIA	Es dos-treinta y uno-veintinueve-doce.
MARISA	Muchas gracias. ¿Sabes *(do you know)* qué hora es?
SONIA	Sí, son las dos menos cuarto de la tarde.
MARISA	Uy, tengo que irme. Hasta luego.
SONIA	Adiós.

1. Marisa y Sonia son amigas.
2. Marisa está mal.
3. El correo electrónico de Alicia es ali@bst.hrw.com.
4. El correo electrónico de Jorge es j136@atn.hrw.com.
5. El teléfono de Pilar es 2-31-19-12.
6. Son las 2:15.

3 Salvador Dalí was born in Figueras, Spain, on May 11, 1904. He died on January 23, 1989. He was a leader of the painters called 'surrealists', who liked to show dream-like images in their work. Study the painting and write the following in Spanish.

1. a sentence that tells where the artist is from
2. his birth date
3. a question: *What time is it?*
4. an answer to the time question based on the large clock face
5. names of numbers you see in the painting
6. names of colors you see in the painting
7. the date of the artist's death

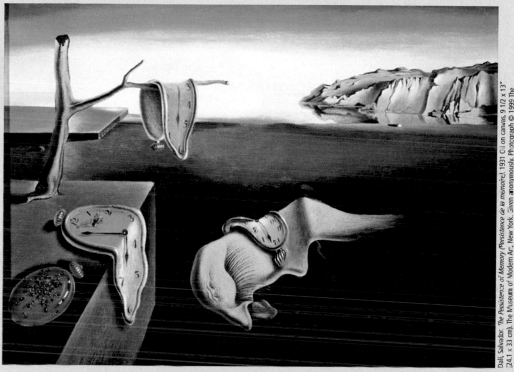

La persistencia de la memoria, de Salvador Dalí (1904–1989)

Dalí, Salvador. *The Persistence of Memory (Persistence de la memoire),* 1931. Oil on canvas, 9 1/2 x 13" (24.1 x 33 cm). The Museum of Modern Art, New York. Given anonymously. Photograph © 1999 The Museum of Modern Art, New York.; © 2003 Salvador Dalí, Gala-Salvador Dalí Foundation/Artists Rights Society (ARS), New York; Digital Image © The Museum of Modern Art/Licensed by SCALA/Art Resource, NY.

4 Situación **I**magine that you have just joined the Spanish Club and are meeting a new friend. Work with a partner. Have a conversation where you:

  ▶ greet each other using appropriate gestures
  ▶ exchange names
  ▶ ask and tell each other how you are doing
  ▶ ask and tell each other where you are from
  ▶ spell out your e-mail addresses and phone numbers for each other
  ▶ close the conversation and say you'll see each other soon

Repaso cumulativo

Video/DVD
GeoVisión

Geocultura
Puerto Rico

▲ **El Viejo San Juan** The buildings and streets of Old San Juan reflect the Spanish colonial period.

▼ **San Juan** The capital of Puerto Rico, San Juan, is on the northeastern coast of the island.

Isabela ●

● Rincón

Río Grande de Añasco

● Mayagüez

Almanac

Population
3,916,632

Capital San Juan

Government
commonwealth associated with the United States

Official Languages
Spanish, English

Currency U.S. dollar

Internet Code
www.[ ].pr

◄ **Jóvenes de Puerto Rico** The different heritage of these students is evidence of Puerto Rico's history.

¿Sabías que...?

Did you know that the island of **Puerto Rico** was first named **San Juan Bautista,** and the capital was named **Puerto Rico** *(rich port)*?

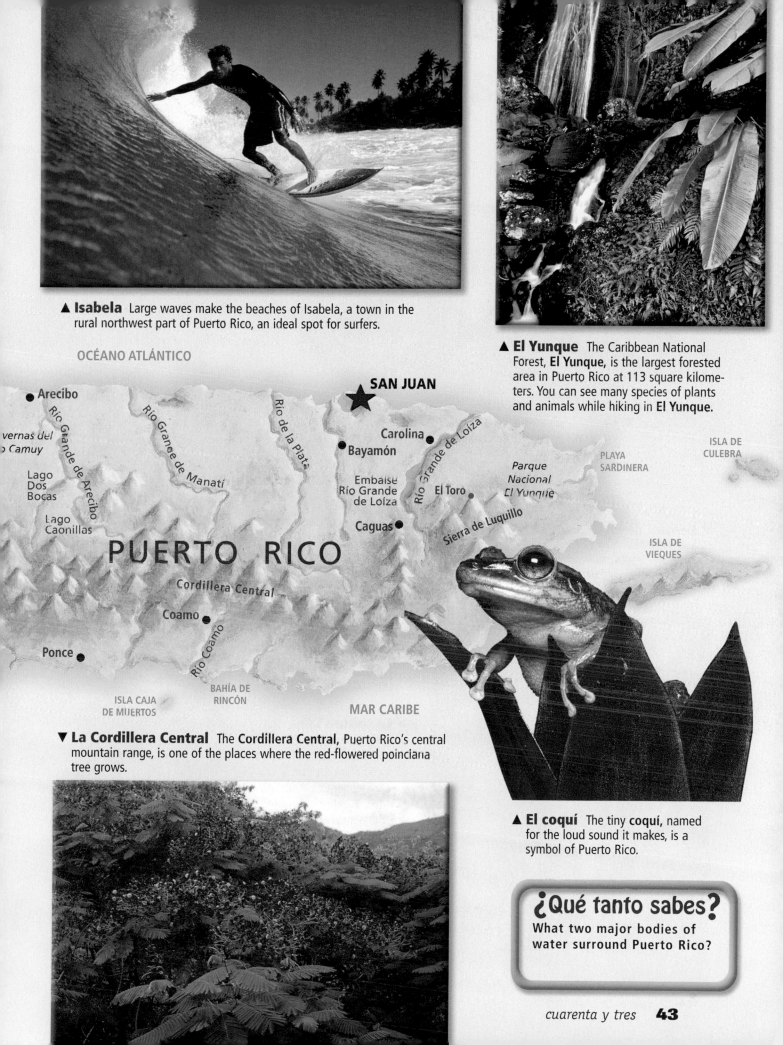

▲ **Isabela** Large waves make the beaches of Isabela, a town in the rural northwest part of Puerto Rico, an ideal spot for surfers.

▲ **El Yunque** The Caribbean National Forest, **El Yunque**, is the largest forested area in Puerto Rico at 113 square kilometers. You can see many species of plants and animals while hiking in **El Yunque**.

OCÉANO ATLÁNTICO

SAN JUAN

Arecibo

Río Grande de Arecibo

Río Grande de Manatí

Río de la Plata

Carolina

Bayamón

Río Grande de Loíza

vernas del Camuy

Lago Dos Bocas

Embalse Río Grande de Loíza

El Toro

Parque Nacional El Yunque

PLAYA SARDINERA

ISLA DE CULEBRA

Lago Caonillas

PUERTO RICO

Caguas

Sierra de Luquillo

ISLA DE VIEQUES

Cordillera Central

Coamo

Río Coamo

Ponce

ISLA CAJA DE MUERTOS

BAHÍA DE RINCÓN

MAR CARIBE

▼ **La Cordillera Central** The **Cordillera Central,** Puerto Rico's central mountain range, is one of the places where the red-flowered poinciana tree grows.

▲ **El coquí** The tiny **coquí**, named for the loud sound it makes, is a symbol of Puerto Rico.

¿Qué tanto sabes?
What two major bodies of water surround Puerto Rico?

A conocer a Puerto Rico

La comida

▲ **El pollo frito con tostones**
Fried chicken with fried plantains is a typical dish in Puerto Rico.

▲ **Las habichuelas** Habichuelas are beans, a Puerto Rican staple often eaten with rice and chicken or beef.

El arte

▼ **Retrato de un oficial del Regimento Fijo (1790)**
This portrait was painted by José Campeche, one of Puerto Rico's most famous artists. It hangs in the Ponce Museum of Art.

► **Las máscaras de vejigante**
Vejigante masks can be made out of a dried coconut shell. They sometimes have horns and are often painted black or red.

► **La cultura taína** The Taino culture was the dominant culture of Puerto Rico before the arrival of Christopher Columbus in 1493. Puerto Rico's pre-Columbian heritage can be seen in Taino art.

Las celebraciones

Interactive TUTOR

Visit Holt Online

go.hrw.com
KEYWORD: EXP1A CH2
Photo Tour

◀ **La Fiesta de Santiago** The Festival of St. James is celebrated in the town of **Loíza** with traditional music, such as the **bomba** and the **plena**.

¿Sabías que...?

Did you know that the culture of Puerto Rico is a mixture of Taino, African, and European influences? What evidence of these cultures do you see in the music and architecture of Puerto Rico?

▶ **El Festival Casals**
The Casals Festival in San Juan, a celebration of classical music, was founded in 1957 by the famous cellist Pablo Casals.

La arquitectura

▲ **El Parque de Bombas** The unique **Parque de Bombas** in Ponce was a fire station from 1883 until 1989. Today it is a museum dedicated to the Ponce fire department.

◀ **El Morro** Construction of this Spanish fortress began in 1539. Its outer walls are six meters thick. The circular sentry boxes, or **garitas,** have become the architectural symbol of Puerto Rico.

2

¡A conocernos!

Objetivos

In Part 1 you will learn to:
- ask what someone is like
- describe someone
- ask about someone's age and birthday
- tell someone your age and birthday
- use **ser** with adjectives
- use gender and adjective agreement
- form questions

In Part 2 you will learn to:
- talk about what you and others like
- describe things
- use singular and plural forms of nouns
- use definite articles
- use the verb **gustar**
- use the words **¿por qué?** and **porque**
- use **de** in different ways

¿Qué ves en la foto?

- **¿De dónde es el muchacho?**

- **¿Cómo son las muchachas?**

- **¿Cómo eres tú ?**

Video/DVD
xpresaVisión

so

El parque Antonia S. Quiñones,
Condado, Puerto Rico

Vocabulario
en acción 1

En un colegio de San Juan

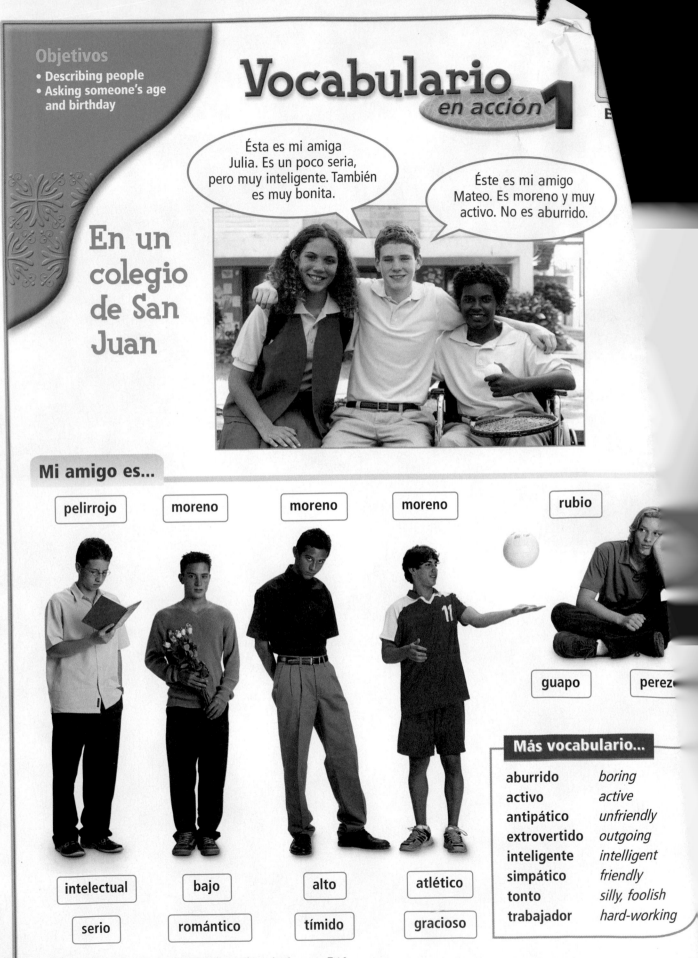

Ésta es mi amiga Julia. Es un poco seria, pero muy inteligente. También es muy bonita.

Éste es mi amigo Mateo. Es moreno y muy activo. No es aburrido.

Mi amigo es...

| pelirrojo | moreno | moreno | moreno | rubio |

guapo   perez[...]

intelectual   bajo   alto   atlético

serio   romántico   tímido   gracioso

Más vocabulario...

aburrido	boring
activo	active
antipático	unfriendly
extrovertido	outgoing
inteligente	intelligent
simpático	friendly
tonto	silly, foolish
trabajador	hard-working

▶ Vocabulario adicional, Palabras descriptivas, p. R10

Mi amiga es...

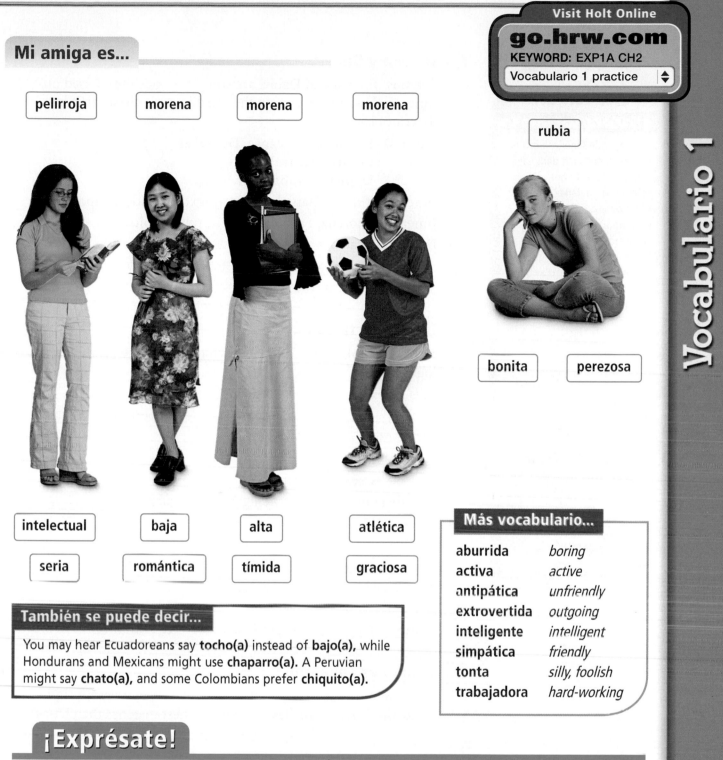

pelirroja · morena · morena · morena · rubia

bonita · perezosa

intelectual · baja · alta · atlética

seria · romántica · tímida · graciosa

Más vocabulario...

aburrida	*boring*
activa	*active*
antipática	*unfriendly*
extrovertida	*outgoing*
inteligente	*intelligent*
simpática	*friendly*
tonta	*silly, foolish*
trabajadora	*hard-working*

También se puede decir...

You may hear Ecuadoreans say **tocho(a)** instead of **bajo(a)**, while Hondurans and Mexicans might use **chaparro(a)**. A Peruvian might say **chato(a)**, and some Colombians prefer **chiquito(a)**.

¡Exprésate!

To ask what someone is like	To describe someone
¿Cómo es Paco? *What's Paco like?*	**Paco es moreno. También es inteligente y un poco tímido.** *Paco has dark hair/a dark complexion. He's also intelligent and a little shy.*
¿Cómo eres? ¿Eres cómico(a)? *What are you like? Are you funny?*	**Sí, soy bastante cómico(a).** *Yes, I'm pretty funny.*

Interactive TUTOR

▶ Vocabulario y gramática, pp. 13–15

Online workbooks

Vocabulario 1

1 Jimena y Daniel

Leamos Jimena and Daniel are complete opposites. Based on Jimena's description, choose the word in parentheses that best describes Daniel.

MODELO Jimena es perezosa. Daniel es ▰▰▰.
(antipático/trabajador)
Daniel es trabajador.

1. Jimena es tímida. Daniel es ▰▰▰. (extrovertido/guapo)
2. Jimena es morena. Daniel es ▰▰▰. (alto/rubio)
3. Jimena es graciosa. Daniel es ▰▰▰. (atlético/serio)
4. Jimena es baja. Daniel es ▰▰▰. (alto/pelirrojo)
5. Jimena es atlética. Daniel es ▰▰▰. (moreno/intelectual)

2 Luis y Marta son...

Leamos/Hablemos Complete each description with the most logical choice.

1. Luis no es moreno. Es...
   a. bajo   **b.** rubio   **c.** perezoso
2. Marta no es antipática. Es...
   a. tímida   **b.** activa   **c.** simpática
3. Luis no es perezoso. Es...
   a. trabajador   **b.** inteligente   **c.** pelirrojo
4. Marta no es tímida. Es...
   a. extrovertida   **b.** morena   **c.** atlética
5. Luis no es bajo. Es...
   a. romántico   **b.** gracioso   **c.** alto
6. Marta no es pelirroja. Es...
   a. morena   **b.** perezosa   **c.** bonita

3 ¿Cómo es cada uno?

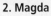
Escuchemos For each picture, you will hear two descriptions. Write the letter of the description that best matches the picture.

| 1. Roberto | 2. Magda | 3. Geraldo | 4. Julieta |

4 ¿Cómo es?

Leamos/Escribamos Read the statements about the picture and respond with **cierto** (*true*) or **falso** (*false*). Rewrite any false statements so they are true.

1. Lucía es baja.
2. La abuela es rubia.
3. Panchito es moreno y activo.
4. Oso es perezoso.
5. El señor Medina es moreno.
6. Lupita Reyes es bonita.
7. El señor Medina es antipático.

Comunicación

5 ¿Quién es?

Hablemos With a partner, take turns describing the characters in the picture above. Have your partner guess who you are describing.

MODELO —Es bonita y morena.
—Es Lupita Reyes.

Más vocabulario...

32	treinta y dos
33	treinta y tres
40	cuarenta
50	cincuenta
60	sesenta
70	setenta
80	ochenta
90	noventa
100	cien

¡Exprésate!

To ask someone's age and birthday	To respond
¿Cuántos años tienes? *How old are you?*	**Tengo quince años.** *I'm 15 years old.*
¿Cuántos años tiene María? *How old is Maria?*	**Ella tiene veintiún años.** *She's 21 years old.*
¿Cuándo es tu cumpleaños? *When is your birthday?*	**Es el 6 de mayo.** *It's May 6th.*
¿Cuándo es el cumpleaños de Ana? *When is Ana's birthday?*	**Es el 24 de noviembre.** *It's November 24th.*

Vocabulario y gramática, pp. 13–15

Online workbooks

6 Respuesta lógica

Leamos Choose the best response to each question.

1. ¿Cuántos años tienes?
2. ¿Cómo eres?
3. ¿Cuándo es tu cumpleaños?
4. ¿Quién es tu mejor amigo?
5. ¿Cómo es?
6. ¿Cuántos años tiene?
7. ¿Cuándo es el cumpleaños de Ana?

a. Es Juan.
b. Mi cumpleaños es el dos de mayo.
c. El cumpleaños de ella es el once de marzo.
d. Soy tímido y serio.
e. Tengo doce años.
f. Tiene trece años.
g. Es rubio(a) y activo(a).

7 Edades y cumpleaños

Escribamos Using the prompts, write questions that ask for the required information. Then write the answers.

MODELO Luisa/13 years old/January 17
—¿Cuántos años tiene Luisa?
—Tiene trece años.
—¿Cuándo es el cumpleaños de Luisa?
—Es el 17 de enero.

1. Mr. López/85 years old/July 15
2. Mrs. García/79 years old/December 12
3. Carmen/26 years old/April 30
4. Francisco/2 years old/September 25
5. you/12 years old/May 6

8 ¿Quién es?

Leamos Daniel has written these notes about family members. Match each description with a picture.

1. El cumpleaños de Carlitos es el 13 de octubre; él tiene dos años.
2. El cumpleaños de Diego es el 24 de marzo y tiene doce años.
3. El cumpleaños de Martina es el 15 de junio. Ella tiene diez años.
4. Todos los primos tienen *(cousins have)* cumpleaños en febrero.
5. El cumpleaños de tía *(aunt)* Juanita es el 31 de agosto; ella tiene treinta y tres años.

Comunicación

HOLT **SoundBooth** ONLINE RECORDING

9 Presentaciones

Hablemos Take turns with two classmates introducing yourselves to each other. First exchange greetings, then ask each other's names, ages, and birthdays. Be prepared to introduce each other to the class and report the information that you just learned.

MODELO —Hola, ¿cómo te llamas?
—Me llamo...
—¿Cuántos años tienes?
—Tengo... años.
—¿Cuándo es tu cumpleaños?
—Es el... de...

Objetivos
• **Ser** with adjectives
• Gender and adjective agreement
• Forming questions

Gramática
en acción 1

GramaVisión

Video/DVD

Ser with adjectives

Interactive TUTOR

1 **Adjectives** are words that describe people or things. You can use the verb **ser** with **adjectives** to describe what someone is like.

Carlos **es simpático.**   Pedro **es pelirrojo.**

Ana **es simpática.**   Rosa y Julio **son inteligentes.**

2 In Spanish, you don't usually need the subject pronoun if it's clear who the subject is.

—¿Cómo **es** el profesor?   —**Es bajo** y **gracioso.**

—¿Cómo **son** Leticia y Diego?   —**Son simpáticos.**

3 To say what someone is not like, put **no** in front of the verb.
No soy bajo. **Soy** alto.

Vocabulario y gramática, pp. 16–18
Actividades, pp. 11–13

Online workbooks

¿Te acuerdas?

Remember that **ser** means *to be.*

yo **soy**	nosotros(as) **somos**
tú **eres**	vosotros(as) **sois**
usted **es**	ustedes **son**
él/ella **es**	ellos/ellas **son**

10 **¿Cómo son...?**

Leamos Complete these sentences about your classmates, your friends, your teacher, and yourself.

1. Yo ===== muy alto(a).
   a. soy   **b.** no soy

2. Profesor(a), usted ===== moreno(a).
   a. es   **b.** no es

3. Tú ===== tímido(a).
   a. eres   **b.** no eres

4. Mi mejor amigo ===== cómico.
   a. es   **b.** no es

5. Mis amigos(as) y yo ===== serios(as).
   a. somos   **b.** no somos

6. Los estudiantes ===== tontos.
   a. son   **b.** no son

7. Mis compañeros de clase ===== perezosos.
   a. son   **b.** no son

11 **Una persona simpática**

Escribamos/Hablemos Roberto always says good things about everyone. What does he say about the following people?

MODELO yo/guapo → **Soy guapo.**
tú/tonta → **No eres tonta.**

1. yo/perezoso
2. tú/bonita
3. mi amigo Carlos/inteligente
4. Profesor Garza, usted/ aburrido

5. nosotros/simpáticos
6. Mari y Gisela/graciosas
7. mis compañeras de clase/antipáticas
8. ustedes/activos

12 **¿Quién es...?**

Escribamos/Hablemos Look at the photos below, and say who is described by each adjective.

MODELO simpático(a)
Felipe es simpático.

Felipe

Gladys

Juan

Rebeca

1. rubio(a)
2. atlético(a)
3. moreno(a)

4. serio(a)
5. intelectual
6. tímido(a)

7. bonita
8. pelirrojo(a)
9. extrovertido(a)

Comunicación

HOLT SoundBooth
ONLINE RECORDING

13 **Yo soy... ¿Y tú?**

Hablemos Write down three adjectives that describe you. If you're male, use the words on page 48. If you're female, use the words on page 49. Then get together in small groups. Record how many students in your group used the same adjectives that you used.

MODELO atlético(a)
—**¿Eres atlético(a)?**
—**Sí, soy atlético(a)./—No, no soy atlético(a).**

Interactive
TUTOR

Gender and adjective agreement

1 Nouns and pronouns in Spanish are divided into genders. Nouns for men and boys are **masculine**. Nouns for women and girls are **feminine**.

> **Masculine:** amigo, él, Juan   **Feminine:** amiga, ella, María

2 Adjectives describe nouns. They have different forms that match, or agree with, the noun or pronoun in gender. The **masculine** form of most adjectives ends in **-o**, while the **feminine** form ends in **-a**.

> **Raúl** es romántic**o**.   **Mari** es romántic**a**.

Adjectives that end in **-e** have the same **masculine** and **feminine** forms.

> **Rafael** es inteligent**e**.   **Carmen** es inteligent**e**.

Adjectives ending in **consonants** do not add an **-a**, unless they end in **-or** or are adjectives of nationality.

> **Lorenzo** es español, intelectual   **Gloria** es española, intelectual
> y trabajad**or**.   y trabajador**a**.

3 Adjectives also agree with nouns in number. An adjective that describes one person or thing is in **singular** form. When it describes more than one person or thing, its form is **plural**. If the singular form ends in a vowel, add **-s** to make it plural. If it ends in a consonant, add **-es**.

> Joaquín es alt**o**.   Paco y Luis son altos.
> Rosa es intelectua**l**.   Mis amigos son intelectual**es**.

To describe a mixed group of men and women, boys and girls, use the **masculine plural** forms of the adjective:

> **Carlos** y **Ana** son romántic**os**.

Vocabulario y gramática, pp. 16–18
Actividades, pp. 11–13

Online workbooks

14 ¿Cómo son los gemelos?

Escribamos Mario and María are twins who are similiar in personality and looks. Say what María is like based on Mario's description. Then describe Gabriel and Gabriela as the opposites of Mario and María, using plural adjectives.

MODELO **Mario es moreno. María es morena también.**
Gabriel y Gabriela son rubios.

1. Mario es bajo.
2. Mario es intelectual.
3. Mario es perezoso.
4. Mario es simpático.
5. Mario es tímido.
6. Mario es serio.

En las calles del Viejo San Juan

15 Mi clase favorita

Leamos/Escribamos A student has only good things to say about her favorite class. Complete her description with the correct forms of the most logical adjective in parentheses.

La clase es muy interesante y la profesora es ___1___ (simpático, antipático). Los estudiantes son ___2___ (perezoso, trabajador). Mis amigas Marta y Gabi son muy ___3___ (tonto, intelectual) y mi amigo Ricardo es muy ___4___ (gracioso, aburrido). ¿Y yo? Soy ___5___ (tonto, inteligente) y ___6___ (activo, perezoso).

16 ¿Cómo son?

Escribamos/Hablemos Describe yourself and people you know by combining words from each column. Use the correct forms of the verb **ser** and the adjectives listed.

MODELO Mis amigas y yo somos graciosas.

1	**2**	**3**	
yo	eres	simpático	activo
mi mejor amigo(a)	es	inteligente	perezoso
mis amigos y yo	son	atlético	interesante
tú (una compañera de clase)	somos	gracioso	trabajador
profesor(a), usted	soy	tímido	serio
ustedes			

Comunicación

HOLT **SoundBooth** ONLINE RECORDING

17 Nuestros compañeros

Hablemos With a partner, take turns describing someone from the picture below and guessing who is being described.

Sócrates   Romeo   Azucena   Linda   Paco   Luis   Jimena

Gramática 1

Question formation

1 To ask a question that may be answered **sí** or **no**, just raise the pitch of your voice at the end of the question. The **subject,** if included, can go before or after the **verb**.

¿Eres extrovertido?	*Are you outgoing?*
¿La profesora es simpática?	*Is the teacher nice?*
¿Es simpática **la profesora?**	*Is the teacher nice?*

2 You can answer a question like this with **sí** or **no.** You say the word **no** twice in your answer: once to mean *no* and another time to mean *not*.

—¿Eres atlético?	*Are you athletic?*
—**Sí**, soy atlético.	*Yes, I'm athletic.*
—**No, no** soy atlético.	*(No, I'm not athletic.)*

3 You can ask for more information by using **question words**. Notice that all question words are written with an accent mark.

¿Cómo es Paco?	*What's Paco like?*
¿Cuándo es tu cumpleaños?	*When is your birthday?*
¿Quién es?	*Who is he (she)?*
¿Quiénes son?	*Who are they?*
¿Qué día es hoy?	*What day is today?*
¿De dónde eres?	*Where are you from?*
¿Cuál es tu teléfono?	*What's your phone number?*

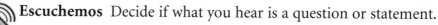

Vocabulario y gramática, pp. 16–18
Actividades, pp. 11–13

Online workbooks

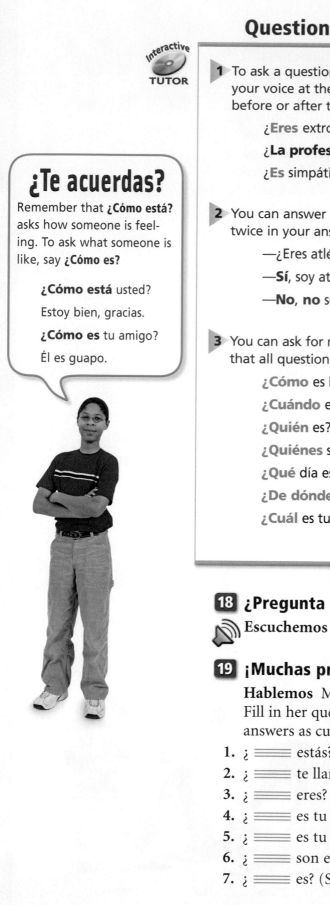

¿Te acuerdas?

Remember that **¿Cómo está?** asks how someone is feeling. To ask what someone is like, say **¿Cómo es?**

¿Cómo está usted?

Estoy bien, gracias.

¿Cómo es tu amigo?

Él es guapo.

---

18 **¿Pregunta o no?**

Escuchemos Decide if what you hear is a question or statement.

19 **¡Muchas preguntas!**

Hablemos María is full of questions for her new neighbor, Jorge. Fill in her questions with the best question word. Use Jorge's answers as cues.

1. ¿ ===== estás? (Estoy bien, gracias.)
2. ¿ ===== te llamas? (Me llamo Jorge.)
3. ¿ ===== eres? (Soy de Puerto Rico.)
4. ¿ ===== es tu cumpleaños? (Es el 10 de enero.)
5. ¿ ===== es tu teléfono? (Es 809-1212.)
6. ¿ ===== son ellos? (Son mis amigos Luisa y Óscar.)
7. ¿ ===== es? (Son las tres. Tengo que irme.)

20 ¿Qué tal?

Leamos/Escribamos Read the e-mail and then answer the questions.

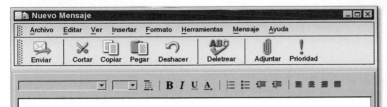

Hola. Me llamo Rocío Sotomayor. Soy de Puerto Rico. Tengo trece años. Soy alta, morena y muy extrovertida. Mi mejor amiga es Carolina. Ella es de Nicaragua. Tiene doce años. Es seria y bastante tímida. Y tú, ¿cómo eres?

Rocío y Carolina en San Juan

1. ¿De dónde es Rocío?
2. ¿Cuántos años tiene?
3. ¿Es rubia o morena?
4. ¿Cómo es Rocío?
5. ¿De dónde es Carolina?
6. ¿Cómo es ella?

21 Entrevista a Gisela

Hablemos/Escribamos On a separate piece of paper, write the missing questions to complete the interview.

MODELO —¿Cómo estás?
—Muy bien, gracias.

1. ¿ ═══ ? —Me llamo Gisela Ríos Perales.
2. ¿ ═══ ? —Soy de Burgos, España.
3. ¿ ═══ ? —No, no soy tímida. Soy extrovertida.
4. ¿ ═══ ? —Son inteligentes, simpáticos y atléticos.
5. ¿ ═══ ? —Tengo once años.
6. ¿ ═══ ? —Mi cumpleaños es el quince de marzo.

Nota cultural

In the United States, a person's 16th and 18th birthdays are important milestones. In most Spanish-speaking countries, the legal driving and voting age is 18. Since Puerto Ricans are U.S. citizens, they can vote when they are 18 years old. They can get their driver's license at age 18 or at 16 with parental consent.

How would your 18th birthday be different if you lived in Puerto Rico?

22 Veinte preguntas

Hablemos Ask your partner to think of a classmate. Guess who he or she is by asking questions that can be answered with **sí** or **no**. Keep trying until you guess correctly. Switch roles.

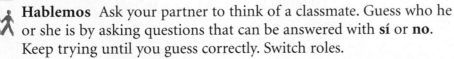

Gramática 1

Cultura

Comparaciones

Un grupo de amigos, San Juan

¿Cómo eres?

There's a saying in Spanish, **"Dime con quién andas y te diré quién eres."** *(Tell me who you spend time with and I'll tell you who you are.)* This saying is like the English expressions "Birds of a feather flock together" and "You're known by the company you keep." These sayings stem from the belief that we choose as friends those who are much like ourselves. Why do you think both English and Spanish have these sayings? Do you think they are true? Why or why not?

Luis
San Juan, Puerto Rico

Luis talks about the interests that he and his best friend have in common. Do you and your best friend have common interests?

Dime, ¿cómo eres tú?

Bueno, pues, yo me considero una persona simpática, graciosa, alegre, un buen amigo y una buena persona.

¿Y qué cosas te gustan?

Me gusta el deporte. Me gusta la música. Me gusta la escuela.

¿Cómo es tu mejor amigo?

Pues, es una persona que es simpática también, amigable, alegre, atleta. Él es moreno. Es bien activo. Me gusta ser amigo de él.

¿Qué cosas le gustan a él?

Le gusta también la música, el deporte. Le gusta la escuela. Y como es una persona alegre, pues no le gusta estar aburrido.

¿Cómo son ustedes?

Pues, tenemos muchos gustos como lo de la música y pues además nos llevamos bien y nos comprendemos en todo.

¿Qué significa la expresión "Dime con quién andas y te diré quién eres"?

Yo pienso que, que es con quien tú te pasas, según esa persona, pues, va a ser tu personalidad.

¿La expresión se aplica en su caso?

Sí.

Océano Atlántico   San Juan
★
PUERTO RICO
Mar Caribe

Cultura

☀ Andrea
Ciudad de México, México

Andrea talks about what she and her friends have in common. Do you and your friends have similiar personalities?

¿Cómo eres tú?

Yo soy alegre, inteligente y divertida.

¿Qué cosas te gustan a ti?

Pues, me gusta el cine, me gustan los libros, la música.

¿Cómo es tu mejor amigo o amiga?

Es alegre también, es divertida y muy inteligente.

¿Qué cosas le gustan a ella?

Le gusta el cine, los libros, bailar.

¿Cómo son ustedes?

Somos muy parecidas.

¿Qué cosas les gustan?

Nos gusta el cine, bailar, cantar.

¿La expresión se aplica en este caso?

Sí, porque somos muy parecidas. Salimos mucho juntas.

Para comprender

1. ¿Qué cosas le gustan a Luis?
2. ¿Qué cosas le gustan a Andrea?
3. ¿A quién le gustan las películas?
4. ¿El amigo de Luis es atlético?
5. ¿Quién es más como su amigo(a), Luis o Andrea?

Para pensar y hablar

Both Luis and Andrea say that the expression **"Dime con quién andas y te diré quién eres"** applies to them and their friends. Based on what they say, do you agree? What are two advantages and disadvantages of being like your friends?

Comunidad
Teaching What We Know

One good way to learn a language is to teach it to someone. Arrange to visit a class to teach some basic Spanish phrases.

◆ When you enter the class, choose a student to talk to.

◆ Greet the student in Spanish, shake hands and get the class to repeat the greeting.

◆ Tell the class your name, and teach everyone to say **Me llamo** + name.

◆ Say goodbye in Spanish, and have the class repeat the expression.

◆ As you leave, thank the teacher and students for letting you visit.

Jóvenes mexicanos conociendo a un nuevo amigo

Vocabulario
en acción 2

ExpresaVisión

Me gusta...

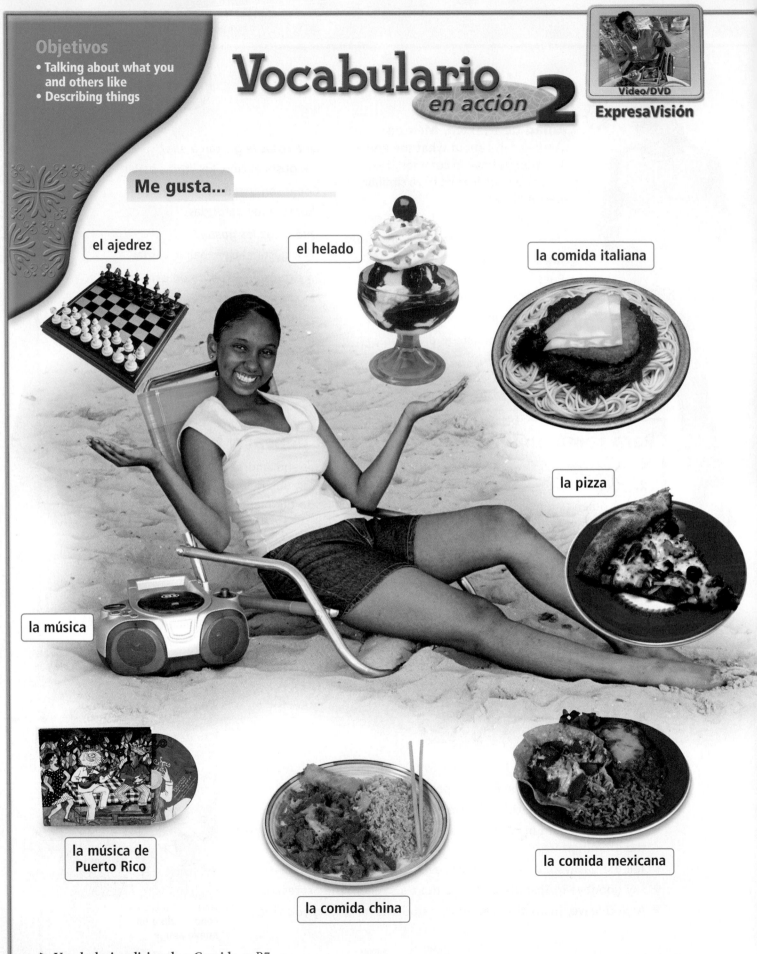

el ajedrez

el helado

la comida italiana

la pizza

la música

la música de Puerto Rico

la comida china

la comida mexicana

▶ Vocabulario adicional — Comida, p. R7

Me gustan...

los libros (de aventuras, de amor)

las películas (de ciencia ficción, de terror, de misterio)

los carros

las fiestas

las hamburguesas

las verduras

las frutas

los deportes

los videojuegos

los animales

¡Exprésate!

To ask someone what he or she likes	To respond
¿Te gusta(n)...? *Do you like . . . ?*	**Sí, me gusta(n) mucho...** *Yes, I like . . . a lot.* **No, no me gusta(n)...** *No, I don't like . . .*
¿Te gusta(n) más...o...? *Do you like . . . or . . . more?*	**Me gusta(n) más...** *I like . . . more.* **Me da igual.** *It's all the same to me.*

Interactive TUTOR

Vocabulario y gramática, pp. 19–21

Online workbooks

▶ **Vocabulario adicional** — Deportes y pasatiempos, p. R8

Vocabulario 2

23 Dime cómo eres

Leamos/Hablemos Based on the descriptions, which item in parentheses would these people say they like or don't like?

MODELO Me llamo Carlos. Soy muy atlético. Me gustan ═══ (los libros/los deportes).
Me gustan los deportes.

1. ¿Qué tal? Soy Marta y soy muy extrovertida. Me gustan ═══ (las fiestas/los libros).

2. Soy Juan y me gusta la pizza. Me gusta ═══ (la comida mexicana/la comida italiana).

3. Buenas tardes. Me llamo Javier y soy muy romántico. Me gustan ═══ (las películas de ciencia ficción/las películas de amor).

4. Hola. Yo soy Samuel y soy intelectual. Me gustan ═══ (los videojuegos/los libros).

5. Soy Carlota y no soy muy activa. Me gustan ═══ (los videojuegos/los deportes).

6. Hola, me llamo Celia. No soy muy atlética. No me gustan ═══ (los deportes/las fiestas).

7. Soy Enrique y soy muy tímido. No me gustan mucho ═══ (los carros/las fiestas).

24 ¿Quiénes hablan?

Escuchemos You will hear four conversations. Decide which conversation goes with each photo.

A

B

C

D

25 ¿Qué te gusta?

Escribamos Write complete sentences to answer these questions.

1. ¿Te gusta el helado?
2. ¿Te gustan los carros?
3. ¿Te gusta más la comida mexicana o la comida italiana?
4. ¿Te gustan más las frutas o las verduras?
5. ¿Te gustan las hamburguesas?
6. ¿Te gustan más los deportes o los videojuegos?

26 ¿Qué les gusta?

Escribamos Imagine that you are working in the cafeteria and you are asking Ana, Gloria, and Beto what they like. Write their answers to the following questions.

MODELO —¿Qué te gusta, Gloria?

—Me gusta la pizza.

1. ¿Qué te gusta, Beto?
2. Gloria, ¿te gusta la fruta?
3. Ana, ¿te gustan las verduras?
4. Beto, ¿te gusta la comida mexicana?
5. ¿Qué te gusta, Ana?

| la pizza | la fruta | las verduras | la comida mexicana | la comida china | el helado |

 Comunicación

27 ¡Entrevista!

Hablemos Interview a classmate. Find out your partner's name, age, birthday, and where he or she is from. Also find out at least three things your partner likes and doesn't like. Be prepared to present your interview to the class.

¿Cómo te llamas?	¿Cuántos años tienes?	¿Qué te gusta?
¿Qué no te gusta?	¿De dónde eres?	¿Cuándo es tu cumpleaños?

¡Exprésate!

To describe something	
¿Cómo es...? *What's . . . like?*	**Es (muy) delicioso(a)/horrible.** *It's (really) delicious/horrible.*
	Es pésimo(a)/fenomenal/formidable. *It's awful/awesome/great.*
	Es algo divertido(a)/interesante. *It's kind of fun/interesting.*
	Es bastante bueno(a)/malo(a). *It's quite good/bad.*

Interactive **TUTOR**

Vocabulario y gramática, pp. 19–21

Online workbooks

28 ¿Qué dice?

Leamos Look at the pictures and choose the word that best completes each of the following sentences.

1. 2. 3. 4.

1. La música es aburrida/divertida.
2. Los libros de amor son muy románticos/no son interesantes.
3. Los videojuegos son pésimos/fenomenales.
4. Las verduras son deliciosas/horribles.

29 En tu opinión

Escribamos/Hablemos Say whether or not you agree with the description of each item. Make sure adjectives agree with the nouns they modify.

MODELO la pizza/bueno
Sí, la pizza es buena. /No, la pizza no es buena.

1. el helado/delicioso
2. la comida china/bueno
3. las verduras/delicioso
4. las películas de terror/horrible
5. los libros de misterio/pésimo
6. los deportes/divertido

30 Descripciones

Escribamos Write answers to each question by describing the things below. Use a different adjective to describe each picture.

1. ¿Cómo es el libro de amor?
2. ¿Cómo son los deportes?
3. ¿Cómo son Chato y Salchicha?
4. ¿Cómo es el videojuego?
5. ¿Cómo es el libro?
6. ¿Cómo es el cumpleaños de Lupe?

1.

2.

3.

4.

5.

6.

Comunicación

HOLT **SoundBooth**
ONLINE RECORDING

31 ¿Te gustan o no?

Hablemos Work with a partner. Find out whether or not your classmate likes the things listed below. Take turns.

MODELO —¿Te gustan los videojuegos?
—Sí, me gustan. Son fenomenales. (No, no me gustan. Son aburridos.)

los videojuegos	los animales	las películas de aventuras
los libros de amor	los deportes	las fiestas

Objetivos
- Nouns with definite articles
- Gustar, ¿por qué? and **porque**
- The preposition **de**

Gramática
en acción 2

GramaVisión

Nouns and definite articles

Interactive TUTOR

1 If a singular noun ends in a **vowel**, add **-s** to make it plural. If a singular noun ends in a **consonant**, add **-es** to make it plural.

estudiant**e** *student*   estudiant**es** *students*
anima**l** *animal*   anima**les** *animals*

2 Adjectives must agree with the **gender** and **number** of the nouns they describe, just as they do when describing people.

La comid**a** mexican**a** es delicios**a**.

3 The **definite articles** can be used to say *the* with a specific noun. They have different forms that agree with the noun in gender and number.

	Masculine	Feminine
SINGULAR	el	la
PLURAL	los	las

—¿Cómo es **el** profesor?   —**El** profesor es simpático.
What is the teacher like?   *The teacher is nice.*

4 Use **definite articles** to talk about a noun as a general category or when saying what you like with **gustar**.

—¿Cómo es **la** pizza?   —Es deliciosa. Me gusta **la** pizza.
What's pizza (in general)   *It's delicious. I like pizza.*
like?

> Vocabulario y gramática, pp. 22–24
> Actividades, pp. 15–17
> **Online** workbooks

En inglés

In English, people and animals are masculine or feminine, but things are always neuter in gender.
The book? It's good!
Ana? She's pretty!

In Spanish, all nouns have gender. With some exceptions, nouns ending in **-o** are masculine, and nouns ending in **-a** are feminine.
el libro
la pizza

Does the English definite article *the* show gender? How do the Spanish definite articles show gender?

32 Los gustos de Luisa

Leamos Luisa wrote a note describing what she likes. Choose the correct answer for each item.

Me gusta ___1___ (el/la) helado porque es ___2___ (delicioso/deliciosa). También me gustan ___3___ (los/las) frutas porque son ___4___ (buenos/buenas). Me gusta mucho ___5___ (el/la) pizza y ¡la comida italiana es ___6___ (fenomenal/fenomenales)! Mi mejor amiga, Juana, es ___7___ (divertido/divertida). Yo soy bastante ___8___ (atlético/atlética). Me gustan mucho ___9___ (los/las) deportes porque son ___10___ (formidable/formidables). Mis amigos y yo somos ___11___ (activos/activas).

33 **Son así...**

Escribamos Write sentences using words from each column.
Remember that articles and adjectives must agree.

1	**2**	**3**	**4**	
El	estudiantes de español	es	serio	aburrido
La	deportes	son	interesante	atlético
Los	helado	somos	bueno	divertido
Las	música mexicana		malo	fenomenal
	fiestas		gracioso	delicioso

34 **¿Te gusta?**

Escribamos Write a sentence saying what
you think each item pictured is like.

MODELO **Las frutas son muy deliciosas.**

1.

2.

3.

4.

5.

6.

7.

8.

Comunicación

HOLT **SoundBooth**
ONLINE RECORDING

35 **Entrevista**

Hablemos Ask three classmates their opinions about the things
in Activity 34. How are their opinions different from yours?

MODELO —¿Cómo son los libros?
—Los libros son horribles/divertidos.

Gramática 2

The verb gustar, ¿por qué?, and porque

En inglés

In English, the definite article *the* is not used when talking about general likes and dislikes.

I like pizza.

How does using *the* change the meaning of a sentence about likes and dislikes?

In Spanish, the definite articles **el, la, los,** and **las** are always used when talking about things you like or dislike.

Me gusta *la* pizza.

1 Use the verb **gustar** to say what people like. If the thing they like is singular, use **gusta**. If it's plural, use **gustan**. Use **¿qué?** with **gusta** to ask what someone likes.

—¿Te **gusta** la pizza?
Do you like pizza?

—Sí, y me **gustan** las verduras.
Yes, and I like vegetables.

—**¿Qué** te **gusta**?
What do you like?

—Me **gustan** los carros.
I like cars.

2 Put one of these **pronouns** before **gustar** to say who likes something.

me gusta(n)	*I like*	**nos** gusta(n)	*we like*
te gusta(n)	*you* (tú) *like*	**os** gusta(n)	*you* (vosotros) *like*
le gusta(n)	*you* (usted) *like, he, she, it likes*	**les** gusta(n)	*you* (ustedes) *like, they like*

3 Notice that **le** can stand for *you* **(usted),** *he, she* or *it;* and **les** can stand for *you* **(ustedes)** or *they.* To ask who is being talked about, use **a quién** or **a quiénes.** To clarify who is being talked about, use **a + name(s).**

—**¿A quién le** gusta la pizza?
Who likes pizza?

—**A Juan le** gusta la pizza.

Juan likes pizza.

—**¿A quiénes les** gusta la pizza?
Who likes pizza?

—**A Juan** y **a Sara les** gusta la pizza.

Juan and Sara like pizza.

4 Put the word **no** before the **pronoun** to say *don't* or *doesn't.*

—¿**Te** gusta la fruta?
Do you like fruit?

—No, **no me** gusta la fruta.
No, I don't like fruit.

5 To ask *why,* say **¿por qué?** Answer with **porque** *(because).*

—¿**Por qué** te gusta el helado?
Why do you like ice cream?

—Me gusta **porque** es delicioso.
I like it because it's delicious.

> Vocabulario y gramática, pp. 22–24
> Actividades, pp. 15–17
> **Online** workbooks

36 El festival de Ponce

Escuchemos Listen to Mari and Josué as they talk about the festival. Decide if the following statements are **cierto** or **falso.**

1. A Mari y a Josué les gusta la fiesta.
2. A Juan no le gusta la fiesta porque no le gusta la comida.
3. A Ana y a Silvia no les gusta la música.
4. A los amigos de Mari les gusta la música.

El festival de Ponce

Capítulo 2 • A conocernos

37 **¿Qué les gusta más?**

Escribamos Based on the descriptions of the following people, which things do they like more?

MODELO Somos muy románticos.
(películas de amor/películas de terror)
Nos gustan más las películas de amor.

1. Eres muy intelectual. (libros/videojuegos)
2. Mis amigos Juan y Beti son atléticos. (música/deportes)
3. Teresa es muy extrovertida. (fiestas/libros)
4. No soy muy atlético. (videojuegos/deportes)
5. Ustedes son bastante serios. (películas de amor/libros de misterio)
6. No somos muy activos. (deportes/películas de aventuras)

Comunicación

HOLT **SoundBooth**
ONLINE RECORDING

38 **La fiesta**

Hablemos You're throwing a party and you want to find out what your guests like. Ask four classmates if they like each of these things. Be prepared to report your findings to the class.

1. ice cream 2. videogames 3. hamburgers 4. fruit 5. music by . . .

39 **¿Por qué te gusta(n)?**

Hablemos With a partner, take turns asking each other if you like the things pictured. Then tell why you like them or not. Be prepared to report to the class what you both like as well as what you disagree about.

MODELO —¿Te gustan los deportes?
—Sí, me gustan los deportes porque son divertidos.

Gramática 2

The preposition de

En inglés

In English, we add **'s** or just an apostrophe **(')** to show ownership.

Chris**'s** class
the teacher**'s** book

How does English use *of* to show possession?

In Spanish, use **de** to show possession.

**la clase de Carlos
los libros de la
profesora**

1 The word **de** is used to tell where someone is from.

Julio es **de** Costa Rica.   *Julio is from Costa Rica.*

2 In addition, **de** can be used to indicate what type of thing you're describing.

los libros **de** aventuras   *adventure books*
las películas **de** misterio   *mystery movies*

3 **De** is also used to show possession or relationship.

Es el carro **de** Ernesto.   *It's Ernesto's car.*

Son los amigos **de** la profesora.   *They're the teacher's friends.*

4 The preposition **de** followed by **el** makes the contraction **del**.

el correo electrónico **del** profesor
the teacher's e-mail address

Vocabulario y gramática, pp. 22–24
Actividades, pp. 15–17

Online workbooks

40 **¿Cómo son?**

Escribamos/Hablemos Complete the statements with **de, del, de la, de los,** or **de las.** Then, decide whether or not each statement is true. Correct the false statements.

MODELO Los animales de los amigos son malos.
No, los animales de los amigos son buenos.

1. El carro ▬▬▬ profesora es fenomenal.

2. La pizza ▬▬▬ Roberto es deliciosa.

3. La fiesta ▬▬▬ amiga de Ana es pésima.

4. El carro ▬▬▬ profesor es bueno.

5. Los videojuegos ▬▬▬ amigas son divertidos.

6. El libro ▬▬▬ profesor es horrible.

41 ¿De o del?

Escribamos Decide whether each blank should be filled with **de, del, de los, de la,** or **de las.**

MODELO Los muchachos son de México.

1. La profesora ===== María es ===== Puerto Rico.
2. A María le gustan los libros ===== aventuras.
3. Las fiestas ===== cumpleaños son fenomenales.
4. Los libros ===== profesora son interesantes.
5. Las películas ===== ciencia ficción son interesantes.
6. El correo electrónico ===== profesor es profesor@xpgs.hrw.edu.
7. Mis compañeros ===== clase son simpáticos.
8. Los libros son ===== estudiantes.

42 La preposición de

Escuchemos As you listen to each sentence, decide how the preposition **de** is being used.

a) to ask about ownership
b) to tell ownership
c) to ask where someone is from
d) to tell where someone is from
e) to describe something

Comunicación

HOLT SoundBooth
ONLINE RECORDING

43 Gustos

Hablemos Work with a partner. Use the drawings to describe Alicia and Rodrigo. Say what they like and dislike.

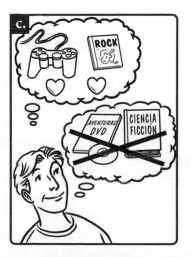

Conexiones culturales

Conexión | Ciencias sociales

1 ¿De dónde son?

Did you know that over 30 million people of Spanish-speaking origin live in the United States? What countries do they come from? Use the information in the pie chart to complete these sentences.

1. Most Spanish speakers in the United States are from ＝＝＝.

2. The three largest Spanish-speaking groups in the United States come from ＝＝＝, ＝＝＝, and ＝＝＝.

3. The largest group of Central American Spanish speakers comes from ＝＝＝.

4. The largest group of South American Spanish speakers comes from ＝＝＝.

Países de origen de los hispanohablantes en Estados Unidos

México	58.5%
Puerto Rico	9.6%
Cuba	3.5%
República Dominicana	2.2%
El Salvador	1.9%
Colombia	1.3%
Guatemala	1.1%
Ecuador	.7%
Perú	.7%
Honduras	.6%
Nicaragua	.5%
Argentina	.3%
Panamá	.3%
Chile	.3%
España	.3%
Venezuela	.3%
Otros países*	17.3%

*Hispanic respondents who did not give a detailed answer in the 2000 census. Due to rounding, sum does not equal 100%

2 ¿De dónde somos?

Work in small groups. Write down what countries each student and his or her father and mother (**padre y madre**), grandparents (**abuelos**), or great-grandparents (**bisabuelos**) came from. Take turns asking and answering in Spanish. You may use a Spanish-English dictionary for additional countries.

MODELO —¿De dónde eres/es...?
　　　　　—Soy de Estados Unidos. Mi padre es de China. Mi madre es de Estados Unidos. Mis bisabuelos son de China.

Alemania *Germany*	**Japón** *Japan*
Australia *Australia*	**Kenia** *Kenya*
Corea *Korea*	**Paquistán** *Pakistan*
China *China*	**Polonia** *Poland*
Francia *France*	**Portugal** *Portugal*
Grecia *Greece*	**Rusia** *Russia*
India *India*	**Sudáfrica** *South Africa*
Inglaterra *England*	**Tanzanía** *Tanzania*
Irlanda *Ireland*	**Turquía** *Turkey*
Italia *Italy*	**Vietnam** *Vietnam*

Conexión Geografía

3 En el mapa

Read the clues below aloud to your partner. Identify where each Spanish-speaking student lives. Use the maps at the end of the book on pages R2 through R6 to figure out what country each student is describing. Use Spanish to tell your partner where each student is from.

Norte

Oeste *Este*

Sur

Conexiones culturales

I'm from South America. My country doesn't have a border next to an ocean. Peru and Chile are to the west and to the east is Brazil. To the south is Argentina.

Me llamo Carolina. Vivo en América del Sur. ¿De dónde soy?

I'm from a country in Central America. To the north is Mexico and to the east, Belize. To the south are El Salvador and the Pacific Ocean.

Me llamo Alberto. Vivo en Centroamérica. ¿De dónde soy?

I'm from the Spanish-speaking half of an island between Cuba and Puerto Rico. It's in the Caribbean Sea. Haiti is the other half of the island.

Me llamo Paloma. Vivo en Europa. ¿De dónde soy?

Me llamo Graciela. Vivo en el Caribe. ¿De dónde soy?

I'm from Europe. They speak Portuguese in the country to the west. To the east is the Mediterranean Sea.

Puerto Rico

setenta y cinco **75**

¿Quién será?

Episodio 2

ESTRATEGIA

Drawing conclusions Drawing logical conclusions based on information you have gathered is an important skill. You draw conclusions about events in a story. Even if things turn out differently than you thought, that does not mean that your conclusion was illogical. Maybe you did not have all the information. As you read the **Novela** or watch the video, gather all the information you can, so that you can draw conclusions about the story and the characters as events unfold.

En España

Marcos meets with la profesora in her office. He reviews Nicolás's files. She describes Nicolás to him, and gives him an assignment.

Francia
Portugal
★ Madrid
ESPAÑA
Mar Mediterráneo
Marruecos   Argelia

1

La profesora Nicolás Ortega García. Le gusta el arte. Es un chico muy simpático. Es de San Juan, Puerto Rico.

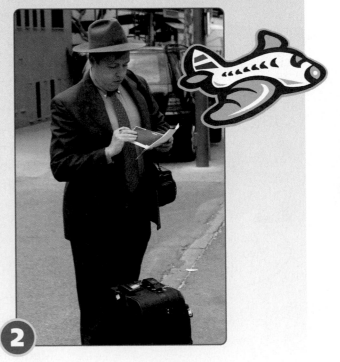

2

Visit Holt Online

go.hrw.com

KEYWORD: EXP1A CH2

Online Edition

An art teacher and a gym coach compare notes about a student they each have in their class.

Océano Atlántico   San Juan

★

PUERTO RICO

Mar Caribe

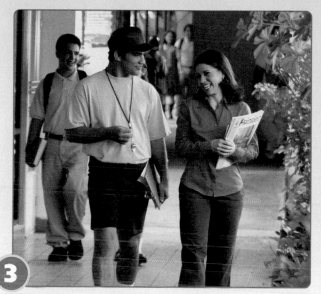

3

Profesora de arte ¿Tienes buenos estudiantes este año?

Entrenador Sí, tengo unos estudiantes muy atléticos este año, y unos que son un poco perezosos.

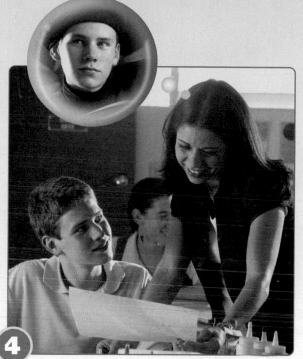

4

Profesora de arte Yo tengo un estudiante que es muy trabajador. Siempre hace las tareas a tiempo. Es un poco serio y también un poco tímido. Pero creo que va a ser muy buen artista.

Entrenador ¿Quién es?

Profesora de arte Se llama Nicolás Ortega García.

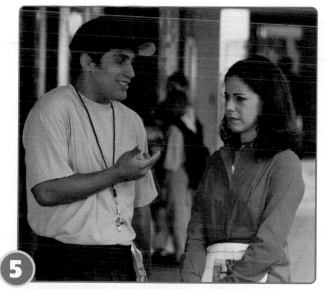

5

Entrenador ¿Nicolás? Dime, ¿cómo es?

Profesora de arte Es alto y rubio.

Entrenador ¿Cuántos años tiene?

Profesora de arte Tiene quince años.

A. CONTESTA

Check your understanding of the **Novela** by answering these questions.

1. Where does the meeting between **la profesora** and her assistant take place?
2. Where is the assistant going to go?
3. What does the art teacher think of the Nicolás Ortega García in her class?

Novela en video

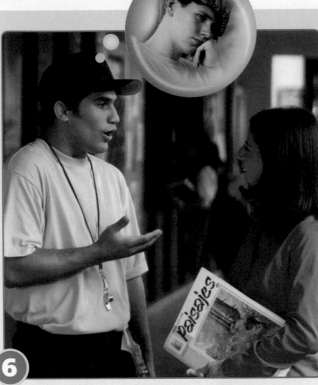

Entrenador Yo también tengo un Nicolás Ortega García en mi clase de educación física.

Profesora de arte ¿Ah, sí?

Entrenador Sí, pero este Nicolás no es trabajador. Es perezoso.

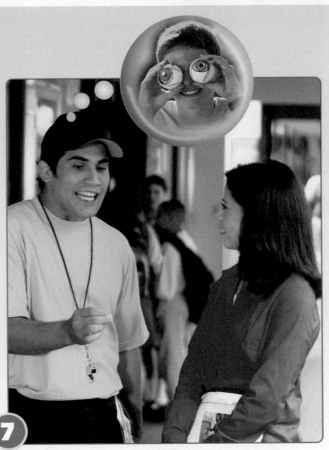

Entrenador No, este Nicolás no es serio. Es cómico.

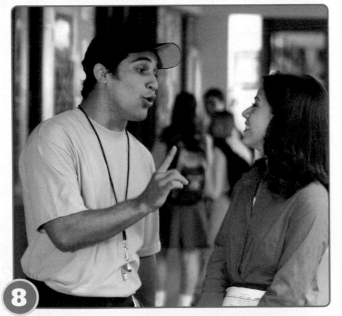

Profesora de arte No es el mismo Nicolás.

Entrenador No, es verdad. Hay dos Nicolás de apellido Ortega García en este colegio, ¿no crees?

Profesora de arte Sí. Así es.

B. CONTESTA

1. What does the gym teacher think of the Nicolás Ortega García in his class?

2. What conclusion do the teachers draw about Nicolás Ortega García?

Actividades

1 Correspondencias

Use the **Novela** to help you match each sentence in English to its corresponding sentence in Spanish.

1. Good morning.
2. He likes art.
3. Who is it?
4. What's he like?
5. It's true.

a. Le gusta el arte.
b. Es verdad.
c. Buenos días.
d. ¿Quién es?
e. ¿Cómo es?

2 ¿Qué dicen?

Find the following sentences in the **Novela** and rewrite the conversation on a separate piece of paper with the missing words.

ENTRENADOR	¿Nicolás? Dime, ¿ __1__ ?
PROFESORA DE ARTE	Es __2__ y rubio.
ENTRENADOR	¿ __3__ años tiene?
PROFESORA DE ARTE	Tiene __4__ años.

3 ¿Comprendes la Novela?

Check your understanding of the events in the story by answering these questions.

1. What information does **la profesora** give Marcos about Nicolás?
2. What do you think Marcos is about to do? Why do you think that?
3. Is the conclusion the two teachers draw about Nicolás logical? Is it correct?
4. What is your conclusion about Nicolás? Which class does he prefer? Why does he act so differently in the two classes?

> **Próximo episodio**
> *Can you predict whether Marcos might be going to Puerto Rico? Why?*
> PÁGINAS 122–125 ▶

Leamos y escribamos

ESTRATEGIA

para leer Inferring is drawing conclusions based on what is only hinted at in what you read. To make inferences, connect what the author writes with your own knowledge and experience. Then draw conclusions based on a combination of the two.

A Antes de leer

Do you think that there is a relationship between someone's personality and the colors he or she likes? On a separate sheet of paper, write two personality traits in Spanish that you would associate with each of the colors blue, red, green, yellow, orange, and black.

¿QUÉ COLOR PREFIERES?

Mi color favorito es el verde.

Si te gusta el color verde, eres una persona muy inteligente, inventiva y lógica. No eres muy extrovertido(a) y no te gusta la rutina. Para ti[1], la naturaleza[2] es importante. Personas famosas: Sócrates, Sherlock Holmes y Thomas Edison.

Mi color preferido es el ANARANJADO.

Si te gusta el anaranjado, eres una persona simpática, graciosa y espontánea. Tienes mucha energía y te fascinan las cosas nuevas, interesantes y diferentes. Para ti, la acción y la diversión[3] son muy importantes. Personas famosas: Winston Churchill y Lucille Ball.

¿Te gusta el color AZUL?

Si te gusta el azul, eres una persona creativa y artística. Eres romántico(a) y sincero(a). Para ti, la armonía entre[4] las personas es muy importante. Personas famosas: Mozart, Indira Gandhi y Thomas Jefferson.

Me fascina el color negro.

Si te gusta el negro, eres una persona seria, elegante y algo misteriosa. También[5] eres disciplinado(a), eficiente y muy independiente. No eres muy extrovertido(a) y no te gustan las personas expresivas. Personas famosas: Cervantes y Abraham Lincoln.

Me gusta el rojo.

Si te gusta el color rojo, eres una persona apasionada, enérgica y activa. Eres muy extrovertido(a) y sociable. Te fascina ser[7] el centro de atención. Personas famosas: Ernest Hemingway, Elizabeth Peña y F. Scott Fitzgerald.

A mí me encanta el color amarillo.

Si te gusta el amarillo, eres intelectual, metódico(a) y analítico(a). Eres tímido(a) y tienes pocos[6] pero buenos amigos. Eres un líder formidable, organizado, eficiente y puntual. Para ti, la familia y las tradiciones son muy importantes. Personas famosas: George Washington y la Madre Teresa.

1. for you   2. nature   3. fun   4. harmony between   5. also   6. few   7. you love being

B Comprensión

Based on the reading, match the colors from Column A with the personality types from Column B. Then draw your own inferences and say what someone might like or dislike based on his or her personality.

A	B	Te gusta(n).../No te gusta(n)...
1. el azul	**a.** Eres tímido(a).	las personas
2. el amarillo	**b.** Eres muy inteligente.	los videojuegos
3. el anaranjado	**c.** Eres romántico(a).	los animales
4. el rojo	**d.** Eres extrovertido(a).	los libros
5. el verde	**e.** Eres serio(a).	las fiestas
6. el negro	**f.** Eres simpático(a).	la música

C Después de leer

1. Did the personality traits you listed for the various colors in **Antes de leer** agree with the reading?

2. Does your favorite color match your own personality? Explain why or why not.

Interactive TUTOR

Taller del escritor

ESTRATEGIA

para escribir Cluster diagrams can help you organize and see how your ideas go together

Yo soy...

Yo no soy...

Me gusta(n)...

No me gusta(n)...

Mi personalidad

Write a paragraph in which you describe yourself and say what you like and don't like. Tell which "personality color" comes closest to your description of yourself.

1 Antes de escribir

Draw four circles. Label the first one **Yo soy...**, the second **Yo no soy...**, the third **Me gusta(n)...**, and the fourth **No me gusta(n)...** Connect other circles to these four and label the new circles with words that describe you, words that do not describe you, things you like, and things you don't like.

2 Escribir y revisar

Use your cluster diagram to organize the information for your paragraph. Include information from each part of the diagram. Read your sentences at least twice. Make sure the paragraph describes you well. Then check spelling and punctuation.

3 Publicar

Get together with three or four classmates. Each member of the group takes someone else's paragraph from the stack and reads it aloud without telling who wrote it. See if the group can guess who wrote each paragraph.

Leamos y escribamos

Prepárate para el examen

Interactive
TUTOR

1 Vocabulario 1
• asking what someone is like
• describing people
• asking how old someone is
pp. 48–53

1 Write descriptions of each person. Give each person a name and an age, then describe his or her appearance. Write some sentences as questions.

1. Leo   2. Mario   3. Paco   4. Eva   5. Ana   6. Luz   7. Pili

2 Gramática 1
• using **ser** with adjectives
• gender and adjective agreement
• question formation
pp. 54–59

2 Complete the following conversations using adjectives, **ser,** and question words. Remember to use the correct adjective and verb forms.

1. —¿===== es tu mejor amigo(a)?
   —===== Paco.

2. —¿===== día es hoy?
   —===== sábado.

3. —¿Cómo ===== tu mejor amigo(a)?
   —Es =====. No es =====.

4. —¿===== eres tú?
   — ===== =====.

5. —¿===== es tu cumpleaños?
   —===== el =====.

3 Vocabulario 2
• talking about what you and others like
• describing things
pp. 62–67

3 Ask your partner if he or she likes the following things and why. Then ask which things he or she likes more. Switch roles.

1.   2.   3.   4.

4 Complete the paragraph, using the correct word in parentheses.

___1___ (El/La) cumpleaños ___2___ (de/del) Fernando y Maribel es ___3___ (el/la) catorce de diciembre. A ellos ___4___ (les gusta/les gustan) mucho las fiestas ___5___ (de/del) cumpleaños. A Maribel ___6___ (le gustan/les gustan) los libros ___7___ (de/de las) aventuras más que ___8___ (los/las) películas. A Fernando ___9___ (le gusta/le gustan) los videojuegos más que ___10___ (el/la) música de Los Hidalgos.

5 Answer the following questions.

1. How do Latin Americans describe someone with dark or light-brown hair and skin?

2. Why are ages sixteen and eighteen important to young people in Puerto Rico?

6 Listen as Patricia reads the e-mail message from Yoli. Then say whether the statements that follow are **cierto** or **falso.**

1. A Yoli no le gustan las clases porque son aburridas.

2. Los compañeros de clase son antipáticos.

3. El cumpleaños de Yoli es el 16 de agosto.

4. A Yoli le gusta la comida china.

Visit Holt Online

go.hrw.com
KEYWORD: EXP1A CH2

Chapter Self-test

4 Gramática 2
- nouns and definite articles
- **gustar, ¿por qué?** and **porque**
- the preposition **de**
  pp. 68–73

5 Cultura
- **Comparaciones**
  pp. 60–61
- **Notas culturales**
  pp. 50, 59, 64
- **Geocultura**
  pp. 42–44

Prepárate para el examen

Conversación

HOLT **SoundBooth** ONLINE RECORDING

7 Role-play the following conversation with a partner. Partner A is a teenage boy at a party and Partner B is his friend.

PARTNER A:	Ask your partner who the dark-haired girl is.
PARTNER B:	Tell your partner her name. Say she is a friend and that she's very nice.
PARTNER A:	Ask how old she is and what she's like.
PARTNER B:	Respond. Use three adjectives to describe the girl.
PARTNER A:	Ask your partner what she likes.
PARTNER B:	Name one thing or food she likes, and one thing she dislikes.
PARTNER A:	Say that you like those things too and ask your partner for her phone number.
PARTNER B:	Answer. Say it's 11:30 and you have to go, then say goodbye.

Gramática 1
- using **ser** with adjectives
  pp. 54–55
- gender and adjective agreement
  pp. 56–57
- question formation
  pp. 58–59

Repaso de Gramática 1

You can use adjectives with the verb **ser** to describe people. Adjectives should agree with the nouns they describe in number and gender. Adjectives are either singular or plural, masculine or feminine.

Carlos es alto.   **Lupe es alta.**   **Carlos y Lupe son altos.**

Form questions by changing your tone of voice or using question words such as **qué, cómo, cuándo, quién, de quiénes, cuál** and **de dónde.**

Gramática 2
- nouns and definite articles
  pp. 68–69
- **gustar, ¿por qué?,** and **porque**
  pp. 70–71
- the preposition **de**
  pp. 72–73

Repaso de Gramática 2

Nouns can be singular or plural, masculine or feminine.

	Masculine	Feminine
SINGULAR	carro	fiesta
PLURAL	carros	fiestas

Use definite articles to say *the* or with a noun used as a general category. Definite articles agree with the nouns they describe in gender and number.

	Masculine	Feminine
SINGULAR	el libro	la pizza
PLURAL	los libros	las pizzas

The verb **gustar** is used to talk about likes and dislikes.

Me gusta la comida italiana. ¿No te gustan los deportes?

The preposition **de** is used to indicate possession, relationship, or where someone is from. It can also describe a type of thing.

Es el libro de Juan.   **Paco es de Perú.**   **Es el amigo del Sr. Tan.**

Letra y sonido

La sílaba tónica
- Words ending in a vowel, **-n,** or **-s** are normally stressed on the next-to-last syllable: **in-te-li-GEN-te, mo-RE-nos, bas-TAN-te.**
- Words ending in a consonant other than **-n** or **-s** are normally stressed on the last syllable: **us-TED, se-ÑOR, es-TOY.**
- All words whose pronunciation doesn't follow these rules are written with an accent mark over the vowel that is stressed: **ca-FÉ, pe-LÍ-cu-la, a-ten-CIÓN.**

Trabalenguas
Tres tristes tigres tragaban trigo en un trigal en tres tristes trastos.

Dictado
Escribe las oraciones de la grabación.

Repaso de Vocabulario 1

Describing people

aburrido(a)	boring
activo(a)	active
alto(a)	tall
antipático(a)	unfriendly
atlético(a)	athletic
bajo(a)	short
bastante	quite, pretty (+ adjective)
bonito(a)	pretty
cómico(a)	funny
¿Cómo eres?	What are you like?
¿Cómo es...?	What is . . . like?
¿Eres...?	Are you . . .?
Es...	He (She, It) is . . .
extrovertido(a)	outgoing
gracioso(a)	witty
guapo(a)	good-looking
intelectual	intellectual
inteligente	intelligent
moreno(a)	dark-haired; dark-skinned
muy	very
pelirrojo(a)	redheaded

perezoso(a)	lazy
romántico(a)	romantic
rubio(a)	blond
serio(a)	serious
simpático(a)	friendly
Soy...	I'm . . .
también	also
tímido(a)	shy
tonto(a)	silly, foolish
trabajador(a)	hard-working
un poco	a little

Asking and saying how old someone is

¿Cuándo es el cumpleaños de...?	When is . . . 's birthday?
¿Cuándo es tu cumpleaños?	When is your birthday?
¿Cuántos años tiene...?	How old is . . .?
¿Cuántos años tienes?	How old are you?
Él (Ella) tiene ... años.	He (She) is . . . years old.
Es el... de...	It's the . . . of . . .
Tengo ... años.	I'm . . . years old.

Numbers 32–100 . . . . See p. 52.

Repaso de Vocabulario 2

Describing things

el ajedrez	chess
los animales	animals
los carros	cars
la comida china (italiana, mexicana)	Chinese (Italian, Mexican) food
los deportes	sports
Es algo divertido(a).	It's kind of fun.
Es bastante bueno(a).	It's quite good.
Es delicioso(a).	It's delicious.
Es pésimo(a).	It's awful.
fenomenal	awesome
las fiestas	parties
formidable	great
las frutas	fruit
las hamburguesas	hamburgers
el helado	ice cream
horrible	horrible

interesante	interesting
los libros (de aventuras, de amor)	(adventure, romance) books
malo(a)	bad
la música (de...)	music (of/by . . .)
las películas (de ciencia ficción, de terror, de misterio)	(science fiction, horror, mystery) movies
la pizza	pizza
las verduras	vegetables
los videojuegos	videogames

Talking about what you and others like

Me da igual.	It's all the same to me.
Me gusta(n)... mucho.	I like . . . a lot.
Me gusta(n) más...	I like . . . more.
No, no me gusta(n)...	No, I don't like . . .
¿Te gusta(n)...?	Do you like . . . ?
¿Te gusta(n) más... o ...?	Do you like . . . or . . . more?

Prepárate para el examen

1 Listen to these statements and match them with the appropriate picture.

A   B   C   D

2 You want to find an Internet pen pal. Read the ads for **Ciberamigos,** and then answer the questions that follow.

ciber@migos

Andrés Vallejo
14 años
avall123@mailmex.hrw.com
Soy cómico y activo. Me gustan las computadoras y las películas de terror. No me gusta la comida italiana. Me gustan las hamburguesas.

Yasmín Herrera
15 años
yazz@telecom.hrw.com.es
¿Qué tal? Soy inteligente y extrovertida. No me gusta la televisión, pero sí me gustan los libros de aventuras y las fiestas.

Liliana Caraval
13 años
lilcar@correo.hrw.com.pr
¡Hola! Soy simpática y seria. No soy aburrida. Me gustan los videojuegos y la música rock. No me gusta la pizza.

1. How old is Andrés? Yasmín? Liliana?
2. What does Liliana like to do? What doesn't she like?
3. Who likes hamburgers? adventure books? videogames?
4. Who is the most active? outgoing? funny?
5. Who would you most like as your pen pal? Why?
6. Based only on the e-mail address, can you guess where each person lives?

3 Imagine that you know the family under the umbrella in the painting. Choose words from the word box to complete the description of these people. Use each word only once.

azul	bajo	sesenta	tiene	tímidas
llama	alto	abril	dos	animales

Es el 12 de ___1___ y el día en San Juan es algo lluvioso *(rainy)*. El paraguas *(umbrella)* del señor es ___2___. Son las ___3___ de la tarde. El señor se ___4___ don Fernando. Tiene ___5___ años. Él es ___6___. El muchacho, Pablo, ___7___ nueve años y no es alto, es ___8___. Las muchachas son Benita y Maribel. Ellas son ___9___ y bajas. A los muchachos les gustan los ___10___.

Día lluvioso en El Viejo San Juan, de Orlando Santiago Correa

Día lluvioso en El Viejo San Juan (Rainy Day in Old San Juan) by Orlando Santiago Correa courtesy of Patrick Santiago

4

Situación Work with a partner to role-play an interview with a famous person. One person is the interviewer, the other is the celebrity. Ask questions to get the following information. Make up any facts that you don't know for sure.

- name, age, and birthday
- where he or she is from
- physical description
- likes and dislikes (food, music, books, and so on)

Take turns playing both roles, and be prepared to present your interviews to the class.

Video/DVD

GeoVisión

Geocultura
Texas

▼ **El Valle de Texas** The Rio Grande valley is where red grapefruit is grown. It's the official state fruit of Texas.

▼ **El Parque Nacional Big Bend** The name "Big Bend" in Big Bend National Park comes from the large "U" formed by the Rio Grande.

NUEVO MÉXICO

El Paso

Ciudad Juárez, México

Almanac

Population
22,859,968

Capital
Austin

Area
266,807 square miles
(691,030 km²)

Economy
chemicals, foodstuffs, vehicles, petroleum products, computers, livestock, fruit

▶ **El Paso** The traditional costumes of these dancers show the influence of neighboring Mexico.

¿Sabías que...?
Did you know that the Rio Grande forms the entire length of the Texas-Mexico border, a total of nearly 1,200 miles (1,930 kilometers)?

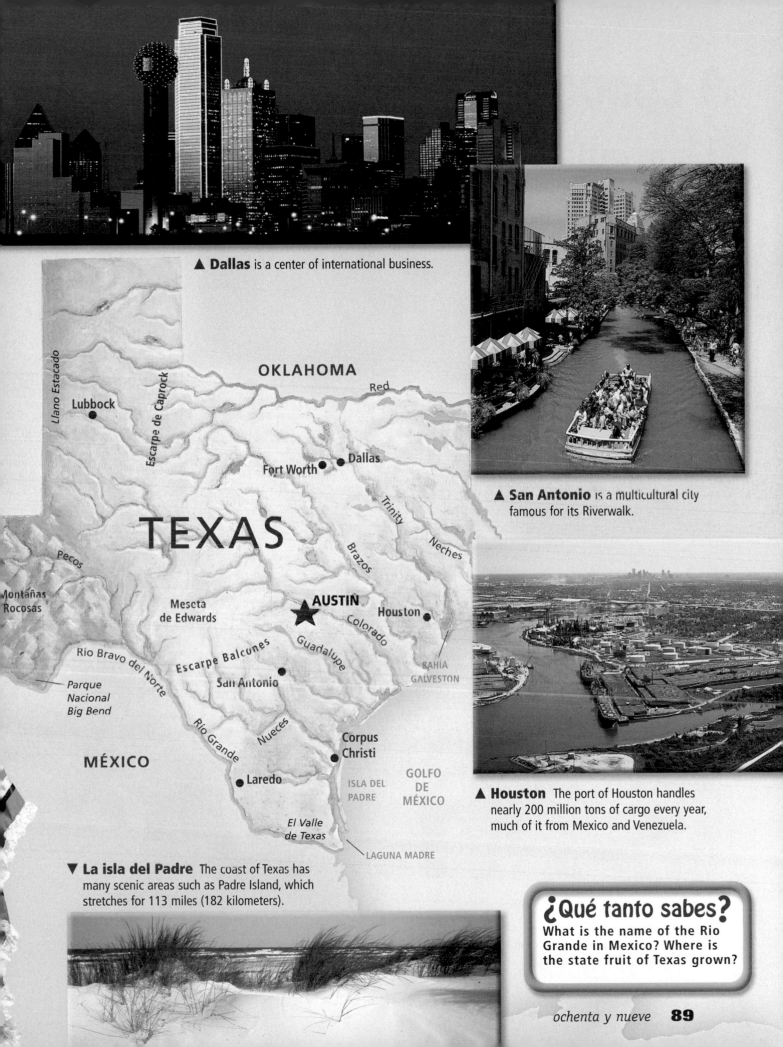

▲ **Dallas** is a center of international business.

▲ **San Antonio** is a multicultural city famous for its Riverwalk.

Map labels

Llano Estacado

Lubbock

Escarpe de Caprock

OKLAHOMA

Red

Fort Worth   Dallas

TEXAS

Trinity

Neches

Pecos

Brazos

Montáñas Rocosas

Meseta de Edwards

AUSTIN

Houston

Colorado

Río Bravo del Norte

Escarpe Balcones

Guadalupe

Parque Nacional Big Bend

San Antonio

BAHIA GALVESTON

MÉXICO

Río Grande

Nueces

Corpus Christi

GOLFO DE MÉXICO

Laredo

ISLA DEL PADRE

El Valle de Texas

LAGUNA MADRE

▲ **Houston** The port of Houston handles nearly 200 million tons of cargo every year, much of it from Mexico and Venezuela.

▼ **La isla del Padre** The coast of Texas has many scenic areas such as Padre Island, which stretches for 113 miles (182 kilometers).

¿Qué tanto sabes?
What is the name of the Rio Grande in Mexico? Where is the state fruit of Texas grown?

A conocer Texas

La arquitectura

▼ **La biblioteca central de San Antonio** San Antonio's Central Library was designed by Ricardo Legorreta, a famous Mexican architect.

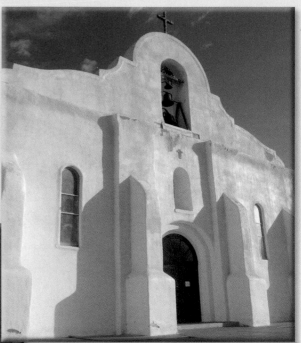

▲ **La capilla de San Elceario** San Elceario Mission, near El Paso, is a fine example of Spanish mission architecture in Texas.

El arte

▲ **Tamalada** was painted by Carmen Lomas Garza (1948–), a Mexican American artist. Many of her paintings show scenes of Mexican American daily life in South Texas.

▶ **Vaquero** is a fiberglass sculpture in front of the El Paso Museum of Art. It was created by Texas artist Luis Jiménez (1940–2006).

La comida

¿Sabías que...?
Did you know that over the course of history, Texas has been ruled by six different governments? Can you name some of them? What influences of these cultures do you see in Texas today?

▲ **La barbacoa al estilo tejano** Barbecue is a typical Texas food.

◀ **Las tostaditas con salsa** Chips and salsa is the official state snack of Texas.

Las celebraciones

◀ **El rodeo** Rodeo is a sport that grew out of the cowhand culture in Texas. Rodeo contestants demonstrate their skills in horseback riding and working with livestock.

▲ **El Cinco de Mayo** The celebration of **Cinco de Mayo** commemorates the Battle of Puebla in 1862, when Mexican troops defeated a French army. Mexican Americans all over Texas celebrate **Cinco de Mayo** with parades, street festivals, and cultural events.

¿Qué te gusta hacer?

Objetivos

In Part 1 you will learn to:
- talk about what you and others like to do
- ask what a friend wants to do and answer
- use the verb **gustar** with infinitives
- place pronouns after prepositions
- use the verb **querer** with infinitives

In Part 2 you will learn to:
- talk about everyday activities
- ask how often someone does something and answer
- form and use regular **-ar** verbs
- use the present tense of **ir** and **jugar**
- talk about the weather

¿Qué ves en la foto?

- **¿Cómo son las muchachas?**

- **¿Cómo es el muchacho?**

- **¿Qué te gusta hacer los fines de semana?**

Amigos mirando hacia El Paso y Juárez desde
las montañas Franklin

Objetivos
- Talking about what you and others like to do
- Talking about what you want to do

Vocabulario
en acción **1**

Video/DVD

ExpresaVisión

A mis amigos y a mí nos gusta...

correr

hacer ejercicio

montar en bicicleta

leer revistas y novelas

escuchar música

dibujar

pasear

patinar

Más vocabulario...

alquilar videos	*to rent videos*	**ir al cine**	*to go to the movies*
bajar archivos	*to download files*	**nadar**	*to swim*
cantar	*to sing*	**navegar por Internet**	*to surf the Internet*
comer	*to eat*	**pasar el rato solo(a)**	*to spend time alone*
escribir cartas	*to write letters*	**platicar en línea**	*to chat online*
hacer la tarea	*to do homework*	**ver televisión**	*to watch television*

Me gusta jugar...

Vocabulario 1

al básquetbol

al béisbol

al fútbol americano

a juegos de mesa

al volibol

al fútbol

al tenis

Más vocabulario...

¿Con quién?	*With whom?*
conmigo	*with me*
contigo	*with you*
con mis amigos(as)	*with my friends*
con mi familia	*with my family*

También se puede decir...

Spanish speakers in Mexico say **el baloncesto** instead of **el básquetbol**, and **andar en bicicleta** instead of **montar en bicicleta**. Many Cubans and Puerto Ricans may refer to **el béisbol** as **la pelota** and say **el balompié** instead of **el fútbol**.

¡Exprésate!

To ask what others like to do	To respond
¿Qué te gusta hacer? *What do you like to do?*	**A mí me gusta salir con amigos.** *I like to go out with friends.*
¿A Juan y a Pablo les gusta ir al centro comercial? *Do Juan and Pablo like to go to the mall?*	**Sí, porque les gusta ir de compras.** *Yes, because they like to go shopping.*

Interactive **TUTOR**

Vocabulario y gramática, pp. 25–27

Online workbooks

▶ **Vocabulario adicional,** Deportes y pasatiempos, p. R8

1 **Les gusta...**

Escuchemos/Leamos Choose the most logical description based on the sentences you hear.

1. Es (extrovertida/tímida).
2. Es (muy activo/perezoso).
3. Es (trabajador/perezoso).
4. Son (atléticos/intelectuales).
5. Es (activa/seria).
6. Son (divertidas/serias).

2 **Me gusta...**

Hablemos Say whether or not you like to do the things pictured.

MODELO Me gusta jugar al béisbol.
(No me gusta jugar al béisbol.)

3 **¿Qué les gusta hacer?**

Escribamos/Hablemos Complete the following sentences.

♻ *¿Se te olvidó?* Gustar, p. 70

1. Me gusta...
2. No me gusta...
3. A mi mejor amigo(a) le gusta...
4. A mi familia y a mí nos gusta...
5. A mis amigos les gusta...
6. A mis amigos y a mí nos gusta...
7. Me gusta salir con...
8. Me gusta ir al cine con...

4 Les gusta jugar...

Leamos/Escribamos Read the questions and write answers in complete sentences based on the pictures.

los amigos

Lili y Ana

Andrés

Paco

las hermanas Núñez

las niñas

José y Raúl

1. ¿A los amigos les gusta jugar al fútbol?
2. ¿A quiénes les gusta jugar al tenis?
3. A Paco le gusta jugar al béisbol, ¿verdad?
4. ¿Qué les gusta hacer a las hermanas Núñez?
5. ¿A quién le gusta jugar al béisbol?
6. ¿A Lili y a Ana les gusta jugar al volibol?
7. ¿Qué les gusta hacer a José y a Raúl?
8. ¿Qué te gusta hacer?

Comunicación

HOLT **SoundBooth** ONLINE RECORDING

5 Actividades

Hablemos Take turns with a partner telling whether or not you like the activities in **Vocabulario 1**. Take notes. Then report to the class one activity that your partner likes and one that he or she does not like.

MODELO —Susana, ¿te gusta escuchar música?
—Sí, me gusta mucho escuchar música.
—A Susana le gusta mucho escuchar música.

¡Exprésate!

To ask what a friend wants to do	To respond
¿Qué quieres hacer hoy? *What do you want to do today?*	**Ni idea.** *I have no idea.*
¿Quieres ir al cine conmigo? *Do you want to go to the movies with me?*	**Está bien.** *All right.*
	No, gracias. No quiero ir al cine hoy. *No, thanks. I don't want to go to the movies today.*

Vocabulario y gramática, pp. 25–27

Online workbooks

Interactive TUTOR

6 Una conversación

Leamos/Escribamos Complete the following conversation.

> montar   jugar   gustar   ir   alquilar   hacer

GERARDO ¿Quieres ___1___ al centro comercial?

MARÍA No, no quiero. ¿Quieres ___2___ videos?

GERARDO No, no quiero. Quiero ___3___ ejercicio.

MARÍA ¿Quieres ___4___ al básquetbol?

GERARDO No, no me gusta el básquetbol. ¿Quieres ___5___ en bicicleta?

MARÍA Está bien. Buena idea.

7 ¿Qué quieres hacer?

Escribamos Write a question for each picture asking if someone likes the activity. Then write a second question asking if that person wants to do the activity with you. Write their answer.

MODELO —¿Te gusta jugar al fútbol? ¿Quieres jugar al fútbol conmigo?
—Sí, quiero jugar al fútbol.

8 Entre amigos

Leamos/Escribamos Rewrite the conversation on a separate sheet of paper, putting the sentences in the correct order.

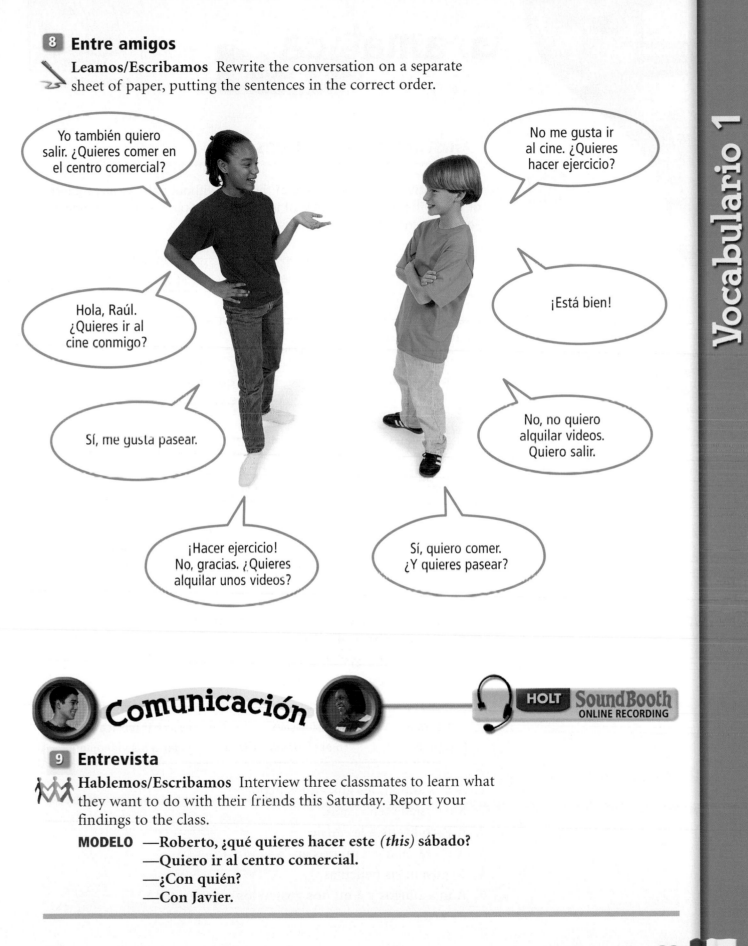

Yo también quiero salir. ¿Quieres comer en el centro comercial?

No me gusta ir al cine. ¿Quieres hacer ejercicio?

Hola, Raúl. ¿Quieres ir al cine conmigo?

¡Está bien!

Sí, me gusta pasear.

No, no quiero alquilar videos. Quiero salir.

¡Hacer ejercicio! No, gracias. ¿Quieres alquilar unos videos?

Sí, quiero comer. ¿Y quieres pasear?

Comunicación

HOLT **SoundBooth**
ONLINE RECORDING

9 Entrevista

Hablemos/Escribamos Interview three classmates to learn what they want to do with their friends this Saturday. Report your findings to the class.

MODELO —Roberto, ¿qué quieres hacer este (this) sábado?
—Quiero ir al centro comercial.
—¿Con quién?
—Con Javier.

Objetivos
- **Gustar** with infinitives
- **Pronouns** after prepositions
- **Querer** with infinitives

Gramática
en acción 1

GramaVisión

Gustar with infinitives

Interactive TUTOR

1 An **infinitive** tells the meaning of the verb without naming any subject or tense. There are three kinds of **infinitives** in Spanish: those ending in **-ar**, those ending in **-er**, and those ending in **-ir**.

-ar infinitives	**-er** infinitives	**-ir** infinitives
cant**ar** to sing	com**er** to eat	escrib**ir** to write

2 Like **nouns**, **infinitives** can be used after a verb like **gustar** to say what you and others like *to do*.

follows gustar

Me **gusta la música.**
I like music.

Me **gusta cantar.**
I like to sing.

3 Always use **gusta** (not **gustan**) with **infinitives**.

Me **gustan los deportes.**
I like sports.

Me **gusta jugar** al tenis.
I like to play tennis.

Vocabulario y gramática, pp. 28–30
Actividades, pp. 21–23

Online workbooks

En inglés

In English, infinitives do not have any special endings, but they almost always have the word **to** in front of them.

to play   to run   to write

In Spanish, infinitives always end in **-ar**, **-er**, or **-ir**.

cantar comer escribir

In the following sentences, find the infinitive.

¿Qué te gusta hacer?
What do you like to do?

10 Gustos

Hablemos/Escribamos Based on the things Carlos and his friends like, what activities do you think they like to do?

¿Se te olvidó? Gustar, p. 70

MODELO A Roberto le gustan las películas.
Le gusta ir al cine.

ir al cine	ver televisión	escuchar música
jugar al tenis	comer comida italiana	jugar a los videojuegos

1. A mis amigos les gustan los deportes.
2. Me gusta la televisión.
3. A Paco le gusta la música.
4. A mi familia y a mí nos gusta la pizza.
5. Te gustan las películas.
6. A mis amigos y a mí nos gustan los videojuegos.

11 Más gustos

Hablemos/Escribamos Based on their personalities, which activity do you think each of these people would like more?

MODELO Raúl es muy activo. (patinar/ver televisión)
Le gusta más patinar.

1. Diego es perezoso. (hacer ejercicio/ver televisión)
2. Mis amigos son atléticos. (nadar y correr/alquilar videos)
3. Elena es trabajadora. (hacer la tarea/escuchar música)
4. Mario es tímido. (ir a fiestas/pasar el rato solo)
5. Mis amigas son románticas. (leer novelas de amor/leer novelas de terror)
6. Soy muy seria. (hacer la tarea/ir a fiestas)
7. Eres muy extrovertido. (salir con amigos/pasar el rato solo)

12 Preguntas y respuestas

Leamos/Escribamos Read the answers that Andrés gave during his interview. Then write the missing questions.

♻ *¿Se te olvidó?* Question words, p. 58

MODELO ¿══? Me gusta leer revistas.
¿Qué te gusta hacer?

1. ¿══? Soy de Chile.
2. ¿══? Tengo trece años.
3. ¿══? Soy extrovertido y gracioso.
4. ¿══? Me gusta ir al cine y hacer deportes.
5. ¿══? Me gusta ir al cine con mis amigos.

Comunicación

HOLT **SoundBooth**
ONLINE RECORDING

13 Preferencias

Hablemos Ask whether your partner likes to do each of the following things. Switch roles. Then tell the class what you found out.

Gramática 1

Pronouns after prepositions

Interactive TUTOR

1 Pronouns can stand for the same noun yet still have different forms, depending on how they're being used in the sentence.

Both stand for Javier

Yo soy Javier. Tengo quince años y **me** gusta dibujar.

2 You already know subject pronouns and the pronouns used with **gustar**. After prepositions such as **a** *(to)*, **de** *(of, from, about)*, **con** *(with)* and **en** *(in, on, at)*, **pronouns** have a different form.

Subject	With **gustar**	After **preposition**
yo	me	**mí**
tú	te	**ti**
usted		**usted**
él	le	**él**
ella		**ella**
nosotros(as)	nos	**nosotros(as)**
vosotros(as)	os	**vosotros(as)**
ustedes		**ustedes**
ellos	les	**ellos**
ellas		**ellas**

3 The pronouns **mí** and **ti** combine with **con** to make the special forms **con**migo and **con**tigo.

4 With **gustar,** the phrase formed by **a** and a pronoun can be added to a sentence to clarify or emphasize who likes something.

adds emphasis   *adds emphasis*   *clarifies*

—¿**A ti** te gusta dibujar?   —**A mí** no me gusta. **A ella** le gusta.

> Vocabulario y gramática, pp. 28–30
> Actividades, pp. 21–23
> **Online** workbooks

Vocabulario y gramática, pp. 28–30
Actividades, pp. 21–23

¿Te acuerdas?

Pronouns take the place of nouns. They can stand for the person talking, the person being talked to, or someone or something that has already been named.

—¿Cuántos años tienes **tú**?

—¿**Yo**? Tengo once años.

Juan es mi amigo.
Él tiene trece años.

14 **María y los amigos**

Leamos/Escribamos On a separate piece of paper, rewrite María's letter choosing the correct prepositions and pronouns.

MODELO Mi amigo Felipe es muy inteligente. A mí me gusta hacer la tarea <u>con él</u>.

Soy extrovertida. **1.** (A mí/A ellos) me gusta pasar el rato con amigos. Mis amigos son muy divertidos. Me gusta mucho salir **2.** (a ellos/con ellos). Mi amigo Jorge es muy activo. **3.** (A él/A mí) no le gusta ver televisión. Mi amiga Laura es muy tímida. **4.** (A ti/A ella) no le gusta ir a fiestas. **5.** (A ellas/A nosotras) nos gusta ir al cine. Juan y Carlos son mis amigos también. **6.** (A ellos/A mí) les gusta jugar a los videojuegos. Y **7.** (a nosotras/a ti), ¿qué te gusta hacer?

15 ¿Te gusta...?

Hablemos Look at the photos and say whether you like to do these activities. Also say what friends you do each activity with.

MODELO Me gusta ir de compras con mi amiga Mari.

1.   2.   3.   4.   5.

16 ¿Qué les gusta?

Leamos/Escribamos Read the description of each person and tell what he or she likes or doesn't like to do.

MODELO Juan es muy activo. Le gustan los deportes.
A él le gusta jugar al béisbol.
(A él no le gusta jugar a los videojuegos.)

1. Sara es muy intelectual. Le gustan los juegos de mesa.
2. Pablo es muy gracioso. Le gustan las fiestas.
3. Lupe es muy extrovertida. No le gusta pasar el rato sola.
4. Alonso es muy serio y tímido. Le gusta pasar el rato solo.
5. A Cristina le gustan las películas. No le gusta salir. Es tímida.
6. Carlos es extrovertido. Le gusta salir con amigos y ver películas.
7. Alicia es muy atlética. Le gusta pasar el rato con amigos.
8. Miguel es muy inteligente y trabajador. Le gustan los libros.

HOLT **SoundBooth**
ONLINE RECORDING

17 Los sábados y los domingos

Escribamos/Hablemos First, write a list of three things you like to do on weekends. Then discuss what you like to do with a small group of classmates and find out what you have in common.

MODELO —Me gusta jugar al fútbol. No me gusta jugar a los videojuegos.

—A mí me gusta jugar a los videojuegos. También me gusta escuchar música.

—Me gustan las fiestas. ¿Les gusta ir a fiestas?

—Sí, nos gusta ir a fiestas.

Present tense of querer with infinitives

Interactive TUTOR

1 To say what you or others *want* or *want to do,* use a form of the verb **querer**. The form you use depends on the subject.

yo **quie**ro	nosotros(as) queremos
tú **quie**res	vosotros(as) queréis
Ud., él, ella **quie**re	Uds., ellos, ellas **quie**ren

2 Just as with **gustar**, you can use a **noun** or an **infinitive** after a form of **querer** to say what you and others want or want to do.

Quiero fruta.
I want some fruit.

Quiero comer.
I want to eat.

—¿Qué **quieres hacer**?
What do you want to do?

—**Quiero escuchar** música.
I want to listen to music.

> Vocabulario y gramática, pp. 28–30
> Actividades, pp. 21–23
> **Online** workbooks

Nota cultural

In Latin America many teens must introduce their friends to their parents before they go out with them. When inviting a friend out, teens are often expected to tell the friend's parents where they are going and when they will return. While this custom may be changing, it is still common in many places.

Is this similar to or different from your parents' rules?

18 ¿Quién quiere?

Leamos/Escribamos Choose the correct form of **querer** to complete the sentences.

1. Marta y yo (quieren/queremos) comer.
2. Yo (quieres/quiero) bajar archivos.
3. Pablo (queremos/quiere) hacer ejercicio.
4. ¿Tú (quieres/quieren) ir al centro comercial?
5. Marco y Felipe (quieren/quiero) navegar por Internet.
6. ¿Ustedes (quieren/queremos) jugar al béisbol?
7. ¿(Quiero/Quiere) usted pasar el rato solo?
8. Juan y Sandra (quieres/quieren) pasear.
9. Tú eres trabajador. (Quieres/Queremos) hacer la tarea.

19 Queremos ir

Leamos/Escribamos Complete the conversation with the correct forms of **querer.**

—Hola, Carla. ¿Qué ___1___ hacer hoy?
—Ni idea. ¿Qué ___2___ hacer tú?
—Bueno, mi familia y yo ___3___ ir al cine.
—¿Y tu amigo Paco no ___4___ ir al cine con ustedes?
—No, Paco y unos amigos ___5___ ir de compras y ___6___ alquilar videos. ¿Y tú? ¿___7___ ir al cine con nosotros?
—Sí, gracias. Yo ___8___ ver una película con ustedes.

20 ¿Qué quieren hacer?

Leamos/Escribamos Say what Juanita and her friends want to do this weekend based on what they like. Use the expressions in the box.

MODELO A mis amigos les gusta la televisión.
Quieren ver televisión.

ver televisión	jugar al ajedrez	comer pizza	leer
comer comida china	alquilar videos	jugar al tenis	escuchar música

1. A mis amigos les gusta la comida china.
2. A ti te gustan los deportes.
3. A mi mejor amigo le gusta la comida italiana.
4. A mí me gustan las novelas.
5. A nosotros nos gustan los juegos de mesa.
6. A mi amiga le gustan las películas.

21 Vamos al centro comercial

Escuchemos Listen to the conversation between Juan and Sofía and decide which photos show what they both want to do.

22 Actividades

Hablemos/Escribamos Imagine that your class is going to have a party. Using the activities listed on pages 94–95, ask three classmates what they want to do at the party. Then write their answers in two lists showing what they want to do and what they don't want to do. Be prepared to share your answers with the class.

MODELO —¿Qué quieres hacer en la fiesta?
—Quiero escuchar música pero no quiero nadar.

Cultura

Comparaciones

¿Qué les gusta hacer a ti y a tus amigos los fines de semana?

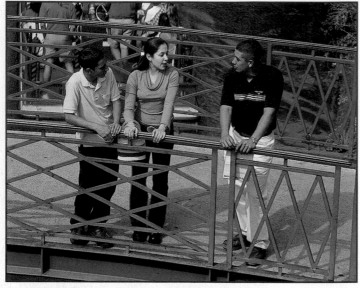

Amigos en el Paseo del Río, San Antonio, Texas

It is common in Spain and Latin America for young people to get together and do things in large groups. Often they will meet up with their friends in a plaza, park, or café to hang out and eat before going shopping or dancing. Many young people also spend a fair amount of time with their families, especially on Sundays, when it is typical to eat a large family meal together. What do you like to do on the weekends, and how is it different from what these people do?

Celina
El Paso, Texas

Celina talks about what she and her friends like to do on a nice day. What do you and your friends like to do when the weather is good?

Dime, ¿adónde vas cuando hace buen tiempo?

Me gusta salir al parque.

¿Vas sola o vas con amigos?

Me gusta ir con amigos.

¿Qué les gusta hacer en el parque?

Nos gusta ir a correr o jugar fútbol; si no, a platicar.

¿Qué no te gusta hacer?

No me gusta pasar el tiempo sola.

¿Por qué no te gusta?

Porque me gusta estar acompañada... con familia y amigos.

106 *ciento seis*

Cultura

☀ Rita
Lima, Perú

Rita talks about her favorite indoor and outdoor activities. Do you always go outside on a nice day? If not, why not?

Dime, ¿adónde vas cuando hace buen tiempo?

Cuando hace buen tiempo voy a la playa, al cine o a acampar.

¿Vas sola o vas con amigos?

Voy con amigos.

¿Qué les gusta hacer en esos lugares?

Cuando vamos a la playa, nos gusta nadar y jugar; cuando vamos al cine, ver películas; y cuando vamos a acampar, hacer fogatas.

¿Qué cosas no te gusta hacer?

No me gusta ir a clase de matemáticas.

¿Por qué no te gusta?

No me gusta porque es aburrido y a veces no entiendo.

Para comprender

1. ¿A quién le gusta hacer ejercicio?
2. ¿A Rita qué le gusta hacer cuando hace buen tiempo?
3. ¿Qué les gusta hacer a Rita y a sus amigos cuando van a la playa?
4. ¿Quién juega al fútbol con sus amigos?
5. A Celina no le gusta pasar el rato sola. ¿Con quién quiere pasar el rato?

Para pensar y hablar

When asked where they go when the weather is good, both Celina and Rita say that they like to spend time outdoors with friends. Do you like to be outside or would you rather do something indoors? Would you rather do things in a group or with just one friend? Do you like spending time alone?

Comunidad
What's the weather?

What are the differences and similarities in weather between your town and towns in the Spanish-speaking world? Create a weather information chart in Spanish with your classmates.

◆ Choose three cities in different parts of the Spanish-speaking world.

◆ Use a newspaper or Web site to find high and low temperatures for the three cities and your town.

◆ Is your town's weather hot, cold, or moderate compared to the other three cities?

**Les gusta salir
cuando llueve.**

Objetivos
• Talking about everyday activities
• Saying how often you do things

Vocabulario
en acción 2

Los fines de semana me gusta...

estudiar

practicar deportes

tocar el piano

descansar

hablar por teléfono

trabajar

bailar

Vocabulario 2

¿Adónde vas los fines de semana?

Voy...

a la piscina

a la iglesia

al gimnasio

a la playa

Más vocabulario...

al baile	to the dance
a la casa de...	to . . . 's house
al colegio	to school
al ensayo	to rehearsal
al entrenamiento	to (sports) practice
a la reunión	to the meeting
al trabajo	to work

También se puede decir...

In Mexico a swimming pool may be called **la alberca**. In Argentina, they may call it **la pileta**.

¡Exprésate!

To ask about everyday activities	To respond
¿Qué haces los fines de semana? *What do you do on weekends?*	**Los sábados, cuando hace buen tiempo, voy con mis amigos al parque.** *On Saturdays, when the weather is nice, I go with my friends to the park.*
¿Qué hace Luis cuando hace mal tiempo? *What does Luis do when the weather is bad?*	**Le gusta escuchar música. No va a ninguna parte.** *He likes to listen to music.* *He doesn't go anywhere.*

Interactive TUTOR

Vocabulario y gramática, pp. 31–33

Online workbooks

▶ **Vocabulario adicional** — Deportes y pasatiempos, p. R8

23 El fin de semana

Leamos Alberto's cousin Margarita is coming for a weekend visit and has asked Alberto what they will be doing. Complete his letter to her by choosing the correct words.

descansar	deportes	baile	gimnasio
iglesia	playa	tiempo	casa

Hola Margarita,

El sábado, si hace buen __1__ quiero ir a la __2__ a nadar. Si hace mal tiempo, quiero ir al __3__ a hacer ejercicio y practicar unos __4__ . El domingo quiero ir a la __5__ a las 12:00 y de las 4:00–6:00 de la tarde quiero __6__ . El domingo a las 8:00 P.M. hay un __7__ en la __8__ de Juan con música muy buena.

Chao, Alberto

24 ¿Qué planes tienes?

Hablemos/Escribamos Using the pictures, complete these sentences.

MODELO Hoy quiero ir...

Hoy quiero ir a la piscina.

1. Me gusta...

2. Quiero...

3. Mañana voy...

4. Cuando hace buen tiempo, quiero ir...

5. ¿Te gusta ir...?

6. Cuando hace mal tiempo, ¿te gusta...?

25 Una conversación telefónica

Leamos/Escribamos Jaime and Gabi are deciding what to do this afternoon. Rewrite their conversation in the correct order on a separate piece of paper.

¡Sí! Me gusta nadar.

Jaime, ¿qué haces hoy? Hace muy buen tiempo.

Hola, Jaime. ¿Qué tal?

Hasta pronto.

Voy a la piscina. ¿Quieres ir conmigo?

Hola, Gabi. Estoy bien.

Está bien. Nos vemos en la piscina.

Comunicación

HOLT SoundBooth
ONLINE RECORDING

26 ¿Adónde vas los fines de semana?

Hablemos Take turns with a partner asking and answering whether you go to these places on weekends. Why or why not?

MODELO al parque
—¿Vas al parque los fines de semana?
—Sí, voy al parque porque quiero correr.
(No, no voy al parque porque quiero descansar.)

1. a la playa
2. al gimnasio
3. al ensayo
4. al colegio
5. al trabajo
6. al cine
7. a la casa de...
8. al entrenamiento
9. a la piscina

¡Exprésate!

To ask how often	To respond
¿Con qué frecuencia vas a la playa? *How often do you go to the beach?*	**Casi nunca. No me gusta nadar.** *Hardly ever. I don't like to swim.*
¿Te gusta salir con amigos? *Do you like to go out with friends?*	**Sí. Después de clases, casi siempre vamos al parque. A veces vamos también a la piscina.** *Yes. After classes, we almost always go to the park. Sometimes we also go to the swimming pool.*

Interactive TUTOR

→ Vocabulario y gramática, pp. 31–33 — **Online workbooks**

Más vocabulario...

los...	on . . .
lunes	*Mondays*
martes	*Tuesdays*
miércoles	*Wednesdays*
jueves	*Thursdays*
viernes	*Fridays*
sábados	*Saturdays*
domingos	*Sundays*
fines de semana	*weekends*
todos los días	*every day*
siempre	*always*
nunca	*never*

27 Un programa de radio

Escuchemos Complete the sentences based on what you hear.

1. La estudiante se llama (Susana Parra/Alicia Hernández).
2. Los jueves le gusta (ir a la casa de amigas/trabajar).
3. Susana va al cine (los sábados y domingos/los lunes).
4. Los sábados Susana va a (nadar/patinar).
5. Los domingos, a Susana le gusta (leer/tocar el piano).
6. A Susana (le gusta/no le gusta) bailar.

28 A mí me gusta...

Escribamos Write about what you like to do. Replace the underlined activities with ones that apply to you.

> **MODELO** Me gusta <u>alquilar videos</u> todos los fines de semana.
> **Me gusta bailar todos los fines de semana.**

1. Todos los días me gusta <u>ir al parque</u>.
2. Nunca quiero <u>trabajar</u> los viernes.
3. Los fines de semana después de hacer la tarea me gusta <u>salir con amigos</u>.
4. Los domingos quiero <u>descansar</u>.
5. No me gusta <u>salir</u> los martes.
6. Los sábados me gusta <u>ir al centro comercial con mis amigos Pablo y Maribel</u>.
7. A veces, los viernes me gusta <u>ir al cine</u>.
8. Nunca quiero <u>tocar el piano</u> los fines de semana.
9. Los viernes después de clases me gusta <u>hablar por teléfono con Ricardo</u>.
10. Después de clases siempre quiero <u>estudiar</u>.

29 Mi agenda

Escribamos Imagine that this is your schedule. Write at least five sentences telling what you like to do and when.

AGENDA

lunes:	practicar el piano	(9:30)
martes:	trabajar en el cine	(4:00)
miércoles:	bailar con amigos en el gimnasio	(7:30)
jueves:	ir a la reunión del Club de español	(8:15)
viernes:	practicar el piano	(9:00)
sábado:	trabajar en el cine	(3:00)
domingo:	ir a la iglesia con mis abuelos	(2:00)

Comunicación

HOLT SoundBooth
ONLINE RECORDING

30 ¿Con qué frecuencia vas...?

Hablemos Work with a partner. Take turns asking how often you each go the following places. Include information about why you go there and what you do there in your answers.

MODELO —¿Con qué frecuencia vas a la playa?
—Nunca voy a la playa. No me gusta nadar.

1.
2.
3.

4.
5.
6.

Objetivos
• Regular **-ar** verbs
• **Ir** and **jugar**
• Weather expressions

Gramática en acción 2

Present tense of regular -ar verbs

Interactive
TUTOR

1 Every verb has a **stem** followed by an ending. The stem tells the verb's meaning. An **infinitive ending** doesn't name a subject.

verb stems
habl	-ar
com	-er
escrib	-ir
infinitive endings

2 To give the verb a subject you **conjugate** it. To conjugate a regular **-ar** verb in the present tense, drop the **-ar** ending of the infinitive and add these **endings**. Each ending goes with a particular subject.

yo cant**o**	nosotros(as) cant**amos**
tú cant**as**	vosotros(as) cant**áis**
Ud., él, ella cant**a**	Uds., ellos, ellas cant**an**

—¿Te gusta **cantar**?
Do you like to sing?
—Sí, **cant**o todos los días.
Yes, I sing every day.

—¿**Nad**an ustedes mucho?
Do you swim a lot?
—No, casi nunca **nad**amos.
No, we hardly ever swim.

3 Since usually the ending of the verb tells the subject, the **subject pronoun** is normally left out. Use **subject pronouns** to add emphasis, or when it wouldn't otherwise be clear who the subject is.

—¿Patinan **ustedes** mucho?
Do you skate a lot?
—**Ellos** patinan. **Yo** nunca patino.
They skate. I never skate.

Vocabulario y gramática, pp. 34–36
Actividades, pp. 25–27
Online workbooks

En inglés

In English, most verbs in the present tense have only two forms. The **subject pronouns** are not left out.

I sing	we sing
you sing	you sing
he, she, it sing**s**	they sing

In Spanish, the verb ending tells you who the subject is.

When do both Spanish and English verb forms change their endings?

31 En el parque

Leamos Complete the sentences that Marcos wrote.

1. Los sábados yo (paso/pasas) el rato con amigos.
2. Y tú, ¿cómo (pasas/pasa) el rato con amigos?
3. Ana (patinan/patina) en el parque con José.
4. Javi y yo (nadan/nadamos) en la piscina.
5. Maribel y Florencia (patinan/patinas) con nosotros.

Unos amigos montan en bicicleta en un parque en Texas.

32 Los fines de semana

Hablemos/Escribamos Based on the pictures, say what each person does on weekends.

MODELO Escucho música y descanso.

yo

1. nosotros

2. Juan

3. ellas

4. mi mejor amiga

33 ¿Cuándo?

Escribamos Write sentences using words from each column to tell what you and your friends do or don't do at certain times during the week.

MODELO Mi mejor amigo (no) descansa los domingos.

mi mejor amigo(a)	practicar deportes	los lunes
mis amigos	pasear	los jueves
ustedes *(to your classmates)*	tocar el piano	los viernes
	escuchar música	los sábados
mis amigos y yo	estudiar	los fines de semana
yo	trabajar	todos los días
tú *(to a classmate)*	navegar por Internet	después de clases
	hablar por teléfono	

Comunicación

HOLT SoundBooth
ONLINE RECORDING

34 ¿Con qué frecuencia vas al cine?

Hablemos Take turns with a partner talking about how often each of you does the activities in **Vocabulario 2**.

MODELO —¿Con qué frecuencia practicas deportes?
—Practico deportes todos los fines de semana. ¿Y tú?
—¿Con qué frecuencia tocas el piano?
—Casi nunca toco el piano. ¿Y tú?

Gramática 2

Present tense of ir and jugar

Interactive TUTOR

1 The **-ar** verbs you have learned are called regular verbs because their conjugations all follow a predictable pattern. Some verbs such as **ir** *(to go)* are called irregular, because they do not follow a clear pattern.

yo **voy**	nosotros(as) **vamos**
tú **vas**	vosotros(as) **vais**
Ud., él, ella **va**	Uds., ellos, ellas **van**

—¿Adónde **vas** los sábados? —**Voy** a la piscina.

2 The verb **jugar** *(to play a sport or game)* has regular **-ar** endings, but the vowel **u** in the stem changes to **ue** in all but the **nosotros** and **vosotros** forms.

yo **jue**go	nosotros(as) jugamos
tú **jue**gas	vosotros(as) jugáis
Ud., él, ella **jue**ga	Uds., ellos, ellas **jue**gan

—¿**Juegan** ustedes en el colegio? —No, no **jugamos** mucho.

3 The preposition **a** is used after **ir** to mean *to*. Use **¿adónde?** to ask *where to*. **A** is also used after **jugar** with a sport. When **a** is followed by **el**, the two words combine to form the contraction **al**.

—¿**Adónde van** los domingos? —**Vamos al** gimnasio. **Jugamos al** básquetbol.

Vocabulario y gramática, pp. 34–36
Actividades, pp. 25–27

Online workbooks

¿Te acuerdas?

When **de** is followed by **el**, the two words combine to form the contraction **del**.

el teléfono **del** profesor
el libro **del** estudiante

35 Sitios

Escribamos Write complete sentences using the correct word or words from the box. Then say whether or not you like the activity and how often you do it. ♻ *¿Se te olvidó?* Definite articles, p. 68

MODELO Me gusta ir a la playa los sábados.
   (No me gusta ir a la playa. Nunca voy a la playa.)

al	a los	a las	a la

1. ir ===== piscina
2. jugar ===== béisbol
3. ir ===== cine
4. ir ===== iglesia
5. ir ===== entrenamiento
6. ir ===== casas de mis amigos
7. jugar ===== ajedrez
8. jugar ===== videojuegos

36 Pasatiempos

Escribamos/Hablemos Based on the pictures, say where these people go in their free time and what game they play there. Use the verbs **ir** and **jugar**.

Sonia

MODELO Sonia va al parque. Juega al tenis.

1. yo   2. tú   3. mi amigo(a)

4. nosotros   5. ellos

37 ¿Con qué frecuencia?

Leamos/Escribamos How often do you, your family, and your friends go to the following places on weekends?

MODELO yo/playa
     Casi nunca voy a la playa los fines de semana.

siempre	a veces	(casi) nunca

1. mi familia y yo/cine
2. mis amigos/piscina
3. mi mejor amigo(a)/iglesia
4. mis amigos y yo/fiestas
5. yo/clase de español
6. los profesores/colegio

Comunicación

HOLT **SoundBooth** ONLINE RECORDING

38 ¿Qué haces?

Escribamos/Hablemos Complete the questions with the correct form of the verb. Then use them to interview a partner.

1. ¿A qué deportes ===== (jugar) tú?
2. ¿Quién ===== (jugar) contigo?
3. ¿Tu mejor amigo y tú ===== (jugar) al ajedrez?
4. ¿Adónde ===== (ir) tú los sábados?
5. ¿Tu mejor amigo(a) y tú ===== (ir) de compras?
6. ¿Adónde ===== (ir) ustedes de compras?

Weather expressions

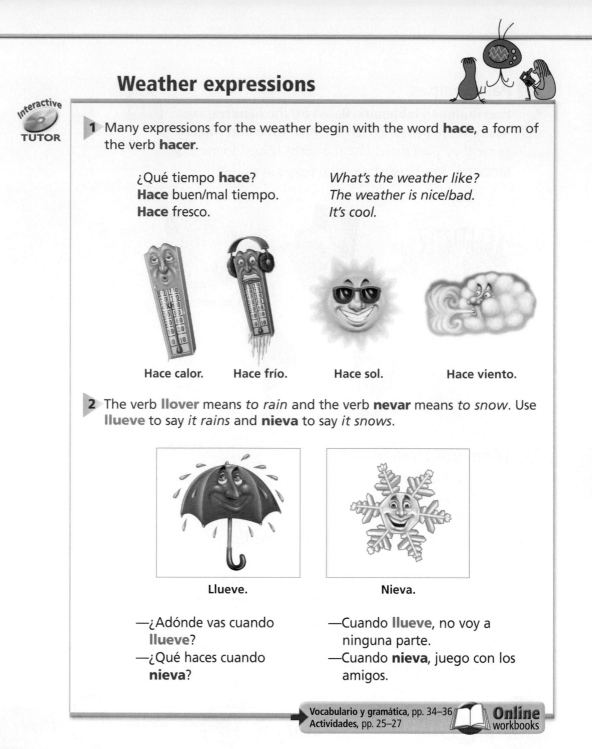

1 Many expressions for the weather begin with the word **hace**, a form of the verb **hacer**.

¿Qué tiempo **hace**?
Hace buen/mal tiempo.
Hace fresco.

What's the weather like?
The weather is nice/bad.
It's cool.

Hace calor.   Hace frío.   Hace sol.   Hace viento.

2 The verb **llover** means *to rain* and the verb **nevar** means *to snow*. Use **llueve** to say *it rains* and **nieva** to say *it snows*.

Llueve.   Nieva.

—¿Adónde vas cuando **llueve**?
—¿Qué haces cuando **nieva**?

—Cuando **llueve**, no voy a ninguna parte.
—Cuando **nieva**, juego con los amigos.

Vocabulario y gramática, pp. 34–36
Actividades, pp. 25–27

Online workbooks

39 ¿Qué tiempo hace?

Leamos/Hablemos Look at the photo. For each set of expressions, choose the one that better describes the photo.

1. **a.** Nieva.   **b.** No nieva.
2. **a.** Hace calor.   **b.** Hace fresco.
3. **a.** Llueve.   **b.** No llueve.
4. **a.** Hace mal tiempo.   **b.** Nieva.
5. **a.** Hace sol.   **b.** No hace sol.
6. **a.** Hace buen tiempo.   **b.** No hace buen tiempo.

Capítulo 3 • ¿Qué te gusta hacer?

40 ¿Cuál?

Escuchemos Listen to six descriptions of the weather. Decide if each one describes picture A, picture B, or neither picture.

41 ¿Qué haces?

Hablemos Say what the weather is usually like in these places during the given months.

MODELO en Texas en abril
En Texas en abril hace muy buen tiempo.

1. en Alaska en enero
2. en Florida en julio
3. en Arizona en mayo
4. en Seattle en febrero
5. en California en mayo
6. en Illinois en diciembre
7. en Texas en agosto
8. en Louisiana en noviembre
9. en Nueva York en abril
10. en Colorado en octubre

Comunicación

HOLT **SoundBooth** ONLINE RECORDING

42 ¿Adónde van?

Hablemos With a partner, use the drawings to say what Miguel and Alicia do on the weekends. Give as many details as you can.

Conexiones culturales

Conexión Música

el charango

la flauta

1 Los instrumentos

People in Spanish-speaking countries play many different musical instruments. Some of these instruments are described here. Look at the photographs as you read the descriptions.

1. La **flauta** azteca es un instrumento muy bonito. Es parecida a *(it looks like)* la flauta dulce *(recorder)*.

2. El **charango** es popular en los Andes. Es parecido a la guitarra.

3. El **güiro** es un instrumento percusivo *(percussion instrument)*. ¡Pero es muy diferente al tambor *(drum)*!

4. En muchos países el **arco** se usa *(is used)* para tocar el violín. En Centroamérica el **arco** es un instrumento musical.

el güiro

el arco

2 ¿Cómo lo harías *(would you do it)*?

People have always made musical instruments from materials that are readily available. For example, people have made pottery flutes from clay and percussion instruments from gourds. If you had to make your own musical instrument from materials you have around your classroom, what materials would you use? What instrument would you make? Share your answers with a partner.

Músicos en la región de Asturias, España, tocando gaitas *(bagpipes)*

Conexión Ciencias naturales

El huracán Hurricanes are violent tropical thunderstorms with extremely heavy rains and high wind speeds of up to 186 mph. Hurricanes usually occur in the Atlantic Ocean, the Gulf of Mexico, and the Caribbean Sea between June 1 and November 30. During the worst hurricanes, streets become rivers, whole cities lose their electricity, and people must sometimes leave their homes and go to higher ground. The word hurricane comes from *hurakán,* the storm god of the Caribbean Taino Indians.

Sección de puente destrozada después del huracán Ivan cerca de Pensacola, Florida

3 ¿Dónde está el huracán?

Use the information in the table to track Hurricane Charley on graph paper. Draw a line connecting the points of the hurricane's path. Put a dot on the map where the latitudes and longitudes listed cross on your graph. Find out which countries it hit. See the example of Hurricane Frances drawn on the map.

Hurricane Charley

Day	Latitude	Longitude
1	17° N	77° W
2	19° N	81° W
3	26° N	82.5° W
4	27° N	80° W

4 ¿Cómo se llama?

Each tropical storm of the season is given a name. The names are chosen ahead of time, and they alternate between female and male names in alphabetical order. For example, the first storm would be Alex, the next Brenda, and so on. Write Spanish names for the first ten tropical storms of the season. Would a hurricane named Rosa be early or late in the hurricane season?

Daño ocasionado por el huracán Charley en Port Charlotte, Florida

Conexiones culturales

¿Quién será?
Episodio 3

E S T R A T E G I A

Understanding subtext People do not always say what they mean. When someone asks, "How are you?," the **text** of your answer (what you say) might be, "I'm just fine." But your **subtext** (what you really mean) may be, "I feel awful, but I don't want to talk about it." As you read the **Novela** or watch the video, listen for Sra. Corona's and Sofía's subtexts.

En México

En casa de Sofía *Sofía and her mother talk about Sofía's interests.*

Estados Unidos

MÉXICO   Golfo de México

Ciudad de México ★

Océano Pacífico

1

Sra. Corona Sofía, a ti te gusta mucho la música, ¿verdad, hija?

Sofía Claro, mamá.

Sra. Corona Y te gusta bailar, ¿no es así, hija?

Sofía Claro, mamá, me gusta mucho bailar.

2

Sra. Corona Vas a tomar clases de ballet los lunes y los viernes en la Academia de Danza Clásica.

Sofía Pero, mamá, ¡no quiero tomar clases de ballet!

Sra. Corona El ballet es música y es baile, hija, las dos cosas que más te gustan en todo el mundo.

3

Sofía ¿Viernes? Mamá, ¡hoy es viernes!

Sra. Corona Sí, hija. Hoy vas a la clase de ballet a las cinco en punto. ¡Adiós, cariño!

4

Sofía ¿Ballet? ¿Yo? ¿Bailarina? ¡Nunca!

Novela en video

5

Roque Hace muy buen tiempo hoy. ¿Por qué no vamos a la piscina a nadar?

Celeste No, no quiero nadar. Quiero ir al cine. Hay una película formidable en el Cineplex que quiero ver.

Sofía Pero, no quiero ir a la piscina. Y tampoco quiero ir al cine.

6

Roque ¡Pero, Sofía! ¡Es viernes! ¡Siempre hacemos algo juntos los viernes!

Sofía Ya lo sé. Pero hoy no quiero hacer nada. Voy a casa a estudiar.

Celeste ¿Qué te pasa, Sofía? ¡Tú casi nunca estudias los viernes por la noche!

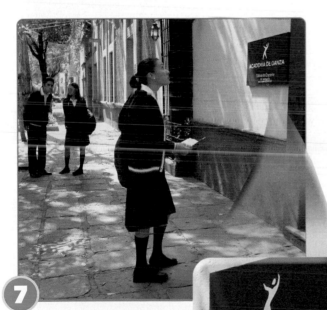

ACADEMIA DE DANZA
Talleres de Coyoacán
TEL. 5634-1170
e-mail: academica@cosmo.com

7

Celeste Hay algo muy raro aquí.

Roque Sí, muy raro. Es viernes y ¡no quiere salir con sus amigos!

A. CONTESTA

Check your understanding of the **Novela** by answering these questions.

1. What does Sofía's mother want her to do after school on Friday? How does Sofía feel about it?
2. Who are Celeste and Roque?
3. What do Celeste and Roque want to do after school on Friday?
4. Why do they find Sofía's behavior odd?

En España

La profesora calls Marcos in Puerto Rico to tell him where he's going next.

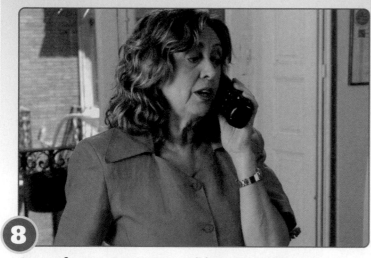

8

La profesora Tengo otra candidata. Es una chica de Texas. Después de Puerto Rico, vas a Texas. A El Paso, Texas.

Cuatro candidatos... Sólo nos faltan seis.

En Puerto Rico

Marcos arrives in Puerto Rico.

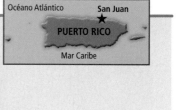

9

B. CONTESTA

1. Where is **la profesora's** assistant supposed to go after this episode?

2. How many **candidatos** have been located? How many are yet to be found?

Actividades

1 ¿Cierto o falso?

Based on the story, tell whether each statement is **cierto** or **falso**.

1. A Sofía le gusta la música.
2. Sofía quiere tomar clases de ballet.
3. Celeste quiere nadar.
4. Sofía no quiere nadar, y tampoco quiere ver una película.
5. El asistente habla por teléfono celular.

2 ¿Listos?

Complete the following sentences with words from the story that la señora Corona says to Sofía.

> viernes   cinco   tomar   colegio

Hija, vas a ___1___ clases de ballet los lunes y ___2___. Hoy vas a la clase de ballet a las ___3___ en punto.

3 ¿Comprendes la Novela?

In **Estrategia** for this episode, you learned that people sometimes say one thing but mean another. What would you say about the following people? Do they mean what they say, or are they saying one thing but meaning another?

1. Sofía's mother, when she talks to Sofía about ballet lessons
2. Sofía, when she answers her mother
3. Sofía, when she is talking to her friends about Friday afternoon

> **Próximo episodio**
> *Can you predict what Marcos will find out about Nicolás?*
> PÁGINAS 168–171 ▶

Leamos y escribamos

para leer Predicting what will happen in a story is a helpful strategy. You will be able to read a story more quickly and easily if you focus your attention on what you expect to happen.

A Antes de leer

The following story is a myth from the southwestern United States. Read the title and the first paragraph of the text and use what you know about myths to predict what will happen in this one.

Los cuatro elementos

Existen cuatro elementos en el mundo[1]: el agua[2], el fuego[3], el viento y el honor. Son amigos inseparables. Son inteligentes, divertidos y graciosos. Siempre pasan el rato juntos y les gusta hablar por horas y horas. Pero un día, el día de la creación, los amigos saben que tendrán que separarse[4]. En una reunión, en la casa del agua, se dicen adiós[5].

El agua dice así: —Vamos a lugares diferentes. En el futuro, si me quieren encontrar[6], búsquenme[7] en los lugares[8] donde llueve. ¡Nado con los océanos!

El fuego dice así: —Ustedes son mis mejores amigos. En el futuro, si me quieren encontrar, búsquenme en los lugares donde hace calor. ¡Paseo con el sol!

El viento dice así: —¡Amigos! No quiero separarme de ustedes. En el futuro, si me quieren encontrar, búsquenme en el aire, en los lugares donde hace mal tiempo. ¡Corro con los tornados y los huracanes!

El honor, el último[9] en hablar, dice así: —Compañeros. ¡Escuchen con atención! En el futuro, si me pierden[10] a mí, ¡no me busquen! ¡No me van a encontrar!

1 world   2 water   3 fire   4 will have to part   5 say goodbye
6 if you want to find me   7 look for me   8 places   9 the last one
10 if you lose me

B Comprensión

Complete the following sentences.

1. Los cuatro elementos en el mundo son...
2. Los elementos son amigos inseparables y les gusta...
3. El día de la creación, los amigos se dicen adiós en...
4. En el futuro el agua, el fuego y el viento se pueden encontrar en los lugares donde...
5. El último elemento dice: "...no me busquen" porque...

C Después de leer

What is the moral of the story? What does this myth tell you about the cultural values of people in the Southwest? Do the people in your community share similar values?

Interactive TUTOR

Taller del escritor

ESTRATEGIA

para escribir When describing things that happen in a certain order, or scheduling activities, it helps first to arrange your ideas. You can use lists, timelines, or charts.

		febrero
viernes	sábado	domingo

Horario de actividades

Imagine a friend is coming to visit for a week and you need to plan activities. Write your friend a letter:

• explain your plans
• describe a few of them
• ask what he or she wants to do.

1 Antes de escribir

Divide a sheet of paper into seven columns, one for each day of the week. Jot down what you want to do with your friend for each day.

2 Escribir y revisar

Using your chart, write a letter to your friend. When and where will the activities take place? Tell your friend why you like these activities. Ask what he or she likes or wants to do. Read your draft at least two times, comparing it with your chart. Did you explain your plans? Are some activities described? Did you ask what your friend likes to do? Check spelling and punctuation.

3 Publicar

Post your letter along with those of your classmates on the bulletin board. Which letter sounds like the best week?

Leamos y escribamos

Prepárate para el examen

Interactive
TUTOR

1 Vocabulario 1
• talking about what you and others like to do
• talking about what a friend wants to do
pp. 94–99

1 Using the pictures below to guide you, say what you like or what you want to do.

2 Gramática 1
• **gustar** with infinitives
• pronouns after prepositions
• **querer** with infinitives
pp. 100–105

2 Choose the correct word in parentheses.

Yo soy Diana. Mi mejor amiga se llama Maribel. Ella es muy atlética y le __1__ (gustan/gusta) jugar al volibol y al básquetbol. A mí __2__ (me/te) gusta más navegar por Internet o ver películas. Me __3__ (gusta/gustan) las películas románticas. A Maribel __4__ (le/me) gustan las películas románticas también. Me gusta ir al cine con __5__ (ella/usted). Pero a nuestras amigas Ana y Rita no __6__ (les/le) gusta ir al cine. Ellas __7__ (quiero/quieren) alquilar videos o ver televisión.

3 Vocabulario 2
• talking about everyday activities
• saying how often you do things
pp. 108–113

3 Complete the sentences with logical answers.
1. Me gustan los deportes. Los sábados me gusta ====.
2. Soy introvertida. Después de clases me gusta ====.
3. Me gusta la música; me gusta ==== el piano.
4. ¿Te gusta ==== por teléfono con amigos todos los días?
5. Cuando hace mal tiempo nos gusta ====.
6. Me gustan las películas. No me gusta ir al cine. Me gusta ==== videos.

4 Complete the paragraph with the correct verb forms.

Yo ___1___ (jugar) al fútbol con amigos los domingos. Me gusta jugar cuando ___2___ (hacer) sol. Después, ellos y yo ___3___ (pasear) y ___4___ (ir) a la piscina. A mí me gusta el cine, y los sábados ___5___ (ir) al cine con mi amigo Leo. A él le gusta la música. Él ___6___ (tocar) el piano y ___7___ (cantar). Cuando ___8___ (hacer) mal tiempo, mis amigos y yo ___9___ (jugar) al básquetbol en el gimnasio. Yo ___10___ (descansar) los lunes y los martes ___11___ (ir) al entrenamiento de fútbol.

4 Gramática 2
- regular **-ar** verbs
- **ir** and **jugar**
- weather expressions
pp. 114–119

5 Answer the following questions.

1. How can Latin American students participate in sports?
2. When do parents expect to meet their teenager's friends? Is this true for you and your parents too?
3. Who pays the bill when friends go out **a la americana?**

5 Cultura
- **Comparaciones** pp. 106–107
- **Notas culturales** pp. 96, 104, 110
- **Geocultura** pp. 88–91

6 Marta is interviewing students for an article for her journalism class. Listen to her interview with Paco. List the days of the week and write what Paco does during the week.

Conversación

HOLT **SoundBooth** ONLINE RECORDING

7 Role-play the following conversation with a partner. Partner A and Partner B are friends talking about what they want to do today.

PARTNER A: Greet your partner. Ask what he or she wants to do.

PARTNER B: Respond. Say you're going to the park in the morning because you want to play basketball. Invite your partner to go with you.

PARTNER A: Say you don't want to go. Say you're going to the mall and ask if your partner wants to go with you.

PARTNER B: Decline the invitation. Ask why your partner doesn't want to play basketball.

PARTNER A: Explain that you don't want to play because it's cold. Ask why your partner doesn't want to go to the mall.

PARTNER B: Explain that you don't want to go to the mall because you don't like to go shopping.

PARTNER A: Suggest going to a movie together in the afternoon.

PARTNER B: Accept the invitation and end the conversation.

Prepárate para el examen

Repaso de Gramática 1

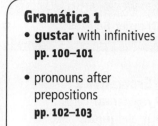

Gramática 1
- **gustar** with infinitives
  pp. 100–101
- pronouns after prepositions
  pp. 102–103
- **querer** with infinitives
  pp. 104–105

Use **gustar** with an **infinitive** to say what you and others like to do.

A mí **me gusta hablar** por teléfono contigo.
Use these pronouns after the prepositions **a, de, en,** and **con.**

mí (conmigo)	nosotros(as)
ti (contigo)	vosotros(as)
usted, él, ella	ustedes, ellos, ellas

Use **querer** with an **infinitive** to say what you and others want to do.

qu**ie**ro	queremos
qu**ie**res	queréis
qu**ie**re	qu**ie**ren

Queremos ir a la playa.

Repaso de Gramática 2

Gramática 2
- regular **-ar** verbs
  pp. 114–115
- **ir** and **jugar**
  pp. 116–117
- weather expressions
  pp. 118–119

hablar		ir		jugar	
habl**o**	habl**amos**	voy	vamos	j**ue**go	jugamos
habl**as**	habl**áis**	vas	vais	j**ue**gas	jugáis
habl**a**	habl**an**	va	van	j**ue**ga	j**ue**gan

Use the verb **hacer** to talk about the weather.

¿Qué tiempo **hace**?
Hace buen/mal tiempo.
Hace frío. **Hace** calor.
Hace sol. **Hace** fresco.
Hace viento.

Use the words **llueve** and **nieva** to say *it rains* and *it snows*.

Letra y sonido (h) (j) (g)

Las letras h, j, g
- The letter **h** in Spanish is silent. It is not pronounced: **h**ola, **h**ora, **h**ablar, **h**acer **h**oy.
- The letter **j** is pronounced much like the English *h*, though sometimes it sounds harsher, a little like the *h* in *hue*. The letter **g** before the vowels **e** and **i** (**ge, gi**) has the same pronunciation: **j**ugar, **j**ueves, **J**osé, **g**eografía, **g**imnasio, e**j**ercicio, pelirro**j**a, inteli**g**ente, a**g**itar.

Trabalenguas
El hipopótamo Hipo
  está con hipo.

Me trajo Tajo tres trajes,
  tres trajes me trajo Tajo.

Dictado
Escribe las oraciones de la grabación.

Repaso de Vocabulario 1

Talking about what you and others like to do

A ellos(as) les gusta...	They like to . . .
A mis amigos y a mí nos gusta...	My friends and I like to . . .
alquilar videos	to rent videos
bajar archivos	to download files
el básquetbol	basketball
el béisbol	baseball
cantar	to sing
el centro comercial	mall
el cine	movie theater
comer	to eat
correr	to run
dibujar	to draw
escribir cartas	to write letters
escuchar música	to listen to music
el fútbol	soccer
el fútbol americano	football
hacer ejercicio	to exercise
hacer la tarea	to do homework
ir al cine	to go to the movies
ir de compras	to go shopping
los juegos de mesa	board games
jugar (ue)	to play
leer revistas y novelas	to read magazines and novels
Me gusta...	I like to . . .
montar en bicicleta	to ride a bike
nadar	to swim
navegar por Internet	to surf the Internet
pasar el rato solo(a)	to spend time alone
pasear	to go for a walk
patinar	to skate
platicar en línea	to chat online
¿Qué te gusta hacer?	What do you like to do?
salir con amigos	to go out with friends
el tenis	tennis
ver televisión	to watch television
el volibol	volleyball

Talking about what you want to do

con mis amigos(as)	with my friends
con mi familia	with my family
conmigo	with me
contigo	with you
Está bien.	All right.
Ni idea.	I have no idea.
¿Qué quieres hacer hoy?	What do you want to do today?
querer (ie)	to want
Quiero ir...	I want to go . . .

Repaso de Vocabulario 2

Talking about everyday activities

¿Adónde vas...?	Where do you go . . .?
bailar	to dance
el baile	dance
la casa de...	. . . 's house
el colegio	school
...cuando hace buen tiempo...	. . . when the weather is good . . .
...cuando hace mal tiempo...	. . . when the weather is bad . . .
descansar	to rest
el ensayo	rehearsal
el entrenamiento	practice
estudiar	to study
el gimnasio	gym
hablar por teléfono	to talk on the phone
la iglesia	church
Le gusta...	He/She likes . . .
No va a ninguna parte.	He/She doesn't go anywhere.
el parque	park
la piscina	pool
la playa	beach
practicar deportes	to play sports
¿Qué hace...?	What does . . . do?
¿Qué haces...?	What do you do . . .?
la reunión	meeting
tocar el piano	to play the piano
trabajar	to work
el trabajo	work

Saying how often

a veces	sometimes
(casi) nunca	(almost) never
(casi) siempre	(almost) always
¿Con qué frecuencia vas...?	How often do you go . . .?
después de clases	after class
todos los días	every day

To say on which day something happens See p. 112.

Prepárate para el examen

Integración

capítulos 1-3

1 Listen to each conversation and match it with the appropriate picture.

A   **B**   **C**   **D**

2 Marisol wants to find an e-mail pen pal. Read her e-mail and then answer the questions.

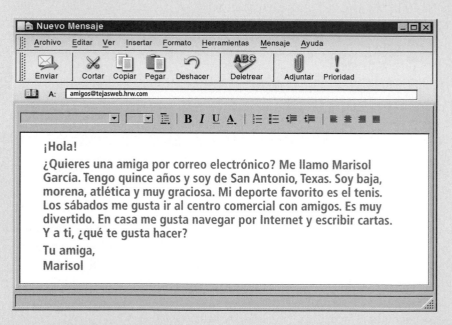

Nuevo Mensaje

Archivo   Editar   Ver   Insertar   Formato   Herramientas   Mensaje   Ayuda

Enviar   Cortar   Copiar   Pegar   Deshacer   Deletrear   Adjuntar   Prioridad

A: amigos@tejasweb.hrw.com

B I U A

¡Hola!

¿Quieres una amiga por correo electrónico? Me llamo Marisol García. Tengo quince años y soy de San Antonio, Texas. Soy baja, morena, atlética y muy graciosa. Mi deporte favorito es el tenis. Los sábados me gusta ir al centro comercial con amigos. Es muy divertido. En casa me gusta navegar por Internet y escribir cartas. Y a ti, ¿qué te gusta hacer?

Tu amiga,
Marisol

1. ¿Cuántos años tiene Marisol y de dónde es?
2. ¿Cómo es Marisol?
3. ¿Qué deporte le gusta más?
4. ¿Cuándo le gusta salir con amigos? ¿Adónde van?
5. ¿Qué le gusta hacer a Marisol cuando pasa el rato sola?

Visit Holt Online

go.hrw.com
KEYWORD: EXP1A CH3

Cumulative Self-test

3 Imagine that you are in Reynosa and are interviewing people at the fair. Write six questions in Spanish that you would use to get the following information. Don't forget to be polite!

1. the name of an adult
2. the age of a child
3. a child's birthday
4. where an adult is from
5. a description of a child
6. if a child likes Mexican food

La feria en Reynosa, de Carmen Lomas Garza (n. 1948)

4 With a partner, take turns role-playing interviewer and one of the people in the painting above. Ask questions similar to those you wrote for Activity 3. Switch roles. Be prepared to tell the class what you learned about your partner.

5

Situación

The Student Council is planning an outdoor teen camp for the summer and wants to have activities ready for whatever weather condition might occur. In groups of three, discuss in Spanish what you like to do in the following weather conditions.

▶ hot and sunny
▶ rainy
▶ cool and windy
▶ cold

List everyone's ideas on the board. With the rest of the class, decide on two activities to plan for each weather condition.

Video/DVD
GeoVisión

Geocultura
Costa Rica

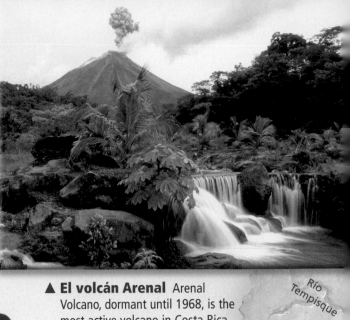

▲ **El volcán Arenal** Arenal Volcano, dormant until 1968, is the most active volcano in Costa Rica. It sits near Lake Arenal.

Río Tempisque

▼ **San José** The capital of Costa Rica lies in the Central Valley. The region around **San José** is the most populated in the country. There are several volcanoes nearby.

Almanac

Population
4,016,173

Capital San José

Government
democratic republic

Official Language
Spanish

Currency colón

Internet code
www.[ ].cr

◀ **Ticos** People in Costa Rica call themselves **ticos**. Here you can see a young **tico** and **tica** wearing traditional dance costumes.

¿Sabías que...?
Protected wilderness and wildlife areas account for 27% of the land in Costa Rica, a far greater percentage than any other country in the world.

NICARAGUA

El perezoso de tres dedos
The three-toed sloth moves very slowly and spends most of its time in forest treetops.

Río San Juan

Río San Carlos

Volcán Arenal

Laguna Arenal

Reserva Biológica del Bosque Nuboso de Monteverde

Río Chirripó

Parque Nacional Tortuguero

MAR CARIBE

Volcán Poás

Volcán Barva

Volcán Irazú

Río Reventazón

Limón

GOLFO DE NICOYA

Puntarenas

Alajuela

Valle Central

Escazú

SAN JOSÉ

Cartago

Cordillera Central

Río Telire

PENÍNSULA DE NICOYA

OCÉANO PACÍFICO

Cerro Chirripó (3819 m)

Cordillera de Talamanca

Río General

COSTA RICA

GOLFO DULCE

Parque Nacional Corcovado

▲ El café Coffee beans are the main crop in Costa Rica's Central Valley.

▲ El Parque Nacional Tortuguero
Tortuguero National Park is on the Caribbean coast of Costa Rica. The park is home to endangered green sea turtles, jaguars, and howler monkeys.

◄ El Parque Nacional Corcovado
Corcovado National Park is located on the rugged Osa Peninsula. Its tropical rain forest gets almost six meters of rain per year.

¿Qué tanto sabes?
Which volcanoes are found near **San José**?

ciento treinta y cinco **135**

A conocer Costa Rica

Las celebraciones

◀ **Las fiestas patronales**
On patron saints' days you can see young people dressed up in **payaso** costumes, dancing to live music.

▶ **El Día de Juan Santamaría**
On April 11, Costa Rica celebrates the memory of national hero **Juan Santamaría,** a drummer boy who died bravely in 1856 during the Battle of Rivas against the invader William Walker.

El arte

◀ **Jorge Jiménez Deredia (1954–)**
This modern artist is world famous for his harmonious sculptures in marble and bronze. He is the first Latin American artist to have a work displayed at St. Peter's Basilica in Rome. The marble sculpture you see here is displayed in **San José**.

▼ **El Día del Boyero** A festival for oxcart drivers, or **boyeros,** is celebrated in **San Antonio de Escazú** on the second Sunday in March. The festival includes a parade of beautifully painted carts pulled by oxen.

La comida

▶ **Olla de carne** Costa Ricans make a traditional stew called **olla de carne** out of meat with vegetables such as sweet potatoes, chayote squash, corn, and potatoes.

¿Sabías que...?

The quetzal is endangered across Central America because its habitat is being destroyed. How are animals and their habitats being protected in Costa Rica?

▼ **La mariposa "el perro de los naranjos"** The giant swallowtail butterfly is commonly seen in March and April.

Los animales

▶ **La lapa roja** The scarlet macaw can be seen on the Osa Peninsula.

◀ **El mono congo** You can easily find the howler monkey in the forest by listening for its loud yell.

▶ **El quetzal** The quetzal lives in cloud forests. This bird is famous for its beautiful green feathers.

4

La vida escolar

Objetivos

In Part 1 you will learn to:
- say what you have and what you need
- talk about school supplies and school subjects
- use indefinite articles and **¿cuánto?, mucho,** and **poco**
- form **tener** and some of its idioms
- use **venir** and **a** + time

In Part 2 you will learn to:
- talk about plans and give invitations
- talk about school events and places
- use **ir a** + infinitive
- form **-er** and **-ir** verbs in the present
- use the tag questions **¿no?** and **¿verdad?**
- use **hacer, poner, saber, traer,** and **ver**
- use **de** with **salir** and **saber**

¿Qué ves en la foto?

- **¿Dónde están los muchachos?**

- **¿Qué hacen?**

- **¿Qué haces tú cuando vas al zoológico?**

Jóvenes en el parque Zoo Ave de
San José, Costa Rica

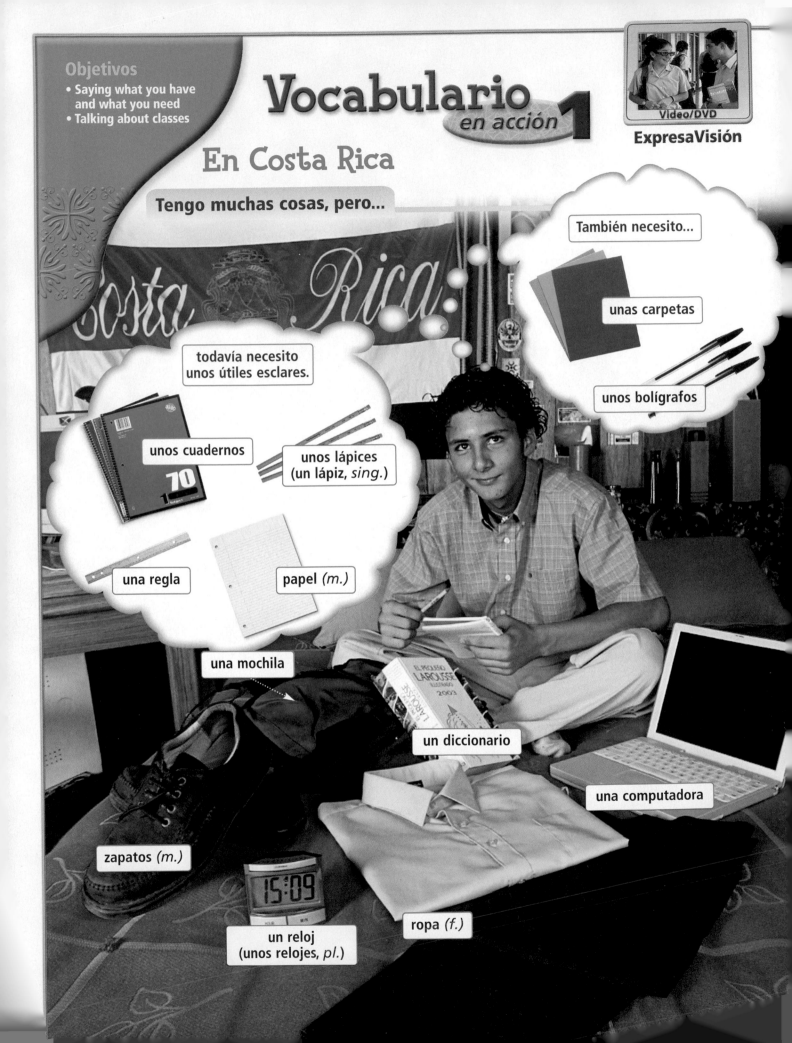

Vocabulario 1

¿Qué clases tienes esta tarde?

Tengo historia...

CENTRO EDUCATIVO NUEVA ESPERANZA
400 mts Oeste del Beneficio La Meseta,
San Juan de Santa Barbara Heredia,
Telfax (Primaria) 506.265.5393
Tel (Secundaria) 506.265.7934

Horas	Clases
8:00	*matemáticas*
8:50	*arte*
9:40	*biología*
10:30	*español*
11:20	*educación física*
12:10	*almuerzo*
13:00	*historia*
13:50	*inglés*

por la mañana

por la tarde

Más vocabulario...

las materias	*school subjects*
el alemán	*German*
las ciencias	*science*
la computación	*computer science*
el francés	*French*
la química	*chemistry*
el taller	*shop, workshop*

También se puede decir...

In Spain, a computer is called **un ordenador**, while in Colombia, many say **un computador**.

Colombians may use either **un esfero** or **un plumero** for **un bolígrafo**. Ecuadoreans may say either **un bolígrafo** or **una pluma**.

¡Exprésate!

To ask what others have or need	To respond
¿Necesitas algo para el colegio? *Do you need anything for school?*	**Sí, necesito muchas cosas.** *Yes, I need a lot of things.*
¿Necesitas algo para la clase de arte? *Do you need anything for art class?*	**No, no necesito nada.** *No, I don't need anything.*
¿Necesitas una calculadora? *Do you need a calculator?*	**Sí, necesito una calculadora.** *Yes, I need a calculator.*
¿Tienes carpetas? *Do you have folders?*	**Sí, tengo un montón./No, no tengo.** *Yes, I have a ton of them./No, I don't have any.*

Interactive TUTOR

▶ **Vocabulario adicional** — Materias, p. R7

Vocabulario y gramática, pp. 37–39

Online workbooks

Costa Rica

1 ¿Qué necesitas y qué tienes?

Escuchemos Listen as Óscar and his mom talk about what school supplies he needs and already has. Choose the picture that shows what they're going to buy.

a.

b.

2 Una carta electrónica

Leamos Lupe wrote to tell Francisco of some supplies he'll need for school. Read the e-mail and answer the questions that follow.

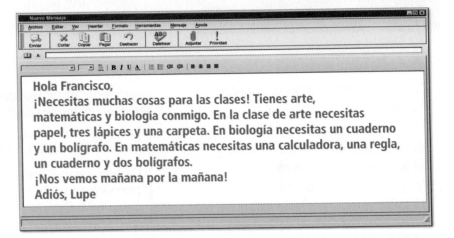

Hola Francisco,
¡Necesitas muchas cosas para las clases! Tienes arte, matemáticas y biología conmigo. En la clase de arte necesitas papel, tres lápices y una carpeta. En biología necesitas un cuaderno y un bolígrafo. En matemáticas necesitas una calculadora, una regla, un cuaderno y dos bolígrafos.
¡Nos vemos mañana por la mañana!
Adiós, Lupe

1. What classes do Lupe and Francisco have together?
2. For which class do they need pencils and paper?
3. What supplies do they need for math class?
4. What do they need to bring for biology?
5. When will Lupe and Francisco see each other next?
6. For which classes do they need a pen?
7. For which class do they need a folder?
8. For which classes do they need a notebook?

3 Necesito muchas cosas

Hablemos Di (*Say*) cuatro cosas que tienes y cuatro cosas que necesitas para el colegio.

MODELO Tengo una mochila. Necesito ropa.

4 Necesito mucho para las clases

Escribamos/Hablemos Use the model and one word from each box to make logical sentences.

MODELO Para la clase de arte, necesito unos lápices.
No necesito una calculadora.

matemáticas	inglés
español	computación
arte	historia

un diccionario	una computadora
unos lápices	unas carpetas
papel	una calculadora

5 ¿Qué tiene Ricardo?

Escribamos Write three sentences that tell what Ricardo has in his locker (**el armario**). Then write two sentences that tell what school supplies he does not have in his locker. Finish with one sentence that tells what item he needs to help him get to class on time.

Comunicación

6 ¿Qué necesitas?

Hablemos What school supplies do you need for your classes? With a partner, take turns asking each other what you need for the following classes. Name at least two items.

MODELO la clase de arte —¿Qué necesitas para la clase de arte?
—Necesito unos lápices y papel.

1. la clase de español
2. la clase de matemáticas
3. la clase de inglés
4. la clase de ciencias
5. la clase de computación

¡Exprésate!

To ask about classes	To respond
¿Qué clases tienes esta tarde/después del almuerzo? *What classes do you have this afternoon/ after lunch?*	**Primero tengo español y después tengo computación.** *First I have Spanish and afterwards I have computer science.*
¿Cuál es tu materia preferida? *What's your favorite subject?*	**Mi materia preferida es matemáticas. Es fácil. No me gusta la clase de inglés porque es difícil.** *My favorite subject is math. It's easy. I don't like English because it's hard.*

Vocabulario y gramática, pp. 37–39

Online workbooks

Interactive TUTOR

Nota cultural

Students in public schools in some Spanish-speaking countries have fewer elective classes than students in the United States. In Costa Rica, high school students take the same classes for the first three years. In their third year, they take a national exam to see if they will continue a college preparatory program, or attend a technical or vocational program for their last two years.

How is this different from your school?

7 Muchas materias

Leamos/Escribamos Imagine this is your class schedule. Answer the questions that follow.

Día	lunes	martes	miércoles	jue
Horario				
8:45	historia	biología	historia	bio
9:40	matemáticas	computación	matemáticas	com
10:35	ed. física	arte	ed. física	arte
11:30	español	ciencias	español	cier
12:25	almuerzo	almuerzo	almuerzo	alm
12:55	química	inglés	química	ingl
1:50	taller	francés	taller	frar

400 mts Oeste del Beneficio La Meseta, San Juan de Heredia. Telfax 506.265.5393 Tel 506.265.7934

1. ¿Qué clases tienes los lunes por la mañana?
2. ¿Qué tienes primero los martes?
3. ¿Qué días tienes educación física?
4. ¿Qué clase tienes después de química los miércoles?
5. ¿Qué clases tienes por la tarde los martes?

8 Mis clases

Leamos/Escribamos Complete the paragraph, describing your own schedule.

Por la mañana tengo ___1___ clases. Primero, tengo la clase de ___2___. Después, tengo ___3___ y ___4___. Me gusta la clase de ___5___ porque es ___6___. Después de ___7___ tengo el almuerzo. Por la tarde tengo la clase de ___8___. La profesora es ___9___. Para la clase de español, necesito ___10___ y para la clase de matemáticas, necesito ___11___. Mi materia preferida es ___12___.

Comunicación

HOLT **SoundBooth** ONLINE RECORDING

9 ¿Qué clases tienes?

Hablemos Work with a partner. Take turns asking if your partner has the classes indicated below. Answer with the day of week and the time of day (morning or afternoon).

MODELO arte — ¿Tienes clase de arte?

— Sí, tengo arte los lunes y miércoles por la mañana.

(No, no tengo clase de arte.)

arte

francés

computación

almuerzo

historia

ciencias

matemáticas

alemán

educación física

taller

inglés

español

10 ¿Cómo es tu horario?

Hablemos Write your school schedule. Include the days, times, and classes. With a partner, talk about your classes, using the schedules you've created. Mention at least three classes and say why you like or dislike them.

MODELO — ¿Qué clase tienes primero los jueves?

— Primero, tengo la clase de... Me gusta porque...

Objetivos
- Indefinite articles, ¿cuánto?, mucho and poco
- Tener and some tener idioms
- Venir and a la/las with time

Gramática
en acción 1

GramaVisión

Interactive TUTOR

Indefinite articles; ¿cuánto?, mucho, and poco

1 The **indefinite articles** **un** and **una** are used to say *a* or *an* before a singular noun, while **unos** and **unas** are used to say *some* before a plural noun. The indefinite articles can sometimes be left out, especially when the noun is plural.

Necesito **un** diccionario.	*I need a dictionary.*
¿Tienes (**unos**) lápices?	*Do you have (some) pencils?*

2 The indefinite articles agree with the noun in gender and number.

	Masculine	Feminine
SINGULAR	**un** libro	**una** mochila
PLURAL	un**os** libr**os**	un**as** mochil**as**

3 To talk about amounts of things, use the following adjectives. These words also agree with the nouns they describe in gender and number.

SINGULAR	¿cuánto(a)? how much?	mucho(a) a lot of, much	poco(a) little, not much
PLURAL	¿cuántos(as)? how many?	muchos(as) a lot of, many	pocos(as) few, not many

—¿**Cuánta** tare**a** tienes?	*How much homework do you have?*
—Tengo **mucha**.	*I have a lot.*

> Vocabulario y gramática, pp. 40–42
> Actividades, pp. 31–33
>
> **Online** workbooks

En inglés

In English, adjectives generally go before the nouns they modify.

It's an **awful** book.

Think of an example in English where the adjective follows the noun it modifies.

In Spanish, adjectives like ¿cuánto(a)?, mucho(a) and poco(a) go before the noun.

¿Cuánta tarea tienes?

Tengo muchas mochilas.

Hay poca tarea hoy.

However, most other adjectives follow the noun they modify.

Es un libro pésimo.

11 ¿Tienes o necesitas?

Hablemos Give the correct indefinite article for the following nouns. Then say whether you need these items or whether you already have them.

MODELO <u>una</u> regla
Necesito una regla. (Tengo una regla.)

1. ═══ cuaderno
2. ═══ calculadora
3. ═══ lápices
4. ═══ bolígrafos
5. ═══ carpetas
6. ═══ mochila
7. ═══ diccionario
8. ═══ computadora
9. ═══ reloj

12 **¿Cuánto?**

Hablemos Ask a friend how many of these items he or she has. Use **cuánto, cuántos, cuánta,** or **cuántas.**

MODELO **¿Cuántas mochilas tienes?**

1. ¿===== ropa tienes?
2. ¿===== lápices tienes?
3. ¿===== relojes tienes?
4. ¿===== reglas tienes?
5. ¿===== cuadernos tienes?
6. ¿===== carpetas tienes?
7. ¿===== papel tienes?
8. ¿===== libros tienes?

13 **¿Mucho o poco?**

Escribamos/Hablemos Now answer the questions from Activity 12, using the correct forms of **mucho** and **poco.**

MODELO **Tengo muchas (pocas) mochilas.**

14 **Útiles escolares**

Escuchemos Gabi is helping her younger sister, Verónica, figure out what school supplies she still needs. Look at the picture and decide if what she says is **cierto** or **falso.**

 Comunicación

HOLT SoundBooth ONLINE RECORDING

15 **¿Qué necesitamos?**

Hablemos You and your partner need to prepare a report that includes pictures, graphs, and mathematical calculations. Talk about the supplies you have and make a list of the supplies you need.

MODELO —¿Necesitamos papel?
—No, tengo mucho papel pero *(but)* necesitamos revistas.

Gramática 1

Present tense of tener and some tener idioms

Interactive TUTOR

1 Use the verb **tener** to tell what someone *has.* To conjugate the **yo** form, drop the **-er** ending and add **-go.** To conjugate all the other forms except **nosotros(as)** and **vosotros(as),** change the **-e** in the stem of **tener** to **-ie.**

yo ten**go**	nosotros(as) tenemos
tú t**ie**nes	vosotros(as) tenéis
Ud., él, ella t**ie**ne	Uds., ellos, ellas t**ie**nen

—¿T**ie**nes un bolígrafo? *Do you have a pen?*
—No. Ten**go** un lápiz. *No. I have a pencil.*

2 Use **tener que** + **infinitive** to talk about what you have to do.

Tengo que ir a un ensayo. *I have to go to a rehearsal.*

Vocabulario y gramática, pp. 40–42
Actividades, pp. 31–33
Online workbooks

Some other commom tener idioms	
tener ganas de + infinitive	*to feel like doing something*
tener prisa	*to be in a hurry*
tener (mucha) hambre	*to be (very) hungry*
tener (mucha) sed	*to be (very) thirsty*

En inglés

In English, we use the verb *to be* to say how old we are, or to say we're hungry or thirsty.

I am 15 years old.

We are hungry and thirsty.

In Spanish, use a form of **tener** *(to have)* with a noun for these expressions.

Tengo 15 años.

Tenemos hambre y sed.

Give examples where **ser** means *to be* and **tener** means *to have.*

16 ¿De quién habla?

Escuchemos Listen as Ana Mari talks about some of her friends. Match each picture to each statement she makes.

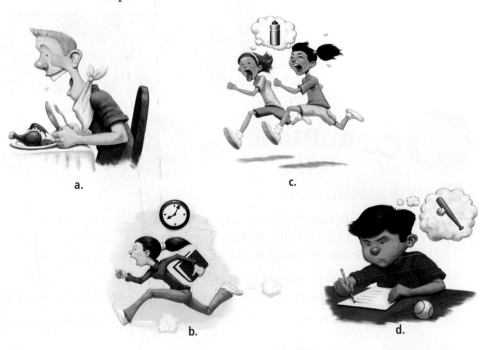

a.

c.

b.

d.

17 ¿Qué planes tienes?

Leamos Complete the conversation between Elena and her friend with the correct forms of **tener** and **tener que.**

—Elena, necesito un favor. ¿ __1__ un diccionario?

—No, pero la señora López __2__ muchos diccionarios en el salón de clase.

—Buena idea. __3__ irme. ¿Nos vemos por la tarde?

—¿Hoy? ¿Qué __4__ hacer (tú)?

—Nosotras __5__ un examen de alemán mañana y __6__ estudiar.

—Está bien. Nos vemos a las 4:00.

18 Rompecabezas

Escribamos Use the correct form of **tener** and a phrase from each puzzle piece to form six logical sentences.

1	**2**	**3**
Quiero salir. ¿(Tú)...?	tener	pasear conmigo
Es tarde y el profesor...	tener que	hoy por la tarde
Hace calor. (Yo)...	tener ganas de	prisa
Y ustedes, ¿qué clases...?		nadar
		sed
		los lunes

Comunicación

HOLT SoundBooth ONLINE RECORDING

19 Planes

Hablemos Look at the pictures. With a partner, take turns asking each other if you either want to or have to do these things today.

MODELO —¿Tienes ganas de ir al baile hoy por la noche?
—Sí, tengo ganas de bailar.

The verb venir and a + time

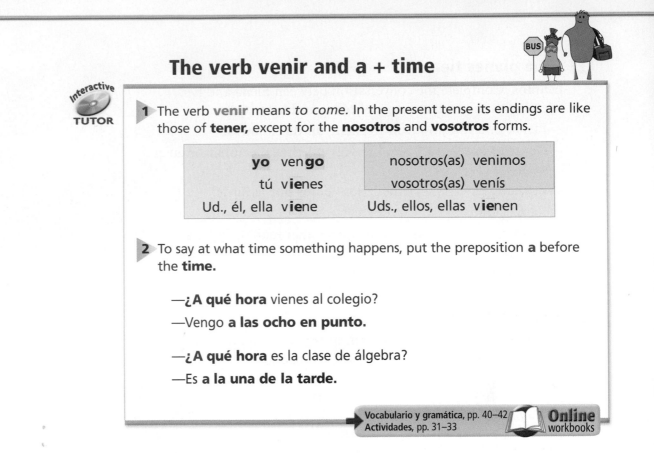

Interactive TUTOR

1 The verb **venir** means *to come*. In the present tense its endings are like those of **tener,** except for the **nosotros** and **vosotros** forms.

yo ven**go**	nosotros(as) venimos
tú v**ie**nes	vosotros(as) venís
Ud., él, ella v**ie**ne	Uds., ellos, ellas v**ie**nen

2 To say at what time something happens, put the preposition **a** before the **time.**

—**¿A qué hora** vienes al colegio?

—Vengo **a las ocho en punto.**

—**¿A qué hora** es la clase de álgebra?

—Es **a la una de la tarde.**

Vocabulario y gramática, pp. 40–42
Actividades, pp. 31–33

Online workbooks

20 Mi fiesta

Escuchemos Listen as Marta plays the messages on her answering machine. On a sheet of paper, write down at what time Marta's friends are coming to her party tonight.

1. Jorge
2. Juliana
3. Anabel
4. Valentín
5. Marisol y Chema
6. Gabi

21 ¿Vienes conmigo?

Escribamos/Hablemos Write sentences or questions using words from each of the word boxes below. Remember to use the correct form of the verb.

MODELO (tú) **¿Vienes a la clase de español esta tarde?**

yo tú nosotros el profesor (la profesora) ustedes usted	(no) venir	a la clase de español al colegio a la clase de... a la reunión de...	los fines de semana los lunes y... los... a veces todos los días

Unos amigos llegan a una fiesta de cumpleaños, San José.

22 ¿A qué hora viene el autobús?

Escribamos/Hablemos Given the situations below, use the bus schedule to find the earliest bus that goes to Chirripó National Forest. Follow the model.

MODELO Son las once y veinte. Roberto está en San Isidro.
El autobús cincuenta y seis viene a las once y media.

1. Es mediodía. Juan está en San Isidro.
2. Son las nueve en punto. Ángela está en Cartago.
3. Es la una y cuarto. Mónica está en San Isidro.
4. Son las ocho y diez. Antonio está en San José.
5. Son las diez y cinco. Carlos está en Cartago.
6. Son las once menos cuarto. Jorge está en Cartago.
7. Son las nueve y treinta y cinco. Amalia está en San José.
8. Son las nueve y veinticinco. Raúl está en San José.

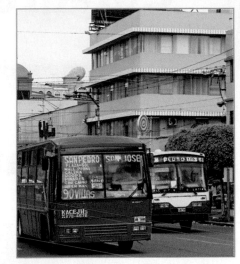

Autobuses, San José

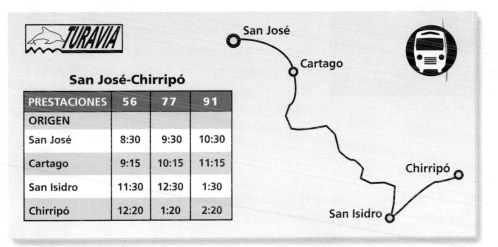

San José-Chirripó

PRESTACIONES	56	77	91
ORIGEN			
San José	8:30	9:30	10:30
Cartago	9:15	10:15	11:15
San Isidro	11:30	12:30	1:30
Chirripó	12:20	1:20	2:20

Comunicación

HOLT SoundBooth ONLINE RECORDING

23 En el colegio

Hablemos Ask your classmate when he or she comes to school, what classes he or she has, and at what time. Then switch roles.

MODELO —¿A qué hora vienes al colegio?
—Vengo a las ocho y media.
—¿Qué clases tienes?
—Tengo español, matemáticas, historia...
—¿A qué hora es la clase de...?
—Es a las...

Cultura

 **Comparaciones** Interactive **TUTOR**

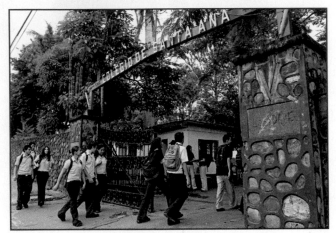

En el Colegio de Santa Ana, Costa Rica

¿Cómo es un día típico en tu colegio?

Students in the United States usually have certain classes they must take, as well as a few elective classes such as choir, drama, shop, and so on. Most schools have after-school activities as well, such as sports or band. In Spain and Latin America, all classes tend to be obligatory, and there aren't many school-sponsored clubs or teams that meet after school. Listen as the following speakers talk about what a typical day is like at their schools. How is their day similar to or different from yours?

 Julio
San José, Costa Rica

Julio talks about his school schedule, required classes, and electives.

¿A qué colegio asistes?

Yo asisto al colegio de Santa Ana.

¿Cómo es un día típico en tu colegio?

Un día típico es entrar a las siete de la mañana, salir a las once y veinte de la mañana, ir a almorzar, regresar de nuevo a las doce y de ahí hasta las cuatro y veinte de la tarde. Luego ya retorna uno a la casa de uno.

¿Qué materias tienes?

A nosotros nos dan matemáticas, inglés, francés, español, estudios sociales.

¿Son materias obligatorias u opcionales?

Hasta el tercer año inglés y francés son obligatorias y de cuarto a quinto, uno puede escoger entre inglés y francés.

¿Cuál es tu materia favorita y por qué?

Mi materia favorita es matemáticas. Es más fácil para mí desarrollarla.

Cultura

☀ Jasna
Santiago, Chile

¿A qué colegio asistes?

Asisto al Colegio Carmen Macfi.

¿Cómo es un día típico en tu colegio?

Bueno, entro en la mañana, ocho y media, y bueno, tenemos distintas materias durante los días y tenemos recreo, luego el almuerzo y después salgo a las tres. Y me voy a mi casa y estudio.

¿Qué materias tienes?

Tengo castellano, historia, matemáticas, inglés, los electivos y

ciencias que es química, física y biología.

¿Son materias obligatorias u opcionales?

Los electivos son opcionales. Yo en mi caso tomé ciudad contemporánea y problemas del conocimiento. Y cuando estás en cuarto medio, con ciencias puedes eliminar una que en mi caso yo eliminé física.

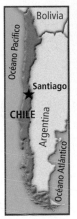

Para comprender

1. ¿A qué hora va Julio al colegio?
2. ¿Estudia Julio ciencias?
3. ¿Qué hace Jasna después de ir a casa?
4. ¿Jasna estudia ciencias?
5. ¿Te gusta más el día escolar de Julio o Jasna? ¿Por qué?

Para pensar y hablar

Make a list of three classes that Julio and Jasna have in common. Do you also have these classes? Why or why not? Both Julio and Jasna are required to study English as a foreign language. Does your school require you to study a foreign language, or is it an elective? Do you think requiring a foreign language is a good idea? Why or why not?

Comunidad
¿Cómo se dice ... en español?

You can help everyone at your school learn some school-related Spanish vocabulary. Ask permission from the principal to label things and places in your school with nicely-made vocabulary labels. If there are some native speakers in your class, ask their assistance with vocabulary you don't know.

◆ Brainstorm with your class places and things to label in Spanish.

◆ Print each word neatly by hand or using a computer.

◆ Tape the labels in the appropriate places.

◆ Check with students periodically to see if they can remember the Spanish names for items you posted.

Canyon Vista Middle School, Austin, Texas

Objetivos
- Talking about plans
- Inviting someone to do something

Vocabulario
en acción **2**

Video/DVD

ExpresaVisión

En Costa Rica

En mi colegio este fin de semana hay...

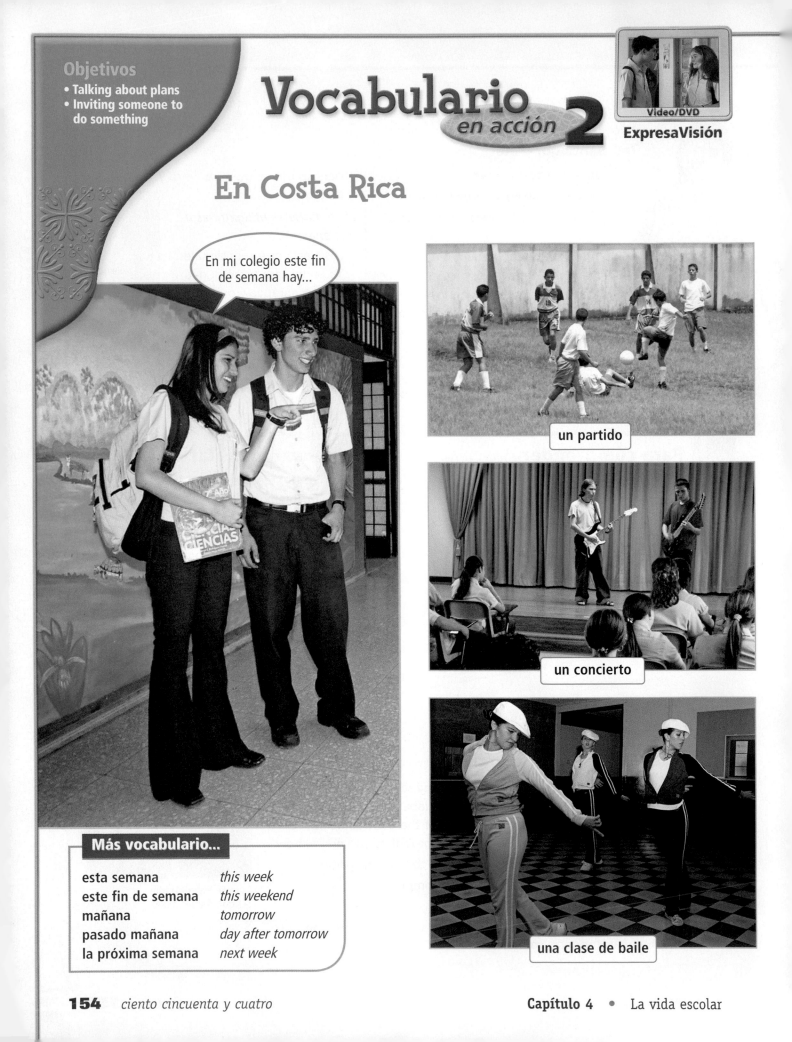

un partido

un concierto

una clase de baile

Más vocabulario...

esta semana	*this week*
este fin de semana	*this weekend*
mañana	*tomorrow*
pasado mañana	*day after tomorrow*
la próxima semana	*next week*

En el colegio

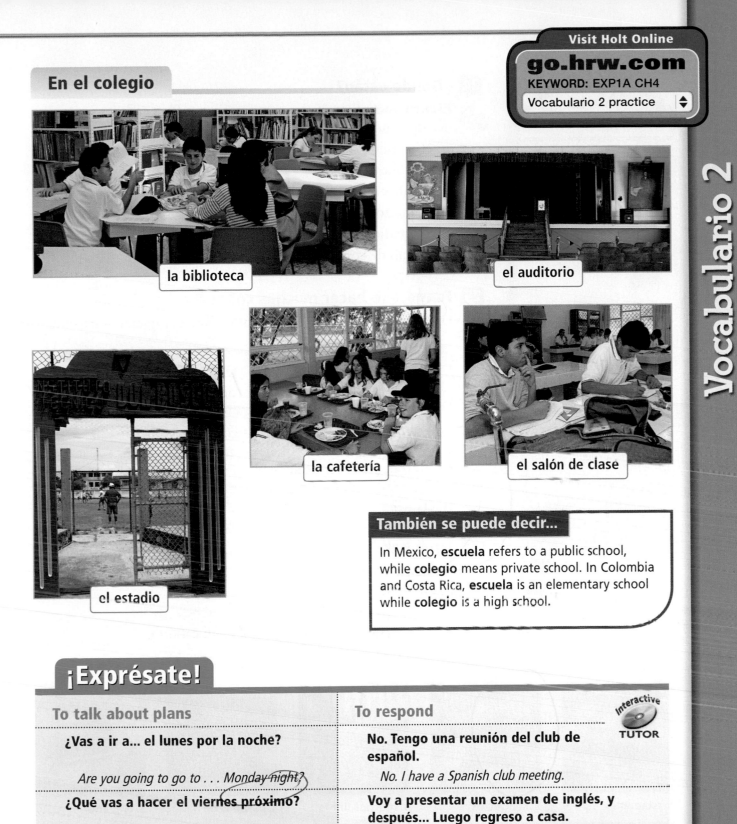

la biblioteca

el auditorio

la cafetería

el salón de clase

el estadio

También se puede decir...

In Mexico, **escuela** refers to a public school, while **colegio** means private school. In Colombia and Costa Rica, **escuela** is an elementary school while **colegio** is a high school.

¡Exprésate!

To talk about plans	To respond
¿Vas a ir a... el lunes por la noche?	**No. Tengo una reunión del club de español.**
Are you going to go to . . . Monday night?	*No. I have a Spanish club meeting.*
¿Qué vas a hacer el viernes próximo?	**Voy a presentar un examen de inglés, y después... Luego regreso a casa.**
What are you going to do next Friday?	*I'm going to take an English test, and afterwards . . . Then I'm going back home.*
¿A qué hora vas a llegar al partido?	**Voy a llegar temprano (a tiempo). No me gusta llegar tarde.**
What time are you going to get to the game?	*I'm going to get there early (on time). I don't like to be late.*

Vocabulario y gramática,
pp. 43–45

Online workbooks

Vocabulario 2

VALORACIÓN DE LOS APRENDIZAJES Y DE LA CONDUCTA					
PERIODOS ASIGNATURAS	I	II	III	PROMEDIO ANUAL	CONDICIÓN
Estudios Sociales	80	84	86	83	Aprobada
Cívica					
Matemática	83	75	72	77	Aprobada
Español	89	84	93	90	Aprobada
Biología	86	74	88	83	Aprobada
Química	79	89	88	85	Aprobada
Física					
Inglés	82	80	79	80	Aprobada
Educación Física	78	85	93	85	Aprobada
Educación Musical	80	96	100	92	Aprobada
Psicología Ética Profesional	65	85	81	77	Aprobada
Educación Religiosa	100	95	98	97	Aprobada
Conducta	91	99	99	97	Aprobada
ESPECIALIDAD	Secretariado				
Sub área	I	II	III	PROMEDIO ANUAL	CONDICIÓN
Prá. de la OF Secre	89	99	95	94	Aprobada
Téc. Exc. en el desarrollo Secre	96	93	100	96	Aprobada
Automatización	79	84	87	83	Aprobada

* Consignar el nombre de cada sub área

Libreta de calificaciones de un colegio de Costa Rica

24 ¿Dónde están?

Escuchemos Escucha las conversaciones. Para cada conversación decide dónde están las personas.

a. en el salón de clase
b. en la biblioteca
c. en la cafetería
d. en el auditorio
e. en el estadio
f. en el club de computación

25 Tengo que hacer muchas cosas

Leamos Usa las palabras del cuadro para completar el párrafo.

luego	partido	tarde	presentar
auditorio	regresar	club	pasado

Esta semana voy a hacer muchas cosas. Hoy por la ___1___, a las 2:30, voy a ___2___ el examen de química y ___3___ voy a ir a la reunión del ___4___ de alemán. Mañana a las 5:00 tengo un ___5___ de béisbol. ___6___ mañana voy a ir al ensayo de piano en el ___7___ del colegio. Voy a ___8___ a casa tarde.

26 ¿Qué haces?

Hablemos Use **hay** (*there is, there are*) and the photos to say where these things are at your school.

MODELO partidos de fútbol
Hay partidos de fútbol en el estadio.

1. exámenes

2. conciertos

3. muchos libros

4. partidos de béisbol

5. el piano

6. ensayos

7. partidos de básquetbol

8. comida

9. computadoras

10. bailes

27 ¿Adónde tienen que ir?

Escribamos You're helping some students figure out where to go for different activities. Based on what you read in each item, write a sentence telling where each person has to go. For item 7, think of what you want to do and tell where you have to go.

MODELO Martín quiere hablar con el profesor de ciencias.

Martín tiene que ir al salón de clase.

1. Quiero jugar al básquetbol.
2. Blanca y Ángel quieren estudiar.
3. Paula necesita ir a un ensayo.
4. Paco y David tienen hambre.
5. Marisol quiere hacer la tarea en la computadora.
6. Luis Miguel necesita presentar el examen de química.
7. ¿Tú?

28 ¿Vas a la biblioteca?

Hablemos Take turns with a partner asking if he or she is going to go to the places or events listed. Answers should include when you are going to that place or event and your reason for going.

MODELO la biblioteca —¿Vas a la biblioteca?

—Sí, voy a las 5:00 de la tarde.
Tengo que estudiar.

1. la cafetería
2. el auditorio
3. el estadio
4. el concierto
5. el gimnasio
6. la reunión del club de español

¡Exprésate!

To invite someone to do something	To respond
¿Qué tal si vamos al partido de fútbol? *How about if we go to the soccer game?*	**No sé. ¿Sabes qué? No tengo ganas.** *I don't know. You know what? I don't feel like it.*
Vienes conmigo a la cafetería, ¿no? *You're coming with me to the cafeteria, aren't you?*	**¡Claro que sí! Tengo mucha hambre.** *Yes, of course! I'm very hungry.*
Hay un concierto. Vas a ir, ¿verdad? *There's a concert.* *You're going to go, right?*	**No, no voy a ir. Tengo que estudiar.** *No, I'm not going to go.* *I have to study.*

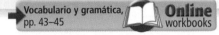

Vocabulario y gramática, pp. 43–45

Online workbooks

29 Invitaciones

Escuchemos/Escribamos Listen to the conversations. On a separate piece of paper, write down what each person is invited to do, then tell whether the invitation is accepted or not.

1. Raquel   2. Andrés   3. Silvia   4. Marta

30 Esta noche

Leamos Marta and Fernando are deciding what to do tonight. Read their conversation and choose the correct word for each sentence.

> FERNANDO ¿Qué vas a (hacer/hablar) esta noche?
>
> MARTA No sé. ¿No hay un (practicar/partido) de fútbol en el estadio?
>
> FERNANDO Sí hay, pero no tengo (ganas/hambre) de ir.
>
> MARTA ¿Quieres ir (a la clase/al concierto) en el auditorio?
>
> FERNANDO Está bien, yo (voy/vienes) contigo. Pero, ¿sabes qué? ¡Tengo hambre!
>
> MARTA Vamos primero a la (biblioteca/cafetería.)
>
> FERNANDO ¡Buena idea!

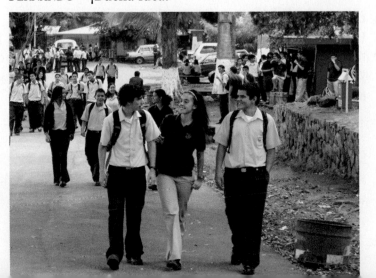

Saliendo de clase,
San José, Costa Rica

31 ¿Qué tal si...?

Hablemos/Escribamos Use the expressions below to invite a
friend to each event.

MODELO ¿Qué tal si vamos al gimnasio el martes por la tarde?

1

¿Qué tal si vamos...?
¿Quieres ir conmigo...?
Vas a ir... ¿verdad?
Vienes conmigo...¿no?

2

al gimnasio
a la cafetería
al concierto de piano
al baile del colegio
al partido de volibol
a la reunión del club de alemán

3

el martes por la tarde
el sábado próximo
pasado mañana a las 4:30
el viernes por la noche
el miércoles a las 12:00
el lunes próximo por la mañana

32 ¿Sabes qué?

Hablemos Now turn down your friend's invitations from
Activity 31 by saying you have to do what is pictured.

MODELO ¿Sabes qué? Tengo que ir al partido de fútbol.

A   B   C   D

Viernes:
examen
de historia

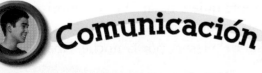 **Comunicación**

33 ¿Vienes conmigo?

Hablemos Choose three school events you'd like to attend, and
then invite three different classmates to each of them. They will
accept or turn down the invitation.

MODELO —Hay un baile el viernes por la noche en el colegio.
¿Quieres ir conmigo?

—¡Claro que sí! Me gustan los bailes.

Objetivos
- **Ir a** with infinitives
- **-er** and **-ir** verbs, tag questions
- **-er** and **-ir** verbs with irregular **yo** forms

Gramática
en acción 2

Ir a with infinitives

Interactive TUTOR

1 To talk about what someone is or isn't going to do, use the present tense of **ir** with **a** followed by an **infinitive**.

—¿**Vas a estudiar**? 　　　　—No, **voy a descansar**.
Are you going to study? 　　*No, I'm going to rest.*

—¿**Van a salir**? 　　　　　—Sí, **vamos a comer**.
Are you going to go out? 　*Yes, we're going to eat.*

2 To say that you are going to do something on a certain day of a particular week, use **el** before the **weekday**.

El sábado voy a ir de compras.
On Saturday I'm going to go shopping.

Vocabulario y gramática, pp. 46–48
Actividades, pp. 35–37
Online workbooks

¿Te acuerdas?

Use **los** and a plural form of the day of the week to say you do something on that day every week.

¿Qué haces los sábados?
What do you (usually) do on Saturdays?

34 Planes diferentes

Escuchemos Say whether Roberto and Nora are talking about **a)** plans for the weekend or **b)** about things they do every weekend.

35 ¿Qué van a hacer?

Leamos/Escribamos Complete the sentences with the correct form of **(no) ir a** based on the cues.

MODELO Yo ═══ descansar el sábado. Tengo que trabajar.
　　　　Yo no voy a descansar el sábado.

1. Mi mejor amigo casi siempre quiere pasar el rato conmigo. Él ═══ comer conmigo este fin de semana.
2. Mis amigos y yo ═══ salir el viernes por la noche. Nos gusta salir.
3. Mi familia y yo ═══ ir al cine el domingo. Tenemos que ir a una reunión el domingo.
4. Yo ═══ comer en la cafetería hoy. No tengo hambre.
5. Los estudiantes de la clase de español ═══ estudiar mucho esta tarde. Van a presentar un examen mañana.
6. Mi mejor amiga ═══ ir de compras el domingo. Siempre va de compras los sábados.

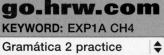

Gramática 2

36 ¿Cuándo vas a...?

Hablemos Use the pictures to say what these people are going to do and when. Then say whether or not you're going to do the same things and when.

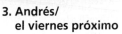

Sara
mañana

MODELO Sara va a estudiar mañana. Yo no. Voy a estudiar pasado mañana.

1. Lucía/ el sábado próximo 2. Enrique/ el domingo 3. Andrés/ el viernes próximo 4. Mario y Lola/ el lunes

37 ¿Sabes qué van a hacer?

Escribamos/Hablemos Say whether the following people are going to do the activities listed. For items 4 and 5, guess what another student and your teacher are going to do.

MODELO yo (salir con amigos esta noche, ver televisión)
No voy a salir con amigos esta noche.
Voy a ver televisión.

1. yo (hacer ejercicio hoy, tocar el piano después de clases)
2. mis amigos y yo (salir este fin de semana, ir al cine el sábado)
3. mi mejor amigo(a) (pasar el fin de semana conmigo, jugar al básquetbol esta semana)
4. tú (llegar temprano al colegio mañana, ir a una reunión hoy)
5. usted (venir al colegio mañana, alquilar un video esta noche)

HOLT SoundBooth
ONLINE RECORDING

38 ¡Cuántos planes!

Hablemos Ask your classmate what he or she is going to do on Friday, Saturday, and Sunday. After he or she invites you along, say whether you want to go or do something else. Switch roles.

MODELO —¿Qué vas a hacer el viernes por la noche?
—El viernes por la noche voy a bailar. ¿Quieres venir conmigo?
—Sí. Me gusta bailar. (No. El viernes voy a nadar.)

-er and -ir verbs; tag questions

1 To conjugate a regular **-er** or **-ir** verb in the present tense, drop the **-er** or **-ir** of the infinitive and add these **endings**.

	comer *to eat*	**escribir** *to write*
yo	com**o**	escrib**o**
tú	com**es**	escrib**es**
Ud., él, ella	com**e**	escrib**e**
nosotros(as)	com**emos**	escrib**imos**
vosotros(as)	com**éis**	escrib**ís**
Uds., ellos, ellas	com**en**	escrib**en**

2 A **tag question** is attached to the end of a sentence to make it a question. If you expect someone to answer *yes*, use **¿no?** or **¿verdad?** When the expected answer is *no*, use **¿verdad?**

—Vienes a la fiesta, **¿no? (¿verdad?)**
You're coming . . . aren't you?

—**Sí**, voy a ir.
Yes, I'm going to go.

—No vas al partido, **¿verdad?**
You're not going . . . right?

—**No**, no voy.
No, I'm not going.

Some **-er** and **-ir** verbs	
abrir	to open
asistir (a)	to attend
beber (algo)	to drink (something)
interrumpir	to interrupt

Vocabulario y gramática, pp. 46–48
Actividades, pp. 35–37

Online
workbooks

Nota cultural

Private schools in Costa Rica start in the morning and run until early afternoon, similar to what happens in U.S. schools. On the other hand, public schools in Costa Rica have three sessions: **el turno matutino** is four hours of classes in the morning, **el turno vespertino** is four hours in the afternoon, and **el turno nocturno** is four hours in the evening.

How would your life be different if you had classes in the evenings?

---

39 **¿Cierto o falso?**

Leamos/Escribamos Complete each sentence with the correct verb from the box.

comen	asistimos	lee	escriben	corro
escribimos	bebes	abre	corres	abro

1. Mis amigas y yo ===== al colegio en julio.
2. Mis compañeros de clase ===== muchas cartas en español.
3. Yo casi nunca ===== en la clase de educación física.
4. Mis amigos ===== conmigo en la cafetería.
5. El (La) profesor(a) ===== revistas interesantes en clase.
6. Tú a veces ===== algo en la clase.
7. La biblioteca ===== a las 9:00 de la mañana.

40 En la clase de español

Escribamos/Hablemos Using the words from each word box, say whether or not these things happen in your school. Remember to conjugate the verbs.

MODELO Muchos estudiantes comen en la cafetería.

muchos (pocos) estudiantes	comer	muchas (pocas) cartas en español
el profesor (la profesora)	beber	algo (nada) en clase
yo	interrumpir	temprano (tarde) los viernes
nosotros	(no) leer	pocas (muchas) revistas
tú	escribir	al colegio en diciembre
ustedes	asistir	a los estudiantes/al profesor/a la profesora
la cafetería (la biblioteca)	abrir	en la cafetería

41 Un día típico en el colegio

Leamos/Escribamos Complete the sentences with an activity pictured below.

MODELO A veces los profesores comen en la cafetería.

1. Yo nunca...
2. Con frecuencia el (la) profesor(a)...
3. Mis compañeros de clase y yo...
4. La biblioteca siempre...
5. Todos los días mi mejor amigo(a)...
6. Cuando tienen educación física, los estudiantes...

42 En nuestra escuela

Hablemos Ask a classmate questions using the pictures in Activity 41 and tag questions. Have your partner answer the questions. Switch roles.

MODELO —La biblioteca del colegio abre a las 10:00, ¿verdad?

—No, la biblioteca abre a las 9:00.

Some -er/-ir verbs with irregular yo forms

Interactive TUTOR

1 The following **-er** and **-ir** verbs have irregular **yo** forms.

	hacer *to do, to make*	poner *to put*	traer *to bring*
yo	ha**go**	pon**go**	trai**go**
tú	haces	pones	traes
Ud., él, ella	hace	pone	trae
nosotros(as)	hacemos	ponemos	traemos
vosotros(as)	hacéis	ponéis	traéis
Uds., ellos, ellas	hacen	ponen	traen

	saber *to know information*	ver *to see*	salir *to go out*
yo	**sé**	**veo**	sal**go**
tú	sabes	ves	sales
Ud., él, ella	sabe	ve	sale
nosotros(as)	sabemos	vemos	salimos
vosotros(as)	sabéis	veis	salís
Uds., ellos, ellas	saben	ven	salen

2 The preposition **de** is used after **salir** to talk about leaving a place. It is used after **saber** to say how much someone knows about something.

Salgo de mi casa a las siete.   *I leave my house at seven.*
No **sé** mucho **de** arte.   *I don't know much about art.*

→ Vocabulario y gramática, pp. 46–48
Actividades, pp. 35–37

Online workbooks

43 Y tú, ¿qué haces?

Leamos Complete these sentences with the correct verb.

1. ¿Tú ===== del colegio a las 5:30?
   a. hago   **b.** sales   **c.** salgo
2. Yo ===== mis papeles en mi mochila.
   a. pongo   **b.** vemos   **c.** salgo
3. Mi amigo ===== su tarea por la noche.
   a. ponen   **b.** pone   **c.** hace
4. A veces mis amigas ===== su almuerzo de casa.
   a. traigo   **b.** ponen   **c.** traen
5. Nosotros nunca ===== películas en la cafetería.
   a. sé   **b.** sabemos   **c.** vemos
6. Yo no ===== mucho de computadoras.
   a. salgo   **b.** sé   **c.** hace

Estudiantes del colegio Franco-Costarricense

44 Un amigo de Internet

Leamos/Escribamos Rogelio posts this e-mail on a pen pal Web site. Read the e-mail and decide if the statements that follow are **cierto** or **falso**. Then write Rogelio and tell him about your interests.

1. Rogelio sale con amigos los fines de semana.
2. Rogelio lee libros de misterio.
3. Rogelio hace ejercicio a veces.
4. A Rogelio no le gusta el Internet.
5. A veces, Rogelio tiene conciertos.
6. A Rogelio le gusta ir al cine.

> Me llamo Rogelio y tengo 14 años. Los fines de semana salgo con mis amigos o hago ejercicio. Leo revistas de deportes y me gusta navegar por Internet. Con frecuencia tengo conciertos de piano. No me gusta ir al cine, pero sí traigo videos para ver en casa. Y a ti, ¿qué te gusta hacer?

45 Las fiestas

Hablemos/Escribamos Answer these questions about what you do with your friends on weekends.

1. ¿Sales con amigos los fines de semana?
2. ¿Vas a la casa de tus amigos?
3. ¿Qué hacen ustedes? ¿Escuchan música o ven videos?
4. ¿Traen comida? ¿Salen a comer? ¿Qué les gusta comer?
5. ¿Les gusta ir al cine? Cuando van al cine, ¿a qué hora salen?
6. ¿Qué más haces con ellos?

Comunicación

46 Después de clases

Hablemos/Escribamos With a partner, take turns describing this student's day after school. Include as many details as possible.

Gramática 2

Conexiones culturales

Misiones españolas Franciscan friars founded missions in northern New Spain between the 1500s and 1700s in what are today the states of California, Arizona, Texas, New Mexico, and Florida. These missions were founded in order to claim land for Spain and to convert the native people to Catholicism.

Misión San José was built in 1720 in what is now San Antonio, Texas. At one time, the compound housed up to 350 people. The mission had fields and a farm nearby, and a large cattle and sheep ranch 25 miles to the southwest.

1. Church	7. Housing	13. Granary
2. Friar Housing	8. Bastion	14. Carpentry Shop
3. Convent Garden	9. Southeast Gate	15. Kilns
4. Garden Well	10. Southwest Gate	16. Mill
5. Well	11. Ovens	17. Vat
6. East Gate	12. West Gate	18. Aqueduct

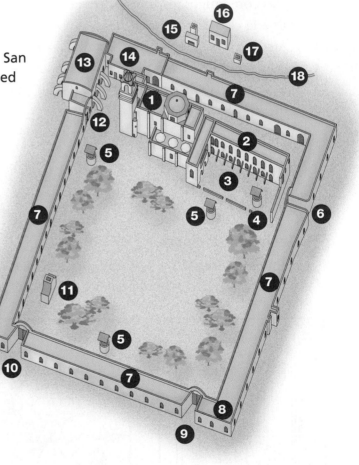

1 ¿Producir o comprar?

According to the paragraph above and the drawing, what food and supplies could the people who lived in the mission compound produce for themselves? What other supplies might they have needed to buy? Use the list below.

chicken	vegetables
beef	water
coffee	wool blankets
salt	horseshoes
corn	clothes

2 El trabajo

From the drawing above, what work would most interest you if you had lived in the San José mission? Building furniture? sewing clothes? shearing sheep? Explain your reasons.

Conexión Geografía

Las misiones de Alta California San Diego de Alcalá Mission was founded in 1769 in what is now San Diego, California. In 1770, San Carlos Borromeo de Carmelo was founded, 650 miles to the north in what is now the town of Carmel. In the beginning, mules were used to deliver food and supplies between San Diego and Carmel. Since the trip was both difficult and dangerous, a chain of missions was founded along **El Camino Real** to provide rest, shelter, and protection for travelers. Each mission was about one day's journey from another by mule.

Conexión Matemáticas

3 Cincuenta millas en mula

1. San Carlos Borromeo de Carmelo is 650 miles to the north of San Diego de Alcalá. If a mule travels about fifty miles in one day, how many missions should the friars establish between San Diego de Alcalá and San Carlos Borromeo de Carmelo?

2. Count the missions from San Diego de Alcalá to San Carlos Borromeo de Carmelo on the map. How many missions were constructed? Is the number of missions the same as the number in your answer for item 1?

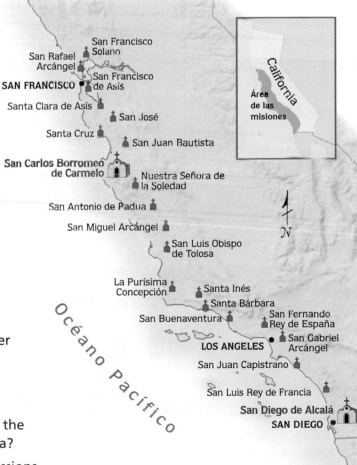

4 Las primeras misiones

1. Which missions were built first, the missions in Texas or in California?

2. Why do you think they built missions in that region first?

Conexiones culturales

¿Quién será?

Episodio 4

ESTRATEGIA

Comparing and contrasting When you compare and contrast two or more things, you look for similarities and differences. For example, you can look for similarities or differences in how the students in Mexico and those in Puerto Rico dress and behave. You can also compare and contrast the Puerto Rican and Mexican students with yourself and students in your school. What are some similarities and differences you notice as you read the **Novela** or watch the video?

En Puerto Rico

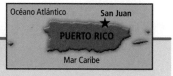
Océano Atlántico   San Juan ★
PUERTO RICO
Mar Caribe

Marcos is trying to gather information on Nicolás. Nicolás is completely unaware.

1

3

Nicolás ¿Qué necesitas?
Mateo Necesito un lápiz... una goma... una regla... y papel.

Mateo Oye, Nicolás, ¿a qué hora es tu clase de matemáticas?
Nicolás Tengo matemáticas a la una de la tarde. ¿Por qué?
Mateo Porque yo tengo matemáticas ahora y necesito muchas cosas.

2

4

Mateo ¿Qué tal si vamos al partido de béisbol después de clases?
Julia Claro que sí.
Nicolás No, no tengo ganas.
Mateo ¿No tienes ganas? ¿Qué vas a hacer?
Nicolás Voy a... voy a... voy a...

Tengo que irme.
¡Nos vemos!

5

Julia ¿Vas a qué? ¿Vas a hacer ejercicio?

Nicolás No, nunca hago ejercicio los lunes,
¿sabes? Los lunes son para...

Mateo ¿Para qué? ¿Qué vas a hacer?

Nicolás Voy a ver televisión. Mi programa
favorito... esta noche...

Julia ¿Cuál es tu programa preferido?

6

Mateo ¿Y mañana? ¿Vas al concierto en el
gimnasio?

Julia ¿Y pasado mañana?

After school, Mateo and Julia decide to follow Nicolás to see where he's going.

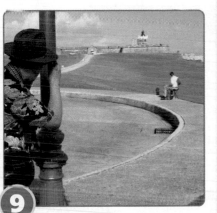

7

Mateo ¿Quieres ver adónde
va Nicolás?

Julia Sí, pero, ¿el partido de
béisbol?

Mateo No importa, vamos.

8

Mateo ¿Qué hace Nicolás?

Julia No sé. Pero...

9

Julia ¿Qué hace ese
señor?

A. CONTESTA

Answer the questions about the **Novela**. If you are not sure, make an
educated guess!

1. Where are Nicolás and Mateo as the story begins?

2. Who has all his school supplies with him? Which student does not have
any of the supplies that he needs?

3. Why does Nicolás try to get away from his friends after school?

En España

La profesora tells Marcos about her next candidate and his next trip.

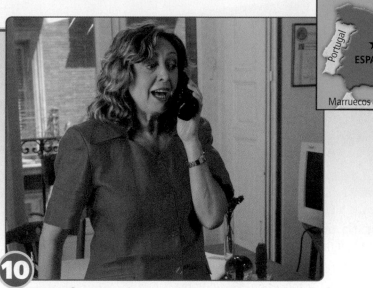

10

La profesora Ahora tengo un candidato de Costa Rica, Marcos. Sí, sí, después de Puerto Rico vas a El Paso y después de El Paso, a San José.

En Puerto Rico

11

B. CONTESTA

1. What is **la profesora's** assistant doing at the end of the story?
2. What does she tell him on the phone this time?

Actividades

1 ¿Quién es?

Match the name of the person with the sentence that best describes him or her.

1. Nicolás
2. Mateo
3. Julia
4. Marcos

a. Tiene cámara y teléfono.
b. Tiene ganas de ir al partido de béisbol.
c. Necesita muchas cosas para la clase de matemáticas.
d. Tiene matemáticas a la una.

2 ¿Qué dice...?

Based on information in the **Novela**, complete each of the following questions or statements.

1. ¿Qué necesitas...
2. ¿Qué vas a hacer?
3. Y mañana, ¿vas al...
4. ¿Cuál es...
5. Ahora tengo...

a. tu programa preferido?
b. para la clase de matemáticas?
c. un candidato de Costa Rica.
d. concierto en el gimnasio?
e. Voy a ver televisión.

3 ¿Comprendes la Novela?

Check your understanding of the events in the story by answering these questions.

1. Contrast Nicolás's preparation for math class with Mateo's.
2. Does Nicolás answer his friends truthfully about his after-school plans? How can you tell?
3. Can Mateo and Julia tell what Nicolás is doing? Who else is there? What is he doing?
4. Compare and contrast the actions of Sofía in **Episodio 3** and of Nicolás in this episode. What about the actions of their friends?

Próximo episodio
Can you predict what Marcos will do in Costa Rica?

PÁGINAS 214–217 ▶

A Antes de leer

Read the title and the first paragraph of the story. Can you answer at least one of each of the questions in the **Estrategia para leer?**

Pepito, el niño precoz

Pepito es un niño gracioso, inteligente y precoz[1]. Tiene siete años y hoy es su primer día de colegio. Cuando viene a casa por la tarde, los padres de Pepito tienen muchas preguntas: ¿Te gusta el colegio?, ¿Cómo es tu profesora?, ¿Cuál es tu materia preferida? Pepito dice[2] que le gusta mucho el colegio: sus compañeros de clase son divertidos, la profesora es simpática y no es muy estricta y su materia preferida es matemáticas.

Por la noche, a la hora de comer, su mamá pone un plato con dos huevos[3] en la mesa. Pepito, siempre precoz, esconde[4] uno de los dos huevos y después de un minuto pregunta:

—Papá, ¿cuántos huevos ves en el plato?

—Pues, uno—contesta[5] el padre.

Pepito pone entonces el otro huevo en el plato y pregunta:

—Y ahora, papá, ¿cuántos huevos ves?

—Dos—contesta el padre.

—¡Magnífico! —exclama Pepito—los dos huevos que ves ahora y el otro huevo de antes,[6] son tres huevos, ¿verdad?

Su papá está un poco confundido.[7] Sólo ve dos huevos en el plato y no tres. Pero la mamá de Pepito, que escucha todo esto y que también es muy inteligente y graciosa dice:

—¡Claro que sí, Pepito! Hay tres huevos. El primero es para mí, el segundo[8] es para tu papá, y el tercero[9] es para ti.

1 precocious   2 says   3 eggs   4 hides   5 answers   6 from before
7 confused   8 second   9 third

B Comprensión

Contesta las siguientes preguntas.

1. ¿Cuántos años tiene Pepito y cómo es?
2. ¿Cuál es la materia preferida de Pepito?
3. ¿Cómo es la profesora de Pepito? ¿Y los compañeros de clase?
4. ¿Qué pone la mamá en la mesa y qué hace el niño?
5. ¿Qué le pregunta Pepito a su papá? ¿Qué dice él?
6. ¿Qué dice la mamá de Pepito?

C Después de leer

How would you describe Pepito? Which sentences in the story give you clues about his personality? What about his parents? What are they like? Do they have a sense of humor? Explain.

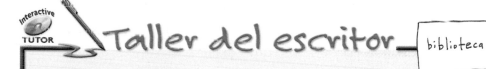

Taller del escritor

ESTRATEGIA

para escribir Using drawings can help organize your writing. If you can picture the setting in which the events occur, your writing may be clearer to your readers.

Un recorrido con nuevos estudiantes

Imagine you're helping with orientation at your school and you're taking two new students on a tour. Create a conversation based on your first meeting with them.

- Explain what classes they will take and when.
- Include questions new students might ask.
- Invite them to attend a club meeting, play, or another school activity.

1 Antes de escribir

Sketch the layout of your school. Label the places you would show new students. Draw arrows to show the route you plan to take.

2 Escribir y revisar

Begin your conversation based on the route you drew. The places you go should be based on the new students' questions and your explanations. End the conversation with an invitation and the students' responses.

Read over the questions, explanations, and answers. Check for correct use of grammar, spelling, and punctuation.

3 Publicar

Display your conversation and sketch on the bulletin board. You may wish to act out your conversations in groups of three classmates.

Prepárate para el examen

Interactive TUTOR

1 Completa la conversación de manera lógica.

—¿Qué clases tienes esta tarde?

—Tengo ___1___ , ___2___ y ___3___ .

—¿Cuál es tu materia preferida?

—Bueno, me gusta ___4___ porque es ___5___ . Y tú, ¿cuál es tu materia preferida?

—Es ___6___ . Bueno, ¿qué necesitas para la clase de inglés?

—Necesito ___7___ y ___8___ .

2 Answer the following questions about you and your friends.

1. ¿A qué hora vienen ustedes al colegio por las mañanas?
2. ¿Generalmente tienen prisa ustedes cuando vienen al colegio?
3. ¿Cuántas clases tienes en un día?
4. ¿Necesitas muchas cosas para las clases?
5. ¿Qué cosas necesitas para la clase de español?
6. ¿Qué tienes que hacer después de clases?
7. ¿Qué tienes ganas de hacer este fin de semana? ¿y tu mejor amigo(a)?

3 Invite your partner to each of the events pictured. Your partner will accept or turn down each invitation.

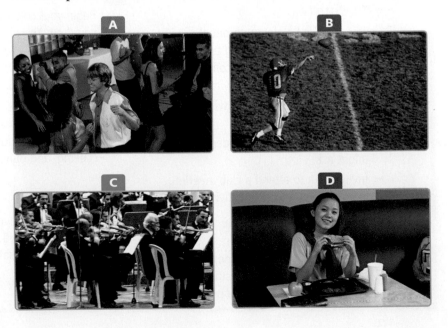

4 Answer these questions about your weekend plans.

1. ¿Vas a ir a un concierto este fin de semana?
2. ¿Ves televisión los sábados?
3. ¿Va un amigo a tu casa el domingo?
4. ¿Van a hacer la tarea en casa tu amigo y tú?
5. ¿Vas a ir a un partido de béisbol el sábado?
6. ¿Sales mucho con amigos los viernes?
7. ¿Sales a comer comida china los domingos?

4 **Gramática 2**
• **ir a** with infinitives
• **-er** and **-ir** verbs and tag questions
• **-er** and **-ir** verbs with irregular **yo** forms

5 Answer the following questions.

1. How are programs of study in Latin America similar to or different from those in the United States?
2. What advantages or disadvantages are there in students repeating a semester if they fail two classes and the final exam?
3. What are the three class sessions in Costa Rican public schools called? When do they begin?

5 **Cultura**
• **Comparaciones** pp. 152–153
• **Notas culturales** pp. 142, 144, 156
• **Geocultura** pp. 134–137

6 Escucha las preguntas y escribe las respuestas en tu papel.

Conversación

7 Role-play the following conversation with a partner. Partner A and Partner B are talking about classes and after school plans.

PARTNER A: Greet your partner. Ask what classes he/she has after lunch.

PARTNER B: Respond to your partner's greeting and question.

PARTNER A: Ask if he or she feels like going to the mall after school.

PARTNER B: Say yes, want to go because you need to buy a lot of things at the bookstore.

PARTNER A: Say you need a lot of things, too. Ask when your partner is going to do his or her homework.

PARTNER B: Explain that you are going to do your homework this evening. Ask what he or she is doing tomorrow.

PARTNER A: Say you are going to the soccer game tomorrow at the park. Ask if your partner wants to go with you.

PARTNER B: Say yes, thank you. Say you will see each other tomorrow at the park.

Prepárate para el examen

Repaso de Gramática 1

Gramática 1

• indefinite articles; **¿cuánto?, mucho, poco** pp. 146–147

• present tense of **tener** and some **tener** idioms pp. 148–149

• **venir** and **a** + time pp. 150–151

	Masculine		Feminine	
SINGULAR	un	mucho	una	mucha
	cuánto	poco	cuánta	poca
PLURAL	unos	muchos	unas	muchas
	cuántos	pocos	cuántas	pocas

tengo	tenemos		vengo	venimos
tienes	tenéis		vienes	venís
tiene	tienen		viene	vienen

The preposition **a** followed by the **time** tells at what time something happens.

—¿Vienes a mi casa **a las 8:15**? —Sí. Tenemos clase **a las 9 en punto**.

Repaso de Gramática 2

Gramática 2

• **ir a** + infinitive pp. 160–161

• present tense of **-er** and **-ir** verbs and tag questions pp. 162–163

• **-er** and **-ir** verbs with irregular **yo** forms pp. 164–165

The verb **ir** followed by **a** and an **infinitive** tells what is going to happen in the near future. Tag questions such as **¿no?** and **¿verdad?** ask the person listening to agree with the person speaking.

Vas a bailar en la fiesta, **¿no?**

Sí, también **voy a cantar.**

comer		escribir	
como	comemos	escribo	escribimos
comes	coméis	escribes	escribís
come	comen	escribe	escriben

Some irregular **yo** forms are **tengo, traigo, hago, sé, veo, salgo,** and **pongo.**

Letra y sonido S Z C qu

Las letras s, z, c y qu

• In Spanish, the letter **s** sounds like the English *s* in *sun:* **s**al**s**a, **s**e**s**o, **s**illa, **s**olo, **s**u**s**.

• The letters **z** (before **a, o, u**), and **c** (before **e, i**) sound like the English *c* in the word *center:* **z**apatos, **z**ona, a**z**ul, **c**entro, **c**ien**c**ias.

• In most of Spain, **z** and **c** in these combinations sound much like the English *th* in *think.*

• The letters **c** (before **a, o, u**) and **qu** (before **e** and **i**) sound like the English *k:* **c**arpeta, **c**oro, **c**uaderno, **qu**erer, **qu**ién.

Trabalenguas

Cuca Seco cose en casa de Coco Suca.

Cuando cuentes cuentos, cuenta cuántos cuentos cuentas.

Dictado

Escribe las oraciones de la grabación.

Repaso de Vocabulario 1

Saying what you have and need

el **bolígrafo**	pen
la **calculadora**	calculator
la **carpeta**	folder
la **computadora**	computer
el **cuaderno**	notebook
el **diccionario**	dictionary
el **lápiz**/los **lápices**	pencil/pencils
la **mochila**	backpack
mucho(a)	a lot of, much
muchos(as)	a lot of, many
¿**Necesitas algo para el colegio/la clase de arte?**	Do you need anything for school/art class?
No, no necesito nada.	No, I don't need anything.
el **papel**	paper
poco(a)	little, not much
pocos(as)	few, not many
la **regla**	ruler
el **reloj**/los **relojes**	clock, watch/clocks, watches
la **ropa**	clothes
Sí, necesito muchas cosas.	Yes, I need a lot of things.
Sí, tengo un montón.	Yes, I have a ton of them.
¿**Tienes...?**	Do you have . . . ?
un/una	a, an
unos/unas	some
los **útiles escolares**	school supplies
los **zapatos**	shoes

Talking about classes

el **alemán**	German
el **almuerzo**	lunch
el **arte, las artes**	art, the arts
la **biología**	biology
las **ciencias**	science
la **computación**	computer science
¿**Cuál es tu materia preferida?**	What's your favorite subject?
la **educación física**	physical education
Es fácil/difícil.	It's easy/hard.
el **español**	Spanish
el **francés**	French
la **historia**	history
el **inglés**	English
las **matemáticas**	mathematics
las **materias**	school subjects
Mi materia preferida es...	My favorite subject is . . .
Primero tengo..., y después tengo...	First I have . . ., and afterwards I have . . .
por la mañana/tarde	in the morning/afternoon
¿**Qué clases tienes esta tarde?**	What classes do you have this afternoon?
la **química**	chemistry
el **taller**	shop, workshop
tener	to have
venir	to come

Prepárate para el examen

Repaso de Vocabulario 2

Talking about plans . . . . *See p. 155.*

el **auditorio**	auditorium
la **biblioteca**	library
la **cafetería**	cafeteria
la **clase de baile**	dance class
el **concierto**	concert
el **estadio**	stadium
esta semana	this week
este fin de semana	this weekend
hacer	to do, to make
hay	there is, there are
llegar	to get there, to arrive
mañana	tomorrow
el **partido de...**	. . . game
pasado mañana	day after tomorrow
poner	to put

presentar un examen	to take a test
la **próxima semana**	next week
saber (de)	to know information, to know about
salir (de)	to go out, to leave
el **salón de clase**	classroom
traer	to bring
ver	to watch, to see
el **viernes próximo**	next Friday

Inviting someone to do something . . . . *See p. 158.*

Integración
capítulos 1-4

1 Match each picture to the statements that best describe Lorenzo's busy day.

a.   b.   c.   d.

2 Manuel has been accepted as an exchange student in the United States. Read his e-mail to his host parents and then tell whether each statement is **cierto** or **falso.** Correct the false statements.

Nuevo Mensaje

Archivo   Editar   Ver   Insertar   Formato   Herramientas   Mensaje   Ayuda

Enviar   Cortar   Copiar   Pegar   Deshacer   Deletrear

A: medina@serviciosanjose.hrw.com.cr

Cc:

Asunto:

B *I* <u>U</u> <u>A</u>

Estimados Señores Medina,

Me llamo Manuel. Vivo en San José, Costa Rica. Soy alto, atlético, extrovertido y tengo muchos amigos. Mis materias preferidas son computación y matemáticas. No me gusta la clase de francés porque es muy aburrida. Monto en bicicleta, corro y practico básquetbol y fútbol. Me gusta escuchar música y también toco el piano. Me gusta comer hamburguesas y pizza.
Quiero ir a Texas porque me gusta el inglés y quiero saber más sobre la cultura de Estados Unidos.

Hasta luego,
Manuel

---

1. Manuel es alto, atlético y tiene pocos amigos.

2. A Manuel le gustan más las clases de computación y matemáticas.

3. A Manuel no le gusta la clase de francés porque es difícil.

4. Manuel quiere ir a Costa Rica.

5. Manuel tiene ganas de visitar Estados Unidos.

3 Imagine that you lived at the time of this painting, were traveling along this path, and met these people. Write a description of the scene, answering the following questions.

1. ¿Qué colores ves?
2. ¿Qué tiempo hace?
3. ¿Qué día de la semana es?
4. ¿Cuántas personas hay?
5. ¿Adónde van?
6. ¿Tienen prisa?

Víctor Hugo Fernández, Gráficos del Globo, S.A., Costa Rica

Domingueando, de Tomás Povedano de Arcos (1847–1943)

4

Situación

With a partner, role-play a scene in a school supplies store. One of you is a student shopping for supplies on the first day of school, the other is the storekeeper. Through questions and answers, say:

▶ what classes the student has
▶ what supplies the student already has
▶ what supplies the student needs
▶ when the student's first class is
▶ what the student's favorite class is

Repaso cumulativo

179

GeoVisión

Geocultura Chile

▲ **La costa del Pacífico** Chile's Pacific coastline is 6,000 kilometers long, but the country is less than 185 kilometers wide. The city of **Viña del Mar** is a destination for sunbathers.

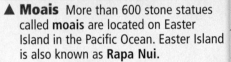

▼ **Santiago** Chile's capital was founded in 1541 by the Spanish explorer Pedro de Valdivia. This city of 5.5 million people lies at the foot of the Andes Mountains.

▲ **Moais** More than 600 stone statues called **moais** are located on Easter Island in the Pacific Ocean. Easter Island is also known as **Rapa Nui.**

Almanac

Population
15,980,912

Capital
Santiago

Government
republic

Currency
Chilean peso

Official Language
Spanish

Internet Code
www.[ ].cl

▼ **Volantines**
Flying these small kites is popular in the springtime.

¿Sabías que...?
Chile has over 2,000 volcanoes. 55 of them are active, and in some parts of the country these volcanoes cause almost weekly tremors.

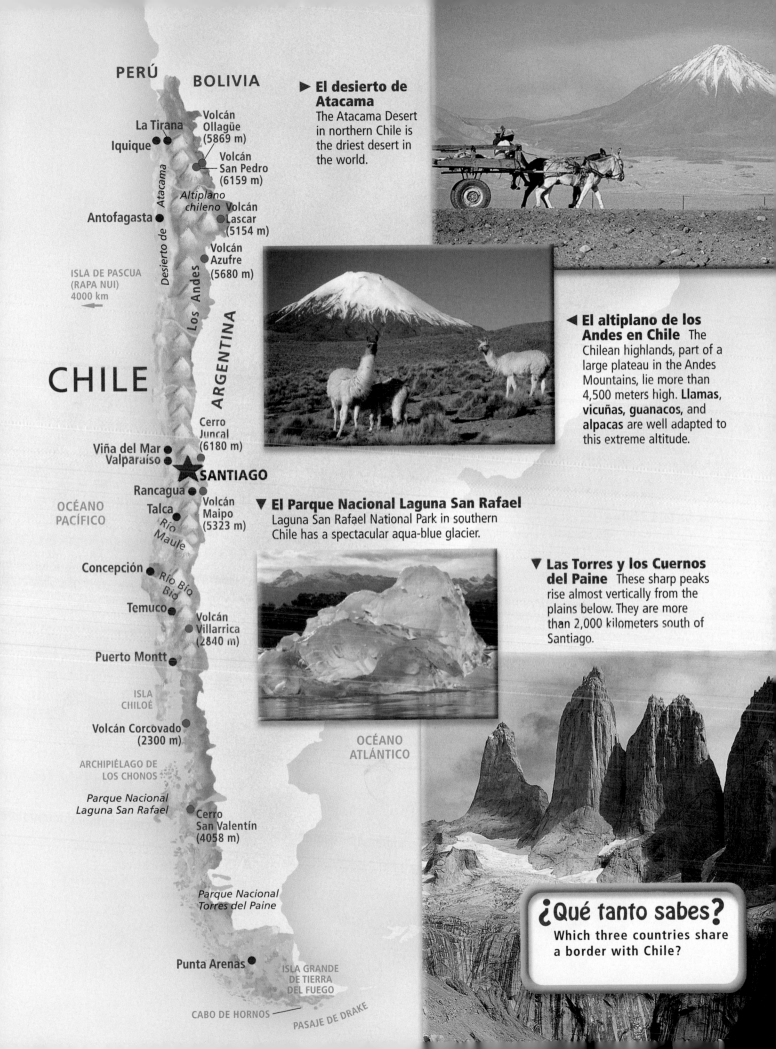

PERÚ

BOLIVIA

► **El desierto de Atacama**
The Atacama Desert in northern Chile is the driest desert in the world.

Volcán Ollagüe (5869 m)

La Tirana

Iquique

Volcán San Pedro (6159 m)

Desierto de Atacama

Antofagasta

Altiplano chileno

Volcán Lascar (5154 m)

Volcán Azufre (5680 m)

ISLA DE PASCUA (RAPA NUI) 4000 km

Los Andes

ARGENTINA

◄ **El altiplano de los Andes en Chile** The Chilean highlands, part of a large plateau in the Andes Mountains, lie more than 4,500 meters high. **Llamas, vicuñas, guanacos,** and **alpacas** are well adapted to this extreme altitude.

CHILE

Cerro Juncal (6180 m)

Viña del Mar

Valparaíso

★ SANTIAGO

Rancagua

OCÉANO PACÍFICO

Talca

Volcán Maipo (5323 m)

Río Maule

▼ **El Parque Nacional Laguna San Rafael**
Laguna San Rafael National Park in southern Chile has a spectacular aqua-blue glacier.

Concepción

Río Bío Bío

Temuco

Volcán Villarrica (2840 m)

Puerto Montt

ISLA CHILOÉ

▼ **Las Torres y los Cuernos del Paine** These sharp peaks rise almost vertically from the plains below. They are more than 2,000 kilometers south of Santiago.

Volcán Corcovado (2300 m)

ARCHIPIÉLAGO DE LOS CHONOS

Parque Nacional Laguna San Rafael

Cerro San Valentín (4058 m)

OCÉANO ATLÁNTICO

Parque Nacional Torres del Paine

Punta Arenas

ISLA GRANDE DE TIERRA DEL FUEGO

CABO DE HORNOS

PASAJE DE DRAKE

¿Qué tanto sabes?
Which three countries share a border with Chile?

A conocer Chile

La arquitectura

▲ **La Isla Chiloé** Houses on the southern island of **Chiloé** are often painted in vivid colors. Some houses called **palafitos** are built on stilts.

▲ **Lo moderno y lo antiguo** Colonial architecture from the past contrasts with modern architecture in the capital city of Santiago, giving it a European feel.

La comida

▼ **Los mariscos** Chileans eat a great variety of seafood from the Pacific Ocean. This dish is called **curanto.**

▲ **El pastel de choclo** This Chilean meat pie is topped with mashed corn. The word **choclo** means *corn* in the Mapuche language.

Las celebraciones

¿Sabías que...?

Mapuche defenders halted Spanish armies at the **Río Bío Bío** for over 300 years. How can you see the effects of the Mapuche and Spanish cultures on architecture, food, and celebrations in Chile today?

▲ **La Fiesta de La Tirana** The town of La Tirana near Iquique holds this major festival each July. The festival has its roots in Incan ceremonies, Chinese carnivals, and Spanish fiestas.

▶ **Los mapuches** The culture of the Mapuche people can be seen in their customs, handicrafts, traditional dress, and festivals.

Las bellas artes

▲ **Pablo Neruda (1904–1973) y Gabriela Mistral (1889–1957)** These two famous Chilean poets each won a Nobel Prize in Literature.

▶ **Pedro Lira (1845–1912)** Chilean artist Pedro Lira gained international fame for this painting, *The Founding of Santiago.*

En casa con la familia

Objetivos

In Part 1 you will learn to:
- describe people and family relationships
- use possessive adjectives
- form **o** to **ue** stem changing verbs
- use verbs with an **e** to **ie** stem change

In Part 2 you will learn to:
- talk about where you and others live
- talk about responsibilities
- form **estar** and use it with prepositions
- say where people and things are using prepositions
- make sentences negative using **nunca, tampoco, no, nadie,** and **nada**
- form and use the verbs **tocar** and **parecer**

¿Qué ves en la foto?

- ¿Qué colores ves en la foto?

- ¿Qué les toca hacer a los muchachos?

- ¿Qué te parece tener que ayudar en casa?

Una familia de Santiago, Chile

Vocabulario
en acción 1

La familia Pérez de Santiago

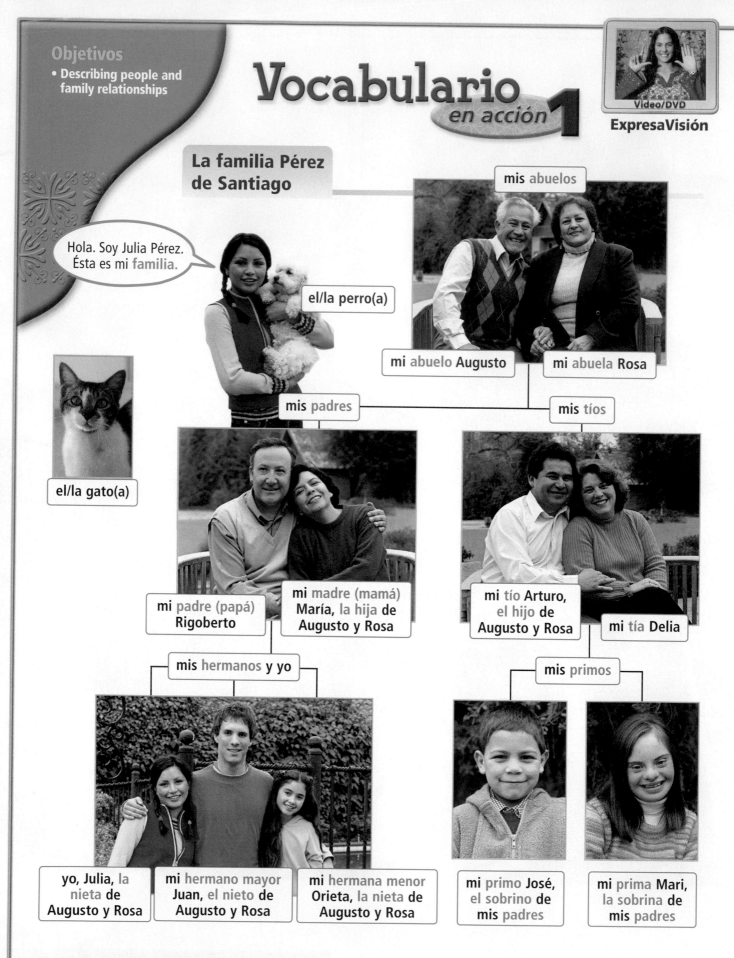

mis abuelos

Hola. Soy Julia Pérez. Ésta es mi familia.

el/la perro(a)

mi abuelo Augusto

mi abuela Rosa

el/la gato(a)

mis padres

mis tíos

mi padre (papá) Rigoberto

mi madre (mamá) María, la hija de Augusto y Rosa

mi tío Arturo, el hijo de Augusto y Rosa

mi tía Delia

mis hermanos y yo

mis primos

yo, Julia, la nieta de Augusto y Rosa

mi hermano mayor Juan, el nieto de Augusto y Rosa

mi hermana menor Orieta, la nieta de Augusto y Rosa

mi primo José, el sobrino de mis padres

mi prima Mari, la sobrina de mis padres

▶ Vocabulario adicional — La familia, p. R9

Tiene los ojos...

azules

verdes

negros

de color café

Tiene el pelo...

castaño

canoso

negro

largo

corto

Más vocabulario...

¿Cómo es?		*What is he/she like?*	
ciego(a)	*blind*	**sordo(a)**	*deaf*
gordo(a)	*fat*	**travieso(a)**	*mischievous*
joven	*young*	**viejo(a)**	*old*

También se puede decir...

In Spanish, there are several words for *eyeglasses:* **los lentes, los anteojos,** and **las gafas.**

People from the Dominican Republic may refer to brown or hazel eyes as **ojos marrones** or **ojos galanos.** Cubans may call hazel eyes **ojos carmelitas,** and Colombians may use **ojos castaños.**

¡Exprésate!

To ask about people and family relationships	To respond
¿Cuántas personas hay en tu familia? *How many people are in your family?*	**En mi familia somos cuatro personas.** *There are four people in my family.*
¿Cómo es tu familia? *What is your family like?*	**Somos delgados y tenemos el pelo rubio. Todos usamos lentes. Mi hermana María está en una silla de ruedas.** *We are thin and have blond hair. We all wear glasses. My sister María is in a wheelchair.*
¿Cómo es tu tía? *What is your aunt like?*	**Es profesora. Es una persona callada. Ella y mi tío tienen dos hijos pero no tienen nietos.** *She's a teacher. She's a quiet person. She and my uncle have two children, but don't have any grandchildren.*

Vocabulario y gramática, pp. 49–51

Online workbooks

▶ **Vocabulario adicional** — Profesiones, p. R10

Chile

ciento ochenta y siete **187**

Vocabulario 1

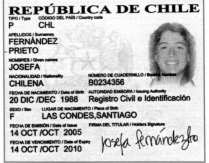
1 ¿Cierto o falso?

Escuchemos Mira el árbol genealógico (*family tree*) y escucha las oraciones. Indica si cada oración es **cierta** o **falsa**.

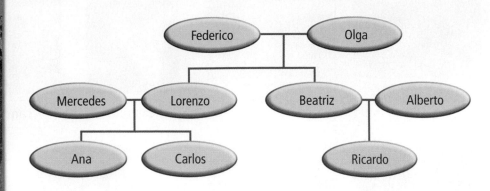

2 ¿Quién es quién?

Leamos Answer the questions based on the family tree in Activity 1.

1. ¿Quién es la hermana de Lorenzo?
2. ¿Cómo se llama el tío de Ricardo?
3. ¿Cómo se llama la abuela de Ana?
4. ¿Quién es la madre de Carlos?
5. ¿Cuántos nietos tienen Federico y Olga?
6. ¿Cómo se llama el padre de Ricardo?
7. ¿Cuántos hijos tienen Mercedes y Lorenzo?
8. ¿Quién es el primo de Carlos?

3 Descripciones

Leamos/Escribamos Completa la descripción de cada foto con una respuesta lógica.

1. Mi abuelo es ═══. Tiene el pelo ═══ y ═══.
2. Mi tío es ═══. Tiene un ═══ inteligente.
3. Mi papá es ═══. Usa ═══.
4. Mi ═══ se llama Barrigón. Es muy ═══, ¿no?

1. mi abuelo

2. mi tío

3. mi papá

4. Barrigón

4 La familia Herrera

Leamos Imagine that your friend is an exchange student in Chile. He has sent you this photo of his host family, the Herreras. Finish the description of the Herrera family.

En la familia Herrera hay ___1___ personas. La abuela está en una ___2___. El abuelo es ___3___ y ___4___ y tiene el pelo ___5___. Hay ___6___ hijas y ___7___ hijo. El hijo tiene un ___8___. La hija mayor y la mamá tienen el pelo ___9___. Me gusta esta familia, ellos son muy ___10___.

La familia Herrera de Valparaíso, Chile

Comunicación

HOLT **SoundBooth** ONLINE RECORDING

5 ¿Quién es cómico?

Hablemos Work in pairs. Ask your partner questions using **¿Quién en tu familia es...?** and the adjectives below. Then switch roles. Remember to use the correct form of adjectives in your answers!

MODELO cómico —¿Quién en tu familia es cómico?
—Mi hermana Anita es cómica.

1. serio(a)
2. viejo(a)
3. joven
4. delgado(a)
5. travieso(a)
6. alto(a)
7. atlético(a)
8. callado(a)

6 **Retrato de familia**

Leamos Read the sentences below. For each sentence, write the name of the family described.

MODELO **Mi hermano se llama Alberto. (Canales)**

1. Somos ocho en casa.
2. Somos seis personas en mi familia: mis padres, mi tía, mis dos hermanos y yo.
3. Somos tres hermanas, dos hermanos, mis padres y mi abuelo.
4. Mi hermana menor tiene tres años y es rubia.
5. La hermana de mi papá se llama Rosa.
6. Mi papá es rubio y tiene los ojos azules.
7. Tengo cinco nietos.
8. Tengo tres sobrinos.
9. El padre de mi papá usa lentes.
10. Mi hermana menor se llama Zenaida.

la familia Andrade

abuelo

papá   mamá

Leticia   Andrés   Rosa

Felipe   Esperanza

la familia Canales

tía Rosa   papá   mamá

Alberto   Rosario   Zenaida

7 **¿Quién eres?**

Escribamos Pretend you are a member of either the Canales or the Andrade family. Write five sentences that give clues to your identity.

MODELO **Tengo dos hermanos y dos hermanas.**

8 ¿Cómo son?

Escribamos Use words from each list to write at least three sentences about yourself and your family members.

MODELO Mi hermano tiene doce años. Es bajo y tiene el pelo rubio. Es travieso.

yo	tener	═══ años	delgado(a)
mi hermano(a)	(no) usar	los ojos	gordo(a)
mi abuelo(a)	ser	el pelo	travieso(a)
mi padre		lentes	serio(a)
mi madre		alto(a)	joven
mi perro		bajo(a)	viejo(a)
mi gato		ciego(a)	trabajador(a)
		sordo(a)	perezoso(a)

Comunicación

HOLT SoundBooth ONLINE RECORDING

9 Adivina... ¿quiénes son?

Escribamos/Hablemos With a partner, write three sentences about each family below. Talk about how the people look, their family relationships to each other, and activities they do together. Then get together with another pair of classmates and exchange papers. See if you can guess correctly which of their sentences match each photo.

1. la familia Howard 2. la familia Ruiz 3. la familia Takeda 4. la familia Dean

10 Entrevista

Hablemos Ask three classmates the following questions. Based on their answers, who is most like you? Report your findings to the class.

♻ *¿Se te olvidó?* The preposition de, p. 72

1. ¿Cuántas personas hay en tu familia?
2. ¿Con quién de tu familia te gusta más pasar el rato? ¿Cómo es?
3. ¿Cuántos hermanos mayores tienes? ¿Cuántos menores? ¿Cómo son?
4. ¿Tienes perro o gato? ¿Cómo se llama(n)?

Objetivos
• Possessive adjectives
• Stem-changing verbs:
  o → ue
• Stem-changing
  verbs: e → ie

Gramática en acción 1

GramaVisión

Possessive adjectives

Interactive TUTOR

1 **Possessive adjectives** show ownership or relationships between people. They are placed before the noun.

Owner		Owner	
yo	**mi** libro / **mis** libros	nosotros(as)	**nuestro** libro/**nuestra** casa / **nuestros** libros/**nuestras** casas
tú	**tu** libro / **tus** libros	vosotros(as)	**vuestro** libro/**vuestra** casa / **vuestros** libros/**vuestras** casas
usted / él / ella	**su** libro / **sus** libros	ustedes / ellos / ellas	**su** libro / **sus** libros

2 While **possessive adjectives** refer to the **owner,** their form agrees in gender and number with the noun that comes after them.

refers to   *agrees grammatically*

Martín vive con **su**s abuelo**s**.

refers to   *agrees grammatically*

Carlos y yo vivimos con **nuestr**a abuel**a**.

3 **Su** and **sus** can take the place of a phrase with **de + a person**.

—¿De dónde es la madre **de Juan**? —**Su** madre es de Puebla.

> Vocabulario y gramática, pp. 52–54
> Actividades, pp. 41–43
> **Online** workbooks

En inglés

In English, the possessive adjectives *his, her,* and *their* tell whether something belongs to a male, a female, or more than one person.

Which possessive adjective in English can stand for one person or more than one person?

In Spanish, the possessive adjective **su** has many possible meanings *(his, her, its, your, their),* but context usually makes the meaning clear.

11 Nuestras cosas

Leamos Complete the sentences to say that each person is looking for his or her own belongings.

1. Busco (mi/su) libro de español.
2. Buscamos (sus/nuestros) cuadernos.
3. Ellos buscan (tus/sus) mochilas.
4. Mi hermana menor busca (mis/sus) lentes.
5. Buscas (tus/vuestros) lápices.
6. Mamá busca (su/tu) reloj.
7. Mis amigos y yo buscamos (vuestra/nuestra) tarea.

12 **¿De Carolina o de Marta?**

Escuchemos Listen to the following sentences. Then, based on the photos, decide whether each sentence refers to Carolina's family or Marta's family.

la familia de Carolina

la familia de Marta

13 **En mi familia**

Leamos/Escribamos Juan is talking about his family with a friend. Fill in the blanks in the conversation with the correct possessive adjective and then tell the class about Juan's family.

—Juan, ¿cuántas personas hay en ___1___ família?

—Somos cinco en mi familia: ___2___ padres, ___3___ hermana mayor, ___4___ hermano menor y yo.

—¿Dónde trabajan ___5___ padres?

—___6___ madre es profesora. ___7___ trabajo es muy interesante. ___8___ padre trabaja con ___9___ padre, mi abuelo. A mis padres les gusta mucho ___10___ trabajo.

—Ustedes tienen una casa verde, ¿verdad?

—No, ___11___ casa no es verde pero ___12___ carro es verde.

14 **La familia de mi amigo**

Hablemos Interview a classmate about someone from his or her extended family. Find out the family member's name, what he or she is like, and what your classmate and he or she like to do together.

MODELO —¿Cómo se llama tu abuelo?

—Se llama Robert Miller.

—¿Y cómo es?

—Es alto, delgado y muy simpático.

Gramática 1

Stem-changing verbs: o → ue

1 Verbs with vowel variations in their stems are called **stem-changing verbs.** You have already learned **jugar** where the **u** changes to **ue**. In the verb **dormir** *(to sleep),* the **o** of the stem changes to **ue** in all forms except **nosotros(as)** and **vosotros(as).**

yo d**ue**rmo	nosotros(as) dormimos
tú d**ue**rmes	vosotros(as) dormís
Ud., él, ella d**ue**rme	Uds., ellos, ellas d**ue**rmen

El perro **duerme** mucho.   *The dog sleeps a lot.*

2 Other verbs that follow this pattern are **almorzar** *(to have lunch),* **volver** *(to go back* or *come back),* and **llover** *(to rain).*

Cuando **llueve, vuelvo** a casa en el autobús.
When it rains, I come home on the bus.

3 Use **dormir hasta** to say you *sleep until* a certain time.

Los domingos **dormimos hasta** las once.

> Vocabulario y gramática, pp. 52–54
> Actividades, pp. 41–43

Online workbooks

Interactive **TUTOR**

¿Te acuerdas?

In Spanish, regular -ar, -er, and -ir verbs have **regular stems** and regular endings.

hablar

hablo	**habl**amos
hablas	**habl**áis
habla	**habl**an

comer

como	**com**emos
comes	**com**éis
come	**com**en

escribir

escribo	**escrib**imos
escribes	**escrib**ís
escribe	**escrib**en

15 ## Su rutina diaria

Leamos Complete the e-mail with the missing verbs. Each word is used once.

duermo	almuerzo	vuelvo	jugamos	almorzamos
duerme	almuerza	vuelve	dormimos	volvemos

Nuevo Mensaje

Archivo Editar Ver Insertar Formato Herramientas Mensaje Ayuda

Enviar Cortar Copiar Pegar Deshacer Deletrear Adjuntar Prioridad

Nosotros casi siempre ____1____ en la cafetería. Mi hermano ____2____ a las once y media y yo ____3____ a la una. Siempre tengo mucha hambre. Mi hermano ____4____ a casa en su bicicleta a las dos y media y yo ____5____ a las tres. A veces nosotros ____6____ a videojuegos después de volver y a veces yo ____7____ un poco en el sofá. A las cuatro y media vamos al parque por una hora. Nosotros ____8____ del parque a las cinco y media. Después de cenar hacemos nuestra tarea. Los sábados nosotros ____9____ hasta tarde. El perro siempre ____10____ conmigo.

16 Un fin de semana típico

Leamos/Escribamos Complete each sentence with the correct form of the underlined verb. Sometimes the sentence requires a conjugated form and sometimes an infinitive.

1. Cuando <u>llueve</u> no tengo ganas de salir, pero no va a ════ mañana.

2. Voy a <u>almorzar</u> en el centro comercial. Yo siempre ════ con mis primos en el centro comercial los sábados.

3. Luego mi prima Juana viene a mi casa y <u>jugamos</u> al tenis. A ella le gusta ════ conmigo.

4. Después Juana y yo ════ al centro comercial. Nos gusta ir de compras. Pero nuestros amigos no <u>vuelven</u>.

5. Luego yo ════ a mi casa y Juana <u>vuelve</u> a su casa.

6. Cuando vuelvo a casa por la tarde siempre quiero <u>dormir</u> un poco. Yo ════ mucho por la tarde los sábados.

7. Los sábados <u>duermo</u> hasta las diez. A mi hermano no le gusta ════ hasta las diez.

8. Quiero <u>jugar</u> al fútbol hoy. No voy a ════ porque va a llover.

9. Mi hermana y yo vamos a <u>almorzar</u> después de jugar al tenis. Ella y yo siempre ════ a la una y media.

Comunicación

17 ¿Quién de tu familia...?

Hablemos Interview your partner using the photos and question words as a guide. Your partner should talk about what he or she and at least two other family members do. Then switch roles.

¿con qué frecuencia?

MODELO —¿Con qué frecuencia juegan al básquetbol?
—Mi hermano y yo a veces jugamos al básquetbol.
Mi madre nunca juega al básquetbol.

a. ¿dónde? b. ¿con qué frecuencia? c. ¿mucho? ¿poco? d. ¿a qué hora?

Stem-changing verbs: e → ie

Interactive TUTOR

1 Some verbs show a vowel stem change from **e** to **ie**, such as **empezar** (*to begin, to start*), **merendar** (*to have a snack*), **entender** (*to understand*), and **querer** (*to want*). The **e** changes to **ie** in all but the **nosotros(as)** and **vosotros(as)** forms.

yo emp**ie**zo	nosotros(as) empezamos
tú emp**ie**zas	vosotros(as) empezáis
Ud., él, ella emp**ie**za	Uds., ellos, ellas emp**ie**zan

—¿A qué hora **empieza** la película? —**Empieza** a las siete.
What time does the movie start? *It starts at seven o'clock.*

Tengo que estudiar más. No **entiendo** nada en la clase de matemáticas.
I have to study more. I don't understand anything in math class.

2 You can also use **empezar a** followed by an **infinitive** to say what you or others start to do.

—¿A qué hora **empiezan a trabajar** tus padres?

—**Empiezan a trabajar** a las ocho de la mañana.

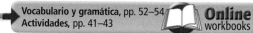
Vocabulario y gramática, pp. 52–54
Actividades, pp. 41–43
Online workbooks

¿Te acuerdas?

The verb t**e**ner is also an **e** → **ie** stem-changing verb. It is irregular in the **yo form**.

tengo	tenemos
t**ie**nes	tenéis
t**ie**ne	t**ie**nen

18 **Después de clases**

Leamos/Hablemos Complete the conversation using the correct verbs from the box. One verb will be used twice.

jugamos quieres merendamos tengo tienes empieza entiendo

—Hola, Guillermo.

—Hola, Fernando. ¿Cómo estás?

—Más o menos. Esta tarde ___1___ mucha hambre.

—Sí, yo también. ¿Qué tal si ___2___ algo? Hay fruta en la mesa.

—Sí, buena idea. Y después de comer, ¿(tú) ___3___ ir al cine conmigo? La película "El perro invisible" ___4___ a las cinco.

—No, no ___5___ ganas de ver una película.

—Si no ___6___ ganas de ir al cine, ¿quieres jugar al básquetbol? Tengo un partido mañana y necesito practicar.

—Sí, está bien. ¿Qué tal si ___7___ una hora? Luego tengo que estudiar.

—¿Por qué tienes que estudiar esta tarde?

—Porque mañana hay un examen en la clase de historia y yo no ___8___ nada. Es una clase difícil.

19 ¿A qué hora?

Leamos/Hablemos Look at the pictures and answer the following questions. ♻ *¿Se te olvidó?* A + time, p. 150

6:30 A.M.

MODELO ¿Hasta qué hora ducrme Gabi los lunes?
Los lunes Gabi duerme hasta las seis y media de la mañana.

1. ¿A qué hora empieza la primera clase de Gabi?
2. ¿A qué hora almuerza?
3. ¿A qué hora tiene su ensayo de banda?
4. ¿A qué hora merienda?
5. ¿A qué hora empieza a hacer su tarea?
6. ¿Qué quicre hacer Gabi después de hacer su tarea?

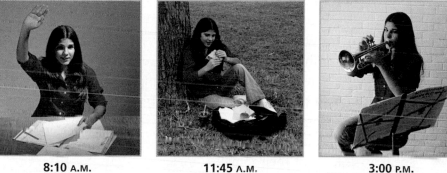

8:10 A.M.   11:45 A.M.   3:00 P.M.

4:20 P.M.   7:00 P.M.   8:30 P.M.

Comunicación

HOLT **SoundBooth** ONLINE RECORDING

20 Entrevista

Hablemos Use the questions from Activity 19 to ask your partner about his or her daily routine. Then report to the class what you found out.

MODELO —¿Hasta qué hora duermes los lunes?
—Los lunes duermo hasta las seis y media.

Gramática 1

Cultura

Comparaciones

Una familia unida de Santiago

¿Quiénes son los miembros de tu familia y cómo son?

In Spain and in Latin America, it is not uncommon to see extended families sharing a house or an apartment. Young adults often continue to live at home with their parents even after graduating from college. One reason for this is the cost of housing relative to income in Spain and Latin America. Many young people simply don't make enough money to live in their own homes or apartments. What advantages and disadvantages do you see to having a large extended family living together? Think about this question as you listen to several Spanish speakers talk about their families.

Amaru
Santiago, Chile

Amaru describes members of her family. How would you describe your family?

¿Quiénes son los miembros de tu familia?

Bueno, está mi papá, mi mamá y tengo dos hermanos y una hermana.

¿Cómo son ellos?

Bueno, mi mamá es muy trabajadora. Ella es pequeña y es muy linda. Mi hermano pequeño es muy grande, muy simpático, pero un poco travieso.

¿Tienes mascotas?

Tengo dos gatos y dos perros.

¿Con qué frecuencia ves a tus tíos y a tus primos?

Bueno, los veo más o menos un domingo al mes.

¿Se llevan bien ustedes?

Bueno, no nos vemos mucho pero nos llevamos bien.

Cultura

☀ Cristian
Buenos Aires, Argentina

Christian talks about how often he sees his extended family. Do you visit relatives often?

¿Quiénes son los miembros de tu familia?

Bueno, los miembros de mi familia son mi papá, mi mamá, y mi hermana mayor. Después estoy yo. Me llamo Cristian. Y después está mi hermanito más chiquito.

¿Cómo son ellos?

Mi papá es un hombre alto como yo. Tiene el pelo negro, los ojos marrones y es un poco gordo. Mi hermana es una chica linda. Tiene los ojitos claros, pecas, el pelo castaño, y es un poquito más baja que yo.

¿Tienes mascotas?

Sí. Dos perros.

¿Con qué frecuencia ves a tus tíos y a tus primos?

A mis tíos y a mis primos, los veo en las fiestas una vez por mes, dos veces.

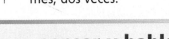

Chile

Buenos Aires

ARGENTINA

Océano Atlántico

Para comprender

1. ¿Quién es travieso de la familia de Amaru?
2. ¿Cuántas mascotas tiene Amaru?
3. ¿Cómo es el papá de Cristian?
4. ¿Cómo es la hermana de Cristian?
5. ¿Quién tiene la familia más grande? ¿Amaru o Cristian?
6. ¿Quién ve más a sus tíos y a sus primos? ¿Amaru o Cristian?

Para pensar y hablar

Do you think Amaru's and Cristian's families are large or small? Are families in your community typically larger or smaller than theirs? Name two advantages to having a large family (six or more) and two advantages to having a small family (three or four).

Comunidad

Surnames and Family Trees

Genealogy is a fascinating way to learn more about the history and cultures of Spanish speakers in your area. Research the background of a Hispanic family. It may be your own, or that of a famous Hispanic explorer, such as Pedro Menéndez de Avilés or Juan de Oñate.

- Use English and Spanish resources of state or local genealogical societies.
- Use the genealogical resources on the National Archives Web site.
- Present your findings to the class.

✠ FLORIDA

IV CENTENARIO DE

MENÉN-
DEZ DE
AVILÉS

2 PTAS

The Granger Collection, New York

Pedro Menéndez de Avilés

Objetivos
- Talking about where you and others live
- Talking about responsibilities

Vocabulario *en acción* 2

Video/DVD

ExpresaVisión

Una casa en Santiago

la cocina

el baño

la sala

el garaje

la ventana

las plantas

la puerta

el sofá

la habitación

el comedor

la silla

la cama

el escritorio

la mesa

¿Dónde vives?

en la ciudad

en el pueblo

en las afueras

en el campo

Vocabulario 2

También se puede decir...

The word for *bedroom* has many regional variations: **la alcoba, la recámara, el dormitorio, la pieza, el cuarto.**

In Mexico, **el departamento** is usually the preferred word for *apartment.*

Other words for **quehaceres** are **labores** and **deberes.**

¡Exprésate!

Interactive TUTOR

To ask about where someone lives	To respond
¿Dónde viven ustedes? *Where do you live?*	**Vivimos en un apartamento pequeño. Está en un edificio de diez pisos.** *We live in a small apartment. It's in a ten-story building.*
¿Cuál es tu dirección? *What's your address?*	**Es calle Valdivia, número 56.** *It's 56 Valdivia Street.*
¿Cómo es tu casa? *What's your house like?*	**Es bastante grande. Tiene cuatro habitaciones, y un patio y jardín muy bonitos.** *It's quite large. It has four bedrooms and a very pretty patio and garden.*

Vocabulario y gramática, pp. 55–57

Online workbooks

21 ¿Dónde?

Leamos/Hablemos Complete each sentence with a logical place.

1. El carro y las bicicletas están en...
   a. el garaje.   b. la sala.
2. Almorzamos en...
   a. el baño.   b. el comedor.
3. Hay muchas plantas en las ventanas...
   a. de la sala.   b. del jardín.
4. Descanso y veo películas en...
   a. la sala.   b. el garaje.
5. Preparamos el desayuno en...
   a. la cocina.   b. la habitación.
6. Hay dos habitaciones en...
   a. la sala.   b. la casa.
7. Hay un escritorio y una cama en...
   a. el jardín.   b. la habitación.

22 La casa de Mónica

Leamos/Escribamos Read Mónica's letter to Raquel, an exchange student from Spain who is coming to live at her house next year. Mónica is telling Raquel about her house. Answer the questions that follow.

Querida Raquel,

Nuestra casa es bastante grande. La dirección es Calle Hidalgo, número 365. Está en las afueras de la ciudad. La casa tiene dos pisos, con garaje, patio y jardín. Tiene una cocina, un comedor, cuatro habitaciones y tres baños. Vas a dormir en mi habitación. Tengo dos camas. Mi familia y yo pasamos las noches en la sala, donde nos gusta ver televisión o escuchar música.

¡Hasta luego!
Mónica

Casa en las afueras de Viña del Mar, Chile

1. ¿Dónde está la casa?
2. ¿Cuántas habitaciones hay? ¿baños?
3. ¿Hay más cuartos? ¿Cuáles son?
4. ¿Qué hace la familia en la sala?
5. ¿Dónde va a dormir Raquel?

Comunicación

23 Cuestionario sobre la familia

Leamos/Hablemos Based on what you read in the questionnaire below, work with your partner to describe the family. Then take turns answering the questionnaire for yourselves and comparing answers.

1. En la familia Young hay tres ═══.
2. La ═══ es Calle Ortega, número 75.
3. El hermano ═══ tiene 16 años.
4. La hermana ═══ tiene 12 años.
5. Kelly ═══ la cama todos los días.
6. Mike a veces corta el ═══.
7. La madre siempre ═══.
8. Lynn saca la ═══ los sábados.

Información Personal

1 Datos personales

a. Nombre completo:

   Apellido   Young
   Nombre(s)   Kelly

b. Edad: 14   años

c. Dirección: Calle Ortega, número 75

2 Vivo...

a. en una casa ☐
b. en un apartamento ☒
c. en la ciudad ☒
d. en las afueras ☐

3 Datos familiares

a. ¿Tienes hermanos?   sí
   ¿Cuántos?   ?
b. ¿Cuántos años tiene cada uno?

   Mi hermano mayor Mike tiene 16 años.

   Mi hermana menor Lynn tiene 12 años.

4 Los quehaceres

a. hacer la cama   yo, todos los días
b. arreglar el cuarto
c. cocinar   mi madre, siempre
d. limpiar el garaje
e. cortar el césped   mi hermano, a veces
f. sacar la basura   mi hermana, los sábados

Chile

Vocabulario 2

¡Exprésate!

To ask about responsibilities	To respond
¿Qué te parece tener que ayudar en casa? *What do you think about having to help out at home?*	**A veces tengo que cuidar a mis hermanos, pero me parece bien. No es gran cosa.** *Sometimes I have to take care of my brothers and sisters, but it's all right with me. It's no big deal.* **A mí siempre me toca pasar la aspiradora en la sala. ¡Qué lata!** *I always have to vacuum the living room. What a pain!*
¿Qué te toca hacer a ti? *What do you have to do?*	**A menudo tengo que arreglar mi cuarto.** *I often have to pick up my room.*
¿Y a Juan? *And Juan?*	**A Juan nunca le toca lavar los platos. Me parece injusto.** *Juan never has to do the dishes. It seems unfair to me.*

Interactive TUTOR

▶ Vocabulario y gramática, pp. 55–57 **Online** workbooks

24 En la casa

Escuchemos Match each sentence you hear with the picture to which it corresponds. Not every sentence will have a matching picture.

a.　　　　b.　　　　c.　　　　d.

25 Los quehaceres

Escribamos Write complete sentences telling who does these chores in your home. Use the words **casi siempre, a veces, casi nunca,** or **nunca.** Be sure to conjugate the verb in each sentence.

MODELO Mi padre casi siempre corta el césped.

1. cortar el césped
2. pasar la aspiradora
3. limpiar el baño
4. lavar los platos
5. cocinar

6. hacer la cama
7. arreglar la sala
8. sacar la basura
9. cuidar a los hermanos
10. limpiar la cocina

26 Mi mascota *(pet)* increíble

Escribamos Write a description of your real or imaginary dog or cat to be entered in the "Pet of the Week" contest. Write at least five sentences. Be sure to mention your dog or cat's name, age, size, color, and at least one interesting thing your pet does.

27 ¡A Adela le toca hacer mucho!

Leamos/Escribamos Adela's friends are coming over tomorrow for a birthday party and sleepover. Based on what you see below, rewrite her list of chores to do before they arrive.

MODELO el cuarto
Tengo que arreglar el cuarto.

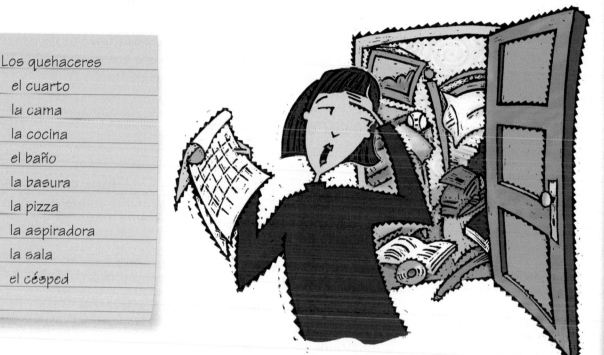

Los quehaceres
el cuarto
la cama
la cocina
el baño
la basura
la pizza
la aspiradora
la sala
el césped

 **Comunicación**

28 ¿Qué haces tú?

Hablemos Work with a partner. Ask each other what you do to help out at home. Tell how often and when you do various chores. Mention at least two things you do, and one thing you do not do.

MODELO —¿Qué haces para ayudar en casa?
—A veces paso la aspiradora. Limpio la cocina todos los días. Nunca saco la basura.

Objetivos
- **Estar** with prepositions
- Negation with **nunca, tampoco, nadie,** and **nada**
- **Tocar** and **parecer**

Gramática en acción 2

Video/DVD
GramaVisión

Interactive TUTOR

Estar with prepositions

1 You've already used some forms of the verb **estar** to talk about how someone is feeling. **Estar** is irregular in the present tense.

yo **estoy**	nosotros(as) **estamos**
tú **estás**	vosotros(as) **estáis**
Ud., él, ella **está**	Uds., ellos, ellas **están**

2 The verb **estar** is also used with some **prepositions** to say where someone or something is in relation to someone or something else. Some prepositions are made up of more than one word.

—¿Dónde **está** tu apartamento?
—**Está detrás de** un edificio grande.

Vocabulario y gramática, pp. 58–60
Actividades, pp. 45–47
Online workbooks

Some prepositions			
al lado de	next to	**detrás de**	behind
cerca de	close to, near	**encima de**	on top of, above
debajo de	underneath	**lejos de**	far from
delante de	in front of		

29 Un día escolar

Leamos/Escribamos Complete the conversation with the correct forms of **estar**. Then rewrite the conversation, answering the questions about yourself.

—¿Con quiénes almuerzas en el colegio?

—Almuerzo con mis amigos Raquel y Joel.

—¿A qué hora __1__ ustedes en la cafetería?

—__2__ en la cafetería a las doce y media.

—¿Dónde __3__ (tú) a las dos de la tarde?

—__4__ en mi clase de matemáticas.

—¿Y después de clases? ¿__5__ (tú) en casa o en el colegio?

—__6__ en el entrenamiento de volibol. Vuelvo a la casa a las cinco.

—¿Tu casa __7__ cerca del colegio?

—No, __8__ bastante lejos.

Una casa del sur de Chile

30 ¿Dónde están?

Escribamos Look at the drawing. Write complete sentences telling where the first thing is in relation to the second.

> **MODELO** la mochila/el bolígrafo
> La mochila está lejos del bolígrafo.

1. la computadora/el escritorio
2. la mochila/el perro
3. la silla/el escritorio
4. la planta/la ventana
5. el gato/la planta
6. los lentes/las revistas
7. la computadora/el bolígrafo
8. el perro/la silla
9. el diccionario/las revistas
10. las revistas/los lentes

31 En nuestra familia

Hablemos/Escribamos Tell where you and your family members are at the following times.

> **MODELO** Los lunes a las diez de la mañana, mi padre está en su trabajo.

1. Los viernes a las ocho de la noche, yo…
2. Los sábados a la seis de la mañana, mi madre…
3. Los miércoles a la una de la tarde, yo…
4. Los lunes a las diez de la mañana, mis hermanos…
5. Los martes a las dos de la mañana, mi familia y yo…
6. Los domingos a las tres de la tarde, mi padre…
7. Los jueves a las seis de la tarde, mis padres…
8. Los fines de semana a las diez de la noche, yo…

 **Comunicación**

32 ¿Qué es?

Hablemos Pick five things in the classroom. Tell your partner where they are, using prepositions. Your partner guesses what you're talking about. Switch roles.

> **MODELO** —Está cerca de la ventana.
> —¿Es la computadora?
> —Sí, es la computadora.

Negation with nunca, tampoco, nadie, and nada

1 **Nunca** (*never*) and **tampoco** (*neither, not either*) can take the place of **no**, or they can be added toward the end of a sentence that already has **no**.

No voy a la playa.	*I don't go to the beach.*
Nunca voy a la playa.	*I never go to the beach.*
No voy a la playa **nunca**.	*I never go to the beach.*
Tampoco voy a la piscina.	*I don't go to the pool either.*
No voy a la piscina **tampoco**.	*I don't go to the pool either.*

2 The word **nada** means *nothing* when it is the subject of a sentence and *not anything* or *nothing* when it goes after the verb. When **nada** is after the verb, **no** must be placed before the verb.

Nada es fácil.	**No** quiero **nada** hoy.
Nothing is easy.	*I don't want anything today.*

3 Use **nadie** to say *nobody* or *not anybody*. When **nadie** is after the verb, **no** must be placed before the verb.

Nadie quiere ir al cine.	**No** hay **nadie** aquí.
Nobody wants to go to the movies.	*There isn't anybody here.*

Vocabulario y gramática, pp. 58–60
Actividades, pp. 45–47

Online workbooks

¿Te acuerdas?

The word **no** means *not, do not,* or *don't*. Place it before the verb or the pronouns that go with **gustar**.

No soy de Madrid.

A mí **no** me gusta la pizza.

---

33 **Después de cenar**

Escuchemos Escucha las oraciones y decide si son **ciertas** o **falsas** según (*according to*) las fotos.

la hija

el hijo

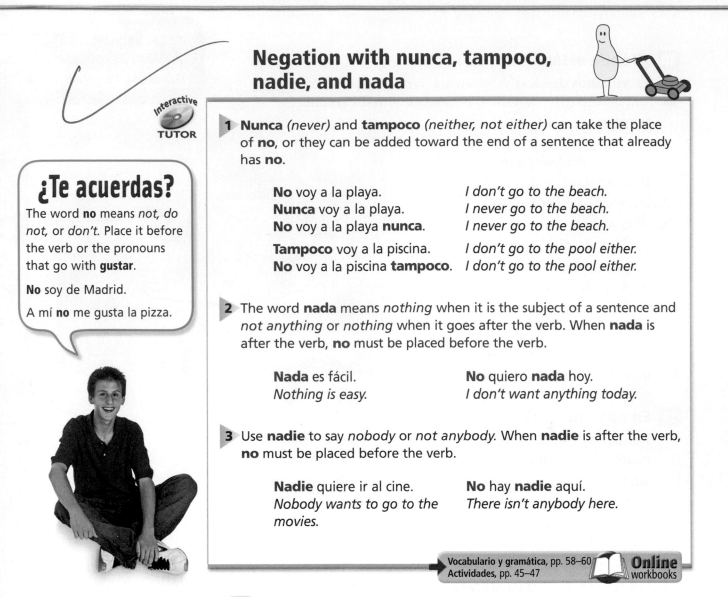
la madre

34 No queremos hacer nada

Leamos Choose the best word to complete each sentence.

1. Mis primos no van a la playa. No voy a la playa (también/tampoco).

2. No quiero hacer (nada/nunca) hoy.

3. Mis padres, mis hermanos y yo tenemos el pelo castaño. (Siempre/Nadie) en mi familia tiene el pelo rubio.

4. Cuando llueve y hace frío, mi perro no quiere salir. A mí (tampoco/nada) me gusta salir cuando hace mal tiempo.

5. Siempre preparamos la cena en la cocina. (Nunca/Tampoco) cocinamos en el patio.

6. Después de cenar, me toca lavar los platos. (Tampoco/Nadie) me ayuda.

Un cine en Viña del Mar, Chile

35 ¿Vas a hacer algo hoy?

Leamos Complete the conversation with your friend about this weekend using words from the box.

tampoco	siempre	también
nada	nunca	algo

— ¿Vas a hacer ___1___ el sábado?

—No, no voy a hacer ___2___ . ¿Y tú?

—Casi ___3___ voy al cine los sábados. ¿Quieres ir conmigo?

—Sí, yo ___4___ quiero ir al cine. ¿Sales mucho los sábados?

—Sí. Casi ___5___ paso los fines de semana en casa.

—Yo ___6___ paso los fines de semana en casa. Siempre salgo con mis amigos y mis primos.

Comunicación

36 ¿Y tú?

Hablemos Interview a classmate using the following questions.

1. ¿Qué días siempre tienes mucho que hacer?
2. ¿Qué quehaceres casi siempre te toca hacer en casa?
3. ¿Quién te ayuda con los quehaceres?
4. ¿Qué haces cuando no tienes tarea?
5. ¿Qué haces cuando no tienes nada que hacer?

Tocar and parecer

1 To say what you have to do, what your duties are, or whose turn it is to do something, use the verb **tocar** followed by an **infinitive**. **Tocar** may be used like **gustar**.

me	toca(n)	**nos**	toca(n)
te	toca(n)	**os**	toca(n)
le	toca(n)	**les**	toca(n)

—A ti **te toca sacar** la basura hoy.
It's your turn to take out the trash today.

—¿A mí? No. Hoy **le toca** a Fernando.
My turn? No. It's Fernando's turn today.

2 The verb **parecer** means *to seem* and may also be used like **gustar.** It's very common to use this verb when asking for and giving opinions.

me	parece(n)	**nos**	parece(n)
te	parece(n)	**os**	parece(n)
le	parece(n)	**les**	parece(n)

Siempre me toca a mí **lavar** los platos. **Me parece** injusto.
I always have to wash the dishes. It seems unfair to me.

A mi papá **le parece** una lata **cortar** el césped.
My dad thinks cutting the grass is a pain.

Vocabulario y gramática, pp. 58–60
Actividades, pp. 45–47

Online workbooks

¿Te acuerdas?

The verb **gustar** uses these **pronouns** for the person who likes something. The verb agrees with what is liked.

me gusta(n)	**nos** gusta(n)
te gusta(n)	**os** gusta(n)
le gusta(n)	**les** gusta(n)

37 ¡Qué lata!

Escuchemos For each picture you'll hear two sentences. Tell whether they are **cierto** or **falso.**

mi hermana

mi hermano

mi papá y mi hermano menor

mi mamá y yo

38 ¿A quién le toca?

Hablemos/Escribamos Tell your sister it's her turn to do the chores and your turn to have fun.

MODELO A ti te toca limpiar el baño. A mí me toca jugar.

1. descansar/cortar el césped
2. lavar los platos/ir de compras
3. cocinar/ver televisión
4. jugar/hacer la cama
5. leer/limpiar la casa
6. limpiar el baño/cantar

39 ¿Qué les parece?

Hablemos/Escribamos Say how the following activities seem to you. Then name someone you know who has a different opinion.

MODELO A mí me parece divertido ir de compras. Pero a mi padre le parece aburrido.

divertido	fácil	muy bien	interesante
difícil	aburrido	fenomenal	pésimo

1. trabajar en el jardín
2. vivir en el campo
3. jugar con los perros
4. ir al centro comercial
5. jugar a videojuegos
6. hablar por teléfono
7. bailar
8. hacer ejercicio

Comunicación

HOLT SoundBooth ONLINE RECORDING

40 Mi familia

Hablemos Take turns with a partner. Imagine that one of you is the teenage girl in the drawings below. Ask and answer questions about the girl's family, her house, and her family's activities.

nuestra casa   la casa de abuela

Conexiones culturales

Conexión Arte

La familia The word "family" has different meanings for different people. **La familia extendida** *(extended family)* includes relatives such as grandparents, aunts and uncles, and cousins. When Spanish speakers talk about **mi familia,** they often include their extended family.

Look at the two portraits of families, one by Miguel Cabrera and the other by Joan Miró. Miguel Cabrera lived in Mexico in the 1700s. He is famous for his paintings of families. Joan Miró, born near Barcelona, Spain, in 1893, is famous for his playful drawings and paintings.

1 La familia y el arte

Work with a partner to answer these questions about the family portraits.

1. How many people are in each family?

2. Identify the family members.

3. What perspectives on families and family life are presented in each painting?

2 Un dibujo

Draw a picture of your idea of family. Show your drawing to a classmate and explain it. How does your drawing compare to your classmate's? How does your drawing compare with the paintings on this page?

Miguel Cabrera, from *Español y mestiza, castiza,* 1763

Joan Miró, *La familia,* 1924, Chalk on glass paper. 29 1/2"x 41", The Museum of Modern Art, New York

Conexión Historia

Un árbol genealógico Have you ever seen your own family tree? How many relatives can you think of in your family? Family trees can be drawn in many different ways. Gabriela's family tree goes from the top (the past) down the page to the present.

La familia de Gabriela

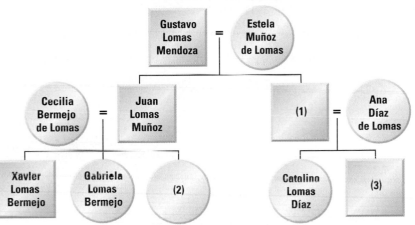

3 ¿Cómo se llaman?

1. ¿Cómo se llama el hermano de Gabriela?
2. ¿Cómo se llaman sus abuelos paternos (los padres de su padre)?
3. ¿Cómo se llama la tía de Gabriela?

4 La familia de Gabriela

Copy the family tree above on your own paper. Then, using the information in the following sentences, write the complete names of the missing relatives on the family tree.

1. El hermano de Juan es Antonio.
2. La sobrina de Ana es Leticia.
3. El primo de Gabriela es Pablo.

5 ¡Te toca a ti!

Work with a partner to draw your own real or imaginary family trees. Use your own symbols for marriages, divorces, deaths, and other important events. Compare the last names in your family tree with the last names in the family tree on this page.

Conexiones culturales

Chile

¿Quién será?

Episodio 5

Understanding humor Understanding humor is an important part of enjoying a story on video. Sometimes humor can be created by contrasting what a character is actually experiencing with what a character *feels* like he or she is experiencing. As you read the **Novela** or watch the video, compare Sofía's and Nicolás's real household chores with how they see those chores. Does the comparison make you laugh? Do you feel the same way about household chores?

En México

Estados Unidos
MÉXICO   Golfo de México
Ciudad de México ★
Océano Pacífico

Es sábado, un día que a veces no le gusta mucho a Sofía...

Sofía, ¡tienes que pasar la aspiradora en tu habitación y en la sala también!

1

Sofía Hoy es sábado. Los sábados mi familia y yo hacemos el quehacer.

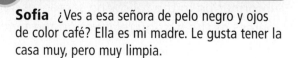

2

Sofía ¿Ves a esa señora de pelo negro y ojos de color café? Ella es mi madre. Le gusta tener la casa muy, pero muy limpia.

Check your understanding of the **Novela** by answering the questions.
1. What does Sofía's family do on Saturdays?
2. What does Sofía's mother want Sofía to do?

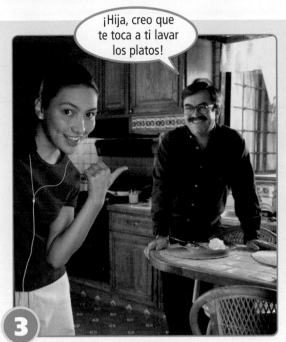

¡Hija, creo que te toca a ti lavar los platos!

3

Sofía ¿Ves a ese señor canoso con los lentes y la sonrisa graciosa? Es mi padre. No le gusta lavar los platos.

¡Sofía! ¡Sofía! ¡Cara de tortilla! ¡Tienes que sacar la basura!

4

Sofía ¿Ves a ese niño travieso? Es Quique, mi hermano. A Quique no le toca hacer los quehaceres. ¡Me parece injusto!

5

Sofía ¡Qué lata! No puedo descansar nunca.

B. CONTESTA

1. What does Sofía's father want Sofía to do?
2. Does Sofía's brother also have to do chores? If not, why not?
3. What is Sofía thinking about when she says, **"No puedo descansar nunca."**?

*Es sábado en la casa de Nicolás,
en San Juan...*

¡Nicolás! Tienes que cortar el césped hoy. Vienen tus tíos y tus primos.

Océano Atlántico San Juan
★
PUERTO RICO
Mar Caribe

6 **Nicolás** Hoy es sábado. Quiero salir de casa antes de que...

7 **Nicolás** ¡El césped! ¡Ay, no! Mi abuela es muy exigente. ¡Quiere todo perfecto!

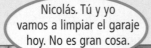

Nicolás. Tú y yo vamos a limpiar el garaje hoy. No es gran cosa.

8 **Nicolás** Mi papá es mecánico. ¡Está loco por los carros! Le gusta tener el garaje muy organizado.

9 **Nicolás** Un sábado bonito ¡arruinado! Y, ¿para qué? ¡Para hacer labores! ¡Me parece injusto!

As Marcos learns more about the Chilean candidate, he gets a call from la profesora telling him to go to Mexico next.

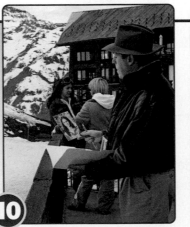

10

Bolivia

Océano Pacífico

★ Santiago

CHILE

Argentina

Océano Atlántico

C. CONTESTA

1. What does Nicolás's grandmother want him to do?

2. What does his father want him to do?

3. Why does he look so frustrated?

Actividades

1 ¿Cómo son ellos?

Match each name with a description that fits based on information in the **Novela.**

1. El Sr. Corona   **a.** es muy travieso.
2. La Sra. Corona   **b.** tiene el pelo negro.
3. Quique   **c.** tiene muchos quehaceres.
4. Sofía   **d.** es canoso.

2 En casa de Nicolás

Find the information in the **Novela** to complete the paragraph.

La ___1___ de Nicolás quiere todo perfecto. Nicolás tiene que ___2___ el césped y ___3___ el garaje. Su padre quiere el ___4___ muy organizado. A Nicolás le parece ___5___ tener que hacer los quehaceres los sábados.

3 ¿Comprendes la Novela?

Check your understanding of the events in the story by answering these questions.

1. Which statement by Sofía tells you something about her mother's personality?
2. Why does Sofía think her father doesn't like to wash dishes?
3. Why does Sofía call her little brother **"ese niño travieso"**?
4. Is Sofía right when she feels that she is being treated unjustly?
5. How does Nicolás end up spending his Saturday?
6. Why are the attitudes of Sofía and Nicolás amusing?

Leamos y escribamos

A Antes de leer

Scan the following ads. What can you find out about the prices and the locations of the properties?

CASAS Y APARTAMENTOS

AGENCIA INMOBILIARIA[1]

Zamora + Asociados
Calle Loma Linda 546
Tel: 5-55-69-32
www.vivienda[2]enlínea.hrw.com

A. Se vende[3] casa, estilo chalet, en pueblo tranquilo. 5 dormitorios, 3 baños, gran sala/comedor, sala de juegos, oficina, cocina moderna, garaje doble y piscina. ¡Precio incomparable!

B. Se alquila[4] apartamento remodelado. Av. Providencia 3192. 2 dormitorios, 2 baños, sala, cocina/comedor y garaje. A sólo tres cuadras[5] de la universidad. ¡Un sitio ideal!

C. Se vende casa en las afueras de la ciudad. El Rosal, calle Margarita 89. Aire y calefacción[6] central. 2 dormitorios, 1 baño, sala, comedor, cocina, garaje y magnífico jardín. Precio negociable.

D. Se alquila apartamento amueblado[7]. Nuevo edificio en el centro de la ciudad. Perfecto para hombre o mujer profesional. 1 habitación, 1 baño, sala, cocina y balcón con magnífica vista[8] de la ciudad. ¡Gran oportunidad!

E. Se vende pequeño condominio en zona residencial. Enfrente de un parque y cerca de la Escuela Primaria Salazar. 3 dormitorios, 2 baños, sala con chimenea, comedor, cocina y garaje. ¡Gran precio!

1 real estate company   **2** properties   **3** for sale   **4** for rent   **5** blocks   **6** heating   **7** furnished   **8** view

B Comprensión

Based on each person's profile, match these prospective home buyers or tenants with the properties in the previous ads.

1. Una abuela que vive con su nieto de cuatro años y un gato.

2. Dos hermanos que empiezan sus estudios en la universidad.

3. Una mujer de negocios joven.

4. Una familia con tres hijos y dos perros grandes.

5. Una familia pequeña con dos hijos de siete y nueve años.

C Después de leer

What kinds of things, other than size and cost, do people take into consideration when looking for a home to rent or buy? Describe the ideal home for your real family or an imaginary one. Explain why the features of your prospective home make it ideal.

Interactive TUTOR

Taller del escritor

ESTRATEGIA

para escribir Draw bubbles and list in them the characteristics of the things you describe. Then connect the bubbles to each other to help you see your writing plan.

> A mi mamá le gusta trabajar en el jardín.

> A mi mamá le toca cortar el césped.

> Mamá

¿Qué les toca hacer?

Think of your dream home. Write a paragraph describing it. Explain:

- where it is and what it's like
- who lives there with you
- what each person likes and dislikes doing
- each person's chores.

1 Antes de escribir

Draw a bubble and inside of it write the name of a person living with you in the dream home. Link that bubble to another in which you write that person's likes and dislikes. (**A mi papá le gusta cocinar.**) Draw another line linking the person to a bubble that lists her or his chores. (**A mi papá le toca limpiar la cocina.**) Do this for each

person. Also draw linked bubbles describing your home. (**En mi casa ideal hay...**)

2 Escribir y revisar

Begin with a detailed description of your dream home. Explain why the location is ideal. Then write about the people who live there, their likes and dislikes, and each person's chores.

Read your draft at least twice. Check for spelling, punctuation, and correct grammar.

3 Publicar

You may want to include a drawing of your dream home with your paragraph. How does it compare to your classmates' dream homes?

Leamos y escribamos

Prepárate para el examen

Interactive
TUTOR

1 Imagine that these photos come from your family album. Describe the family members and tell how old they are. Write at least three sentences for each picture.

1. mis hermanos   2. mi abuelo   3. mis padres   4. mi gato

1 Vocabulario 1
• describing people and family relationships
pp. 186–191

2 Gramática 1
• possessive adjectives
• stem-changing verbs
pp. 192–197

2 Pablo is describing his and his family's activities. Complete his description with the correct form of the verb or possessive adjective.

Los domingos, ___1___ (mis/tus) hermanos y yo ___2___ (empezar/volver) el día muy temprano. Mi hermano corre por el parque y después ___3___ (empezar/volver) a casa y ayuda a ___4___ (tus/mis) padres en el jardín. Vamos a la iglesia y ___5___ (volver/dormir) a la una. A la una y media mi familia y yo ___6___ (almorzar/merendar). Después de almorzar, los abuelos ___7___ (volver/jugar) a juegos de mesa. Yo nunca ___8___ (volver/jugar) con ellos. Me gusta más salir con ___9___ (nuestro/mis) amigos. A mis amigos y a mí nos gusta ___10___ (arreglar/merendar) a las tres y media.

3 Vocabulario 2
• talking about where you and others live
• talking about your responsibilities
pp. 200–205

3 Tell how often you have to do the following chores. If you never do them, say who does.

1. hacer las camas
2. lavar los platos
3. sacar la basura
4. limpiar el baño
5. cuidar a mis hermanos
6. cocinar
7. cortar el césped
8. pasar la aspiradora

4 Complete the following sentences.

1. A mí me ▨▨▨▨ (tocar/parecer) hacer todo en casa.
2. Los libros de mi papá ▨▨▨▨ (hacer/estar) encima del sofá.
3. A mi hermano le ▨▨▨▨ (tocar/parecer) fenomenal salir con sus amigos.
4. El perro no quiere jugar ▨▨▨▨ (siempre/nunca).
5. Mis amigos nunca hacen nada. Yo no hago nada ▨▨▨▨ (también/tampoco).

5 Answer the following questions.

1. What information do Latin American last names provide?
2. How do culture and climate influence home architecture?
3. When Spanish speakers talk about their **familia,** are they referring to an immediate or an extended family?

6 Complete the paragraph based on what you hear.

La casa de Sara está en ___1___. En la familia son ___2___ personas. Hay ___3___ habitaciones en la casa. A Sara le toca ___4___. Le parece ___5___. A su hermano nunca le toca ___6___. A Sara le parece ___7___.

Visit Holt Online

go.hrw.com
KEYWORD: EXP1A CH5
Chapter Self-test

4 Gramática 2
- using **estar** with prepositions
- negation
- **tocar** and **parecer**
  pp. 206–211

5 Cultura
- **Comparaciones**
  pp. 198–199
- **Notas culturales**
  pp. 188, 190, 206
- **Geocultura**
  pp. 180–183

Prepárate para el examen

Conversación

HOLT **SoundBooth**
ONLINE RECORDING

7 Role-play the following conversation with a partner. Partner A and Partner B are friends talking about chores.

PARTNER A: Name three chores you have to do and complain about them. Ask what chores your partner does.

PARTNER B: Respond and ask your partner what his or her brother has to do.

PARTNER A: Name some chores your brother does. Complain about having to clean your room. Say it seems unfair.

PARTNER B: Say that your partner's brother does a lot of chores. Ask why your partner thinks it's unfair.

PARTNER A: Say it's unfair because your mom cleans your brother's room.

PARTNER B: Say it seems fine to you. Ask if your partner wants to do his or her brother's chores.

PARTNER A: Answer no, then ask what chores your partner's brother does.

PARTNER B: Say your brother doesn't do any chores because he's two.

Repaso de Gramática 1

Gramática 1
- possessive adjectives
  pp. 192–193
- o → ue stem-changing verbs
  pp. 194–195
- e → ie stem-changing verbs
  pp. 196–197

Possessive adjectives show ownership or relationship between people.

mi/s	**nuestro/a/os/as**
tu/s	**vuestro/a/os/as**
su/s	**su/s**

Almorzar, dormir, llover, and **volver** are **o → ue** stem-changing verbs. **Empezar, entender, querer,** and **merendar** are **e → ie** stem-changing verbs.

alm**ue**rzo	almorzamos	emp**ie**zo	empezamos
alm**ue**rzas	almorzáis	emp**ie**zas	empezáis
alm**ue**rza	alm**ue**rzan	emp**ie**za	emp**ie**zan

Repaso de Gramática 2

Gramática 2
- **estar** with prepositions
  pp. 206–207
- negation with **nunca, tampoco, nadie,** and **nada**
  pp. 208–209
- **tocar** and **parecer**
  pp. 210–211

Use **estar** with **prepositions** to say where someone or something is located.

estar		prepositions of location		
estoy	estamos	**al lado de**	**delante de**	**encima de**
estás	estáis	**cerca de**	**detrás de**	**lejos de**
está	están	**debajo de**		

Negation

nada	nunca	nadie	no	tampoco

tocar				parecer			
me toca(n)		**nos** toca(n)		**me** parece(n)		**nos** parece(n)	
te toca(n)		**os** toca(n)		**te** parece(n)		**os** parece(n)	
le toca(n)		**les** toca(n)		**le** parece(n)		**les** parece(n)	

Letra y sonido b v

Las letras b y v

- The letters **b** and **v** follow these rules: At the beginning of a sentence, and after **m** or **n**, both are pronounced as *b* in the English word *boy*. **V**oy a casa., ¿**B**ailas mucho?, dicie**m**bre, un **b**aile

- Everywhere else, their pronunciation is softer with the lips barely touching: vi**v**ir, a**b**uelo, re**v**ista, a**b**urrido

Trabalenguas

El buen abuelo Vicente vende bonitas boinas baratas, baberos babosos, bolillos verdes, botas bellas y revistas aburridas.

Dictado

Escribe las oraciones de la grabación.

Repaso de Vocabulario 1

Describing people and family
relationships . . . . See p. 159.

los **abuelos**	grandparents	**menor**	younger
el/la **abuelo(a)**	grandfather, grandmother	**merendar (ie)**	to have a snack
almorzar (ue)	to have lunch	**negro(a)**	black
callado(a)	quiet	el/la **nieto(a)**	grandson, granddaughter
canoso(a)	gray-haired	los **nietos**	grandsons, grandchildren
castaño(a)	dark brown	el **padre**	father
ciego(a)	blind	los **padres**	parents
corto(a)	short	el **pelo**	hair
de **color café**	brown	el/la **perro(a)**	dog
delgado(a)	thin	la **persona**	person
dormir (ue)	to sleep	el/la **primo(a)**	cousin
empezar (ie)	to begin, to start	los **primos**	cousins
entender (ie)	to understand	la **silla de ruedas**	wheelchair
el/la **gato(a)**	cat	el/la **sobrino(a)**	nephew, niece
gordo(a)	fat	los **sobrinos**	nephews, nieces and nephews
hasta	until	**sordo(a)**	deaf
el/la **hermano(a)**	brother, sister	**tener (ie) los ojos azules**	to have blue eyes
los **hermanos**	siblings	el/la **tío(a)**	uncle, aunt
el/la **hijo(a)**	son, daughter	los **tíos**	aunts and uncles
los **hijos**	children, sons	**todos(as)**	everyone, all of us
joven	young	**travieso(a)**	mischievous
largo(a)	long	**usar lentes**	to wear glasses
la **madre**	mother	**verde**	green
mayor	older	**viejo(a)**	old
		volver (ue)	to go back or come back

Repaso de Vocabulario 2

Talking about where you and others live

las **afueras**	outskirts	**hacer los quehaceres**	to do the chores
el **apartamento**	apartment	el **jardín**	garden
el **baño**	bathroom	**limpiar**	to clean
la **calle**	street	la **mesa**	table
el **campo**	countryside	**nadie**	nobody, not anybody
la **ciudad**	city	el **patio**	patio, yard
la **cocina**	kitchen	**pequeño(a)**	small
cocinar	to cook	las **plantas**	plants
el **comedor**	dining room	el **pueblo**	town, village
cortar el césped	to cut the grass	la **puerta**	door
la **dirección**	address	**sacar la basura**	to take out the trash
el **edificio (de diez pisos)**	(ten-story) building	la **sala**	living room
el **escritorio**	desk	la **silla**	chair
el **garaje**	garage	el **sofá**	couch
grande	big, large	**tampoco**	neither, not either
la **habitación**	bedroom	la **ventana**	window
hacer la cama	to make the bed	**vivir**	to live

Talking about your responsibilities . . . . . . See p. 2[

Prepárate para el examen

Integración
capítulos 1-5

1 Listen to Josefina talk about her family and then match her descriptions with the correct photo.

A **B** **C** **D**

2 Esteban is writing to "Metida," an advice columnist. Read his letter and then answer the questions that follow.

Querida Metida, ...

> "Quiero salir más con mis amigos los fines de semana, pero no tengo tiempo. Los viernes por la tarde practico fútbol en el estadio. No llego a casa hasta las 8:00. Los sábados tengo un montón que hacer en casa. Arreglo mi cuarto y corto el césped. Ayudo a lavar los platos después de comer. Los domingos cuido a mi hermano menor porque mis padres juegan al tenis. Por la noche tengo que hacer la tarea. Me parece injusto pero, ¿qué puedo hacer?"
>
> —Esteban

1. ¿Qué problema tiene Esteban?
2. ¿Por qué no sale los viernes?
3. ¿Qué le toca hacer a Esteban los sábados?
4. ¿Cuándo salen los padres de Esteban? ¿Qué hacen?
5. ¿Qué le toca hacer a Esteban cuando salen sus padres?
6. ¿Qué necesita hacer Esteban? En tu opinión, ¿qué consejos (advice) le va a escribir "Metida" a él para resolver (solve) su problema?

3 Imagine you are in an art gallery looking at the painting below. Use your imagination to think about what the artist wanted to express. Then write answers to the following questions.

1. ¿Qué colores ves?

2. ¿Qué tiempo hace?

3. ¿Dónde están las personas?

4. ¿Son una familia? ¿Quiénes son?

5. ¿Cuántos años tiene cada *(each)* persona?

6. ¿Cómo son ellos?

Esperando a los pescadores, de Isidoro Molleda (n. 1930)

4

Situación

In small groups, create an imaginary family. Decide on roles; each person takes on the identity of a family member. Take turns introducing a member of your "family" to the class by giving the following information:

▶ name and age

▶ role in the family (father, son, aunt, and so on)

▶ physical description of the imaginary family member

▶ what chores he or she does and when the chores are done

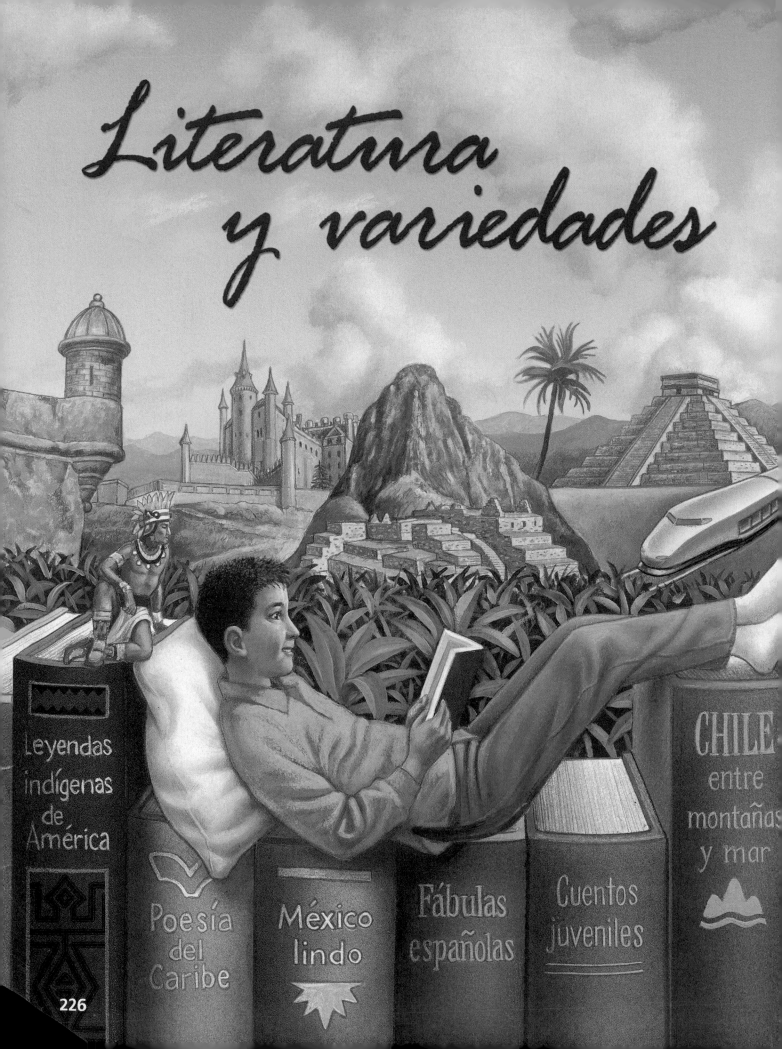

Literatura y variedades

Leyendas indígenas de América

Poesía del Caribe

México lindo

Fábulas españolas

Cuentos juveniles

CHILE entre montañas y mar

Las
maravillas
de la
naturaleza

España
a través
de su
arte

España

El Museo del Prado 🔊

The Prado Museum, in downtown Madrid, Spain, is one of the largest and best-known art museums in the world. It houses over 9,000 works of art. The collection is so vast that only a tenth of it can be displayed at any one time. Although most of its paintings and sculptures are by European artists, it holds works by artists from around the world and reveals centuries of history through art. Read the following information in the visitor brochure and the descriptions of the paintings by three famous Spanish artists to learn more about the Prado and its collection.

ESTRATEGIA

Look for cognates (words with similar meanings and spellings in English and Spanish) to help you understand some of the words you do not know.

MUSEO NACIONAL DEL **PRADO**

ESPAÑOL

Plano del Museo
Localización de colecciones

MUSEO NACIONAL DEL **PRADO**

Ruiz de Alarcón, 23. 28014 Madrid
http://museoprado.mcu.es
Teléfono: +34 913 30 28 00
Fax: +34 913 30 28 56

Información General:

Dirección:
Ruiz de Alarcón, 23, 28014 Madrid

Teléfono:
34 913 30 28 00

Correo electrónico:
museo.nacional@prado.mcu.es

Internet:
http://museoprado.mcu.es

Horario:

martes a domingo:
9.00-19.00 h

24 y 31 de diciembre:
9.00-14.00 h

Cerrado[1]:
los lunes; 1 de enero; Viernes Santo, 1 de mayo y 25 de diciembre

Precio de Entrada:[2]

Público general:
3,01 Euros

Menores[3] de 18 años:
gratuito[4]

1 closed 2 admission 3 younger 4 free

Cesto Con Flores¹

Juan de Arellano, famoso pintor español, se especializó en la pintura² de flores. Esta obra es una de muchas obras que pintó con ese tema³. Como puedes ver, es una composición magnífica. Las flores están iluminadas en el centro para acentuar⁴ los colores y la belleza⁵.

1 basket with flowers   2 painting   3 theme   4 to highlight
5 beauty

La Familia de Carlos IV

Esta obra es de Francisco de Goya y Lucientes, uno de los artistas más famosos y el artista oficial de la Corte¹ de España. Es de la Familia Real y se llama *La Familia del Rey Carlos IV*. Los colores en esta pintura son extraordinarios. Hay muchas obras de Goya en el Prado.

1 Court

El Caballero¹

Esta pintura es de El Greco, uno de los más famosos pintores² españoles. En realidad, el verdadero nombre de El Greco es Doménikos Theotokópoulos. La mayoría de los temas de sus pinturas son religiosos y los colores en estas pinturas son vívidos y vibrantes. También son importantes sus retratos³, como éste de un caballero.

1 knight   2 painters   3 portraits

Después de leer

1. What time does the Prado generally close?
2. How much is admission to the museum?
3. What is the subject of many of Arellano's paintings?
4. Who are the people in Goya's painting?
5. What is El Greco's real name?

Puerto Rico

El coquí 🔊

Puerto Rico's Yunque rainforest covers 28,000 acres and is one of the oldest reserves in the Western Hemisphere. It is the only tropical rainforest in the U.S. National Forest System. The rainforest averages 240 inches of rain a year. The Yunque is home to 13 species of a tiny frog called the **coquí**. These frogs are considered a national symbol for the island. Read the following article to learn more about this unique amphibian.

Estruendo[1] musical

La voz[2] más famosa de Puerto Rico es la de una pequeña especie de rana que se llama coquí. Hay dieciséis especies de coquíes en Puerto Rico y trece de ellas viven en el Parque Nacional del Yunque. Se llama coquí porque por la noche miles de estas ranas salen y emiten un coro de cantos[3], "co-quí". El estruendo es muy fuerte porque una sola rana puede emitir hasta 100 decibeles, igual que una guitarra eléctrica. ¡Imagina un concierto de miles de guitarras eléctricas en tu vecindario[4] cada noche! El canto del coquí se oye por toda la isla de Puerto Rico.

1 racket   **2** voice   **3** calls, songs   **4** neighborhood

230

No soy renacuajo[1]

El coquí es una especie de rana muy interesante porque nunca pasa por una etapa[2] de renacuajo. La madre, o hembra[3], pone aproximadamente 28 huevos[4]. El padre, o macho[5], cuida de[6] los huevos. Después salen los coquíes bebés, ¡ya en forma de rana!

De muchos colores

Algunas personas, aun los puertorriqueños, piensan que el coquí es solamente[7] verde. La verdad[8] es que hay coquíes de muchos colores: marrones, grises, amarillos, azules, verdes o anaranjados, como el coquí dorado en esta foto. El coquí es muy importante en Puerto Rico porque come gran cantidad de insectos como mosquitos. Es un símbolo nacional y su música resuena[9] por toda la isla.

1 tadpole   2 stage   3 female   4 eggs   5 male
6 takes care of   7 only   8 the truth   9 resonates

Después de leer

1. What is **El Yunque**?
2. How did the **coquí** get its name?
3. Given the tiny size of the **coquí,** what is surprising about its call?
4. In what way are **coquíes** different from other frogs?
5. What color is the **coquí**?
6. Why is the **coquí** important in Puerto Rico?

Obras de Carmen Lomas Garza 🔊

Carmen Lomas Garza is one of the best-known Mexican American painters. In 1990 she published her first children's book, *Cuadros de familia*, in which she combines her paintings with her own warm writing style. She uses the book to explain her work and describe her childhood in Kingsville, Texas, near the border with Mexico. In her second book, *En mi familia*, 1996, Lomas Garza once again shares her memories of growing up in a traditional Mexican American community and family.

Read the following excerpts from these two books to experience a slice of life on the Texas border.

ESTRATEGIA

Actively picture in your mind what you are reading—the setting, the way the characters look and are dressed, their actions and speech. Visualization helps you create a context for what you are reading.

Tamalada de *Cuadros de familia*

Ésta es una escena de la cocina de mis padres. Todos están haciendo tamales. Mi abuelo tiene puesto rancheros[1] azules y camisa azul. Yo estoy al lado de él, con mi hermana Margie. Estamos ayudando a remojar[2] las hojas secas[3] del maíz[4]. Mi mamá está esparciendo la masa[5] de maíz sobre las hojas, y mis tíos están esparciendo la carne[6] sobre la masa. Mi abuelita está ordenando los tamales que ya están enrollados, cubiertos y listos[7] para cocer[8]. En algunas familias sólo las mujeres preparan tamales, pero en mi familia todos ayudan.

▲ *Tamalada* (1990)

---

1 overalls   **2** soak   **3** dry leaves   **4** corn   **5** spreading the dough   **6** meat   **7** rolled, covered, and ready   **8** to cook

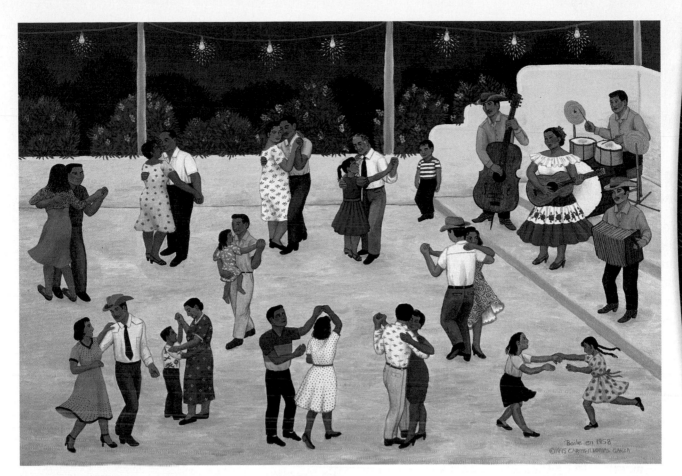

▲ **Baile en el Jardín** (1995)

Baile en el Jardín de En mi familia

Ésta es una noche de sábado en El Jardín, un restaurante familiar de mi pueblo natal[1].
Es verano y hace tanto calor que la gente baila afuera[2]. Un conjunto[3] toca con
tambora[4], acordeón, guitarra y bajo[5]. Ésta es la música con la que crecí[6]. Todos bailan
formando un gran círculo: las parejas[7] jóvenes, las parejas más grandes[8], y los viejitos
bailan con adolescentes o criaturas[9]. Hasta los bebés se ponen a bailar.

Para mí, el baile representa fiesta, celebración. Aquí está la música, los hermosos
vestidos, y todos los miembros de la familia bailan juntos. Es como el cielo. Es la gloria.

1 hometown
2 outside
3 band
4 drum
5 bass
6 I grew up with
7 couples
8 older
9 little ones

Después de leer

1. Name the four steps to making tamales that the author mentions.

2. In Lomas Garza's family, who makes the tamales?

3. In **Baile en el Jardín**, what is the weather like?

4. What instruments are in the band?

5. Who is dancing in **El jardín**?

6. Why does Lomas Garza like the dance?

Costa Rica

La artesanía chorotega 🔊

The small village of Guaitil is one of the centers of Costa Rican folk art. Nearly the entire town is dedicated to making pottery using the methods, tools, and designs that their ancestors, the Chorotegas, used hundreds of years ago. The craftsmen of Guaitil use natural paints and basic colors like red, black, white, and brown to decorate their pottery with traditional symbols of nature and daily life. Learn more about Chorotega artistry in the following interview with Gustavo, who is one of the youngest and most famous potters in the village.

E S T R A T E G I A

Many words can be understood based on how they are used in the sentence or paragraph. When you come to an unknown word, try to guess its meaning based on context (the other words around it).

Gustavo

¿Desde cuándo ayudas a tus padres en el taller[1] de cerámica?

Siempre me ha gustado ayudar a mi madre, Luz Marina; pero cuando era[2] pequeño lo que más me gustaba era modelar, hacer figuritas.

¿Y ahora?

Ahora pintar y decorar las piezas.

¿De dónde sacas estas ideas?

Bueno, los dibujos[3] que yo hago son aquellos que están en los libros antiguos[4] pero hay veces que invento otros dibujos para cambiar[5] y esos los saco de la mente[6], sólo de la mente.

¿Se te ocurren cuando estás pintándolas, o las pintas antes en un papel?

No, las pinto directamente sobre la tinaja[7].

---

1 workshop   **2** I was   **3** drawings   **4** old   **5** to change
6 mind   **7** ceramic jar

¿Hay algún sitio donde enseñan esta artesanía[1]?

Sí, la cooperativa de artesanos[2] del pueblo tiene una escuela y ahí se enseñan los diseños[3] que hacían nuestros antepasados[4] chorotegas.

¿Tienes en casa libros de dibujos precolombinos?

No, yo los diseños los tengo grabados[5] en la mente.

¿Cuánto tardas en pintar una tinaja grande?

Normalmente media hora, o tal vez un poco más.

¿Cuántas horas dedicas a esto?

Bueno, a veces mis padres tienen mucho trabajo y todos tenemos que colaborar[6]. Entonces puedo hacer hasta 20 vasijas medianas en un día. Pero cuando hay menos trabajo, pinto en mis ratos libres.

¿Te quieres dedicar exclusivamente a esto?

Ahora estoy empezando y me gusta mucho. Es posible que siga[7] con el taller de mis padres.

---

1 folk art
2 craftmen's cooperative
3 designs
4 ancestors
5 etched
6 to help out
7 that I may continue

Después de leer

1. What did Gustavo like to do when he was a small child?

2. What does he do now?

3. Does Gustavo draw his designs on paper first?

4. Where does Gustavo get his ideas for his designs?

5. How long does it take him to paint a piece of pottery?

Chile

Las novelas de Isabel Allende

Isabel Allende is from Peru, but she was raised in Chile. She is one of the most famous modern Latin American writers. Her novels and stories are read throughout the world. Her family is the theme of many of her stories and often her relatives are the inspiration for the characters in her novels. Today, Isabel Allende lives with her husband and family in California. Read the following commentary and the excerpt from one of her novels to learn more about her work and life in Chile.

ESTRATEGIA

Look at the title, the photos, and the important words in the text. Then read the first sentence of each paragraph. Skimming helps you understand the main ideas.

En 1981, Isabel Allende empezó[1] a escribir una carta a su abuelo en Chile. Un año más tarde esta carta de 500 páginas se convirtió[2] en su primera novela, *La casa de los espíritus (The House of the Spirits,* 1982).

Su novela *Paula* (1994) es la historia de su vida. Es dedicada a su hija, Paula, quien murió[3] a la edad[4] de 24 años, después de estar en el hospital por un año.

Vas a leer un fragmento de su libro *Mi país inventado,* en el que escribe sobre su familia y la historia de Chile. A través de[5] sus propios parientes[6] ilustra el carácter de los chilenos.

---

1 began   **2** became   **3** died   **4** age
5 by means of   **6** her own relatives

Por encima de[1] los clanes está la familia, inviolable y sagrada,[2] nadie escapa a sus deberes[3] con ella. Por ejemplo, el tío Ramón suele llamarme por teléfono a California, donde vivo, para comunicarme que murió un tío en tercer grado,[4] a quien no conocí,[5] y dejó[6] una hija en mala situación. La joven quiere estudiar enfermería,[7] pero no tiene medios[8] para hacerlo. Al tío Ramón, como el miembro de más edad del clan, le corresponde ponerse en contacto con cualquiera que tenga lazos de sangre con el difunto,[9] desde los parientes cercanos hasta los más remotos, para financiar los estudios de la futura enfermera. Negarse sería un acto vil,[10] que sería recordado[11] por varias generaciones.

---

1 at the top of   2 sacred   3 obligations   4 distant   5 hadn't met
6 left   7 nursing   8 means   9 whomever is related to the deceased
10 would be despicable   11 would be remembered

Después de leer

1. What is the theme of Isabel Allende's novels?
2. How did her first novel begin?
3. Who is Paula?
4. To whom do Chileans have obligations?
5. What does the daughter of Allende's uncle want to study?
6. Who helps her?

La Península Ibérica

FRANCIA

ANDORRA

MAR CANTÁBRICO

OCÉANO ATLÁNTICO

MAR MEDITERRÁNEO

Islas Baleares

Menorca

Mallorca
Palma

Ibiza

Gerona

Barcelona

Cataluña

Los Pirineos

Huesca

Zaragoza

Aragón

Río Ebro

San Sebastián
Bilbao
Santander

Asturias
Oviedo

Cordillera Cantábrica

Cantabria

País Vasco

Pamplona

Navarra

La Rioja
Logroño

Río

Castilla y León

León

Valladolid

Río Duero

Salamanca

Madrid

Madrid

Sierra de Guadarrama

Río Tajo

ESPAÑA

Comunidad Valenciana

Valencia

Alicante

Murcia
Murcia
Cartagena

Castilla-La Mancha

Toledo

Cáceres

Extremadura

Río Guadiana

Badajoz

Andalucía

Córdoba
Granada

Sierra Nevada

Río Guadalquivir

Sevilla

Málaga

Gibraltar (R.U.)

Estrecho de Gibraltar

Ceuta (Esp.)

Melilla (Esp.)

MARRUECOS

PORTUGAL

Lisboa

La Coruña

Galicia

OCÉANO ATLÁNTICO

Islas Canarias

MARRUECOS

Fuenteventura

Gran Canaria

Las Palmas

Santa Cruz de Tenerife

Tenerife

La Palma

OCÉANO ATLÁNTICO

N

100 Kilómetros

100 Millas

50

50

0

0

R2

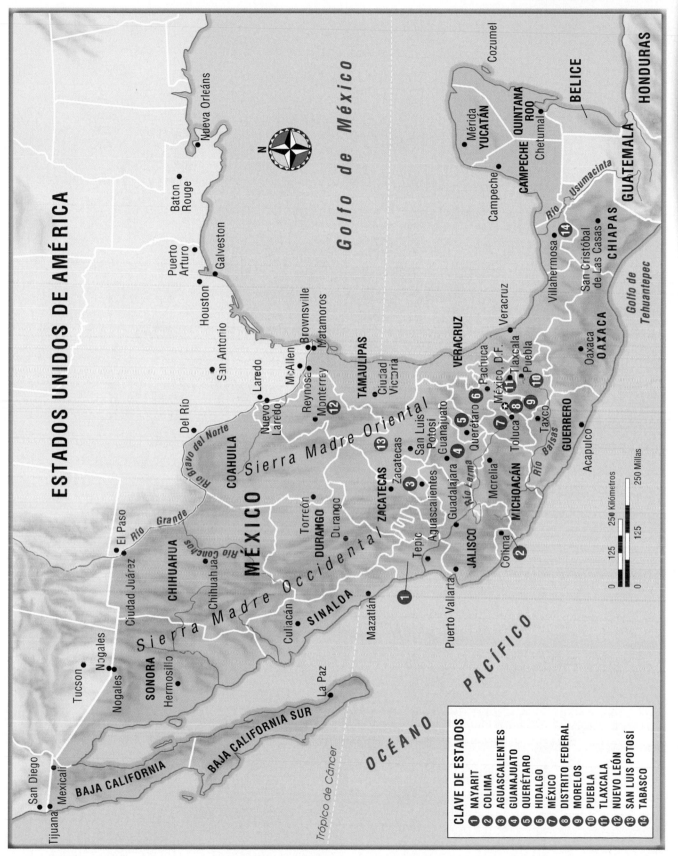

México

ESTADOS UNIDOS DE AMÉRICA

Golfo de México

San Diego
Tijuana
Mexicali
Nogales
Tucson
Nogales
SONORA
Hermosillo
La Paz
BAJA CALIFORNIA
BAJA CALIFORNIA SUR
Trópico de Cáncer

El Paso
Ciudad Juárez
CHIHUAHUA
Chihuahua
Río Grande
Río Bravo del Norte
Río Conchos
Sierra Madre Occidental
MÉXICO
COAHUILA
Sierra Madre Oriental
Del Río
Torreón
DURANGO
Durango
Nuevo Laredo
Laredo
Nuevo Laredo
Reynosa
McAllen
Matamoros
Brownsville
TAMAULIPAS
Ciudad Victoria

Mazatlán
Culiacán
SINALOA
Tepic
Aguascalientes
ZACATECAS
Zacatecas
San Luis Potosí
Guanajuato

Puerto Vallarta
JALISCO
Guadalajara
Colima
Río Lerma
Querétaro
MICHOACÁN
Morelia
Río Balsas
Toluca
Taxco
GUERRERO
Acapulco

México, D.F.
Pachuca
Tlaxcala
Puebla
VERACRUZ
Veracruz
OAXACA
Oaxaca
Villahermosa
Golfo de Tehuantepec

San Antonio
Houston
Puerto Arturo
Galveston
Baton Rouge
Nueva Orleáns

Mérida
YUCATÁN
Campeche
CAMPECHE
QUINTANA ROO
Cozumel
Chetumal
BELICE
Río Usumacinta
San Cristóbal de Las Casas
CHIAPAS
GUATEMALA
HONDURAS

OCÉANO PACÍFICO

CLAVE DE ESTADOS
1 NAYARIT
2 COLIMA
3 AGUASCALIENTES
4 GUANAJUATO
5 QUERÉTARO
6 HIDALGO
7 MÉXICO
8 DISTRITO FEDERAL
9 MORELOS
10 PUEBLA
11 TLAXCALA
12 NUEVO LEÓN
13 SAN LUIS POTOSÍ
14 TABASCO

0 125 250 Kilómetros
0 125 250 Millas

R3

Estados Unidos de América

Golfo de San Lorenzo

OCÉANO ATLÁNTICO

CUBA

CANADÁ

ESTADOS UNIDOS DE AMÉRICA

MÉXICO

OCÉANO PACÍFICO

Augusta
Boston
Quebec
Nueva York
Montreal
Ottawa
Filadelfia
Río Hudson
Baltimore
Washington, D.C.
Bahía Chesapeake
Richmond
Raleigh
Charlotte
Columbia
Cataratas de El Niágara
Lago Ontario
Buffalo
Cleveland
Lago Erie
Toledo
Detroit
Columbus
Cincinnati
Louisville
Nashville
Atlanta
Montgomery
Tallahassee
Orlando
Cabo Cañaveral
Lago Okeechobee
Miami
Cayos de La Florida
Cayo Hueso
La Habana
Lago Hurón
Lago Michigan
Milwaukee
Chicago
Indianápolis
San Luis
Memphis
Jackson
Baton Rouge
Nueva Orleáns
San Petersburgo
Lago Superior
Río Misisipi
Des Moines
Kansas City
Topeka
Wichita
Tulsa
Little Rock
Oklahoma City
Dallas
Austin
Houston
Golfo de México
Mineápolis
Lincoln
Lago Winnipeg
Fargo
Winnipeg
Rapid City
Cheyenne
Colorado Springs
Denver
Pueblo
Santa Fe
Albuquerque
Amarillo
El Paso
Ciudad Juárez
San Antonio
Laredo
Nuevo Laredo
Brownsville
Matamoros
Monterrey
Hermosillo
Chihuahua
Río Grande
Helena
Boise
Montañas Rocosas
Gran Cañón
Gran Lago Salado
Salt Lake City
Provo
Río Colorado
Phoenix
Tucson
Nogales
Nogales
Mexicali
Tijuana
San Diego
San Bernardino
Los Ángeles
Las Vegas
Reno
Sacramento
San Francisco
San José
Fresno
Santa Bárbara
Sierra Nevada
Cordillera de las Cascadas
Vancouver
Seattle
Portland
Salem
Península de Baja California
Golfo de California

N
300 Kilómetros 600
0 300 600 Millas
0

Islas Hawaii
Honolulú
Kailua Kona

Río Yukón
Meseta de Alaska
Anchorage
Juneau
Golfo de Alaska
Bethel
Mar de Bering

América Central y las Antillas

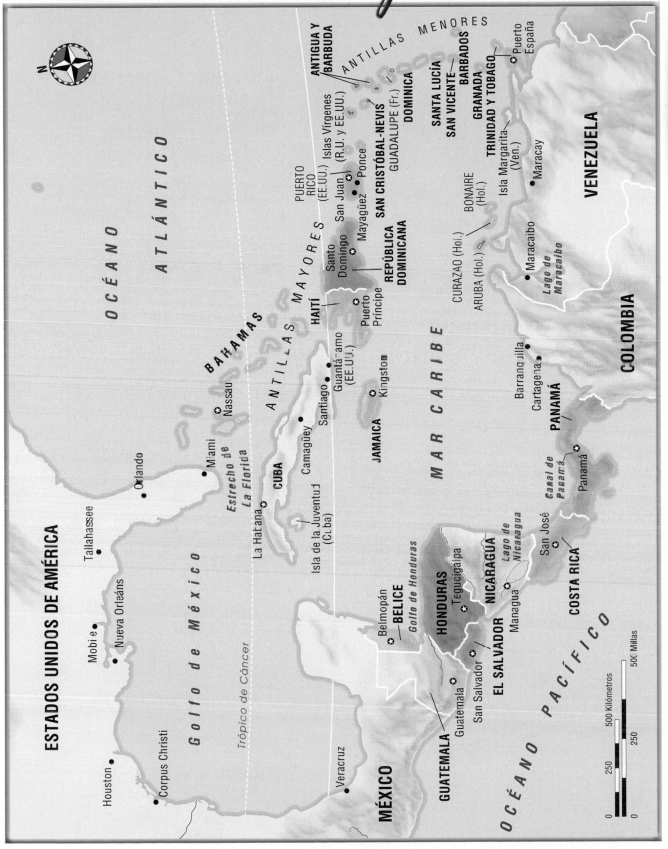

América del Sur

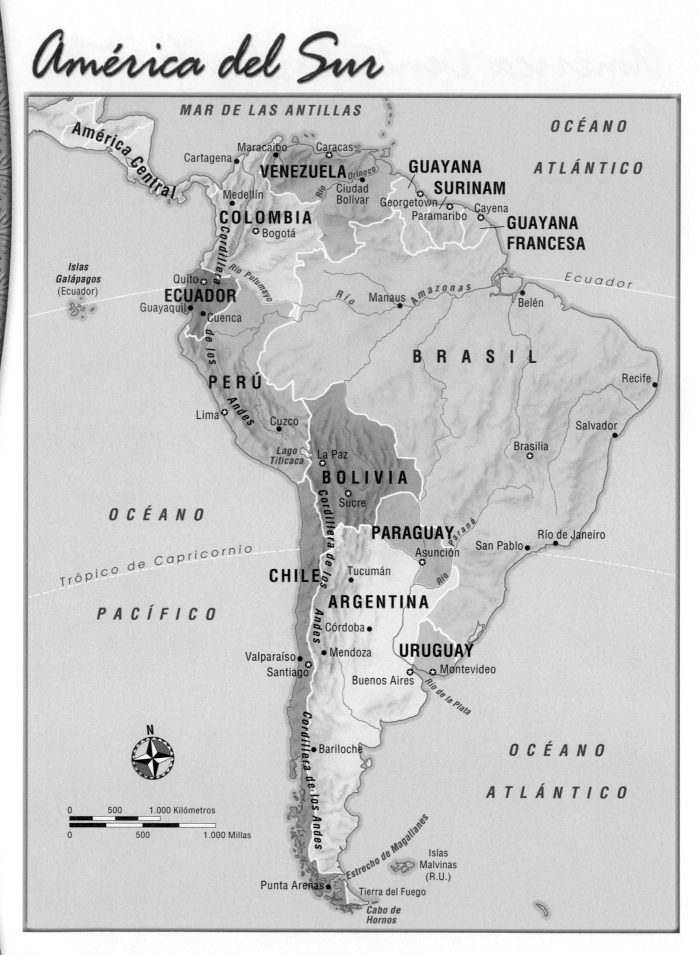

MAR DE LAS ANTILLAS

América Central

OCÉANO

ATLÁNTICO

Cartagena
Maracaibo
Caracas
VENEZUELA
Orinoco
GUAYANA
SURINAM
Medellín
Ciudad Bolívar
Georgetown
Cayena
COLOMBIA
Paramaribo
GUAYANA
Bogotá
FRANCESA

Islas Galápagos (Ecuador)

Quito
ECUADOR
Río Putumayo
Ecuador
Guayaquil
Cuenca
Río
Amazonas
Manaus
Belén

PERÚ
B R A S I L
Recife

Lima
Andes
Cuzco
Salvador

Lago Titicaca
La Paz
Brasilia

BOLIVIA
Sucre

OCÉANO
Paraná
PARAGUAY
Río de Janeiro

Trópico de Capricornio
CHILE
Asunción
San Pablo
Tucumán
Río

PACÍFICO
ARGENTINA
Córdoba
URUGUAY
Valparaíso
Mendoza
Montevideo
Santiago
Buenos Aires
Río de la Plata

N

Cordillera de los Andes
Bariloche

OCÉANO

ATLÁNTICO

0   500   1.000 Kilómetros
0   500   1.000 Millas

Estrecho de Magallanes
Islas Malvinas (R.U.)
Punta Arenas
Tierra del Fuego

Cabo de Hornos

Vocabulario adicional

This list includes additional vocabulary that you may want to use to personalize activities. If you can't find a word you need here, try the Spanish-English and English-Spanish vocabulary sections, beginning on page R23.

Materias (School Subjects)

el álgebra	algebra
el cálculo	calculus
la contabilidad	accounting
la física	physics
la geometría	geometry
el italiano	Italian
el japonés	Japanese
el latín	Latin
la literatura	literature
el ruso	Russian

Celebraciones (Celebrations)

el bautizo	baptism
la canción	song
El Día de los Reyes	Three Kings Day
la Pascua Florida	Easter
las Pascuas	Christmas
el Ramadán	Ramadan
Rosh Hashaná	Rosh Hashanah

Comida (Food)

el ají picante (el chile)	hot pepper
el aguacate	avocado
las arvejas	peas
el azúcar	sugar
la banana (el guineo)	banana
la batida, el batido	milkshake
la cereza	cherry
la coliflor	cauliflower
el champiñón (el hongo)	mushroom
los condimentos	seasonings
los fideos	noodles
el filete de pescado	fish fillet
la lechuga	lettuce
la mayonesa	mayonnaise
el melón	cantaloupe
la mostaza	mustard
la pimienta	pepper
la piña	pineapple
el plátano	plantain

la sal	salt
el yogur	yogurt

Computadoras (Computers)

arrastrar	to drag
la búsqueda	search
buscar	to search
comenzar la sesión	to log on
la contraseña, el código	password
el disco duro	hard drive
en línea	online
grabar	to save
hacer clic	to click
la impresora	printer
imprimir	to print
el marcapáginas, el separador	bookmark
el ordenador	computer
la página Web inicial	homepage
el ratón	mouse
el reproductor de MP3	MP3 player
la Red	the Net
subir archivos	to upload files
la tecla de aceptación	return key
la tecla de borrar, la tecla correctora	delete key
el teclado	keyboard
terminar la sesión	to log off
la unidad de CD-ROM	CD-ROM drive
el Web, la Telaraña Mundial	World Wide Web

De compras (Shopping)

cobrar	to charge
el dinero en efectivo	cash
el descuento	discount
en venta	for sale
la rebaja	sale, sale price
regatear	to bargain
la tarjeta de crédito	credit card
la tarjeta débito	debit card
el (la) vendedor, -ora	salesperson

Deportes y pasatiempos
(Sports and Hobbies)

el anuario	yearbook
las artes marciales	martial arts
la astronomía	astronomy
el ballet	ballet
el boxeo	boxing
coleccionar sellos (monedas, muñecas)	to collect stamps (coins, dolls)
coser	to sew
el drama	drama
la fotografía	photography
la gimnasia	gymnastics
jugar a las cartas	to play cards
jugar a las damas	to play checkers
la orquesta	orchestra
el patinaje en línea, (sobre hielo)	inline (ice) skating

En el cine o el teatro
(At the Movies or Theater)

el actor	actor
actuar	to act
la actriz	actress
aplaudir	to applaud
la butaca	box seat
la escena	scene
el escenario	stage
el espectáculo	performance, show
la estrella	star
la pantalla	screen
el telón	curtain

En el consultorio (At the Clinic)

la alergia	allergy
el antibiótico	antibiotic
ponerle a uno una inyección	to give someone a shot
el dolor	pain
los escalofríos	chills
estornudar	to sneeze
la gripe	flu
la medicina	medicine
las pastillas, las píldoras	pills, tablets
el síntoma	symptom
la tos	cough
toser	to cough

En el zoológico (At the Zoo)

el ave, las aves	bird, birds
el canguro	kangaroo
la cebra	zebra
el cocodrilo	crocodile
el delfín	dolphin
el elefante	elephant
el gorila	gorilla
el hipopótamo	hippopotamus
la jirafa	giraffe
el león	lion
la foca	seal
el mono, el chango	monkey
el oso	bear
el oso polar	polar bear
el pingüino	penguin
la serpiente	snake
el tigre	tiger

En la casa (Around the House)

la alfombra	rug, carpet
el ático	attic
el balcón	balcony
las cortinas	curtains
el despertador	alarm clock
las escaleras	stairs
el espejo	mirror
el estante	bookcase
el fregadero	kitchen sink
la galería	porch
la lámpara	lamp
el lavamanos	bathroom sink
la lavadora	washing machine
la mesita de noche	nightstand
los muebles	furniture
la secadora	dryer

el sillón	easy chair
el sótano	basement
el timbre	doorbell
el tocador	dresser

En las afueras y en la ciudad
(Places around Town)

la autopista	highway
el banco	bank
la esquina	street corner
la estación de autobuses (trenes)	bus (train) station
la fábrica	factory
la ferretería	hardware store
la farmacia	drugstore
la gasolinera	gas station
el hospital	hospital
la mezquita	mosque
el mercado	market
la oficina	office
la parada de autobuses	bus stop
la peluquería	barbershop
el puente	bridge
el rascacielos	skyscraper
el salón de belleza	beauty salon
el semáforo	traffic light
el supermercado	supermarket

Instrumentos musicales
(Musical Instruments)

el acordeón	accordion
el arpa, las arpas	harp
la armónica	harmonica
el bajo	bass
la batería	drum set
el clarinete	clarinet
la flauta dulce	recorder
la flauta	flute
la guitarra	guitar
la mandolina	mandolin
las maracas	maracas
el oboe	oboe
el saxofón	saxophone
el sintetizador	synthesizer
el tambor	drum
el trombón	trombone
la trompeta	trumpet
la tuba	tuba
la tumbadora	conga drum
la viola	viola
el violín	violin

La familia (Family)

el (la) ahijado(a)	godson, goddaughter
el (la) bisabuelo(a)	great-grandfather, great-grandmother
el (la) biznieto(a)	great-grandson, great-granddaughter
el (la) cuñado(a)	brother-in-law, sister-in-law
el (la) hijastro(a)	stepson, stepdaughter
la madrina	godmother
la madrastra	stepmother
la nuera	daughter-in-law
el padrino	godfather
el padrastro	stepfather
el (la) suegro(a)	father-in-law, mother-in-law
el yerno	son-in-law

Palabras descriptivas
(Descriptive Words)

amistoso(a)	friendly
la barba	beard
bien educado(a)	well-mannered
el bigote	mustache
calvo(a)	bald
la estatura	height
flaco(a)	skinny
lindo(a)	pretty
las pecas	freckles
las patillas	sideburns
el pelo lacio	straight hair
el pelo rizado	curly hair
pesar	to weigh
tranquilo(a)	quiet

Partes del cuerpo (Parts of the Body)

la barbilla	chin
las cejas	eyebrows
la cintura	waist
el codo	elbow
la frente	forehead
los labios	lips
la muñeca	wrist
el muslo	thigh
las pestañas	eyelashes
la rodilla	knee
la sien	temple
el tobillo	ankle
la uña	nail

Profesiones (Professions)

el (la) abogado(a)	lawyer
el (la) arquitecto(a)	architect
el (la) bombero(a)	firefighter
el (la) cartero(a)	mail carrier
el (la) cocinero(a)	cook
el (la) conductor, -ora	driver
el (la) constructor, -ora	builder
el (la) decorador, -ora	interior decorator

el (la) dentista	dentist
el (la) detective	detective
el (la) enfermero(a)	nurse
el (la) escritor, -ora	writer
el hombre (la mujer) de negocios	businessman, businesswoman
el (la) ingeniero(a)	engineer
el (la) médico(a)	doctor
el (la) piloto(a)	pilot
el (la) (mujer) policía	police officer
el (la) secretario(a)	secretary

Regalos (Gifts)

la agenda	agenda, daily planner
el álbum	album
el animal de peluche	stuffed animal
los bombones	chocolates
el calendario	calendar
los claveles	carnations
la colonia	cologne
las flores	flowers
el llavero	key chain
el perfume	perfume
el rompecabezas	puzzle
las rosas	roses

Ropa (Clothes)

la bata	robe
la bufanda	scarf
el chaleco	vest
las chancletas	flip-flops
la corbata	tie
los guantes	gloves
las medias	socks, stockings, hose
las pantuflas, las zapatillas	slippers
el pañuelo	handkerchief
el paraguas	umbrella
la ropa interior	underwear
los tacones, los zapatos de tacón	high heels

Temas de actualidad (Current Issues)

el bosque tropical	rain forest
la contaminación	pollution
el crimen	crime
los derechos humanos	human rights
la economía	economy
la educación	education
la guerra	war

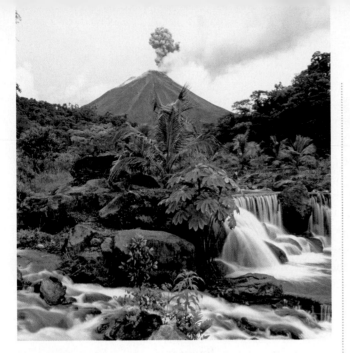

el medio ambiente	environment
el mundo	world
las noticias	news
la paz	peace
la política	politics
la tecnología	technology
la violencia	violence

Vacaciones (Vacation)

la agencia de viajes	travel agency
el andén	train platform
el asiento	seat
los cheques de viajero	traveler's checks
hacer una reservación	to make a reservation
el horario	schedule, timetable
el mar	sea

la parada	stop
el pasillo	aisle
reservado(a)	reserved
la ventanilla	window
la visa	visa
visitar los lugares de interés	to sightsee
volar	to fly

Refranes (Proverbs)

Más vale pájaro en mano que cien volando.
A bird in the hand is worth two in the bush.

Hijo no tenemos y nombre le ponemos.
Don't count your chickens before they're hatched.

Quien primero viene, primero tiene.
The early bird catches the worm.

Más vale tarde que nunca.
Better late than never.

El hábito no hace al monje.
Clothes don't make the man.

Más ven cuatro ojos que dos.
Two heads are better than one.

Querer es poder.
Where there's a will, there's a way.

Ojos que no ven, corazón que no siente.
Out of sight, out of mind.

No todo lo que brilla es oro.
All that glitters is not gold.

Caras vemos, corazones no sabemos.
You can't judge a book by its cover.

Donde una puerta se cierra, otra se abre.
Every cloud has a silver lining.

En boca cerrada no entran moscas.
Silence is golden.

Dime con quién andas y te diré quién eres.
Birds of a feather flock together.

Al mal tiempo buena cara.
When life gives you lemons, make lemonade.

Antes que te cases mira lo que haces.
Look before you leap.

Expresiones de ¡Exprésate!

Functions are the ways in which you use a language for particular purposes. In specific situations, such as in a restaurant, in a grocery store, or at school, you will want to communicate with those around you. In order to do that, you have to "function" in Spanish: you place an order, make a purchase, or talk about your class schedule.

Here is a list of the functions presented in *¡Exprésate! 1A* for Chapters 1–5 along with the Spanish expressions you'll need to communicate in a wide range of situations. Following each function is the chapter and page number from the book where it is introduced.

Socializing

Greetings
Ch. 1, p. 8
> Buenos días, señor.
> Buenas noches, señora.
> Buenas tardes, señorita.

Saying Goodbye
Ch. 1, p. 8
> Adiós.
> Tengo que irme.
> Hasta luego.
> Buenas noches.
> Hasta mañana.
> Nos vemos.
> Hasta pronto.

Asking how someone is and saying how you are
Ch. 1, p. 8
> Hola, ¿cómo estás?
> ¿Cómo está usted?
> ¿Qué tal?
> Estoy bien/regular/mal.
> ¿Y usted?
> Más o menos. ¿Y tú?

Introducing people
Ch. 1, p. 10
> Éste(a) es... Es un(a) compañero(a) de clase.
> Encantado(a).
> Mucho gusto.
> Igualmente.
> Ésta es... (Ella) es mi profesora de...
> Éste es... (Él) es mi profesor de...

Inviting others to do something
Ch. 4, p. 158
> ¿Qué tal si vamos a...?
> No sé. ¿Sabes qué? No tengo ganas.
> Vienes conmigo a..., ¿no?
> ¡Claro que sí! Tengo mucha hambre.

> Hay un concierto.
> Vas a ir, ¿verdad?
> No, no voy a ir. Tengo que...

Exchanging Information

Asking and giving names
Ch. 1, p. 6
> ¿Cómo te llamas?
> ¿Cómo se llama usted?
> Me llamo... ¿Y tú?
> Soy...
> ¿Quién es...?
> Él (Ella) es...
> ¿Cómo se llama (él/ella)?
> (Él/Ella) se llama...

Saying where you and others are from
Ch. 1, p. 11
> ¿De dónde eres?
> ¿De dónde es usted?
> Soy de...
> ¿De dónde es...?
> Es de...

Asking and giving phone numbers
Ch. 1, p. 19
> ¿Cuál es tu teléfono?
> Es tres-dos-cinco-uno-dos-tres-uno.
> ¿Cuál es el teléfono de...?
> Es...

Saying what time it is
Ch. 1, p. 20
> ¿Qué hora es?
> Son las seis y cuarto de la mañana.
> Es la una en punto.
> Son las... y trece de la tarde.
> Son las... y media de la tarde.
> Son las... menos cuarto.

Son las... menos diez de la noche.
Es mediodía.
Es medianoche.

Asking and giving the date and the day
Ch. 1, p. 21

¿Qué fecha es hoy?
Es el primero (dos, tres...) de enero.
¿Qué día es hoy?
Hoy es...

Asking how words are spelled and giving e-mail addresses
Ch. 1, p. 23

¿Cómo se escribe...?
Se escribe...
¿Cuál es tu correo electrónico?
Es...
¿Cuál es el correo electrónico de...?
Es eme punto ge-o-ene-zeta-a-ele-o arroba
ere-e-de punto hache-cre-uve doble punto a-ere.

Describing people
Ch. 2, p. 49

¿Cómo es...?
... es moreno(a). También es... y un poco...
¿Cómo eres? ¿Eres cómico(a)?
Sí, soy bastante cómico(a).

Asking and saying how old someone is
Ch. 2, p. 52

¿Cuántos años tienes?
Tengo ... años.
¿Cuántos años tiene...?
... tiene ... años
¿Cuándo es tu cumpleaños?
Es el 6 de mayo.
¿Cuándo es el cumpleaños de...?
Es el...

Describing things
Ch. 2, p. 66

¿Cómo es...?
Es...
Es (muy)...
Es bastante...
Es algo...

Talking about what you and others want to do
Ch. 3, p. 98

¿Qué quieres hacer hoy?
Ni idea.
¿Quieres ir a... conmigo?
Está bien.
No, gracias. No quiero ir a... hoy.

Talking about everyday activities
Ch. 3, p. 109

¿Qué haces los fines de semana?
Los sábados, cuando hace buen tiempo, voy...
¿Qué hace... cuando hace mal tiempo?
Le gusta...
No va a ninguna parte.

Asking and saying how often
Ch. 3, p. 112

¿Con qué frecuencia vas a...?
Casi nunca. No me gusta...
¿Te gusta...?
Sí. Después de clases, casi siempre vamos a...
A veces vamos también a...

Talking about what you and others have or need
Ch. 4, p. 141

¿Necesitas algo para el colegio?
Sí, necesito muchas cosas.
No, no necesito nada.
¿Necesitas algo para la clase de...?
Sí, necesito...
¿Tienes...?
Sí, tengo un montón.
No, no tengo.

Talking about classes
Ch. 4, p. 144

¿Qué clases tienes...?
Primero tengo... y después tengo...
¿Cuál es tu materia preferida?
Mi materia preferida es... Es fácil.
No me gusta la clase de... porque es difícil.

Talking about plans
Ch. 4, p. 155

¿Vas a ir a... el... por la...?
No. Tengo...
¿Qué vas a hacer el... próximo?
Voy a... y después... Luego regreso...
¿A qué hora vas a llegar a...?
Voy a llegar temprano (a tiempo).
    No me gusta llegar tarde.

Describing people and family relationships
Ch. 5, p. 187

¿Cuántas personas hay en tu familia?
En mi familia somos... personas.
¿Cómo es tu familia?
Somos delgados y tenemos el pelo rubio.
    Todos usamos lentes. Mi... está en una
    silla de ruedas.

¿Cómo es tu...?
Es... Es una persona... (Él/Ella) y mi...
   tienen... hijos pero no tienen...

Describing where someone lives
Ch. 5, p. 201
   ¿Dónde viven ustedes?
   Vivimos en un apartamento. Está en un edificio
      de... pisos.
   ¿Cuál es tu dirección?
   Es calle..., número...
   ¿Cómo es tu casa?
   Es bastante... Tiene... habitaciones y un... y...
      muy bonitos.

Talking about your responsibilities
Ch. 5, p. 204
   ¿Qué te parece tener que ayudar en casa?
   A veces tengo que..., pero me parece bien.
      No es gran cosa.
   ¿Qué te toca hacer a ti?
   A mí siempre me toca... ¡Qué lata!
   A menudo tengo que...
   A... nunca le toca... Me parece injusto.

Expressing Attitudes and Opinions

Talking about what you and others like
Ch. 2, p. 63
   ¿Te gusta(n)...?
   Sí, me gusta(n) mucho.
   No, no me gusta(n).
   ¿Te gusta(n) más... o...?
   Me gusta(n) más...
   Me da igual.

Talking about what you and others like to do
Ch. 3, pp. 94–95
   ¿Qué te gusta hacer?
   A mí me gusta...
   ¿A... les gusta...?
   Sí, porque les gusta...

Síntesis gramatical

NOUNS AND ARTICLES

Gender of Nouns

In Spanish, nouns (words that name a person, place, or thing) are grouped into two classes or genders: masculine and feminine. All nouns, both persons and objects, fall into one of these groups. Most nouns that end in **-o** are masculine, and most nouns that end in **-a, -ción, -tad,** and **-dad** are feminine. Some nouns, such as **estudiante** and **cliente,** can be either masculine or feminine.

Masculine Nouns	Feminine Nouns
libro	casa
chico	universidad
cuaderno	situación
bolígrafo	mesa
vestido	libertad

FORMATION OF PLURAL NOUNS

	Add **-s** to nouns that end in a vowel.		Add **-es** to nouns that end in a consonant.		With nouns that end in **-z,** the **-z** changes to a **-c.**	
SINGULAR	libro	casa	profesor	papel	vez	lápiz
PLURAL	libro**s**	casa**s**	profesor**es**	papel**es**	ve**ces**	lápi**ces**

Definite Articles

There are words that signal the gender of the noun. One of these is the *definite article.* In English, there is one definite article: *the.* In Spanish, there are four: **el, la, los, las.**

SUMMARY OF DEFINITE ARTICLES

	Masculine	Feminine
SINGULAR	**el** chico	**la** chica
PLURAL	**los** chicos	**las** chicas

CONTRACTIONS

a + el → **al**
de + el → **del**

Indefinite Articles

Another group of words that are used with nouns are the *indefinite articles:* **un, una,** (*a* or *an*) and **unos, unas** (*some* or *a few*).

	Masculine	Feminine
SINGULAR	**un** chico	**una** chica
PLURAL	**unos** chicos	**unas** chicas

Pronouns

Subject Pronouns	Direct Object Pronouns	Indirect Object Pronouns	Objects of Prepositions	Reflexive Pronouns
yo	me	me	mí	me
tú	te	te	ti	te
él, ella, usted	lo, la	le	él, ella, usted	se
nosotros, nosotras	nos	nos	nosotros, nosotras	nos
vosotros, vosotras	os	os	vosotros, vosotras	os
ellos, ellas, ustedes	los, las	les	ellos, ellas, ustedes	se

ADJECTIVES

Adjectives are words that describe nouns. The adjective must agree in gender (masculine or feminine) and number (singular or plural) with the noun it modifies. Adjectives that end in -e or a consonant only agree in number.

		Masculine	Feminine
Adjectives that end in **-o** or **-a**	SINGULAR	chico alt**o**	chica alt**a**
	PLURAL	chicos alt**os**	chicas alt**as**
Adjectives that end in **-e**	SINGULAR	chico inteligent**e**	chica inteligent**e**
	PLURAL	chicos inteligent**es**	chicas inteligent**es**
Adjectives that end in a consonant	SINGULAR	examen difícil	clase difícil
	PLURAL	exámenes difícil**es**	clases difícil**es**

Demonstrative Adjectives

	Masculine	Feminine		Masculine	Feminine
SINGULAR	**este** chico	**esta** chica	SINGULAR	**ese** chico	**esa** chica
PLURAL	**estos** chicos	**estas** chicas	PLURAL	**esos** chicos	**esas** chicas

When demonstratives are used as pronouns, they match the gender and number of the noun they replace and are written with an accent mark: **éste, éstos, ésta, éstas, ése, ésos, ésa, ésas.**

Possessive Adjectives

These words also modify nouns and show ownership or relationships between people (*my* car, *his* book, *her* mother).

SINGULAR		PLURAL	
Masculine	Feminine	Masculine	Feminine
mi libro	**mi** casa	**mis** libros	**mis** casas
tu libro	**tu** casa	**tus** libros	**tus** casas
su libro	**su** casa	**sus** libros	**sus** casas
nuestro libro	**nuestra** casa	**nuestros** libros	**nuestras** casas
vuestro libro	**vuestra** casa	**vuestros** libros	**vuestras** casas

Comparatives

Comparatives are used to compare people or things. With comparisons of inequality, the same structure is used with adjectives, adverbs, or nouns. With comparisons of equality, **tan** is used with adjectives and adverbs, and **tanto/a/os/as** with nouns.

COMPARISONS OF INEQUALITY

$$\left. \begin{array}{c} \textbf{más} \\ \textbf{menos} \end{array} \right\} + \left\{ \begin{array}{c} \text{adjective} \\ \text{adverb} \\ \text{noun} \end{array} \right\} + \textbf{que} \quad \left. \begin{array}{c} \textbf{más} \\ \textbf{menos} \end{array} \right\} + \textbf{de} + \text{number}$$

COMPARISONS OF EQUALITY

tan + adjective or adverb + **como**
tanto/a/os/as + noun + **como**

These adjectives have irregular comparative forms.

bueno(a) *good*	malo(a) *bad*	joven *young*	viejo(a) *old*
mejor(es) *better*	**peor(es)** *worse*	**menor(es)** *younger*	**mayor(es)** *older*

Ordinal Numbers

Ordinal numbers are used to express ordered sequences. They agree in number and gender with the noun they modify. The ordinal numbers **primero** and **tercero** drop the final **o** before a singular, masculine noun. Ordinal numbers are seldom used after 10. Cardinal numbers are used instead: **Alfonso XIII, Alfonso Trece.**

1st primero/a	5th quinto/a	9th noveno/a
2nd segundo/a	6th sexto/a	10th décimo/a
3rd tercero/a	7th séptimo/a	
4th cuarto/a	8th octavo/a	

Affirmative and Negative Expressions

Affirmative	Negative
algo	nada
alguien	nadie
alguno (algún), -a	ninguno (ningún), -a
o ... o	ni ... ni
siempre	nunca

Interrogative words

¿Adónde?	¿Cuándo?	¿De dónde?	¿Qué?
¿Cómo?	¿Cuánto(a)?	¿Dónde?	¿Quién(es)?
¿Cuál(es)?	¿Cuántos(as)?	¿Por qué?	

Adverbs

Adverbs make the meaning of a verb, an adjective, or another adverb more definite. These are some common adverbs of frequency.

siempre	*always*	**casi nunca**	*almost never*
nunca	*never*	**a veces**	*sometimes*
todos los días	*every day*		

Prepositions

Prepositions are words that show the relationship of a noun or pronoun to another word. These are common prepositions in Spanish.

a	*to*	**delante de**	*before*	**hacia**	*toward*
al lado de	*next to*	**desde**	*from*	**hasta**	*until*
antes de	*before*	**detrás de**	*behind*	**para**	*for, in order to*
con	*with*	**en**	*in, on*	**por**	*for, by*
de	*of, from*	**encima de**	*over, on top of*	**sin**	*without*
debajo de	*under*				

VERBS

Present Tense of Regular Verbs

In Spanish, we use a formula to conjugate regular verbs. The endings change in each person, but the stem of the verb remains the same.

Infinitive	habl**ar**		com**er**		escrib**ir**	
Present	habl**o**	habl**amos**	com**o**	com**emos**	escrib**o**	escrib**imos**
	habl**as**	habl**áis**	com**es**	com**éis**	escrib**es**	escrib**ís**
	habl**a**	habl**an**	com**e**	com**en**	escrib**e**	escrib**en**

Verbs with Irregular *yo* Forms

hacer		poner		saber		salir		traer	
hago	hacemos	**pongo**	ponemos	**sé**	sabemos	**salgo**	salimos	**traigo**	traemos
haces	hacéis	pones	ponéis	sabes	sabéis	sales	salís	traes	traéis
hace	hacen	pone	ponen	sabe	saben	sale	salen	trae	traen

tener		venir		ver		conocer	
tengo	tenemos	**vengo**	venimos	**veo**	vemos	**conozco**	conocemos
tienes	tenéis	vienes	venís	ves	veis	conoces	conocéis
tiene	tienen	viene	vienen	ve	ven	conoce	conocen

Verbs with Irregular Forms

ser		estar		ir	
soy	somos	estoy	estamos	voy	vamos
eres	sois	estás	estáis	vas	vais
es	son	está	están	va	van

Present Progressive

The present progressive in English is formed by using the verb *to be* plus the *-ing* form of another verb. In Spanish, the present progressive is formed by using the verb **estar** plus the **-ndo** form of another verb.

-ar verbs	**-er** and **-ir** verbs
hablar → estoy habl**ando**	comer → está com**iendo**
trabajar → estás trabaj**ando**	escribir → estamos escrib**iendo**

For **-er** and **-ir** verbs with a stem that ends in a vowel, the **-iendo** changes to **-yendo**:

leer → están le**yendo**

Stem-Changing Verbs

In Spanish, some verbs have an irregular stem in the present tense. The final vowel of the stem changes from e → ie, o → ue, u → ue, and e → i in all forms except **nosotros** and **vosotros**.

e → ie		o → ue		u → ue		e → i	
preferir		**poder**		**jugar**		**pedir**	
pref**ie**ro	preferimos	p**ue**do	podemos	j**ue**go	jugamos	p**i**do	pedimos
pref**ie**res	preferís	p**ue**des	podéis	j**ue**gas	jugáis	p**i**des	pedís
pref**ie**re	pref**ie**ren	p**ue**de	p**ue**den	j**ue**ga	j**ue**gan	p**i**de	p**i**den

Some **e → ie** stem-changing verbs are:		Some **o → ue** stem-changing verbs are:		Some **e → i** stem-changing verbs are:
empezar	**venir**	**almorzar**	**dormir**	**vestirse**
pensar	**merendar**	**llover**	**probar**	**servir**
querer	**calentar**	**encontrar**	**acostarse**	
nevar	**tener**	**volver**	**costar**	

The Verbs *gustar* and *encantar*

The verb endings for **gustar** and **encantar** always agree with what is liked or loved. The indirect object pronouns always precede the verb forms.

gustar (to like)		encantar (to really like or love)	
one thing: **me** **te** **le** **nos** **os** **les** } gusta	more than one: **me** **te** **le** **nos** **os** **les** } gustan	one thing: **me** **te** **le** **nos** **os** **les** } encanta	more than one: **me** **te** **le** **nos** **os** **les** } encantan

Verbs with Reflexive Pronouns

If the subject and object of a verb are the same, include the reflexive pronoun with the verb.

lavarse		ponerse		vestirse	
me lavo	**nos** lavamos	**me** pongo	**nos** ponemos	**me** visto	**nos** vestimos
te lavas	**os** laváis	**te** pones	**os** ponéis	**te** vistes	**os** vestís
se lava	**se** lavan	**se** pone	**se** ponen	**se** viste	**se** visten

Here are other verbs with reflexive pronouns.

acostarse	**bañarse**	**maquillarse**	**secarse**
afeitarse	**levantarse**	**peinarse**	**sentirse**

Preterite of Regular and Irregular Verbs

The preterite is used to talk about what happened at a specific point in time.

Infinitive	Preterite of Regular Verbs	
hablar	hablé	hablamos
	hablaste	hablasteis
	habló	hablaron
comer	comí	comimos
	comiste	comisteis
	comió	comieron
escribir	escribí	escribimos
	escribiste	escribisteis
	escribió	escribieron

hacer	ir	ser	ver
hice	fui	fui	vi
hiciste	fuiste	fuiste	viste
hizo	fue	fue	vio
hicimos	fuimos	fuimos	vimos
hicisteis	fuisteis	fuisteis	visteis
hicieron	fueron	fueron	vieron

sacar	llegar	comenzar
saqué	llegué	comencé
sacaste	llegaste	comenzaste
sacó	llegó	comenzó
sacamos	llegamos	comenzamos
sacasteis	llegasteis	comenzasteis
sacaron	llegaron	comenzaron

Imperative Mood

The imperative is used to tell people to do things. Its forms are sometimes referred to as *commands*. Regular affirmative commands are formed by dropping the **s** from the end of the **tú** form of the verb. For negative commands, switch the **-as** ending to **-es** and the **-es** ending to **-as**.

(tú) hablas → habla (no hables)	you speak → speak (don't speak)
(tú) escribes → escribe (no escribas)	you write → write (don't write)
(tú) pides → pide (no pidas)	you ask for → ask for (don't ask for)

Some verbs have irregular **tú** imperative forms.

tener → ten (no tengas)	ser → sé (no seas)
venir → ven (no vengas)	hacer → haz (no hagas)
poner → pon (no pongas)	salir → sal (no salgas)
ir → ve (no vayas)	decir → di (no digas)

The Verbs *ser* and *estar*

Both **ser** and **estar** mean *to be*, but they differ in their uses.

Use **ser**:
1. with nouns to identify and define the subject
   La mejor estudiante de la clase es Katia.
2. with **de** to indicate place of origin, ownership, or material
   Carmen es de Venezuela.
   Este libro es de mi abuela.
   La blusa es de algodón.
3. to describe identifying characteristics, such as physical and personality traits, nationality, religion, and profession
   Mi tío es profesor. Es simpático e inteligente.
4. to express the time, date, season, or where an event is taking place
   Hoy es sábado y la fiesta es a las ocho.

Use **estar**:
1. to indicate location or position of the subject
   Lima está en Perú.
2. to describe a condition that is subject to change
   Maricarmen está triste.
3. with the present participle (**-ndo** form) to describe an action in progress
   Mario está escribiendo un poema.
4. to convey the idea of *to look, to feel, to seem, to taste*
   Tu hermano está muy guapo hoy.
   La sopa está deliciosa.

Common Expressions

EXPRESSIONS WITH *TENER*

tener ... años	to be . . . years old	tener (mucha) prisa	to be in a (big) hurry
tener mucho calor	to be very hot	tener que	to have to
tener ganas de...	to feel like . . .	tener (la) razón	to be right
tener mucho frío	to be very cold	tener mucha sed	to be very thirsty
tener mucha hambre	to be very hungry	tener mucho sueño	to be very sleepy
tener mucho miedo	to be very afraid	tener mucha suerte	to be very lucky

EXPRESSIONS OF TIME

To ask how long someone has been doing something, use:
 ¿Cuánto tiempo hace que + present tense?

To say how long someone has been doing something, use:
 Hace + quantity of time + **que** + present tense.
 Hace **seis meses** que **vivo en Los Ángeles.**
You can also use:
 present tense + **desde hace** + quantity of time
 Vivo en Los Ángeles desde hace **seis meses.**

WEATHER EXPRESSIONS

Hace muy buen tiempo.	The weather is very nice.
Hace mucho calor.	It's very hot.
Hace fresco.	It's cool.
Hace mucho frío.	It's very cold.
Hace muy mal tiempo.	The weather is very bad.
Hace mucho sol.	It's very sunny.
Hace mucho viento.	It's very windy.
But:	
Está lloviendo mucho.	It's raining a lot.
Hay mucha neblina.	It's very foggy.
Está nevando.	It's snowing.
Está nublado.	It's overcast.

Vocabulario español-inglés

This vocabulary includes almost all words in the textbook, both active (for production) and passive (for recognition only). An entry in **boldface** type indicates that the word or phrase is active. Active words and phrases are practiced in the chapter and are listed on the **Repaso de gramática** and **Repaso de vocabulario** pages at the end of each chapter. You are expected to know and be able to use active vocabulary.

All other words are for recognition only. These words are found in exercises, in optional and visual material, in **Instrucciones** on pages xviii–xix, in **Geocultura**, which is referenced by chapter (1G), **Comparaciones, Leamos y escribamos, También se puede decir,** and **Literatura y variedades.** You can usually understand the meaning of these words and phrases from the context or you can look them up in this vocabulary index. Many words have more than one definition; the definitions given here correspond to the way the words are used in *¡Exprésate!*.

Nouns are listed with definite articles and plural forms when the plural forms aren't formed according to general rules. The number after each entry refers to the chapter where the word or phrase first appears or where it becomes an active vocabulary word. This vocabulary index follows the rules of the **Real Academia,** with **ch** and **ll** in the same sequence as in the English alphabet.

Stem changes are indicated in parentheses after the verb: **poder (ue).**

a *to,* 3; *on,* 4; *at,* 8; **a base de** *based on,* 6; **a continuación** *that follows,* 7; **a finales** *at the end,* 10G; **a la (última) moda** *in the (latest) style,* 8; **a la vez** *at the same time,* 8; **a la vuelta** *around the corner,* 10; **A ...les gusta...** *They like to ...,* 3; **a menudo** *often,* 5; **¿A qué hora vas a...?** *What time are you going to ...?,* 4; **a tiempo** *on time,* 4; **a todo dar** *great,* 9; **Estuvo a todo dar.** *It was great.,* 9; **a través de** *through,* 5G; **a veces** *sometimes,* 3
abordar *to board,* 10
abrazar *to hug,* 9
el abrazo *hug,* 9
el abrigo *(over)coat,* 8
abril *April,* 1
abrir *to open,* 4; **abrir regalos** *to open gifts,* 9
la abuela *grandmother,* 5
el abuelo *grandfather,* 5
los abuelos *grandparents,* 5
aburrido(a) *boring,* 2; **estar aburrido(a)** *to be bored,* 7
acabar de *to just (have done something),* 7
acampar *to camp,* 3
acariciar *to caress,* 7

la acción *action,* 2
el aceite de oliva *olive oil,* 1G
el acento *accent,* 1; el acento ortográfico *written accent,* 8
acerca de *about,* 8
acompañar *to go with,* 6; *to accompany,* 1G; estar acompañada *to be accompanied,* 3
acordarse (ue) *to remember,* 9
acostarse (ue) *to go to bed,* 7
la actividad *activity,* 3
activo(a) *active,* 2
la actualidad *present time,* 6
el acuerdo *agreement;* **Estoy de acuerdo.** *I agree.,* 6; **No estoy de acuerdo.** *I disagree.,* 6
adaptado(a) *adapted,* 5G
además *besides,* 8
Adiós. *Good-bye.,* 1
adivinar *to guess,* 2
el adjetivo *adjective,* 5
la admiración *admiration,* 1
admirar *to admire,* 10
el adolescente *adolescent,* 3
¿adónde? *where?,* 8; **¿Adónde fuiste?** *Where did you go?,* 8; **¿Adónde vas...?** *Where do you go...?,* 3
la aduana *customs,* 10
el adulto *adult,* 7
los aeróbicos *aerobics,* 7; hacer aeróbicos *to do aerobics,* 7
el aeropuerto *airport,* 10
afeitarse *to shave,* 7
afuera *outside,* 3
las afueras *suburbs,* 5

la agencia inmobiliaria *real estate agency,* 5
el agente, la agente *agent,* 10
agitar *to shake,* 3
agosto *August,* 1
el agua (f.) *water,* 6
el águila (f.) *eagle,* 7
ahí *there,* 4
ahora *now,* 9
ahorrar *to save money,* 8
el aire *air,* 3; el aire central *central air conditioning,* 5; el aire libre *open air,* 8
el ajedrez *chess,* 2
el ají *hot pepper,* 10G
el ajo *garlic,* 6
ajustado(a) *tight-fitting,* 8
al (a + el) *to, to the,* 3; *upon,* 6; al fin *finally,* 10; **al lado de** *next to,* 5
la alberca *swimming pool,* 3
alcanzar *to reach,* 7G
la alcoba *bedroom,* 5
alegre *happy,* 2
el alemán *German,* 4
el alfabeto *alphabet,* 1
algo *something, anything,* 4; **algo +** adjective *kind of +* adjective, 2
el algodón *cotton,* 8; **de algodón** *made of cotton,* 8
algún día *some day,* 10
algunas *some,* 2
el alimento *food,* 6
alistarse *to get ready,* 7
allá *there,* 8
allí *there,* 10

el **almacén** *department store*, 8
el **almanaque** *almanac*, 1G
almorzar *to have lunch*, 5
el **almuerzo** *lunch*, 4
Aló *Hello. (telephone greeting)*, 8
el **alpinismo** *mountain climbing*, 7
alquilar *to rent*, 3; **alquilar videos** *to rent videos*, 3
alrededor *around*, 6
el **altiplano** *high plateau*, 10G
alto(a) *tall*, 2
la **altura** *height*, 6G
amanecer *to dawn*, 9
el **amarillo** *yellow*, 1G
amarillo(a) *yellow*, 8
el **ambiente** *atmosphere*, 5G
ambos *both*, 5G
amigable *friendly*, 2
el **amigo(a)** *friend*, 1; **mi mejor amigo(a)** *my best friend*, 1
el **amor** *love*, 8; **de amor** *romance*, 2
amueblado(a) *furnished*, 5
analítico(a) *analytical*, 2
anaranjado(a) *orange*, 8
ancho *width*, 5G; *wide*, 8
andar *to walk, to go*, 2; andar en bicicleta *to ride a bike*, 3; dime con quien andas y te diré quien eres *a person is known by the company he/she keeps*, 2
andino(a) *of the Andes*, 7G
el **anfibio** *amphibian*, 2G
la **anguila** *eel*, 7
el **ángulo** *angle*, 7
el **anillo** *ring*, 8
el **animal** *animal*, 2
el **aniversario** *anniversary*, 9
el **año** *year*, 2; **el Año Nuevo** *New Year*, 9; **el año pasado** *last year*, 9; **¿Cuántos años tiene...?** *How old is . . .?*, 2; **¿Cuántos años tienes?** *How old are you?*, 2
anoche *last night*, 9
anteayer *day before yesterday*, 8
anterior *previous*, 9
antes *before*, 1; **antes de** *before*, 7; de antes *from before*, 4
antiguo(a) *old*, 6G
antipático(a) *unfriendly*, 2
añadir *to add*, 6
aparecer *to appear*, 6
el **apartamento** *apartment*, 5
apasionado(a) *passionate*, 2
apellido *last name*, 2
apetecer *to appeal*, 6
aplicar *to apply*, 2
aportar *to contribute*, 8G
aprender *to learn*, 1
apropiado(a) *appropriate*, 7
aproximadamente *approximately*, 2
los **apuntes** *notes*, 8
aquella *that*, 6
aquello *that*, 4
aquí *here*, 6

árabe *Arab*, 5G
el **árbol** *tree*, 1; la copa del árbol *top of the tree*, 4G
los **aretes** *earrings*, 8
la **argamasa** *mortar*, 10G
argentino(a) *Argentine*, 7
árido(a) *dry*, 10G
la **armonía** *harmony*, 2
armonizar *to harmonize*, 7G
el **arquitecto** *architect*, 3G
arquitectónico(a) *architectural*, 10G
la **arquitectura** *architecture*, 2G
arreglar *to pick up*, 5; **arreglar el cuarto** *to pick up the room*, 5
el **arrendamiento** *rental*, 10
la **arroba** *@*, 1
el **arroz** *rice*, 6
el **arte** *art*, 4; las artes plásticas *sculpture*, 2
la **artesanía** *crafts*, 4
el **artista, la artista** *artist*, 1
artístico(a) *artistic*, 2
asegurar *to reassure*, 6
el **asentamiento** *colony, settlement*, 8G
el **aseo** *restroom*, 10
así *like this*; así que *so*, 8; Así es., *That's how it is.*, 2
asistente *assistant*, 10
asistir (a) *to attend*, 4
asomar *to peek out*, 9
el **asterisco** *asterisk*, 7
atlético(a) *athletic*, 2
el **atole** *Mexican drink made of cornmeal, milk or water, and flavoring*, 6
atraer *to attract*, 1G
atravesar *to cross*, 10G
atreverse *to dare*, 9
el **atún** *tuna*, 6
los **audífonos** *headphones*, 8
el **auditorio** *auditorium*, 4
aun *even*, 2
aún *still*, 10
aunque *even though*, 6
el **autobús** *bus*, 10
el **autor** *author*, 7
el **autorretrato** *self-portrait*, 6G
avanzado(a) *advanced*, 10G
el **ave (pl. las aves)** *bird*, 4G
la **aventura** *adventure*, 2
averiguar *to find out*, 10
el **avión** *airplane*, 10; por avión *by plane*, 10
¡Ay no! *Oh, no!*, 6
¡ay! *ouch!*, 8
ayer *yesterday*, 8
el **aymara** *indigenous language in Peru*, 10G
la **ayuda** *help*, 6
ayudar *to help*, 5; **ayudar en casa** *to help out at home*, 5; Estamos ayudando. *We are helping.*, 3
el **azúcar** *sugar*, 6

el **azul** *blue*, 1G
azul *blue*, 5

la **bahía** *bay*, 8G
bailar *to dance*, 3; bailando *dancing*, 1; ponerse a bailar *to start dancing*, 3
la **bailarina** *dancer (fem.)*, 3
el **baile** *dance*, 3
bajar *to descend*, 7; **bajar archivos** *to download files*, 3; **bajar de peso** *to lose weight*, 7
bajo(a) *short*, 2
balanceado(a) *balanced*, 6
el **balcón** *balcony*, 5
balear *to shoot*, 5
el **ballet** *ballet*, 1
el **baloncesto** *basketball*, 3
bañarse *to bathe*, 7
la **bandeja** *platter*, 7G
la **bandera** *banner*, 9
el **bandido** *bandit*, 5
el **baño** *bathroom*, 5; *restroom*, 10
barato(a) *inexpensive*, 8
la **barbacoa** *barbecue*, 3G
el **barco** *boat*, 10; el barquito *little boat*, 5
la **barranca** *cliff*, 6G
el **barrio** *neighborhood*, 7G
básico(a) *basic*, 6
el **básquetbol** *basketball*, 3
basta *it's enough*, 5
bastante + adjective *quite, pretty* + adjective, 2
la **basura** *trash*, 5; **sacar la basura** *to take out the trash*, 5
la **batalla** *battle*, 3G
el **batido** *milkshake*, 8
el **bebé, la bebé** *baby*, 1
beber (algo) *to drink (something)*, 4; **beber ponche** *to drink punch*, 9
la **bebida** *drink*, 6
la **beca** *scholarship*, 10
el **béisbol** *baseball*, 3
bello(a) *beautiful*, 2G
la **biblioteca** *library*, 4
la **bicicleta** *bike*, 3; **montar en bicicleta** *to ride a bike*, 3
bien *all right, fine*, 1; *really*, 2; bien dicho *well said*, 6; **Está bien.** *All right.*, 3; **Estoy bien.** *I'm fine.*, 1; **Me parece bien.** *It's all right with me.*, 5; **quedar bien** *to fit well*, 8; **Que te vaya bien.** *Hope things go well for you.*, 9
bienvenido *welcome*, 10
el **billete** *ticket*, 10
la **billetera** *wallet*, 10

la **biología** *biology*, 4
blanco(a) *white*, 8; **en blanco**
   blank, 8
el blanquillo *egg*, 6
la **blusa** *blouse*, 8
la **boca** *mouth*, 7
el bocadillo *sandwich (Spain)*, 6;
   finger food (Dom. Rep.), 9
el bocadito *small servings of food*, 7G
las bocas *finger food (Costa Rica)*, 9
la **boda** *wedding*, 9
la boleta *ticket*, 10
el boleto de avión *plane ticket*, 10
el bolígrafo *pen*, 4
la **bolsa** *purse*, 8; *bag*, 8; *travel bag*, 10
la bomba *music and dance style*, 2G
la bombilla *straw used for sipping*
   mate, 7
bonito(a) *pretty*, 2
el borde *edge*, 7G
el borrador *rough draft*, 1
el bosque *forest*, 2G; el bosque
   húmedo *rain forest*, 4G
la botana *finger food (Mex.)*, 9
botar *to throw out*, 5
las botas *boots*, 8
el bote *boat*, 9G; **el bote de vela**
   sailboat, 10; **pasear en bote de vela**
   to go out in a sailboat, 10
el brazo *arm*, 7
brillar *to shine*, 7
brindar *to offer*, 5
el brócoli *broccoli*, 6
bueno(a) *good*, 2; **Buenas noches.**
   Good evening., Good night., 1;
   Buenas tardes. *Good afternoon.*,
   1; **Buenos días.** *Good morning.*, 1
Bueno. *Hello. (telephone greeting)*, 8
burlarse de *to make fun of*, 8
el burro *donkey*, 1
buscar *to look for*, 7; **buscar un**
   pasatiempo *to find a hobby*, 7;
   búsquenme *look for me*, 3

el caballo de paso *horse with high-*
   stepping gait, 10G
caber *to fit*, 10G
la **cabeza** *head*, 7
el cacao *cocoa*, 6G
cada *each*, xxii; cada uno(a) *each*
   one, 6; cada vez *each time*, 8
el café *coffee*, 6; *brown*, 1G; **el café**
   con leche *coffee with milk*, 6; **de**
   color café *brown*, 5
la **cafetería** *cafeteria*, 4; *coffee shop*, 6
la caída de agua *waterfall*, 7G
el caimán *caiman (reptile)*, 7G

la caja *box*, 9
el **cajero automático** *automatic teller*
   machine, 10
la calabaza *squash, pumpkin*, 6G; la
   calabacita *gourd used for* ***mate***
   tea, 7G
los **calcetines** *socks*, 8; **un par de**
   calcetines *a pair of socks*, 8
la **calculadora** *calculator*, 4
la calefacción *heating*, 5; la
   calefacción central *central*
   heating, 5
el calendario *calendar*, 1
calentar (ie) *to heat up*, 6
caliente *hot*, 6
callado(a) *quiet*, 5
la **calle** *street*, 5
el calor *heat*, 3; **Hace calor.** *It's hot.*,
   3; **tener calor** *to be hot*, 7
la caloría *calorie*, 6
la **cama** *bed*, 5; **hacer la cama** *to*
   make the bed, 5
la **cámara** *camera*, 10; **la cámara**
   desechable *disposable camera*, 10
el camarero *waiter*, 6
cambiar *to change*, 4
cambiar dinero *to change money*, 10
el cambio *change*, 9
caminar *to walk*, 7
el camino *path*, 10G
el camión *bus (Mex.)*, 10
la **camisa** *shirt*, 8
la **camiseta** *T-shirt*, 8; la camiseta
   deportiva *sport shirt*, 8
el camote *sweet potato*, 4G
el **campo** *countryside*, 5
la canción *song*, 8
candidato(a) *candidate*, 4
la **canoa** *canoe*, 10
el cañón *canyon*, 6G
canoso(a) *gray-haired*, 5
cansado(a) *tired*, 7; **estar**
   cansado(a) *to be tired*, 7
cantar *to sing*, 3; cantaba *he sang*, 9
el cantar *singing*, 2
la cantidad *amount*, 2; *quantity*, 6; las
   cantidades *large numbers*, 6
el canto *song*, 1G
la capilla *chapel*, 3G
la capital *capital*, 1G
el capítulo *chapter*, 1
la **cara** *face*, 7; cara de tortilla *tortilla*
   face, 1
el carácter *character*, 5
la característica *characteristic*, 6
caracterizar *to characterize*, 5G
la cárcel *jail*, 8
caribeño(a) *Caribbean*, 4G
el cariño *affection; (addressing*
   someone) dear, 3; con cariño
   affectionately, 10
la **carne** *meat, beef*, 6; la carne de res
   beef, 6; la carne molida *ground*
   beef, 6

el **carnet de identidad** *ID*, 10
caro(a) *expensive*, 8
la **carpeta** *folder*, 4
la carreta *cart*, 4G
el carro *car*, 2
la carroza *float*, 9G
la **carta** *letter*, 3
la **casa** *house*, 5; **ayudar en casa** *to*
   help out at home, 5; **la casa de...**
   ...'s house, 3; **decorar la casa**
   to decorate the house, 9
el casabe *flat, dry bread made from*
   manioc, 9G
casarse *to get married*, 10
la cascada *waterfall*, 2G
la cáscara *shell*, 2G
casi *almost*, 3, **casi nunca** *almost*
   never, 3, **casi siempre** *almost*
   always, 3
el caso *case*, 2
castaño(a) *dark brown*, 5
las castañuelas *castanets*, 1G
el castellano *Spanish*, 1G
el castillo *castle*, 2G
el catalán *language from Catalonia,*
   Spain, 1G
el catálogo *catalog*, 8
la catarata *cataract, waterfall*, 7G
la catedral *cathedral*, 1G
catorce *fourteen*, 1
el cayo *key (island)*, 8G
el cazador *hunter*, 7G
la cebolla *onion*, 10G
celebérrimo(a) *most famous*, 8
la celebración *celebration*, 1
celebrar *to celebrate*, 9; celebrará
   will celebrate, 8; se celebra *is*
   celebrated, 2G
célebre *famous*, 8
celeridad *speed*, 8
celta *Celtic*, 1G
la **cena** *dinner*, 6
cenar *to eat dinner*, 6
el **centro** *downtown*, 10; *center*, 3G
el **centro comercial** *mall*, 3
el **cepillo de dientes** *toothbrush*, 7
la cerámica *pottery*, 4
cerca de *close to, near*, 5
cercano(a) *close*, 5
los **cereales** *cereal*, 6
el cerebelo *cerebellum*, 8
el cerebro *brain*, 8
la ceremonia *ceremony*, 6
cero *zero*, 1
cerrado(a) *closed*, 1
cerrar (ie) *to close*, 8
el césped *grass*, 5
la cesta de paja *straw basket*, 8G
el ceviche *dish made with seafood,*
   lemon, and seasonings, 10G
chao *Bye*, 9
la **chaqueta** *jacket*, 8
charlar *to talk, chat*, 9
el chayote *type of squash*, 4G

la chica *girl*, 8
chicano(a) *Mexican that has emigrated to the United States*, 3G
el chile *hot pepper*, 6G; chile en nogada *hot peppers in walnut and spice sauce*, 6G
el chileno *Chilean*, 5
la chimenea *fireplace*, 5
el chiste *joke*, 9
el choclo *corn on the cob*, 5G
el chocolate *chocolate*, 6; *hot chocolate*, 6
el churro *sugar-coated fritter*, 6
el ciclismo *cycling*, 1
ciego(a) *blind*, 5
el cielo *heaven*, 3
cien *one hundred*, 2
la ciencia ficción *science fiction*, 2
las ciencias *science*, 4; **...de ciencias** *science . . .*, 1
el científico *scientist*, 6
ciento un(o) *one hundred one*, 8
cierto(a) *true*, xxii
la cifra *number*, 8
la cima *mountain top*, 7G
cinco *five*, 1
cincuenta *fifty*, 2
el cine *movie theater*, 3
el cinturón *belt*, 8
el círculo *circle*, 3
el citrón *lemon*, 6
la ciudad *city*, 5
¡Claro que sí! *Of course!*, 4
claro(a) *clear*, 6G
la clase *class*, 3; **después de clases** *after class*, 3; **la clase de baile** *dance class*, 4
clasificar *to classify*, 6
clavar *to nail*, 10
el clavo *nail*, 10
el cliente, la cliente *client*, 8
el club de... *the . . . club*, 4
el cobre *copper*, 6G
cocer *to cook*, 3
el coche *car*, 10
la cocina *kitchen*, 5; *cooking*, 3G
cocinar *to cook*, 5
el coco *coconut*, 2G
el cocodrilo *crocodile*, 8G
el código *code*, 2G
cohabitar *to live together*, 8G
la cola *line*, 10
el colectivo *bus (Bol., Perú, Ecuador)*, 10
el colegio *school*, 3
colgar *to hang*, 9
la colina *hill*, 9G
la colonia *colony*, 7G
el colonizador *colonist*, 6G
el color *color*, 8
el colorido *coloring*, 7G
colorido(a) *colorful*, 4G
la columna *column*, xxii
los combates *battles*, 10

la combinación *combination*, 1
combinar *to combine*, 5G
el comedor *dining room*, 5
comenzar (ie) *to start*, 10; **comenzar un viaje** *to begin a trip*, 10; comiencen *begin*, 8
comer *to eat*, 3; se comen *are eaten*, 2G
el comercio *commerce*, 3G
el comestible *food*, 3
cómico(a) *funny*, 2
la comida *food*, 2; *lunch*, 6; **la comida china (italiana, mexicana)** *Chinese (Italian, Mexican) food*, 2; la comida típica *traditional food*, 6
como *like*, 2; *as*, 9; **como siempre** *as always*, 9
cómo *how?, what?*, 1; **¿Cómo eres?** *What are you like?*, 2; **¿Cómo es...?** *What is . . . like?*, 2; **¿Cómo está(s)?** *How are you?*, 1; **¿Cómo me quedan...?** *How does . . . look?*, 8; **¿Cómo se escribe...?** *How do you spell . . .?*, 1; **¿Cómo se llama?** *What's his (her/your) name?*, 1; **¿Cómo te llamas?** *What's your name? (fam.)*, 1
la compañera de clase *classmate (female)*, 1; **una compañera de clase** *a (female) classmate*, 1
el compañero de clase *classmate (male)*, 1; **un compañero de clase** *a (male) classmate*, 1
la comparación *comparison*, 1
comparar *to compare*, 8
compasivo(a) *compassionate*, 6
el complemento directo *direct object*, 6
completar *to complete*, xxii
completo *complete*, 6; por completo *completely*, 6
comprar *to buy*, 8; comprarías *you would buy*, 8
las compras *shopping*, 2; estar de compras *to be on a shopping trip*, 8; **ir de compras** *to go shopping*, 3
la comprensión *comprehension*, 10
comprender *to understand*, 2; nos comprendemos *we understand each other*, 2
la computación *computer science*, 4
la computadora *computer*, 4
común *common*, 9
comunicar *to communicate*, 5
la comunidad *community*, 1
con *with*, 3; con base en *based on*, xxii; **con mis amigos** *with my friends*, 3; **con mi familia** *with my family*, 3; con motivo de *on the occasion of*, 9; **¿Con qué frecuencia vas...?** *How often do you go . . .?*, 3; con relación a *in relation to*, 5
el concierto *concert*, 4

el concurso *competition*, 9G
el condominio *condominium*, 5
conectar *to connect*, 8G
confundido(a) *confused*, 4
confundir *to confuse*, 10
el conjunto *musical group*, 3G
conmemorar *commemorate*, 3G
conmigo *with me*, 3
conocer *to know, to meet, be familiar with*, 9; **conocimos...** *we visited . . .*, 10; **Quiero conocer...** *I want to see . . .*, 10; se conoce *is known*, 2G
conocido(a) *known*, 2G
el conocimiento *knowledge*, 7
conquistar *to conquer*, 10
conseguir (i, i) *to get*, 10
el consejo *advice*, 7
conservar *to preserve*, 2G
considerar *to consider*, 2; *to regard*, 9
constituir *to make up*, 6
construir *to build*, 3G; construye *construct*, 10; fue construido *was built*, 3G
el consultorio médico *doctor's office*, 7
consumir *to consume*, 6; se consumen *are consumed*, 6
el consumo *consumption*, 6
contar *to count*, 1; *to tell*, 4; contando *counting*, 1; **contar (ue) chistes** *to tell jokes*, 9; contar con *to count on*, 10; cuenta *tells*, 6; cuentan *it is told*, 6
contemplar *to contemplate*, 9
contemporáneo *contemporary*, 1G
contener (ie) *to contain*, 10G; que contengan *that contain*, 10
contento(a) *happy*, 7; **estar contento(a)** *to be happy*, 7
contestar *to answer*, xxii
contigo *with you*, 3
el continente *continent*, 6
continuo *continual*, 8
contra *against*, 10
al contrario *to the contrary*, 6
la contribución *contribution*, 2G
contribuir *to contribute*, 8G
el control de seguridad *security checkpoint*, 10
controlar *to control*, 3G
el convento *convent*, 3G
la conversación *conversation*, xxii
convertirse *to become*, 10
la copa *treetop*, 4
el coquí *small tree frog*, 2G
el corazón *heart*, 7G
la cordillera *mountain range*, 2G
el coro *chorus*, 2
correcto(a) *right, correct*, xxii
corregir *to correct*, xxii
el correo electrónico *e-mail address*, 1; **¿Cuál es el correo electrónico de...?** *What is . . .'s e-mail address?*, 1; **¿Cuál es tu correo electrónico?**

los **deportes** *sports*, 2
  deportivo(a) (adj.) *sports*, 8
la **derecha** *right*, 1
el **desarrollo** *development*, 7G
  desarrollar *to develop*, 4
el **desastre** *disaster*, 9
  desayunar *to eat breakfast*, 6
el **desayuno** *breakfast*, 6
  descansar *to rest*, 3
el **descendiente** *descendant*, 10
  describir *to describe*, 5
  descubrir *to discover*, 8; **fue descubierto** *was discovered*, 7G
  desde *since*, 4; *from*, 10; ¿desde cuándo? *since when?*, 4; desde hace *since*, 6; desde joven *since her youth*, 8; desde luego *of course*, 7
  desear *to want, to wish for, to desire*, 6; **deseando** *wanting to*, 8
  desechable *disposable*, 10
  desembarcar *to disembark, to deplane*, 10
  desembocar *to flow*, 10G
el **deseo** *desire*, 9
  desesperado(a) *desperate*, 6
el **desfile** *parade, procession*, 4G
el **desierto** *desert*, 5G
la **despedida** *farewell*, 9; la fiesta de despedida *goodbye party*, 10
  despertarse (ie) *to wake up*, 7
  despierto(a) *awake*, 7
  después *after*, 3; *afterwards*, 4; **después de** *after*, 7; **después de clases** *after class*, 3
  destinado(a) *destined*, 6
el **destino** *destination*, 10
el **detalle** *detail*, 7
  determinar *to determine*, 7
  detrás de *behind*, 5
  devolver (ue) *to return something*, 8
  di *say*, 8
el **día** *day*, 1; **algún día** *some day*, 10; **el Día de Acción de Gracias** *Thanksgiving Day*, 9; **el Día de la Independencia** *Independence Day*, 9; **el Día de la Madre** *Mother's Day*, 9; **el día de la semana** *day of the week*, 1; **el Día de los Enamorados** *Valentine's Day*, 9; **el Día del Padre** *Father's Day*, 9; **el día de tu santo** *your saint's day*, 9; **el día festivo** *holiday*, 9; ¿Qué día es hoy? *What day is today?*, 1
  diablado(a) *devilish*, 5G
el **diablo** *devil*, 7G
el **diálogo** *dialog*, xxii
  diario(a) *daily*, 3G
  dibujar *to draw*, 3
el **dibujo** *drawing*, xxii
el **diccionario** *dictionary*, 4
  dice (inf. decir) *(he/she) says*, 4

la **dicha** *happiness*, 9
  diciembre *December*, 1
el **dictado** *dictation*, 1
  diecinueve *nineteen*, 1
  dieciocho *eighteen*, 1
  dieciséis *sixteen*, 1
  diecisiete *seventeen*, 1
los **dientes** *teeth*, 7
la **dieta** *diet*, 7; **seguir una dieta sana** *to eat a balanced diet*, 7
  diez *ten*, 1
  diferente *different*, 2
  difícil *difficult*, 4; **Es difícil.** *It's difficult.*, 4
  Diga. *Hello. (telephone greeting)*, 8
el **dinero** *money*, 8
el **dinosaurio** *dinosaur*, 1
  dios *god*, 6; **gracias a Dios** *thank goodness*, 6
la **dirección** *address*, 5; **Mi dirección es...** *My address is . . .*, 5
  directamente *directly*, 4
  director (-a) *director*, 10
el **directorio de teléfono** *phone book*, 1
  disciplinado(a) *disciplined*, 2
el **disco** *record*, 8
el **disco compacto** *compact disc*, 8; **el disco compacto en blanco** *blank compact disc*, 8
  diseñar *to design*, 3G; fue diseñado(a) *was designed*, 3G
el **diseño** *design*, 5G
el **disfraz** *costume*, 9G
  disfrazar *to wear a costume*, 4G
  disfrutar *to enjoy*, 2G
  disponible *available*, 7
  dispuesto(a) *willing*, 6G
la **distancia** *distance*, 10
  distinguirse *to distinguish oneself*, 10
  distinto(a) *different*, 6G
la **diversión** *fun*, 2
  diverso(a) *diverse*, 6
  divertido(a) *fun*, 2; ¡Qué divertido! *What fun!*, 10
  divertirse *to have fun*, 1; diviértanse *have a good time* (pl.), 1; que me divierta *to have fun*, 9
  doblado(a) *folded*, 9
  doble *double*, 5
  doce *twelve*, 1
el **documento** *document*, 1
el **dólar** *dollar*, 8
  doler (ue) *to hurt*, 7; **Me duele(n)...** *My . . . hurt(s).*, 7; ¿Te duele algo? *Does something hurt?*, 7; **Le duele...** *His (Her) . . . hurts.*, 7
el **domingo** *Sunday*, 1; **los domingos** *on Sundays*, 3
  dominicano(a) *Dominican*, 9
  donde *where*, 8
  ¿dónde? *where?*, 5; ¿Dónde se puede...? *Where can I . . .?*, 10

  dorado(a) *golden*, 2
  dormido(a) *asleep*, 7
  dormir (ue) *to sleep*, 5; **dormir la siesta** *to take a nap*, 7; **dormir lo suficiente** *to get enough sleep*, 7
el **dormitorio** *bedroom*, 5
  dos *two*, 1
  dos mil *two thousand*, 8
  dos millones (de) *two million*, 8
  doscientos *two hundred*, 8
  dramatizar *to dramatize, to role-play*, xxii
la **duda** *doubt*, 6; sin duda *without a doubt*, 6
  dulce *sweet*, 7
el **dulce** *candy*, 9
la **duración** *duration*, 7
  durante *during*, 10; *throughout*, 6G
  durar *to last*, 10G
el **durazno** *peach*, 6
el **DVD** *DVD*, 8

E

  e *and*, 5
la **economía** *economy*, 3G; la economía doméstica *home economics*, 6G
la **edad** *age*, 2G; de más edad *the oldest*, 5
el **edificio** *building*, 5; **el edificio de... pisos** *. . . story building*, 5
la **educación física** *physical education*, 4
  eficaz *efficient*, 10G
  eficiente *efficient*, 2
el **ejemplo** *example*, 3G
el **ejercicio** *exercise*, 3; **hacer ejercicio** *to exercise*, 3
  el *the* (masc.), 2
  él *he*, 1; **Él es...** *He is . . .*, 1; **Él se llama...** *His name is . . .*, 1
el **elefante** *elephant*, 1
la **elegancia** *elegance*, 5G
  elegante *elegant*, 2
el **elemento** *element*, 1
  elevar *to raise*, 5G
la **elite** *elite*, 6
  ella *she*, 1; A ella le gusta + infinitive *She likes to . . .*, 3; **Ella es...** *She is . . .*, 1; ella misma *herself*, 6; **Ella se llama...** *Her name is . . .*, 1
  ellas *they (f.)*, 1
  ellos *they (m.)*, 1
el **elote** *corn on the cob (Mexico)*, 6
  emitir *to emit*, 2
  emocionado(a) *excited*, 9
la **empanada** *turnover-like pastry*, 9
el **emparedado** *sandwich*, 6

empezar (ie) *to start*, 5

el **empleado, la empleada** *employee*, 7

el **empleo** *job*, 9

emplumado(a) *feathered*, 6

en *on, in, at*, 1; **en frente** *in front*, 3G; **en blanco** *blank*, 8; **en las cuales** *about which*, 8; **en negrilla** *bold*, 9; **en punto** *on the dot*, 1; **en que** *in which*, 8; **¿En que le puedo servir?** *Can I help you?*, 8

enamorado(a) *in love*, 10

Encantado(a). *Pleased to meet you., Nice to meet you.*, 1

encantar (me encanta(n)) *to really like, to love*, 6

encerrar *to lock up*, 10

encima de *on top of, above*, 5

encontrar (ue) *to find*, 7; encontrará *will find*, 10; se encuentra *is/it's located* 1G; se encuentran *they can be found*, 6

encontrarse con alguien *to meet up with someone*, 10

energético(a) *energetic*, 2

la **energía** *energy*, 2

enero *January*, 1

la **enfermera** *nurse*, 5

enfermo(a) *sick*, 7

en frente *in front*, 10

enhorabuena *congratulations*, 10

enojado(a) *angry*, 7

enojarse *to get angry*, 7

enrollado(a) *rolled up*, 3

la **ensalada** *salad*, 6

el **ensayo** *rehearsal*, 3

enseñar *to show, to teach*, 4; **enseñar fotos** *to show photos*, 9

entender *to understand*, 5

enterarse *to find out*, 10

entonces *then*, 4

entrar *to enter*, 4

entre *between*, 2; *in, within*, 6; *among*, 7

entregar *to hand over*, 9

los **entremeses** *appetizers*, 9

la **entrenadora** *trainer*, 7

el **entrenamiento** *practice*, 3

entrenar(se) *to work out*, 7

la **entrevista** *interview*, 2

entrevistar *to interview*, 2

enviar *to send*, 1

la **envoltura** *wrapping*, 9

la **época** *era*, 6; la época colonial *Spanish colonial era*, 2G

el **equipaje** *luggage*, 10

el **equipo** *equipment*, 3G; *team*, 9G; el equipo de transporte *transportation equipment*, 3G

¿Eres...? *Are you...?*, 2

la **erupción** *eruption*, 6G

Es... *He (She, It) is...*, 2; **Es algo divertido.** *It's kind of fun.*, 2; **Es bastante bueno.** *It's pretty good.*, 2; **Es de...** *He (She) is from...*, 1;

Es delicioso. *It's delicious.*, 2; **Es el... de...** *It's the... of...*, 2; **Es fácil/difícil** *It's easy/hard*, 4; **Es el primero (dos, tres) de...** *It's the first (second, third) of...*, 1; **Es la una.** *It is one o'clock.*, 1; **Es pésimo.** *It's awful.*, 2; **Es que...** *It's because; It's just that...*, 7; **¡Es un robo!** *It's a rip-off!*, 8

ese(a) *that*, 5

escapar *to escape*, 5

la **escena** *scene*, 3

escoger *to pick*, 9; *to choose*, 6

escolar *school (adj.)*, 4

esconder *to hide*, 4

escribir *to write*, 1; **¿Cómo se escribe...?** *How do you spell...?*, 1; escribamos *let's write*, 1; **escribir cartas** *to write letters*, 3; **Se escribe...** *It's spelled...*, 1

el **escritor, la escritora** *writer*, 1

el **escritorio** *desk*, 5

escuchar *to listen*, 3; **escuchar música** *to listen to music*, 3; escuchemos *let's listen*, 1; has escuchado *you have heard*, 2; he escuchado *I have heard*, 2

la **escuela** *school*, 2; la escuela primaria *elementary school*, 5; la escuela secundaria *high school*, 9

el **escultor** *sculptor*, 4G

la **escultura** *sculpture*, 2G

ese(a) *that*, 8

eso *that*, 2

esos(as) *those*, 8

espacial *space*, 8G

la **espalda** *back*, 7

el **español** *Spanish*, 1

el **español** *Spaniard*, 6

esparcir *to spread*, 3; está esparciendo *is spreading*, 3

la **especia** *spice*, 8G

la **especialidad** *specialty*, 6

la **especie** *species*, 2G

específico(a) *specific*, 10

los **espejuelos** *glasses*, 5

la **esperanza** *hope*, 9

esperar *to wait*, 8; *to hope*, 10; *to expect*, 10; **Espera un momento.** *Hold on a moment.*, 8; **Espero ver...** *I hope to see...*, 10

las **espinacas** *spinach*, 6

el **espino** *thorn*, 8

espiritual *spiritual*, 9

espontáneo(a) *spontaneous*, 2

la **esposa** *wife*, 9

el **esposo** *husband*, 5

esquiar *to ski*, 10; **esquiar en el agua** *to water-ski*, 10

Está a la vuelta. *It's around the corner.*, 10

ésta, éste *this (pron.)*, 1; **Ésta es.../la señora...** *This is.../Mrs....*, 1;

Éste es.../el señor... *This is... /Mr....*, 1

establecer *to establish*, 8G; fue establecido *was established*, 8G

el **establecimiento** *colony*, 8G

estacionar *to park*, 10

el **estadio** *stadium*, 4

el **estado** *state*, 2G

los **Estados Unidos** *United States*, 1; estadounidense *pertaining to the United States*, 7

estar *to be*, 1; **¿Cómo está(s)?** *How are you?*, 1; **¿Está...?** *Is... there?*, 8; **Está bien.** *All right.*, 3; **Está nublado.** *It's cloudy.*, 3; **Está (un poco) salado(a)** *It's (a little) salty*, 6; **estar a la vuelta** *to be around the corner*, 10; **estar aburrido(a)** *to be bored*, 7; **estar bien** *to be (doing) fine*, 7; **estar cansado(a)** *to be tired*, 7; **estar contento(a)** *to be happy*, 7; **estar mal** *to be (doing) badly*, 7; **estar enfermo(a)** *to be sick*, 7; **estar enojado(a)** *to be angry*, 7; **estar en una silla de ruedas** *to be in a wheelchair*, 5; **estar listo(a)** *to be ready*, 7; **estar nervioso(a)** *to be nervous*, 7; **estar triste** *to be sad*, 7; **¿Está todo listo?** *Is everything ready?*, 9; **Estoy bien, gracias.** *I'm fine, thanks.*, 1; **Estoy de acuerdo.** *I agree.*, 6; **Estoy mal.** *I'm not so good.*, 1; **Estoy regular.** *I'm all right.*, 1; **No está.** *He/She is not here.*, 8; **no estés** *don't be*, 7; **Estuvo a todo dar.** *It was great.*, 9; **No estoy de acuerdo.** *I disagree.*, 6

estas, estos *these (adj.)*, 8

la **estatua** *statue*, 5G

éste *this (pron.)*, 6

este(a) *this*, 8; **este fin de semana** *this weekend*, 4

el **estilo** *style*, 3G

estirarse *to stretch*, 7

el **estómago** *stomach*, 7

el **Estrecho de la Florida** *Strait of Florida*, 8

la **estrella** *star*, 5

el **estrés** *stress*, 7

estricto(a) *strict*, 4

el **estruendo** *noise*, 10

el **estudiante, la estudiante** *student*, 1; el estudiante de intercambio *exchange student*, 10

estudiar *to study*, 3

los **estudios** *studies*, 5; los estudios sociales *social studies*, 4

estupendo(a) *great*, 10; **Fue estupendo.** *It was great.*, 10

la **etapa** *stage*, 2

el **europeo** *European*, 6G

el **evento deportivo** *sporting event*, 1

el **examen**   test, 4; **presentar el examen de...**   to take a . . . test, 4
exclamar   to exclaim, 9
exclusivamente   exclusively, 4
la **excursión**   hike, 10; **ir de excursión**   to go on a hike, 10
la excursión turística   to go on a trip, 1
exigente   strict, 5
existir   to exist, 7
el **éxito**   success, 10
la **experiencia**   experience, 6
el **explorador**   explorer, 5G
exponer   to display, 4G
el **exportador**   exporter, 8G
exportar   to export, 1G
la **exposición**   exposition, 5G; exhibition, 10G
expresar   to express, 6G
la **expresión**   expression, xxii; saying, 2
extender   to cover, 3G; se extiende it extends, 5G
la **extensión**   length, 10G
extranjero(a)   foreign, 10
el **extranjero**   abroad, 10
extraño(a)   strange, 7G
extremo(a)   far, 7G
extrovertido(a)   outgoing, 2

fabuloso(a)   fabulous, 6
fácil   easy, 4; **Es fácil.**   It's easy., 4
facturar el equipaje   to check luggage, 10
la **falda**   skirt, 8
falso(a)   false, xxii
faltar   to be missing, 1; nos faltan we're missing, 3
la **fama**   fame, 5G
la **familia**   family, 3; **En mi familia somos...**   There are . . . people in my family., 5; la Familia Real Royal Family, 1
familiar   pertaining to the family, 7
famoso(a)   famous, 2
fascinar   to love, to like very much, 2
fastidiar   to annoy, 9
favorito(a)   favorite, 1
febrero   February, 1
la **fecha**   date, 1
la **felicidad**   happiness, 9
felicitar   to congratulate, 9
el **felino**   cat, 10G
feliz (pl. felices)   happy, 8; **¡Feliz...!**   Happy (Merry) . . ., 9
fenomenal   awesome, 2
feo(a)   ugly, 8
festejar   to celebrate, 9
festivo   holiday (adj), 9

la **fibra de vidrio**   fiberglass, 3G
la **fiesta**   party, 2; la fiesta patria national holiday, 5G; la fiesta patronal   feast celebrating the patron saint, 4G; **la fiesta sorpresa**   surprise party, 9; **hacer una fiesta**   to have a party, 9
la **figurita**   shape, figurine, 4
fijarse   to notice, 7
el **fin**   end, 9; al fin   finally, 10
el **fin de semana**   weekend, 3; **este fin de semana**   this weekend, 4; **los fines de semana**   weekends, 3
finales: a finales   at the end, 10G
finalmente   finally, 8
financiar   to finance, 5
fino(a)   fine, 2G
el **flan**   flan, custard, 6
las **flautas**   rolled tortillas that are stuffed and fried, 9
la **flor**   flower, 1
las **flores**   flowers, 9
las **fogatas**   campfires, 3
el **folleto**   pamphlet, 7
la **forma**   form, xxii
formaba   formed
la **formación geológica**   geological formation, 7G
formar   to form, 3
formidable   great, 2
la **fortaleza**   fortress, 10
la **fortuna**   fortune, 8
la **foto**   photo, xxii; **enseñar fotos**   to show photos, 9; **sacar fotos**   to take photos, 10
la **fotografía**   photograph, 8
el **fragmento**   excerpt, 5
el **francés**   French, 4
la **frase**   phrase, 8; sentence, 9
la **frecuencia**   frequency, 8; con frecuencia   often, 8; **¿Con qué frecuencia vas...?**   How often do you go . . .?, 3
frecuentado(a)   visited, 1G
frente   front; al frente   to the front, xxii; en frente   in front, 3G
el **fresco**   cool, 3; **Hace fresco.**   It's cool., 3
el **frijol**   bean, 2G
frío(a)   cold, 6; **Hace frío.**   It's cold., 3; **tener frío**   to be cold, 7
la **frontera**   border, 7G
la **fruta**   fruit, 2; la fruta cítrica   citrus fruit, 8G
el **fuego**   fire, 3
¡Fue estupendo!   It was great!, 10
los **fuegos artificiales**   fireworks, 9; **ver los fuegos artificiales**   to see fireworks, 9
fuera   outside, 7G
fuera (inf. ser)   was, 6G
fuerte   loud, 2; strong, 3G
fumar   to smoke, 7; **dejar de fumar**   to stop smoking, 7

el **funcionalismo**   functional architectural style, 6G
funcionar   to work, 10
fundado(a)   founded, 2G
el **fútbol**   soccer, 3
el **fútbol americano**   football, 3
el **futuro**   future, 3
futuro(a)   future, 5

el **gabinete**   cabinet, 9
las **gafas**   glasses, 5
el **gallego**   romance language from Galicia, Spain, 1G
la **galleta**   cookie, 9
la **gana**   desire; **tener ganas de** + infinitive   to feel like doing something, 4
la **ganadería**   cattle raising, 7G
el **ganado**   cattle, 3G
ganar   to win, 5G
la **ganga**   bargain, 8
el **garaje**   garage, 5
la **garganta**   throat, 7
la **garita**   sentry box, 2G
gastar   to spend, 8
el **gato, la gata**   cat, 5
el **gazpacho**   cold tomato soup
la **generación**   generation, 5
generalmente   generally, 8
el **género**   genre, 8G
generoso(a)   generous, 6
la **gente**   people, 3
la **geografía**   geography, 1
geográfico(a)   geographical, 10
geometría   geometry, 4
gigante   giant, 6
el **gimnasio**   gym, 3
el **glaciar**   glacier, 5G
la **gloria**   heaven, 3
glorioso   glorious, 9
el **gobierno**   government, 1G
el **Golfo de México**   Gulf of Mexico, 8G
gordo(a)   fat, 5
la **gorra**   cap, 7
gótico(a)   gothic, 3G
la **grabación**   recording, 1
gracias   thank you, 1, **Estoy bien, gracias.**   I'm fine, thanks, 1; **No, gracias.**   No thanks., 8
gracioso(a)   witty, 2
la **graduación**   graduation, 9
gran   big, 5; great, 5; large, 3
la **granada**   pomegranate, 6
grande   big, large, 5
el **grano**   grain, 6
la **grasa**   fat, 7
gratuito   free, 1
gris   gray, 8

gritar   *to yell*, 7

la grúa   *tow truck*, 9

el grupo   *group*, 6

la guagua   *bus (P.R., Dom. Rep.)*, 10

los guandules   *pigeon peas*, 6

guapo(a)   *good-looking*, 2

guardar   *to store*, 10

la guayabera   *man's short-sleeved shirt*, 8

la guerra   *war*, 7

la guía telefónica   *telephone directory*, 10

guiar   *to guide*, 10; *to drive*, 10

el güiro   *percussive instrument played by scratching with a stick across a rough surface*, 3

el guiso   *stew*, 6

la guitarra   *guitar*, 2; la guitarra eléctrica   *electric guitar*, 2

gustar   *to like*, 2; **A ellos/ellas les gusta...**   *They like...*, 3; **A mis amigos y a mí nos gusta...**   *My friend and I like...*, 3; **Le gusta...**   *He/She likes...*, 3; **Me gusta(n)...**   *I like...*, 2; **Me gusta(n)... mucho.**   *I like... a lot.*, 2; me gustaba   *I liked*, 4; **Me gusta(n) más...**   *I like ... more.*, 2; **Me gustaría...**   *I would like...*, 8; **Me gustaría más...**   *I would prefer...*, 10; Me ha gustado...   *I have liked...*, 4; **No, no me gusta(n)...**   *No, I don't like...*, 2; **¿Te gusta(n)...?**   *Do you like...?*, 2; **¿Te gusta(n) más... o...?**   *Do you like... or... more?*, 2

el gusto   *pleasure*, 9

los gustos   *likes*, 2

haber   *to have;* hubo   *there was*, 10

las habichuelas   *beans*, 2G

la habitación   *bedroom*, 5

habitar   *to inhabit*, 7G

el habla   *speech*, 8

hablar   *to talk, to speak*, 3; **Habla...**   *... speaking (on the telephone)*, 8; **hablar por teléfono**   *to talk on the phone*, 3; Hablemos.   *Let's talk.*, 1

hacer (-go)   *to make, to do*, 4; **estamos haciendo**   *we are making/doing*, 9; están haciendo   *are making*, 3; **Hace buen (mal) tiempo.**   *The weather is nice (bad).*, 3; **Hace calor.**   *It's hot.*, 3; **Hace fresco.**   *It's cool.*, 3; **Hace frío.**   *It's cold.*, 3; Hace más de... años.   *It's more than ... years ago.*, 7G; **Hace sol.**   *It's sunny.*, 3; Hace tanto... que...   *It's so ... that...*, 3; Hace tiempo.   *It's been a long time.*, 9; **Hace viento.**   *It's windy.*, 3; **hacer cola**   *to wait in line*, 10; **hacer ejercicio**   *to exercise*, 3; **hacer la cama**   *to make the bed*, 5; **hacer la maleta**   *to pack your suitcase*, 10; **hacer la tarea**   *to do homework*, 3; **hacer los quehaceres**   *to do the chores*, 5; **hacer una fiesta**   *to have a party*, 9; **hacer un viaje**   *to take a trip*, 10; **hacer yoga**   *to do yoga*, 7; hacían   *they made*, 4; **haz**   *make, do*, 6; hizo   *he/she did*, 9; **no hagas**   *don't do*, 10; **¿Qué están haciendo?**   *What are they doing?*, 9; qué hicieron   *what they did*, 9; **¿Qué hiciste?**   *What did you do?*, 8; se hace   *is made*, 6

hallar   *to find*, 7G

el hambre   *hunger*, 4; **tener hambre**   *to be hungry*, 4

la hamburguesa   *hamburger*, 2

el Hanukah   *Hanukkah*, 9

hasta   *until*, 5; *up to*, 5; **Hasta luego.**   *See you later.*, 1; **Hasta mañana.**   *See you tomorrow.*, 1; **Hasta pronto.**   *See you soon.*, 1

hay (inf. **haber**)   *there is, there are*, 4; **Hay un(a)...**   *There's a...*, 4

haz   *make, do*, 6; Hazme caso.   *Pay attention to me.*, 8

hecho(a)   *made*, 2G

la heladería   *ice cream shop*, 8

el helado   *ice cream*, 2

la hembra   *female*, 2

el hemisferio   *hemisphere*, 7G

la herencia   *inheritance;* la herencia alemana   *German cultural tradition*, 7G; la herencia española   *Spanish cultural tradition*, 10G

la hermana   *sister*, 5

el hermano   *brother*, 5

los hermanos   *brothers, brothers and sisters*, 5

el héroe   *hero*, 4G

la hierba   *grass*, 8G; la hierba fina   *herb*, 8G

la hija   *daughter*, 5

el hijo   *son*, 5

los hijos   *sons, children*, 5

el hipo   *hiccup*, 3; estar con hipo   *to have hiccups*, 3

el hipopótamo   *hippopotamus*, 1

hispano(a)   *Hispanic*, 1

hispanohablante   *Spanish-speaking*, 6

la historia   *history*, 4

el hogar   *home*, 3G

las hojas de maíz   *cornhusks*, 3

hola   *hi, hello*, 1

el hombre   *man*, 8; el hombre de negocios   *businessman*, 5, los hombres   *men, humans*, 6; **para hombres**   *for men*, 8

el hombro   *shoulder*, 7

el homenaje   *tribute*, 1G

hondo(a)   *deep*, 8G

el honor   *honor*, 3

la hora   *hour*, 1; **¿A qué hora vas a...?**   *What time are you going to...?*, 4; **¿Qué hora es?**   *What time is it?*, 1

el horario   *schedule*, 3

la horchata mexicana   *sweet rice drink*, 6

la hormiga   *ant*, 6

el horno   *oven*, 6; el horno microondas   *microwave oven*, 6

horrible   *horrible*, 2; **¡Fue horrible!**   *It was horrible!*, 10

el hotel   *hotel*, 10; **quedarse en un hotel**   *to stay in a hotel*, 10

hoy   *today*, 1; hoy en día   *nowadays*, 6G; **Hoy es...**   *Today is...*, 1; **¿Qué día es hoy?**   *What day is today?*, 1

el huevo   *egg*, 6

húmedo(a)   *damp;* el bosque húmedo   *rainforest*, 4G

el huracán   *hurricane*, 3

la idea   *idea*, 6; la idea principal   *main idea*, 6

el idioma   *language*, 1G; idioma oficial   *official language*, 1G

identificar   *to identify*, 10

la iglesia   *church*, 3

igual que   *same as*, 2

igualmente   *equally*, 8

Igualmente.   *Likewise.*, 1

la iguana   *iguana*, 1

ilustrar   *to illustrate*, 5

imaginar   *to imagine*, 2

el imperativo   *imperative*, 9

el imperio   *empire*, 10G

imponente   *imposing*, 6

importado(a)   *imported*, 5G

la importancia   *importance*, 6

impresionante   *impressive*, 7G

incaico(a)   *Incan*, 10G

incesante   *without stopping*, 8

inclusive   *including*, 8

incluso   *including*, 8G

incomparable   *incomparable*, 5

la independencia   *independence*, 6G

independiente   *independent*, 2

indicar   *to indicate*, xxii

indígena   *indigenous*, 6G

la Infanta   *princess*, 10

la influencia   *influence*, 1G

Inglaterra   *England*, 7G

el inglés   *English*, 4

injusto   *unfair*, 5; **Me parece injusto.**   *It seems unfair to me*, 5

inmediato(a) *immediate*, 10G
inmenso(a) *immense*, 6
el inmigrante *immigrant*, 7G
inmigrar *to immigrate*, 7G
el insecto *insect*, 2
inseparable *inseparable*, 3
inspirar *to inspire*, 1G
el instrumento *instrument*, 8G
intacto(a) *intact*, 10
intelectual *intellectual*, 2
inteligente *intelligent*, 2
la intensidad *intensity*, 7
el interés *of interest*, 10
interesante *interesting*, 2
internacional *international*, 6
interrumpir *to interrupt*, 4
el invasor *invader*, 4G
inventar *to invent*, 4
el inventario *inventory*, 8
inventivo(a) *inventive*, 2
la investigación *research*, 4G
el invierno *winter*, 3
inviolable *inviolable*, 5
la invitación *invitation*, 9; **mandar invitaciones** *to send invitations*, 9
el invitado *guest*, 9; el invitado de honor *guest of honor*, 9
invitar *to invite*, 9
ir *to go*, 2; **¿Adónde fuiste?** *Where did you go?*, 8; **fue** *went*, 8; **fuimos** *we went*, 8; **ir+ a + infinitive** *to be going to (do something)*, 4; **ir de compras** *to go shopping*, 3; **ir de excursión** *to go hiking*, 10; **ir de pesca** *to go fishing*, 10; **ir al cine** *to go to the movies*, 3; **No vayas.** *Don't go.*, 7; **Quiero ir...** *I want to go . . .*, 2; **se va** *leaves*, 6; **¿Vas a...?** *Are you going to . . .?*, 4; **Vas a ir, ¿verdad?** *You're going to go, aren't you?*, 4; **ve** *go*, 6
irse *to leave*, 10
la isla *island*, 10
italiano(a) *Italian*, 6
la izquierda *left*

el jabón *soap*, 7
el jamón *ham*, 6
el jardín *garden*, 5
el jefe *chief*, 10
el jersey *sweater*, 8
la jirafa *giraffe*, 1
joven *young*, 5
el joven, la joven *young person*, 9; **los jóvenes** *young people*, 9
la joyería *jewelry store*, 8
el juego *game*, 3; **el juego de mesa** *board game*, 3; el juego de palabras *word game*, 7
el jueves *Thursday*, 1; **los jueves** *on Thursdays*, 3
el jugador *player*, 2G
jugar (ue) *to play*, 3
el jugo *juice*, 6; **el jugo de** . . . *juice*, 6
el juguete *toy*, 8
la juguetería *toy store*, 8
el juicio *judgment*, 6
julio *July*, 1
junio *June*, 1
juntos(as) *together*, 1
justo(a) *fair, just*, 10

el karate *karate*, 1
el kilómetro *kilometer*, 3
el kiosko *stand or stall*, 9G

la *the* (fem. article), 2
la *you, it,* (pronoun), 6; *you*, 9
las labores *chores*, 5
el lado: por todos lados *everywhere*, 8G
el lago *lake*, 10
la lágrima *tear*, 9
la lana *wool*, 8; **de lana** *made of wool*, 8
la lancha *motorboat*, 10; **pasear en lancha** *to go out in a motorboat*, 10
el lápiz (pl. **los lápices**) *pencil*, 4
largo(a) *long*, 5
las *the* (pl. fem. article), 2
las *you, them* (pronoun), 6
la lástima *pity*, 8; ¡Qué lástima! *What a shame!*, 8
la lata *can*, 9
latinoamericano(a) *Latin American*, 1
lavar *to wash*, 5; **lavar los platos** *to do the dishes*, 5
lavarse *to wash*, 7; **lavarse los dientes** *to brush your teeth*, 7
le *to/for him, her, you*, 2
la leche *milk*, 6
leer *to read*, 3; **al leer** *upon reading*, 6; **antes de leer** *before reading*, 1; **leamos** *let's read*, 1; leer en voz alta *to read aloud*, 6; se leen *are read*, 5; **leer revistas y novelas** *to read magazines and novels*, 3
el legado *legacy*, 8G

lejano(a) *distant*, 10
lejos *far*, 9; **lejos de** *far from*, 5
la lengua *language*, 9
los lentes *glasses*, 5; **usar lentes** *to wear glasses*, 5
lento(a) *slow*, 4G
el león *lion*, 1
les *to/for you* (pl.), *them*, 2
levantar *to lift*, 7; **levantar pesas** *to lift weights*, 7
levantarse *to get up*, 7
la leyenda *legend*, 10
libre *free*, 6G
la librería *bookstore*, 8
el libro *book*, 2; **el libro de amor** *romance book*, 2; **el libro de aventuras** *adventure book*, 2
el líder, la líder *leader*, 2
el limón *lemon*, 6
limpiar *to clean*, 5; limpio(a) *clean*, 5
lindo(a) *beautiful, pretty*, 6
listo(a) *ready*, 7; **estar listo(a)** *to be ready*, 7; **¿Está todo listo?** *Is everything ready?*, 9
llamado(a) *called*, 9G
llamar *to call*, 9; **llamar por teléfono** *to make a phone call*, 8; **Llamo más tarde.** *I'll call back later.*, 8; **Te llamo más tarde.** *I'll call you later.*, 9
la llegada *arrival*, 10
llegar *to arrive, to get there*, 4; **al llegar** *upon arriving*, 6; **ha llegado** *she has come*, 9
llenar *to fill up*, 3
lleno(a) *full*, 9
llevar *to wear*, 8; *to take*, 6; **lo llevó** *took it*, 6G; lleva años trabajando *he has been working for years*, 9
llevarse *to get along*, 2
llover (ue) *to rain*, 3; **llueve (mucho)** *it rains (a lot)*, 3
la lluvia *rain*, 4G
lo *him, it*, 6; *you*, 9; **Lo siento.** *I'm sorry.*, 8
lo: lo de siempre *same as usual*, 9; lo que *what*, 6; lo que pasa *what is happening*, xxii
loco *crazy*, 5
lógico(a) *logical*, 2
el lonche *lunch (Southwest U.S.)*, 6
los *the* (pl. masc.), 2
los *you, them* (pronoun), 6
luchar *to struggle*, 8; *to fight*, 4G
luego *then, later*, 4
el lugar *place*, 1G
los lugares de interés *places of interest*, 10
la luna *moon*, 9
lunes *Monday*, 3; **los lunes** *on Mondays*, 3
la luz *light*, 7G

M

el **macho** *male,* 2
la **madera** *wood,* 5G
la **madre** *mother,* 5
  madrina *godmother,* 1
el **maestro** *master,* 7G
  magnífico(a) *magnificent,* 4
el **maíz** *corn,* 6
  majestuoso(a) *majestic,* 9G
  mal *bad;* **Estoy mal.** *I'm not so
    good.,* 1; **Te veo mal.** *You don't
    look well.,* 7
la **maleta** *suitcase,* 10
  malo(a) *bad,* 2
  malvado(a) *evil,* 10
la **mamá** *mom,* 5
el **mamífero** *mammal,* 4G
la **mañana** *morning,* 4; **de la mañana**
    in the morning, A.M., 1; **por la
    mañana** *in the morning,* 4
  mañana *tomorrow,* 4; **Hasta
    mañana.** *See you tomorrow.,* 1
  mandar *to send,* 9; **mandar
    invitaciones** *to send invitations,*
    9; **mandar tarjetas** *to send cards,* 9
el **mandato** *command,* 6
  manejar *to manage,* 7
la **manera** *way,* 9
la **mano** *hand,* 7
el **manojo** *bunch,* 8
  mantener *to preserve, to keep,* 6
  mantenerse (ie) en forma *to stay
    in shape,* 7
la **manzana** *apple,* 6
el **mapa** *map,* 10
el **maquillaje** *makeup,* 7
  maquillarse *to put on makeup,* 7
  marcado(a) *marked,* 7
  marcar *to set, to dial,* 1
  marcharse *to leave,* 9
el **marisco** *shellfish,* 5G
  marítimo(a) *maritime,* 3G
  marrón *brown,* 2; los ojos
    marrones *brown eyes,* 5
el **martes** *Tuesday,* 1; **los martes** *on
    Tuesdays,* 3
  marzo *March,* 1
  más *more,* 2; **Más o menos.** *So-so.,*
    1; **más que** *more than,* 8; **más...
    que** *more ... than,* 8
la **masa** *dough,* 3
la **máscara** *mask,* 2G
la **mascarada** *masquerade,* 4G
la **mascota** *pet,* 5
el **mate** *Argentinean and Paraguayan
    tea,* 7
las **matemáticas** *mathematics,* 4
la **materia** *subject,* 4; las materias
    obligatorias *required subjects,* 4;
    las materias opcionales *electives,* 4

---

  matutino(a) *(in the) morning,* 4
  mayo *May,* 1
  mayor(es) *older,* 5; *greater,* 3G
la **mayoría** *majority,* 4G
la **mazorca** *corn on the cob,* 6
  me *to/for me,* 2; **Me da igual.**
    It's all the same to me., 2; **Me
    duele(n)...** *My ... hurt(s).,* 7;
    Me gusta(n)... *I like ...,* 2; **Me
    gusta(n) más...** *I like ... more.,* 2;
    Me gusta(n)... mucho. *I like ... a
    lot.,* 2; **Me llamo...** *My name
    is...,* 1; **No, no me gusta(n)...**
    No, I don't like ..., 2; **Me parece
    bien.** *It's all right with me.,* 5; **Me
    parece injusto.** *It seems unfair to
    me.,* 5
  me *me,* 9
  mecánico *mechanic,* 5
la **medalla** *medal,* 5G
  mediano(a) *medium,* 4
la **medianoche** *midnight,* 1
  médico(a) *medical,* 7
  medio(a) *half,* 4; **y media** *half
    past,* 1
los **medios de transporte** *means of
    transportation,* 10
el **mediodía** *midday, noon,* 1
  medir (i) *to measure,* 5G
  mejor(es) *better, best,* 7
el **melocotón** *peach,* 6
  menor(es) *younger,* 5
  menos *less,* 8; **menos cuarto**
    a quarter to..., 1; **menos que** *less
    than,* 8; **menos... que** *less...than,* 8
el **mensaje** *message,* 7G
la **mente** *mind,* 4
el **mercado** *market,* 6; el mercado al
    aire libre *open-air market,* 8
  merendar (ie) *to have a snack,* 5
el **merengue** *music and dance style,* 9G
la **merienda** *snack,* 6
la **mesa** *table,* 5; **poner la mesa** *to set
    the table,* 6
los **meses del año** *months of the year,* 1
  meter *to put in,* 8
  meterse *to set,* 9
  metódico(a) *methodical,* 2
el **metro** *meter,* 1G
el **metro** *subway,* 10
  mezclar *to mix,* 6; mezcla
    mixture, 6
la **mezquita** *mosque,* 1G
  mí *me,* 5; **A mí me gusta +**
    infinitive *I like to...,* 3; **A mí
    siempre me toca...** *I always have
    to...,* 5
  mi(s) *my,* 1; **Mi materia preferida
    es...** *My favorite subject is...,* 4;
    mi mejor amigo(a) *my best friend,*
    1, **mi profesor(-a)** *my teacher,* 1
el **microondas** *microwave,* 6
la **miel** *honey,* 6
el **miembro** *member,* 3

---

  mientras *while,* 6
el **miércoles** *Wednesday,* 1; **los
    miércoles** *on Wednesdays,* 3
  mil *one thousand,* 8; miles
    thousands, 2
la **milla cuadrada** *square mile,* 3
  un millón (de) *one million,* 8; **dos
    millones (de)** *two million,* 8
  mío *mine,* 8
  mirar *to look,* 9; **Nada más estoy
    mirando.** *I'm just looking.,* 8;
    mirar las vitrinas *to window-
    shop,* 8
la **misa** *Mass,* 9
la **misión** *mission,* 3G
  mismo(a) *same,* 6
el **misterio** *mystery,* 2
  misterioso(a) *mysterious,* 2
la **mitad** *half,* 6G
la **mochila** *backpack,* 4
la **moda** *style, fashion,* 8; **a la última
    moda** *in the latest fashion,* 8; muy
    de moda *very fashionable,* 8;
    pasado(a) de moda *out of style,* 8
  modelar *to shape,* 4
  moderno(a) *modern,* 7
el **módulo** *module,* 10
el **mogote** *knoll,* 9G
el **mole** *sauce made with chiles and
    flavored with chocolate,* 6
el **molino** *windmill,* 1G
el **momento** *moment,* 6; **Espera un
    momento.** *Hold on a moment.,* 8
la **monarquía parlamentaria**
    constitutional monarchy, 1G
la **moneda** *currency,* 2; *coin,* 8
el **mono** *monkey,* 4G
la **montaña** *mountain,* 10; **subir a la
    montaña** *to go up a mountain,* 10
  montañoso(a) *mountainous,* 7G
  montar a caballo *to ride a horse,*
    3G; **montar en bicicleta** *to ride
    a bike,* 3
  un montón *a ton,* 4
el **monumento** *monument,* 1G
el **morado** *purple,* 1G
  morado(a) *purple,* 8
  moreno(a) *dark-haired; dark-
    skinned,* 2
  morir (ue) *to die,* 5; murió *died,* 5
el **moro** *rice and beans,* 9G
el **mosaico** *mosaic,* 6G
el **mosquito** *mosquito,* 2
el **mostrador** *counter,* 10
  mostrar (ue) *to show,* 1G
el **movimiento** *movement,* 4G
la **muchacha** *girl,* 1
el **muchacho** *boy,* 1
  mucho *a lot (of),* 2; *much,* 4;
    Mucho gusto. *Pleased/Nice to
    meet you.,* 1
  muchos(as) *a lot of, many,* 4
  mudarse *to move,* 8G
  mudéjar *Moslem,* 5G

la **muerte** *death*, 4G
la **mujer** *woman*, 8; **la mujer de
negocios** *business woman*, 5;
para mujeres *for women*, 8
mundialmente *worldwide*, 6
el mundo *world*, 1G; todo el mundo
everybody, 9
el mural *mural painting*, 6G
la muralla *wall, rampart*, 1G
el museo *museum*, 10
la **música** *music*, 2; **la música de...**
music of/by . . ., 2; la música clásica
classical music, 2G
el músico *musician*, 2
muy *very*, 2

nacer *to be born*, 7G; había nacido
had been born, 7G; nacido(a)
born, 8G
nacional *national*, 1
nada *nothing*, 4; *not anything*, 5
Nada más estoy mirando. *I'm just
looking.*, 8
nadar *to swim*, 3
nadie *nobody, not anybody*, 5
la **naranja** *orange*, 6
el naranjo *orange tree*, 8G
la **nariz** *nose*, 7
la natación *swimming*, 7
nativo(a) *native*, 6
la naturaleza *nature*, 2
la **navaja** *razor*, 7
navegar *to sail*, 5; *to navigate*, 10;
navegar por Internet *to surf the
Internet*, 3
la **Navidad** *Christmas*, 9
la necesidad *necessity*, 7
necesitar *to need*, 4; **¿Necesitas algo?**
Do you need anything?, 4; **Necesito
muchas cosas.** *I need a lot of
things.*, 4; **No, no necesito nada.**
No, I don't need anything., 4
negarse *to refuse*, 5
negociable *negotiable*, 5
el negocio *business*, 9
negro(a) *black*, 5
nervioso(a) *nervous*, 7
nevar (ie) *to snow*, 3
ni *neither, nor*, 7; **Ni idea.** *I have no
idea.*, 3
el nido *nest*, 1
la **nieta** *granddaughter*, 5
el **nieto** *grandson*, 5
los **nietos** *grandsons, grandchildren*, 5
nieva *it snows*, 3

la **niña** *girl*, 1
ninguno(a) *no, none*, 10G;
ninguna parte *nowhere*, 3; **No va
a ninguna parte.** *He/she doesn't
go anywhere.*, 3
el niño *male child*, 8
los **niños** *children*, 8
el nivel del mar *sea level*, 9G
no *no*, 3; *not, do not*, 5; **No debes...**
You shouldn't . . ., 7; **No es gran
cosa.** *It's not a big deal.*, 5; **No
está.** *He/She is not here.*, 8; **No
estoy de acuerdo.** *I disagree.*, 6;
no, gracias *no thank you*, 8; **No
sé.** *I don't know.*, 4; **No, no me
gusta(n)...** *No, I don't like . . .*, 2;
No, no necesito nada. *No, I do
not need anything.*, 4; **No, no voy a
ir.** *No, I'm not going to go.*, 4; **No
seas...** *Don't be . . .*, 7; **No va a
ninguna parte.** *He/She doesn't go
anywhere.*, 3; **No vayas.** *Don't go.*,
7
¿no? *right?*, 4
la **noche** *night*, 1; **de la noche** *at
night*, P.M., 1; **por la noche** *at
night*, 4
la **Nochebuena** *Christmas Eve*, 9
la **Nochevieja** *New Year's Eve*, 9
nocturno(a) *(in the) evening*, 4
nombrado(a) *named*, 9G
el nombre *name*, 10
el noreste *northeast*, 2G
normalmente *normally*, 4
el noroeste *northwest*, 7G
el norte *north*, 5G
norteamericano(a) *North
American*, 8
norteño(a) *northern*, 5G
Noruega *Norway*, 7G
nos *(to/for) us*, 2; **Nos vemos.** *See
you.*, 1
nosotros(as) *we*, 1
la nota *grade*, 6
la noticia *news*, 9
novecientos *nine hundred*, 8
la **novela** *novel*, 3
noventa *ninety*, 2
noviembre *November*, 1
la nube *cloud*, 7
nuestro(a) *our*, 5
nuestros(as) *our*, 5
nuevamente *again*, 9
nueve *nine*, 1
nuevo(a) *new*, 2
las nueces *nuts*, 6
el **número** *number*, 1; *shoe size*, 8
numeroso(a) *numerous*, 2G
nunca *never*, 5; **casi nunca** *almost
never*, 3; nunca más *never again*, 6
la nutricionista *nutritionist*, 7

o *or*, 2
oaxaqueño *from the Mexican state
of Oaxaca*, 6
el objetivo *objective*, 1
el objeto *object*, 1
la obra *work*, 7G; la obra de teatro
play, 6G; la obra maestra
masterpiece, 6G
observar *to observe*, 1
la ocasión *occasion*, 9
occidental *western*, 7G
ochenta *eighty*, 2
ocho *eight*, 1
ochocientos *eight hundred*, 8
el ocio *leisure time*, 8
octubre *October*, 1
el ocupante *occupant*, 10
ocupar *to occupy*, 7G
ocurrir: ¿Se te ocurren? *Do they
occur to you?*, 4
la oficina *office*, 5
la **oficina de cambio** *money
exchange*, 10
la **oficina de correos** *post office*, 10
ofrecer *to offer*, 6
el **oído** *ear*, 7
oír *to hear*, 2; oyes *(you) hear*, 2;
se oye *is heard*, 2
los **ojos** *eyes*, 5; los ojos borrados
hazel eyes, 5; los ojos cafés *brown
eyes*, 5; **tener los ojos azules** *to
have blue eyes*, 5
la ola *wave*, 2G
la olla *pot*, 4G
olor *smell*, 7
olvidar *to forget*, 9; No te olvides.
Don't forget., 8
once *eleven*, 1
la oportunidad *opportunity*, 5
la oración *sentence*, xxii
el orden *order*, 1; el orden
cronológico *chronological order*, 8
ordenar *to organize*, 3; está
ordenando *is organizing*, 3
organizado(a) *organized*, 2
organizar *to organize*, 10
orgulloso(a) *proud*, 6
oriental *eastern*, 10G
el origen *origin*, 6G
originalmente *originally*, 3G
os *(to/for) you* (pl.), 2
el oso *bear*, 1
el otoño *fall*, 3
otro(a) *other, another*, 8
otros(as) *other, others*, 8

P

el **paciente** *patient*, 7
el padre *father*, 5
los padres *parents*, 5; los padres peregrinos *pilgrims*, 8G
  pagar *to pay*, 8; **pagar una fortuna** *to pay a fortune*, 8
la **página** *page*, xxii; la página Web *Web page*, 1
el país *country*, 6; el país de origen *native country*, 6
el **paisaje** *landscape*, 4G
el **pájaro** *bird*, 9
la **palabra** *word*, xxii; la palabra clave *key word*, 1
el **palacio** *palace*, 1
el pan *bread*, 6; **el pan dulce** *pastries*, 6; **el pan tostado** *toast*, 6
la **pantalla** *monitor, screen*, 10
los pantalones (vaqueros) *pants (jeans)*, 8
los pantalones cortos *shorts*, 8
la **pantomima** *pantomime*, 9
la pantorrilla *calf*, 7
el **papá** *dad*, 5
el **Papá Noel** *Santa Claus*, 9
la **papa** *potato*, 6; **las papas fritas** *french fries*, 6
el papel *paper*, 4
las papitas *potato chips*, 9
el **paquete** *package*, 9
el par *pair*, 8
  para *for*, 4; *to, in order to*, 7
el **paraíso** *paradise*, 8G
  parecer *to seem*, 5; *to think*, 8; me parece *it seems to me*, 9; **Me parece bien.** *It's all right with me.*, 5; **Me parece injusto.** *It seems unfair to me.*, 5; No parezco. *I don't seem to be.*, 9; **¿Qué te parece...?** *What do you think of ...?*, 8
  parecido(a) *similar*, 2
la **pared** *wall*, 10G
la **pareja** *pair*; en parejas *in pairs*, xxii; *couple*, 3
el **paréntesis** *parenthesis*, 8
el **pareo** *matching*, 1
el **pariente** *relative*, 5
el parque *park*, 3; **el parque de diversiones** *amusement park*, 10
el **párrafo** *paragraph*, xxii
la **parrilla** *barbecue*, 7
la **parrillada** *Argentine barbecue*, 7G
la **parte** *part*, 6
  participar *to participate*, 1
  particular *particular*, 6
el partido de... *the ... game*, 4
la **pasa** *raisin*, 6
el **pasado** *past*, 8

pasado mañana *day after tomorrow*, 4
pasado(a) *last*, 8; **el año pasado** *last year*, 9
pasado(a) de moda *out of style*, 8
el **pasaje** *ticket*, 10
el pasajero, la pasajera *passenger*, 10
el **pasapalo** *finger food (Ven.)*, 9
el pasaporte *passport*, 10
  pasar *to spend (time, occasion)*, 9; con quien tú te pasas *who you spend time with*, 2; **La pasamos en casa de...** *We spent it at ...'s house*, 9; lo que pasa *what is happening*, 9; **pasar el rato solo(a)** *to spend time alone*, 3; **pasar la aspiradora** *to vacuum*, 5; **pasar por** *to stop at/by*, 10; *to go through*, 2; qué pasa *what's happening*, 6
  pasartelo(la) *to get someone for a telephone call*, 8
el **pasatiempo** *hobby*, 7; **buscar un pasatiempo** *to find a hobby*, 7
  pasear *to go for a walk*, 3; *to go out in*, 10; **pasear en bote de vela** *to go out in a sailboat*, 10; **pasear en lancha** *to go out in a motorboat*, 10
el **pasillo** *corridor*, 10
la pasta de dientes *toothpaste*, 7
el pastel *cake*, 6
el **pastel en hojas** *mashed plantain dough filled with meat and wrapped in plantain leaves*, 9
la **patata** *potato*, 1G; *sweet potato*, 6
el **patinaje en hielo** *ice skating*, 7
  patinar *to skate*, 3
el patio *patio, yard*, 5
la **patrona** *patron*, 9G
la **pava** *kettle used to make mate*, 7
el **pavo** *turkey*, 6G
el **payaso** *clown*, 4G
las pecas *freckles*, 5
el pecho *chest*, 7
  pedir (i) *to order*, 6
  peinarse *to comb your hair*, 7
el **peine** *comb*, 7
la película *film, movie*, 2; **(de ciencia ficción, de terror, de misterio)** *(science fiction, horror, mystery)*, 2
el **peligro de extinción** *danger of extinction*, 8G
  pelirrojo(a) *red-headed*, 2
el pelo *hair*, 5
la **pelota** *ball*, 9G
  pensar (ie) *to think*, 8; **pensar + inf.** *to plan*, 9; **Pensamos...** *We plan to ...*, 9
  peor(es) *worse*, 8
  pequeño(a) *small*, 5; **bastante pequeño(a)** *pretty small*, 5
la **pera** *pear*, 1
  perder (ie) *to lose*, 10; *to miss*, 10; **perder el vuelo** *miss the flight*, 10;

si me pierden *if you lose me*
  perdido(a) *lost*, 10G
  perdone *I'm sorry*, 1
el **perezoso** *sloth*, 4G
  perezoso(a) *lazy*, 2
  perfecto *perfect*, 8
el **periódico** *newspaper*, 8G
la **perla** *pearl*, 2G
  permiso *excuse me*, 9
  permitir *to allow*, 6
  pero *but*, 5
el perro, la perra *dog*, 5
la persona *person*, 2
el **personaje** *character*, 1G; el personaje ficticio *fictional character*, 1G
la **personalidad** *personality*, 2
las pesas *weights*, 7; **levantar pesas** *to lift weights*, 7
la pesca *fishing*, 10; **ir de pesca** *to go fishing*, 10; la pesca comercial *commercial fishing*, 8G
el pescado *fish*, 6
  pescar *to fish*, 10
  pésimo(a) *very bad*, 2
el peso *weight*, 7
el **pez** *fish*, 1
la **picadera** *finger food (Dom. Rep.)*, 9
el **picante** *spice*, 6
  picante *spicy*, 6
el picnic *picnic*, 9; **tener un picnic** *to have a picnic*, 9
el **pico** *peak*, 1G
el **pico de gallo** *spicy relish made with tomatoes, hot peppers, and onions*, 3G
el pie *foot*, 7
la **piedra** *stone*, 5G
la pierna *leg*, 7
la **pieza** *bedroom*, 5; *piece*, 4
la **pileta** *swimming pool (Arg.)*, 3
la piñata *piñata*, 9
el **pingüino** *penguin*, 7G
  pintado(a) *painted*, 2G
  pintar *to paint*; fue pintado *was painted*, 1
el **pintor** *painter*, 2G
  pintoresco(a) *picturesque*, 7G
la **pintura** *painting*, 1; la pintura al óleo *oil painting*, 3G
la pirámide *pyramid*, 10; la pirámide alimenticia *food pyramid*, 7
la piscina *swimming pool*, 3
el piso *floor*, 5; **de... pisos** *... story*, 5
el piyama *pajamas*, 7
la pizza *pizza*, 2
el **placer** *pleasure*, 9
  planes *plans*, 9; **¿Qué planes tienen para...?** *What plans do you have for ...?*, 9
  plano(a) *flat*, 7G
las plantas *plants*, 5
el **plátano** *plantain*, 8G
  platicar en línea *to chat online*, 3

el plato *dish, plate,* 6; **lavar los platos** *to do the dishes,* 5; **el plato hondo** *bowl,* 6; el plato típico *traditional dish,* 2

la playa *beach,* 3

la playera *T-shirt,* 8

la plaza de comida *food court in a mall,* 8

la plena *music and dance style,* 2

la población *population,* 1G

poblado(a) *populated,* 4G

pobre *poor,* 8

poco(a) *few, little, not much,* 4; poco a poco *little by little,* 4; **un poco** *a little,* 2

pocos(as) *not many,* 4

poder (ue) *to be able to, can,* 6

el poema *poem,* 8

la poesía *poetry,* 8

el poeta, la poeta *poet,* 5G

el pollo *chicken,* 6; el pollo frito *fried chicken,* 2G

el ponche *punch,* 9

poner (-go) *to put,* 4; **no pongas** *don't put,* 10; **pon** *put,* 6; poner en orden *to put in order,* xxii; poner huevos *to lay eggs,* 2; poner la comida *to set out the food,* 9; **poner la mesa** *to set the table,* 6; tener puesto(a) *to have on,* 8

ponerse (-go) *to put on,* 7, *to get,* 6; ponerse *to start,* 7; ponerse a bailar *to start dancing,* 3; ponerse en contacto *to get in contact,* 5; ponerse rojo *to flush, to turn red,* 10

por *in, by,* 4; por ejemplo *for example,* 6G; por eso *that's why,* 6; por el estilo *of that sort,* 7; **por favor** *please,* 6; **por fin** *finally,* 10; **por la mañana** *in the morning,* 4; por la noche *at night,* 2; **por la tarde** *in the afternoon,* 4; por lo general *generally,* 8; por lo menos *at least,* 9; por más que *no matter how much,* 7; por medio de *by means of,* 10

¿por qué? *why?,* 2

la porción *portion, serving,* 7

porque *because,* 2

posible *possible,* 4

el postre *dessert,* 6

el pozole *soup made with hominy, meat, and chile,* 6

practicando *practicing,* 7

practicar deportes *to play sports,* 3

el precio *price,* 1; el precio de entrada *entry fee,* 1

precolombino(a) *of the New World era before the arrival of Europeans,* 2G

precoz *precocious,* 4

la preferencia *preference,* 3

preferido(a) *favorite,* 4

preferir (ie) *to prefer,* 6

la pregunta *question,* xxii

preguntar *to ask,* xxii

prehistórico(a) *prehistoric,* 7G

preocuparse *to worry,* 10; **No te preocupes.** *Don't worry.,* 10

preparar *to prepare,* 6

prepararse *to get ready,* 7

los preparativos *preparations,* 9

la preposición *preposition,* 2

la presentación *introduction,* 9

presentar *to present,* 6; *to introduce,* 9; **presentar un examen** *to take a test,* 4; se presentó *was performed,* 10; **Te presento a...** *I'd like you to meet . . .,* 9

presentarse *to present oneself,* 6

el presente *present,* 9

prestar: prestar atención *to pay attention,* 7

el pretérito *preterite,* 8

la primavera *spring,* 3

el primero *first,* 1

primero(a) *first,* 4

el primo, la prima *cousin,* 5; el primo hermano, la prima hermana *first cousin,* 5

los primos *cousins,* 5

la princesa *princess,* 10

principal *main,* 4G; *primary,* 9G

el prisionero *prisoner,* 10

probar (ue) *to try, to taste,* 6

producir *to produce,* 1

el producto *product,* 3G; los productos petroleros *petroleum products,* 3G; los productos químicos *chemicals,* 3G

el profesor *teacher (male),* 1; **mi profesor** *my teacher,* 1

la profesora *teacher (female),* 1; **mi profesora** *my teacher,* 1

prometer *to promise,* 8

el pronombre *pronoun,* 6; el pronombre de complemento directo *direct object pronoun,* 9; el pronombre reflexivo *reflexive pronoun,* 7

pronto *soon,* 1; **Hasta pronto.** *See you soon.,* 1; tan pronto *as soon,* 9

la propiedad *property,* 5

propio(a) *own,* 4

el propósito *purpose,* 6

el provecho *benefit;* Buen provecho. *Enjoy your meal.,* 6

la provincia *province,* 10

próximo(a) *next,* 4; **la próxima semana** *next week,* 4; **el** *(day of the week)* **próximo** *next (day of the week),* 4

el proyecto *project,* 1

publicar *to publish,* 1

el pueblo *town, village,* 5; el pueblo natal *hometown,* 3

¿Puedo...? *Can I . . .?,* 6

el puente *bridge,* 8G

la puerta *door,* 5; *gate,* 10

el puerto *port,* 3G

el puesto *stall,* 9G

la pulsera *bracelet,* 8

el punto *dot,* 1

el punto de vista *point of view,* 9

puntual *punctual, on time,* 2

el puré de papas *mashed potatoes,* 6

que *that;* que me llame después *tell him/her to call me later,* 8; **Que te vaya bien.** *Hope things go well for you.,* 9

¡Qué...! *How . . .!;* **¡Qué bien!** *How great!,* 10; **¡Qué fantástico!** *How fantastic!,* 10; **¡Qué gusto verte!** *It's great to see you!,* 9; **¡Qué lástima!** *What a shame!,* 10; **¡Qué lata!** *What a pain!,* 5; **¡Qué mala suerte!** *What bad luck!,* 10

¿qué? *what?,* 1; **¿Qué clases tienes ...?** *What classes do you have . . . ?,* 4; **¿Qué día es hoy?** *What day is today?,* 1; **¿Qué están haciendo?** *What are they doing?,* 9; **¿Qué fecha es hoy?** *What's today's date?,* 1; **¿Qué hace...?** *What does . . . do?,* 3; **¿Qué haces para ayudar en casa?** *What do you do to help out at home?,* 5; **¿Qué haces...?** *What do you do . . .?,* 3; **¿Qué haces para relajarte?** *What do you do to relax?,* 7; **¿Qué hay de nuevo?** *What's new?,* 9; **¿Qué hiciste?** *What did you do?,* 8; **¿Qué hora es?** *What time is it?,* 1; **¿Qué planes tienen para...?** *What plans do you have for . . .?,* 9; **¿Qué quieres hacer?** *What do you want to do?,* 3; **¿Qué tal?** *How's it going?,* 1; **¿Qué tal...?** *How is . . .?,* 6; **¿Qué tal estuvo?** *How was it?,* 9; **¿Qué tal si...?** *How about (if). . .?,* 6; **¿Qué tal si vamos a...?** *How about if we go to . . .?,* 4; **¿Qué te falta hacer?** *What do you still have to do?,* 7; **¿Qué te gusta hacer?** *What do you like to do?,* 3; **¿Qué te pasa?** *What's wrong with you?,* 7; **¿Qué te toca hacer a ti?** *What do you have to do?,* 5; **¿Qué tiempo hace?** *What's the weather like?,* 3; **¿Qué tiene...?** *What's the matter with . . .?,* 7; **¿Qué tienes que hacer?**

What do you have to do?, 7; **¿Qué vas a hacer?** *What are you going to do?*, 4

el **quechua** *indigenous language in Peru*, 10G

quedar *to fit, to look*, 8; *to remain*, 3G; **¿Cómo me queda...?** *How does it fit?*, 8; **quedar bien/mal** *to fit well/poorly*, 8

quedarse *to stay*, 9; **quedarse en un hotel** *to stay in a hotel*, 10

los **quehaceres** *household chores*, 5; **hacer los quehaceres** *to do the chores*, 5

querer (ie) *to want to*, 3; *to love*, 9; **Quiero conocer...** *I want to see ...*, 10; **queriendo** *wanting to*, 8; **Quiero ir...** *I want to go ...*, 3

querido(a) *dear*, 9

la **quesadilla** *tortillas with melted cheese*, 3G

el **queso** *cheese*, 6

¿quién? *who?*, 1; **¿De parte de quién?** *Who's calling?*, 8; **¿Quién es...?** *Who is ...?*, 1; **¿de quién?** *about whom?*, 1

¿quiénes? *who? (pl.)*, 2

la **química** *chemistry*, 4

quince *fifteen*, 1

la **quinceañera** *girl's fifteenth birthday*, 9

quinientos *five hundred*, 8

el **quiosco** *stand*, 10

Quisiera... *I would like ...*, 6

quitarse *to take off*, 7

las **raciones** *servings*, 6

la **raíz** (pl. las **raíces**) *root*, 1G

rallado(a) *grated*, 6

la **rana** *frog*, 2

los **rancheros** *overalls*, 3

rápidamente *quickly*, 6

rápido(a) *fast*, 8

raro *odd, strange*, 3

el **rato** *time*, 3; el rato libre *free time*, 4

reaccionar *to react*, 10

el **realismo** *realism*, 1

realizar *to carry out*, 10, ha realizado *has carried out*, 10G

el **recado** *message*, 8

la **recámara** *bedroom*, 5

recibir *to receive*, 9; **recibir regalos** *to receive gifts*, 9

reclamar *to reclaim*, 6G

el **reclamo de equipaje** *baggage claim*, 10

recoger *to pick up*, 10

la **recomendación** *recommendation*, 7

reconocido(a) *well-known*, 1G

recordar *to remember*, 6

recorrer *to tour*, 10

el **recorrido** *tour*, 4

el **recreo** *recreation time*, 4

la **red** *network*, 10G

redondo(a) *round*, 7

reducir *to reduce*, 7

referir *to refer*, 3; se refiere *refers*, 3G

reflejar *to reflect*, 1G

el **refrán** *proverb, saying*, 6

el **refresco** *soft drink*, 6

el **refrigerador** *refrigerator*, 6

el **refugio de fauna** *wildlife refuge*, 8G

el **regalo** *gift*, 9; **abrir regalos** *to open gifts*, 9; **recibir regalos** *to receive gifts*, 9

regatear *to bargain*, 8

la **región** *region*, 3

regional *regional*, 6

la **regla** *ruler*, 4

regresar *to return, to go back*, 4

regular *all right*, 1; **Estoy regular.** *I'm all right.*, 1

regularidad: con regularidad *regularly*, 6

reírse *to laugh*, 8; **ríe** *he/she laughs*, 9; se ríen *they laugh*, 8

relajarse *to relax*, 7

religioso(a) *religious*, 1

el **reloj** *clock, watch*, 4

remodelado(a) *remodeled*, 5

remojar *to soak*, 3

remoto(a) *distant*, 5

el **renacuajo** *tadpole*, 2

el **repaso** *review*, 1

representar *to represent*, 3

representativo(a) *representative*, 6

la **respuesta** *answer*, xxii

el **restaurante** *restaurant*, 6

la **república** *republic*, 5G

el **res** *beef*, 6

la **reservación** *reservation*, 6

requerir (ie) *to require*, 7

la **resolución de Año Nuevo** *New Year's resolution*, 9

resolver (ue) *to solve*, 7

respectivo(a) *respective*, 8

responder *to answer*, 9

la **respuesta** *answer*, 3

el **restaurante** *restaurant*, 6

el **restaurante familiar** *family restaurant*, 3

el **retrato** *portrait*, 1G

la **reunión** *meeting*, 3; *reunion*, 9

reunir *to bring together*, 1G

reunirse *to get together*, 9; **reunirse con (toda) la familia** *to get together with the (whole) family*, 9

revisar *to check, to revise, to correct*, 1

la **revista** *magazine*, 3; **la revista de tiras cómicas** *comic book*, 8

el **revolucionario** *revolutionary*, 9G

el **rey** *king*, 1

rico(a) *magnificent*, 9

ridículo(a) *ridiculous*, 8

riguroso(a) *harsh*, 5G

el **río** *river*, 3G

las **riquezas** *riches*, 10

riquísimo(a) *delicious*, 6

el **ritmo** *rhythm*, 5G; el ritmo del momento *the latest rhythm*, 1

el **rito** *ritual*, 6

el **robo** *rip-off*, 8; **¡Es un robo!** *It's a rip-off!*, 8

rodeado(a) *surrounded*, 1G

rodear *to surround*, 7G

el **rodeo** *rodeo*, 3G

rojo(a) *red*, 8

romántico(a) *romantic*, 2

el **rompecabezas** *puzzle*, 4

la **ropa** *clothes*, 4

rubio(a) *blond*, 2

las **ruinas** *ruins*, 10

la **rutina** *routine*, 2

el **sábado** *Saturday*, 1; **los sábados** *on Saturdays*, 3

saber *to know information*, 4; **saber de** *to know about*, 4; no sabe cómo *doesn't know how*, 9; **No sé.** *I don't know.*, 4; **¿Sabes qué?** *You know what?*, 4; **Sé.** *I know.*, 9

el **sabor** *flavor*, 8G

sacar *to take out*, 6; **sacar el dinero** *to get money*, 10; **sacar fotos** *to take photos*, 10; **sacar la basura** *to take out the trash*, 5; sacar una idea *to get an idea*, 4

el **saco** *sportscoat*, 8

sal *go out, leave*, 6

la **sal** *salt*, 6

la **sala** *living room*, 5; **la sala de espera** *waiting room*, 10; la sala de juegos *game room*, 5

salado(a) *salty*, 6; **Está (un poco) salado(a)** *It's (a little) salty.*, 6

la **salida** *departure*, 10; *exit*, 10

salir (-go) *to go out*, 3; *to leave*, 4; **No salgas.** *Don't leave.*, 10; que salga *go out*, 9; **sal** *go out, leave*, 6; salir bien *to work out well*, 7; **salir con amigos** *to go out with friends*, 3

el salón   *room*, 1; **el salón de clase**
   classroom, 4
la salsa   *sauce, gravy*, 6; **la salsa**
   picante   *hot sauce*, 6
el salto   *waterfall*, 2G
el salto en el tiempo   *time warp*, 7
la salud   *health*, 7
   saludable   *healthy*, 6
   saludar   *to greet*, 1
el saludo   *greeting*, 9
   salvarse   *to save oneself*, 10
el salvavidas   *lifeguard*, 1
el sancocho   *stew made with meat,*
   root vegetables, and plantains, 9G
las sandalias   *sandals*, 8
el sándwich de...   *... sandwich*, 6
los sanitarios   *restrooms*, 10
   sano(a)   *healthy*, 7; **seguir (i) una**
   dieta sana   *to eat a balanced diet,*
   7
el santo, la santa   *saint*, 2G
la sartén   *frying pan*, 6
   sé   *be*, 6
la secadora de pelo   *hair dryer*, 7
   secarse   *to dry*, 7
la sección rítmica   *rhythm section*, 8G
   seco(a)   *dry*, 2G
   secreto(a)   *secret*, 1
la sed   *thirst*, 4; **tener (-go, ie) sed**   *to*
   be thirsty, 4
la seda   *silk*, 8; **de seda**   *made of silk,*
   8
   seguir (i)   *to follow*, 10; **seguir (i)**
   una dieta sana   *to eat a balanced*
   diet, 7; sigue el modelo   *follow the*
   model, xxii; siguiéndote   *following*
   you, 8
   según   *according to*, 2
el segundo   *second*, 4
   segundo(a)   *second*, 6
   seis   *six*, 1
   seiscientos   *six hundred*, 8
la selección   *selection*, 6
la selva   *jungle*, 10
la semana   *week*, 4; **el día de la**
   semana   *day of the week*, 1; **esta**
   semana   *this week*, 4; **la próxima**
   semana   *next week*, 4
la Semana Santa   *Holy Week*, 9
el señor   *sir, Mr.*, 1; *gentleman*, 8
el Señor   *the Lord*, 9
la señora   *ma'am; Mrs.*, 1
la señorita   *Miss*, 1
la sensación   *feeling*, 1
   sentarse (ie)   *to sit down*, 10
   sentir (ie)   *to feel*, 9
   sentirse (ie)   *to feel*, 7
   separados   *separately*, 8
   separar   *to separate*, 1G
   septiembre   *September*, 1
   ser   *to be*, 1; **¿Cómo eres?**   *What*
   are you like?, 2; **¿Cómo es...?**
   What is ... like?, 2; No puede ser.

It can't be true., 9; **no seas**   *don't*
   be, 7; **sé**   *be*, 6; **será**   *will be*, 10;
   Soy...   *I'm ...*, 2; **Soy de...**   *I'm*
   from ..., 1
el ser   *being*, 8
la serenata   *serenade*, 9
la serenidad   *serenity*, 1
la serie   *series*, 6G
   serio(a)   *serious*, 2
la serpiente   *serpent*, 6
el servicio   *restroom*, 10
la servilleta   *napkin*, 6
   servir (i)   *to serve*, 6; **¿En qué le**
   puedo servir?   *Can I help you?*, 8
   sesenta   *sixty*, 2
el seso   *brain*, 4
   setecientos   *seven hundred*, 8
   setenta   *seventy*, 2
   si   *if*, 3; **si no**   *otherwise*, 3
   sí   *yes*, 4; **Sí, necesito muchas cosas.**
   Yes, I need a lot of things., 4; **Sí,**
   tengo un montón.   *Yes, I have a*
   ton of them., 4
   siempre   *always*, 5; **casi siempre**
   almost always, 3; **como siempre**
   as always, 9; **lo de siempre**   *same*
   as always, 9
la sierra   *mountain range*, 10G
   siete   *seven*, 1
el siglo   *century*, 3G
el significado   *meaning*, 7
   significar   *to mean*, 2
   siguiente   *following*, 5; **lo siguiente**
   the following, 6
la sílaba   *syllable*, 2
la silla   *chair*, 5; **la silla de ruedas**
   wheelchair, 5
el símbolo   *symbol*, 2
   simpático(a)   *friendly*, 2
   simplemente   *simply*, 6
   sin   *without*, 6; **sin embargo**
   however, 6
la sinagoga   *synagogue*, 9
   sincero(a)   *sincere*, 2
   sino   *but also*, 6
los sirvientes   *servants*, 8
el sistema   *system*, 10G
el sitio   *place*, 3; *site*, 7
la situación   *situation*, 5
   sobre   *over*, 3; *on*, 4; *about*, 2
la sobrina   *niece*, 5
el sobrino   *nephew*, 5
los sobrinos   *nephews, nieces and*
   nephews, 5
   sociable   *social*, 2
el sofá   *sofa*, 5
el sol   *sun*, 3; **Hace sol.**   *It's sunny.*, 3
   solamente   *only*, 3G
el soldado   *soldier*, 6G
   soler   *to usually do*, 5; **suele**
   usually, 5
   sólido(a)   *solid*, 6
   solo(a)   *alone*, 3; **pasar el rato**

   solo(a)   *to spend time alone*, 3
   sólo   *only*, 7
el sombrero   *hat*, 8
   somos (inf. ser)   *we are*, 5; **Somos...**
   personas.   *There are ... people.*, 5
   Son las...   *It's ... o'clock.*, 1
el sonido   *sound*, 2G
la sopa   *soup*, 6; **la sopa de verduras**
   vegetable soup, 6
   sordo(a)   *deaf*, 5
   sorprendido(a)   *surprised*, 8
   Soy... (inf. ser)   *I'm ...*, 2; **Soy de...**
   I'm from ..., 1
   su(s)   *his, her, its, their*, 5
   suave   *soft*, 7
   subir   *to rise*, 7
   subir a la montaña   *to go up a*
   mountain, 10; **subir de peso**   *to*
   gain weight, 7
el subtítulo   *subtitle*, 10
   sucio(a)   *dirty*, 6
el sudeste   *southeast*, 10G
   Suele + inf.   *He (She) usually +*
   verb, 10
el sueño   *dream*, 1G
la suerte   *luck*, 10; **Si tengo suerte...**
   If I'm lucky ..., 10; **Tuviste suerte.**
   You were lucky., 10
el suéter   *sweater*, 8
   suficiente   *enough*, 7; **dormir (ue)**
   lo suficiente   *to get enough sleep*, 7
la sugerencia   *suggestion*, 7
   sugerir   *to suggest*, 6
   Suiza   *Switzerland*, 7G
la superficie   *surface*, 8
el sur   *south*, 2G
   sureño(a)   *southern*, 7G
el surf a vela   *windsurfing*, 9G
   sus   *his/her*, 4; *their, your*, 5
la sustancia   *substance*, 6
   suyo(a)   *his*, 4G

   Tailandia   *Thailand*, 6
   taíno(a)   *belonging to the Tainos,*
   Native Americans dominant in
   early Puerto Rico, 2G
   tal   *such*, 7; **tal vez**   *perhaps*, 4
la talla   *(clothing) size*, 8
   tallado(a)   *carved, cut*, 10G
los tallarines   *noodles*, 7
el taller   *shop, workshop*, 4
la tamalada   *gathering to make*
   tamales, 3G
los tamales   *tamales*, 9
el tamaño   *size*
   también   *also*, 2
la tambora   *drum*, 9G
   tampoco   *neither, not either*, 5
   tan   *so*, 10G

tan sólo   *only,* 9

tan... como   *as . . . as,* 8

tanto   *so much,* 7; *as much,* 1G; tanto... como...   *both . . . and . . . ,* 3G; **Tanto gusto.**   *So nice to meet you.,* 9; **Tanto tiempo.**   *It's been a long time.,* 1; **¡Tanto tiempo sin verte!**   *Long time, no see!,* 9

la tapa   *small servings of food,* 7G

tardar   *to take;* ¿Cuánto tardas?   *How long do you take?,* 4

la tarde   *afternoon, evening,* 1; **de la tarde**   *in the afternoon, evening,* P.M., 1; **esta tarde**   *this afternoon,* 4; **por la tarde**   *in the afternoon,* 4

tarde   *late,* 4; **más tarde**   *later,* 8

la tarea   *homework,* 1; **hacer la tarea**   *to do homework,* 3

la tarjeta   *greeting card,* 8; *card,* 9; **mandar tarjetas**   *to send cards,* 9; **la tarjeta de cumpleaños**   *birthday card,* 8; la tarjeta de crédito   *credit card,* 10; **la tarjeta de embarque**   *boarding pass,* 10; la tarjeta postal   *postcard,* 10; **la tarjeta regalo**   *gift card,* 8

el tataranieto   *great-great-grandson,* 10

el taxi   *taxi,* 10

la taza   *cup,* 6

te   *(to/for) you,* 2; ¿Te duele algo?   *Does something hurt?,* 7; **¿Te gusta(n)...?**   *Do you like . . . ?,* 2; **¿Te gusta(n) más... o...?**   *Do you like . . . or . . . more?,* 2; **Te llamo más tarde.**   *I'll call you later.,* 9; **Te presento a...**   *I'd like you to meet . . . ,* 9; **Te veo mal.**   *You don't look well.,* 7

el teatro   *theater,* 8

el techo de zinc   *sheet-metal roof,* 9G

la tecnología   *technology,* 4

tejano(a)   *Texan,* 3G

el tejido   *weaving,* 10G

la tele   *TV,* 4

el teléfono   *telephone number,* 1; *telephone,* 8; **¿Cuál es el teléfono de...?**   *What's . . . 's telephone number?,* 1; **¿Cuál es tu teléfono?**   *What's your telephone number?,* 1; **hablar por teléfono**   *to talk on the phone,* 3; llamar por teléfono   *to make a phone call,* 8; el teléfono público   *pay phone,* 10

la televisión   *television (TV),* 3; **ver televisión**   *to watch TV,* 3

el tema   *theme,* 6

temblar   *to shake,* 9

tembloroso(a)   *trembling,* 9

la temperatura   *temperature,* 2G

templado(a)   *temperate,* 2G

el templo   *temple,* 9

temprano   *early,* 4

ten   *have,* 6

el tenedor   *fork,* 6

tener (-go, ie)   *to have,* 4; **¿Cuántos años tiene...?**   *How old is . . . ?,* 2; **¿Cuántos años tienes?**   *How old are you?,* 2; **Él (Ella) tiene... años.**   *He's (She's) . . . years old.,* 2; **no tengas**   *don't have,* 10; **ten**   *have,* 6; tendrán que separarse   *will have to separate,* 3; **tener calor**   *to be hot,* 7; **tener catarro**   *to have a cold,* 7; **tener frío**   *to be cold,* 7; **tener ganas**   *to feel like (doing something),* 4; **tener ganas de +** infinitive   *to feel like doing something,* 4; **tener hambre**   *to be hungry,* 4; **tener los ojos azules**   *to have blue eyes,* 5; **tener miedo**   *to be afraid,* 7; **tener prisa**   *to be in a hurry,* 4; tener puesto   *to have on,* 3; **tener que +** infinitive   *to have to do something,* 4; **tener razón**   *to be right,* 8; **tener sed**   *to be thirsty,* 4; **tener sueño**   *to be sleepy,* 7; **tener suerte**   *to be lucky,* 10; **tener un picnic**   *to have a picnic,* 9; **Tengo que irme.**   *I have got to go.,* 1; **Tengo... años.**   *I am . . . years old.,* 2; **Tiene... años.**   *He (She) is . . . years old.,* 2; tuvo   *had,* 7G

el tenis   *tennis,* 3

el tentempié   *snack,* 3G

el tercero   *third,* 4

terminar   *to finish,* 9

la terraza de comidas   *food court in a mall,* 8

el territorio   *territory,* 6G

el terror   *horror,* 2

el testimonio   *testimony,* 6G

el texto   *text,* 6

ti   *you* (emphatic), 3; a ti   *to you,* 6; **A ti te gusta +** infinitive   *You like . . . ,* 3; para ti   *for you,* 2

la tía   *aunt,* 5

el tico   *nickname for Costa Rican,* 4G

el tiempo   *weather,* 3; *time,* 1G; **a tiempo**   *on time,* 4; **cuando hace buen/mal tiempo**   *when the weather's good/bad,* 3

la tienda de...   *. . . store,* 8

tiene   *he/she/it has,* 2; **¿Cuántos años tiene…?**   *How old is . . . ?,* 2; **Él (Ella) tiene... años.**   *He's (She's) . . . years old.,* 2; **Tiene... años.**   *He's (She's) . . . years old.,* 2

tienes   *you have,* 4; **¿Cuántos años tienes?**   *How old are you?,* 2; **¿Tienes...?**   *Do you have . . . ?,* 4

la tierra   *earth,* 6; *land,* 6G

el tigre   *tiger,* 2

la tilde   *wavy line above the ñ,* 1

tímido(a)   *shy,* 2

la tinta   *ink,* 10

el tío   *uncle,* 5

los tíos   *uncles, uncles and aunts,* 5

típico(a)   *typical,* 2G

el tipo   *type;* de todo tipo   *all kinds,* 8; el título   *title,* 5

la toalla   *towel,* 7

tocar   *to play,* 3; *to touch,* 8; **A mí siempre me toca...**   *I always have to . . . ,* 5; **A... nunca le toca...**   *. . . never has to . . . ,* 5; **Le toca a él.**   *It's his turn.,* 5; **¿Qué te toca hacer a ti?**   *What do you have to do?,* 5; **Te toca a ti.**   *It's your turn.,* 5; **tocar el piano**   *to play the piano,* 3; tocar la puerta   *to knock on the door,* 3

el tocino   *bacon,* 6

todavía   *yet,* 10; *still,* 1G; **todavía no**   *not yet,* 10

todo(a)   *all, every,* 2; *whole,* 9; todo el mundo   *everybody,* 9; de todo   *everything,* 8; de todo tipo   *all kinds,* 8; **todos(as)**   *everyone,* 5; **todos los días**   *every day,* 3

tomar   *to drink,* 6; *to eat,* 8; *to take,* 9; siguen tomándolo   *keep drinking it,* 6; *to take,* 7; **tomar el sol**   *to sunbathe,* 10; tomar las cosas con calma   *to take things calmly,* 7; tomar una decisión   *to make a decision,* 9; **tomar un batido**   *to have a milkshake,* 8

el tomate   *tomato,* 6

la tonelada   *ton,* 10

tonto(a)   *silly, foolish,* 2

el tornado   *tornado,* 3

la toronja   *grapefruit,* 3G

la torre   *tower,* 9G

la torta   *sandwich (Mexico),* 6

la tortilla   *Spanish omelet,* 1G; *pancake-like bread made from corn,* 6

la tortuga   *turtle,* 1

el tostón   *fried green plantain,* 2G

trabajador(a)   *hard-working,* 2

trabajar   *to work,* 3

el trabajo   *job,* 3; *work,* 4

el trabalenguas   *tongue twister,* 1

la tradición   *tradition,* 2

tradicional   *traditional,* 1G

traer (-igo)   *to bring,* 4; me trajo   *he/she brought me,* 4; quiero que me traigas   *I want you to bring me,* 9

el tráfico   *traffic,* 3G

tragar   *to swallow,* 2

el traje   *suit,* 3; *dress,* 1G

el traje de baño   *swimsuit,* 8

tranquilo(a)   *quiet,* 5; *calm,* 9

la transpiración   *perspiration,* 8

transportar   *to transport,* 10; fueron transportadas   *were transported,* 10

el transporte   *transportation,* 10

el trasto   *utensil, piece of junk,* 2

tratar   *to try,* 10

travieso(a)   *mischievous,* 5

trece   *thirteen,* 1

treinta   *thirty,* 1

treinta y cinco *thirty-five,* 2
treinta y dos *thirty-two,* 2
treinta y uno *thirty-one,* 1
el **tren** *train,* 10
tres *three,* 1
trescientos *three hundred,* 8
el **trigal** *wheat field,* 2
el **trigo** *wheat,* 2
triste *sad,* 7; **estar triste** *to be sad,* 7
el **trozo** *piece,* 6
tú *you,* 1
tu(s) *your,* 5
el **turismo** *tourism,* 8G
el **turista** *tourist,* 1G
turnarse *to take turns,* xxii
el **turno** *shift,* 4
tutear *to speak to someone informally,* 10
los **tuyos, las tuyas** *yours,* 9

último(a) *latest,* 8; **la última vez** *last time,* 8
el **último, la última** *last one,* 3
un(a) *a, an,* 4; **un poco** *a little,* 2; **un montón** *a ton,* 4
únicamente *only,* 9
único(a) *only,* 4G
la **unidad** *unity,* 3G
la **universidad** *university,* 5
uno *one,* 1
unos(as) *some,* 4
urgente *urgent,* 1
usar *to use, to wear,* 8; **usar el/la...** *to wear size...,* 8; **usar lentes** *to wear glasses,* 5; **usando** *using,* xxii
el **uso** *use,* 6
usted *you* (formal), 1
ustedes *you* (pl.), 1
los **útiles escolares** *school supplies,* 4
utilizar *to use,* 7
la **uva** *grape,* 1
¡Uy! *Oh!,* 1

las **vacaciones** *vacation,* 10
Vale. *Okay.,* 9
valeroso(a) *brave,* 4G
valiente *brave,* 5
la **valija** *suitcase,* 10
el **valle** *valley,* 3G
vamos *let's go, we go,* 3
el **vaquero** *cowboy,* 3G
vaquero(a) *referring to cowboys,* 3G

los **vaqueros** *jeans,* 8
variado(a) *varied,* 7
varias *various,* 6G
la **variedad** *variety,* 6
vas *you are going,* 4; **¿Vas a (a la)...?** *Are you going to the...?,* 4; **Vas a ir, ¿verdad?** *You're going to go, aren't you?,* 4
el **vasco** *language from Basque Provinces, Spain,* 1G
la **vasija** *pot,* 4
el **vaso** *glass,* 6
ve *go,* 6
veces *times,* 7; **a veces** *sometimes,* 3; **hay veces** *there are times,* 4
veinte *twenty,* 1
veintiún *twenty-one,* 1
ven *come,* 6
vencido(a) *defeated,* 6; **no se da por vencido** *doesn't give up,* 6
el **vendedor** *vendor,* 8
vender *to sell,* 8; **se vende** *for sale,* 5; **se venden** *are sold,* 8; **vender de todo** *to sell everything,* 8
venir *to come,* 4; **ha venido** *has come,* 9; **No vengas.** *Don't come.,* 10; **ven** *come,* 6; **venga** *will come,* 9; **Vienes conmigo a...** *You're coming with me to...,* 4
la **ventana** *window,* 5
el **ventanal** *large window,* 6G
la **ventura** *happiness,* 5
ver *to watch, to see,* 4; **nunca ha visto** *never has seen,* 6; **Te veo mal.** *You don't look well.,* 7; **ver televisión** *to watch television,* 3; **vi** *I saw,* 8
el **verano** *summer,* 3
el **verbo** *verb,* xxii
la **verdad** *truth,* 2
¿verdad? *right?,* 4
verde *green,* 5; **verde mar** *sea green,* 5G
las **verduras** *vegetables,* 2
vespertino(a) *(in the) afternoon,* 4
el **vestido** *dress,* 8
vestirse (i) *to get dressed,* 7
vete *go,* 7
vez *time,* 4; **cada vez** *each time,* 8; **hay veces** *there are times,* 4; **la última vez** *last time,* 8
viajar *to travel,* 10
el **viaje** *trip,* 10
el **viajero** *traveler,* 10
la **vida** *life,* 3G
el **video** *video,* 3; **alquilar videos** *to rent videos,* 3
los **videojuegos** *videogames,* 2
los **viejitos** *older folks,* 3
viejo(a) *old,* 5
el **viento** *wind,* 3; **Hace viento.** *It's windy.,* 3
el **viernes** *Friday,* 1; **los viernes** *on Fridays,* 3; **el viernes próximo**

next Friday, 4
el **Viernes Santo** *Good Friday,* 1
el **violín** *violin,* 1
visitar *to visit,* 6
la **vista** *view,* 5
la **vitrina** *shop window,* 8; **mirar las vitrinas** *to window-shop,* 8
vivir *to live,* 5
vivo(a) *bright,* 5G
el **vocabulario** *vocabulary,* xxii
volar *to fly,* 7
el **volcán** *volcano,* 4G
el **volibol** *volleyball,* 3
volver (ue) *to go or come back,* 5; **nunca más volverá** *never will do it again,* 9; **se vuelve** *it becomes,* 6
vosotros(as) *you* (plural; informal), 1
el **vuelo** *flight,* 10
vuestra(s) *your,* 5
vuestro(s) *your,* 5

el **wáter** *restroom,* 10
el **windsurfing** *windsurfing,* 7

y *and,* 1; **y cuarto** *a quarter past,* 1; **y media** *half past,* 1
ya *already,* 10
Ya te lo (la) paso. *I'll get him (her).,* 8
la **yerba mate** *herb used to make Argentinean and Paraguayan tea,* 7
yo *I,* 1
el **yogur** *yogurt,* 7
la **yuca** *yucca,* 8G

la **zanahoria** *carrot,* 6
la **zapatería** *shoe store,* 8
las **zapatillas de tenis** *tennis shoes,* 8
los **zapatos** *shoes,* 4; **los zapatos de tenis** *tennis shoes,* 8
la **zona** *area,* 4; **la zona residencial** *residential area,* 5
el **zoológico** *zoo,* 10
el **zumo** *juice (Spain),* 6

Vocabulario inglés-español

This vocabulary includes all of the words presented in the **Vocabulario** sections of the chapters. These words are considered active—you are expected to know them and be able to use them. Expressions are listed under the English word you would be most likely to look up.

Spanish nouns are listed with the definite article and plural forms, when applicable. If a Spanish verb is stem-changing, the change is indicated in parentheses after the verb: **dormir (ue)**. The number after each entry refers to the chapter in which the word or phrase is introduced.

To be sure you are using Spanish words and phrases in their correct context, refer to the chapters listed. You may also want to look up Spanish phrases in **Expresiones de ¡Exprésate!,** pp. R12–R14.

a little   *un poco,* 2
a lot   *mucho,* 2
a lot of, many   *muchos(as),* 4
a ton   *un montón,* 4
a, an   *un(a),* 4
active   *activo(a),* 2
to **add**   *añadir,* 6
address   *la dirección,* 5; **My address is . . .**   *Mi dirección es...,* 5; e-mail address   *correo electrónico,* 1
adventure   *la aventura,* 2; **adventure book**   *el libro de aventuras,* 2
after   *después,* 3; *después de,* 7; **after class**   *después de clases,* 3
afternoon   *la tarde,* 1; **this afternoon**   *esta tarde,* 4; **in the afternoon**   *de la tarde, P.M.,* 1; *por la tarde,* 4
afterwards   *después,* 4
agent   *el agente, la agente,* 10
agree: I don't agree.   *No estoy de acuerdo.,* 6; **I agree.**   *Estoy de acuerdo.,* 6
airplane   *el avión,* 10; **by plane**   *por avión,* 10
airport   *el aeropuerto,* 10
all   *todas,* 1; *todo(a),* 2
all right   *regular,* 1; **All right.**   *Está bien.,* 3
to **allow**   *dejar,* 3
almost   *casi,* 3; **almost never**   *casi nunca,* 3; **almost always**   *casi siempre,* 3
alone   *solo(a),* 3
alphabet   *el alfabeto,* 1
already   *ya,* 10
also   *también,* 2
always   *siempre,* 5; **almost always**   *casi siempre,* 3; **as always**   *como siempre,* 9
amusement park   *el parque de diversiones,* 10
an   *un, una,* 4
and   *y,* 1
animal   *el animal,* 2
anniversary   *el aniversario,* 9
another   *otro,* 8
any   *cualquier,* 10
anything   *algo,* 4; *nada,* 4
apartment   *el apartamento,* 5
apple   *la manzana,* 6
April   *abril,* 1
Are you . . . ?   *¿Eres...?,* 2
arm   *el brazo,* 7
around the corner   *a la vuelta,* 10
arrival   *la llegada,* 10
to **arrive**   *llegar,* 4
art   *el arte,* 4
as . . . as   *tan...como,* 8
as always   *como siempre,* 9
at   *a(l),* 8; **@**   *la arroba,* 1; *en,* 3
athletic   *atlético(a),* 2
to **attend**   *asistir (a),* 4
auditorium   *el auditorio,* 4
August   *agosto,* 1
aunt   *la tía,* 5
automatic teller machine   *el cajero automático,* 10
awesome   *fenomenal,* 2

back   *la espalda,* 7; **I'll call back later**   *Llamo más tarde,* 8; **to go (come) back**   *volver (ue),* 5
backpack   *la mochila,* 4
bacon   *el tocino,* 6
bad   *malo(a),* 2
bag   *bolsa,* 8
baggage   *el equipaje,* 10; **baggage claim**   *el reclamo de equipaje,* 10
bargain   *la ganga,* 8
baseball   *el béisbol,* 3
basketball   *el básquetbol,* 3

to **bathe**   *bañarse,* 7
bathroom   *el baño,* 5
be   *sé,* 6
to **be able to**   *poder (ue),* 6
to **be**   *estar,* 1; **How are you?**   *¿Cómo está(s)?,* 1; **to be all right**   *estar regular,* 1; **to be angry**   *estar enojado,* 7; **to be around the corner**   *estar a la vuelta,* 10; **to be bored**   *estar aburrido(a),* 7; **to be familiar with**   *conocer,* 9; **to be fine**   *estar bien,* 1; **to be hungry**   *tener hambre,* 4; **to be tired**   *estar cansado(a),* 7; **to be happy**   *estar contento(a),* 7; **to be sick**   *estar enfermo(a),* 7; **to be in a hurry**   *tener prisa,* 7; **to be in a wheelchair**   *estar en una silla de ruedas,* 5; **to be ready**   *estar listo(a),* 7; **to be nervous**   *estar nervioso(a),* 7; **to be right**   *tener razón,* 7; **to be sad**   *estar triste,* 7; **to be scared**   *tener miedo,* 7; **to be sleepy**   *tener sueño,* 7; **to be lucky**   *tener suerte,* 7; **to be thirsty**   *tener sed,* 7; **don't be**   *no estés,* 7
to **be**   *ser,* 1; **don't be**   *no seas,* 7
beach   *la playa,* 3
because   *porque,* 2
bed   *la cama,* 5; **to make the bed**   *hacer la cama,* 5; **to go to bed**   *acostarse (ue),* 7
bedroom   *la habitación,* 5
beef   *la carne,* 6
before   *antes de,* 7
behind   *detrás de,* 5
besides   *además,* 8
best   *el/la/los/las mejor(es),* 1
better   *mejor(es),* 7
big   *grande,* 5
bike   *la bicicleta,* 3; **to ride a bike**   *montar en bicicleta,* 3
bill   *la cuenta,* 6
biology   *la biología,* 4

birthday *el cumpleaños,* 9; **When is
…'s birthday?** *¿Cuándo es el
cumpleaños de…?,* 2; **When is your
birthday?** *¿Cuándo es tu
cumpleaños?,* 2; **…'s birthday** *el
cumpleaños de…,* 2; **birthday card**
la tarjeta de cumpleaños, 8; **girl's
fifteenth birthday** *la
quinceañera,* 9
black *negro(a),* 5
blank *en blanco,* 8
blind *ciego(a),* 5
blond *rubio(a),* 2
blouse *la blusa,* 8
blue *azul,* 5; **to have blue eyes**
tener los ojos azules, 5
board game *el juego de mesa,* 3
to **board** *abordar,* 10
boarding pass *la tarjeta de
embarque,* 10
boat *el barco,* 10
book *el libro,* 2; **adventure book**
el libro de aventuras, 2; **comic book**
la revista de tiras cómicas, 8;
romance book *el libro de amor,* 2
bookstore *la librería,* 8
boots *las botas,* 8
boring *aburrido(a),* 2; **to be bored**
estar aburrido, 7
bowl *el plato hondo,* 6
boy *el muchacho,* 1
bracelet *la pulsera,* 8
bread *el pan,* 6
breakfast *el desayuno,* 6
to **bring** *traer (-igo),* 4
broccoli *el bróculi,* 6
brother *el hermano,* 5
brothers, brothers and sisters *los
hermanos,* 5
brown *castaño(a),* 5; *de color café,* 5
to **brush your teeth** *lavarse los
dientes,* 7
building *el edificio,* 5; **…story
building** *el edificio de… pisos,* 5
bus *el autobús,* 10
but *pero,* 5
to **buy** *comprar,* 8; **you would buy**
comprarías, 8
by plane *por avion,* 10
Bye *chao,* 9

cafeteria *la cafetería,* 4
cake *el pastel,* 6
calculator *la calculadora,* 4
calf *la pantorrilla,* 7
to **call** *llamar,* 9; **I'll call back later.**
Llamo más tarde., 8; **I'll call you
later.** *Te llamo más tarde.,* 9
camera *la cámara,* 10; **disposable
camera** *la cámara desechable,* 10
to **camp** *acampar,* 10

can *poder,* 6
Can I …? *¿Puedo…?,* 6
Can I help you? *¿En que le puedo
servir?,* 8
candy *el dulce,* 9
canoe *la canoa,* 10
car *el carro,* 2
card *la tarjeta,* 8
carrot *la zanahoria,* 5
cat *el gato, la gata,* 5
to **celebrate** *festejar,* 9
cereal *los cereales,* 6
chair *la silla,* 5; **wheelchair** *la silla
de ruedas,* 5
to **change money** *cambiar dinero,* 10
to **chat** *charlar,* 9; **to chat online**
platicar en línea, 3
to **check luggage** *facturar el equipaje,*
10
checkpoint: security checkpoint
control de seguridad, 10
cheese *el queso,* 6
chemistry *la química,* 4
chess *el ajedrez,* 2
chest *el pecho,* 7
chicken *el pollo,* 6
children *los hijos,* 5; *los niños,* 8
chocolate *el chocolate,* 6
chores *los quehaceres,* 5
Christmas *la Navidad,* 9;
Christmas Eve *la Nochebuena,* 9
church *la iglesia,* 3
city *la ciudad,* 5
class *la clase,* 3; **after class** *después
de clases,* 3
classmate (female) *la
(una) compañera de clase,* 1
classmate (male) *el
(un) compañero de clase,* 1
to **clean** *limpiar,* 5
to **clean the room** *arreglar el cuarto,* 5
client *el cliente, la cliente,* 8
climb *subir,* 10
clock *el reloj,* 4
close to *cerca de,* 5
to **close** *cerrar (ie),* 8
clothes *la ropa,* 4
cloudy *nublado,* 7
club *el club de…,* 4
coat *el abrigo,* 8
coffee *el café,* 6; **coffee with milk**
el café con leche, 6; **coffee shop**
la cafetería, 6
cold *frío(a),* 6; **It's cold.** *Hace
frío.,* 3; **to be cold** *tener frío,* 7
to **have a cold** *tener catarro,* 7
color *el color,* 8
comb *el peine,* 7
to **comb your hair** *peinarse,* 7
to **come** *venir,* 4; **come** *ven,* 6; **don't
come** *no vengas,* 10; **to come
back** *volver,* 5; **you're coming
with me to …** *vienes conmigo a…,* 4
comic book *la revista de tiras
cómicas,* 8

compact disc *el disco compacto,* 8;
blank compact disc *el disco
compacto en blanco,* 8
computer *la computadora,* 4;
computer science *la
computación,* 4
concert *el concierto,* 4
to **cook** *cocinar,* 5
cookie *la galleta,* 9
cool *fresco,* 3; **It's cool.** *Hace
fresco.,* 3
corn *el maíz,* 6
to **cost** *costar (ue),* 8; **costs…**
cuesta(n)…, 8; **It will cost.**
Costará., 9
cotton *el algodón,* 8; **made of
cotton** *de algodón,* 8
counter *el mostrador,* 10
country *el país,* 10
countryside *el campo,* 5
court: food court in a mall *la
terraza de comidas,* 8
cousin *el primo, la prima,* 5
custard *el flan,* 6
customs *la aduana,* 10
to **cut** *cortar,* 6; **to cut the grass**
cortar el césped, 5

dad *el papá,* 5
dance *el baile,* 3; **dance class**
la clase de baile, 4
to **dance** *bailar,* 3; **dancing** *bailando,*
1; **to start dancing** *ponerse a
bailar,* 3
dark: dark-skinned; dark-haired
moreno(a), 2
date *la fecha,* 1
daughter *la hija,* 5
day *el día,* 1; **day after tomorrow**
pasado mañana, 4; **day before
yesterday** *anteayer,* 8; **day of the
week** *el día de la semana,* 1;
Father's Day *el Día del Padre,* 9;
holiday *el día festivo,* 9;
Independence Day *el Día de la
Independencia,* 9; **Mother's Day**
el Día de la Madre, 9; **some day**
algún día, 10; **Thanksgiving Day**
el Día de Acción de Gracias, 9;
Valentine's Day *el Día de los
Enamorados,* 9; **What day is
today?** *¿Qué día es hoy?,* 1; **your
saint's day** *el día de tu santo,* 9
deaf *sordo(a),* 5
December *diciembre,* 1
to **decorate** *decorar,* 9; **to decorate
the house** *decorar la casa,* 9
decoration *la decoración,* 9
delicious *delicioso(a),* 2;
riquísimo(a), 6
to **delight** *encantar,* 6

department store   *el almacén,* 8
departure   *la salida,* 10
to desire   *desear,* 6
desk   *el escritorio,* 5
dessert   *el postre,* 6
destination   *el destino,* 10
destined   *destinado(a),* 6
detail   *el detalle,* 7
to determine   *determinar,* 7
dictionary   *el diccionario,* 4
diet   *la dieta,* 7; **to eat a balanced
   diet**   *seguir una dieta sana,* 7
difficult   *difícil,* 4; **It's difficult.** *Es
   difícil.,* 4
dining room   *el comedor,* 5
dinner   *la cena,* 6
disc: compact disc   *el disco
   compacto,* 8; **blank compact disc**
   el disco compacto en blanco, 8
to disembark   *desembarcar,* 10
dish   *el plato,* 6
disposable   *desechable,* 10;
   disposable camera   *la cámara
   desechable,* 10
Do you like . . . ?   *¿Te gusta(n)...?,* 2
to do   *hacer,* 4; **we are doing**   *estamos
   haciendo,* 9; **to do homework**
   hacer la tarea, 3; **to do the chores**
   hacer los quehaceres, 5; **to do the
   dishes**   *lavar los platos,* 7; **to do
   yoga**   *hacer yoga,* 7; **do**   *haz,* 6;
   don't do   *no hagas,* 10; **What are
   they doing?**   *¿Qué están
   haciendo?,* 9; **What did you do?**
   ¿Qué hiciste?, 8
dog   *el perro, la perra,* 5
door   *la puerta,* 5
dot   *el punto,* 1; **on the dot**   *en
   punto,* 1
to download files   *bajar archivos,* 3
downtown   *el centro,* 10
to draw   *dibujar,* 3
dress   *el vestido,* 8
dressed: to get dressed,   *vestirse (i),*
   7
to drink (something)   *beber (algo),* 4;
   tomar, 6; **to drink punch**   *beber
   ponche,* 9
to dry   *secarse,* 7
during   *durante,* 10
DVD   *el DVD,* 8

ear   *el oído,* 7
early   *temprano,* 4
earphones   *los audífonos,* 8
earrings   *los aretes,* 8
easy   *fácil,* 4; **It's easy.**   *Es fácil.,* 4
to eat   *comer,* 3; *tomar,* 8
to eat a balanced diet   *seguir (i) una
   dieta sana,* 7; **to eat breakfast**

desayunar, 6; **to eat dinner**   *cenar,*
   6; **to eat lunch**   *almorzar (ue),* 6
egg   *el huevo,* 6
eight   *ocho,* 1
eight hundred   *ochocientos,* 8
eighteen   *dieciocho,* 1
eighty   *ochenta,* 2
eleven   *once,* 1
e-mail address   *el correo electrónico,*
   1; **What is . . .'s e-mail address?**
   ¿Cuál es el correo electrónico de...?,
   1; **What's your e-mail address?**
   ¿Cuál es tu correo electrónico?, 1
English   *el inglés,* 4
enough   *suficiente,* 7; **to get enough
   sleep**   *dormir (ue) lo suficiente,* 7
evening   *la tarde,* 1; **in the evening,**
   P.M. *de la tarde,* 1
everyone   *todos(as),* 5
everybody   *todos (as),* 5
everything   *todo,* 8
to exercise   *hacer ejercicio,* 3
to expect   *esperar,* 9
expensive   *caro(a),* 8
eyes   *los ojos,* 5; **to have blue eyes**
   tener (ie) los ojos azules, 5

face   *la cara,* 7
fall   *el otoño,* 3
family   *la familia,* 3; **There are . . .
   people in my family.**   *En mi
   familia somos...,* 5
familiar: to be familiar   *conocer,* 9
fantastic: How fantastic!   *¡Qué
   fantástico!,* 10
fat (in food)   *la grasa,* 7
fat (overweight)   *gordo(a),* 5
father   *el padre,* 5; **Father's Day**   *el
   Día del Padre,* 9
favorite   *preferido(a),* 4
flan   *el flan,* 6
February   *febrero,* 1
to feel   *sentirse (ie),* 7; **to feel like
   doing something**   *tener (ie) ganas
   de + infinitive,* 4
few   *pocos(as),* 4
fifteen   *quince,* 1
fifteenth: girl's fifteenth birthday
   quinceañera, 9
fifty   *cincuenta,* 2
film   *la película,* 2
finally   *por fin,* 10
to find   *encontrar (ue),* 7; **to find a
   hobby**   **buscar un pasatiempo,** 7
fine   *bien,* 1; **I'm fine.**   *Estoy bien.,* 1
finger   *el dedo,* 7
finish   *terminar,* 9
fireworks   *los fuegos artificiales,* 9
first   *el primero,* 1
first (adj.)   *primero(a),* 4
fish   *el pescado,* 6

to fish   *pescar,* 10
fishing   *la pesca,* 10; **to go fishing**
   ir de pesca, 10
to fit   *quedar,* 8; **How does it fit?**
   ¿Cómo me queda?, 8
five   *cinco,* 1
five hundred   *quinientos,* 8
flight   *el vuelo,* 10
floor   *el piso,* 5
folder   *la carpeta,* 4
to follow   *seguir (i),* 10
food   *la comida,* 2; **Chinese (Italian,
   Mexican) food**   *la comida china
   (italiana, mexicana),* 2, **food court
   in a mall**   *la plaza (terraza) de
   comida,* 8
foolish   *tonto(a),* 2
foot   *el pie,* 7
football   *el fútbol americano,* 3
for   *para,* 4
for example   *por ejemplo,* 6G
fork   *el tenedor,* 6
fortune   *la fortuna,* 8
forty   *cuarenta,* 2
four   *cuatro,* 1
four hundred   *cuatrocientos,* 8
fourteen   *catorce,* 1
French   *el francés,* 4
French fries   *las papas fritas,* 6
frequency   *la frecuencia,* 8
Friday   *el viernes,* 1; **on Fridays**
   los viernes, 3
friend   *el amigo* (male), *la amiga*
   (female), 1
from   *de,* 1
fruit   *la fruta,* 2
fun   *divertido(a),* 2; **What fun!**
   ¡Qué divertido!, 10
funny   *cómico(a),* 2

to gain weight   *subir de peso,* 7
game: board game   *el juego de
   mesa,* 3; **the . . . game**   *el partido
   de...,* 4
garage   *el garaje,* 5
garden   *el jardín,* 5
German   *el alemán,* 4
to get angry   *enojarse,* 7
to get dressed   *vestirse (i),* 7
to get off a plane   *desembarcar,* 10
to get someone for a telephone call,
   pasártelo(la), 8
to get together   *reunirse,* 9
to get up   *levantarse,* 7
to get   *conseguir (i),* 10
gift   *el regalo,* 9; **gift card**   *la tarjeta
   regalo,* 8
girl   *la muchacha,* 1
girl's fifteenth birthday   *la
   quinceañera,* 9

to give *dar*, 7; **don't give** *no des*, 7
glass *el vaso*, 6
glasses *los lentes*, 5; **to wear glasses** *usar lentes*, 5
go *ve*, 6
to go *ir*, 2; **Where did you go?** *¿Adónde fuiste?*, 8; **to go shopping** *ir de compras*, 2; **to go to the movies** *ir al cine*, 3; **to go hiking** *ir de excursión*, 10; **don't go** *no vayas*, 7; **I want to go . . .** *Quiero ir...*, 3; **Are you going to the . . .?** *¿Vas a...?*, 4; **You're going to go, aren't you?** *Vas a ir, ¿verdad?*, 4
to go back *regresar*, 4; *volver (ue)*, 5
to go for a walk *pasear*, 3
go out *sal*, 6
to go out *salir*, 3; **to go out with friends** *salir con amigos*, 3; **to go out in a sailboat (motorboat)** *pasear en bote de vela (lancha)*, 10
to go to bed *acostarse (ue)*, 7
good *bueno(a)*, 2; **Good evening., Good night.** *Buenas noches.*, 1; **Good afternoon.** *Buenas tardes.*, 1; **Good morning.** *Buenos días.*, 1
good-looking *guapo(a)*, 2
Goodbye. *Adiós.*, 1
graduation *la graduación*, 9
grandchildren *los nietos*, 5
granddaughter *la nieta*, 5
grandfather *el abuelo*, 5
grandmother *la abuela*, 5
grandparents *los abuelos*, 5
grandson *el nieto*, 5
grandsons, grandchildren *los nietos*, 5
grass *el césped*, 5; **to cut the grass** *cortar el césped*, 5
gravy *salsa*, 6
gray *gris*, 8
gray-haired *canoso(a)*, 5
great *formidable*, 2; *estupendo(a)*, 10; *a todo dar*, 10; **It was great.** *Fue estupendo.*, 10
green *verde*, 5
greeting card *la tarjeta*, 8
guest *el (la) invitado(a)*, 9
guitar *la guitarra*, 2
gym *el gimnasio*, 3

H

hair *el pelo*, 5; **to comb your hair** *peinarse*, 7; **hair dryer** *la secadora de pelo*, 7
half *medio*, 1; **half past** *y media*, 1
ham *el jamón*, 6
hamburger *la hamburguesa*, 2
hand *la mano*, 7
hang *colgar (ue)*, 9
Hanukkah *el Hanukah*, 9
happy *contento(a)*, 7; **to be happy**

estar contento(a), 7
Happy (Merry) . . . *¡Feliz...!*, 9
hard *difícil*, 4
hard-working *trabajador(a)*, 2
hat *el sombrero*, 8
to have *tener (-go, ie)*, 4; **have** *ten*, 6; **don't have** *no tengas*, 10; **to have a cold** *tener catarro*, 7; **to have a milkshake** *tomar un batido*, 8; **to have a picnic** *tener un picnic*, 9; **to have blue eyes** *tener los ojos azules*, 5; **to have to do something** *tener que + infinitive*, 4; **I always have to . . .** *A mí siempre me toca...*, 5; **to have a party** *hacer una fiesta*, 9; **to have a snack** *merendar*, 5; **to have lunch** *almorzar*, 5
he *él*, 1; **He is . . .** *Él es...*, 1
head *la cabeza*, 7
health *la salud*, 7
heat *el calor*, 3
to heat *calentar (ie)*, 6
Hello. *Aló.; Bueno.; Diga.*, 8
help *la ayuda*, 6; **to help out at home** *ayudar en casa*, 5
hi, hello *hola*, 1
hike *la excursión*, 10; **to go on a hike** *ir de excursión*, 10
his *su(s)*, 5
history *la historia*, 4
hobby *el pasatiempo*, 7; **to look for a hobby** *buscar un pasatiempo*, 7
holiday *el día festivo*, 9
Holy Week *la Semana Santa*, 9
homework *la tarea*, 3
Hope things go well for you. *Que te vaya bien.*, 9
horrible *horrible*, 2; **It was horrible!** *¡Fue horrible!*, 10
horror *el terror*, 2
hot *caliente*, 6; **hot sauce** *la salsa picante*, 6
hot chocolate *el chocolate*, 6
hotel *el hotel*, 10; **to stay in a hotel** *quedarse en un hotel*, 10
hour *la hora*, 1
house *casa*, 5; **. . .'s house** *la casa de...*, 3; **to decorate the house** *decorar la casa*, 9
household chores *los quehaceres*, 5
how *¿cómo?*, 1; **How about (if) . . .?** *¿Qué tal si...?*, 6; **How are you?** *¿Cómo está(s)?*, 1; **How do you spell . . .?** *¿Cómo se escribe...?*, 1; **How does it fit?** *¿Cómo me queda?*, 8; **How fantastic!** *¡Qué fantástico!*, 10; **How great!** *¡Qué bien!*, 10; **How many . . .?** *¿cuántos(as)?*, 2; **how much?** *¿cuánto(a)?*, 4; **How often do you go . . .?** *¿Con qué frecuencia vas...?*, 3; **How old are you?** *¿Cuántos años tienes?*, 2

hunger *el hambre*, 4
hungry, to be *tener hambre*, 4
to hurt *doler (ue)*, 7; **My . . . hurt(s)** *Me duele(n)...*, 7; **Does something hurt?** *¿Te duele algo?*, 7; **His (Her) . . . hurts.** *Le duele...*, 7

ID *carnet de identidad*, 10
I *yo*, 1
I agree. *Estoy de acuerdo*, 6; **I don't agree.** *No estoy de acuerdo.*, 6
I have no idea. *Ni idea.*, 3
I have to go. *Tengo que irme.*, 1
I want to see . . . *Quiero conocer...*, 10
I would like . . . *Quisiera...*, 6
I'd like you to meet . . . *Te presento a...*, 9
I'll get him (her). *Ya te lo (la) paso.*, 8
I'm fine. *Estoy bien.*, 1
I'm sorry *lo siento*, 8
I'm . . . *Soy...*, 2; **I'm from** *Soy de...*, 1
I'm just looking. *Nada más estoy mirando.*, 8
I'm not so good. *Estoy mal.*, 1
ice cream *el helado*, 2
ice cream shop *la heladería*, 8
Independence Day *El Día de la Independencia*, 9
in front of *delante de*, 5
in the (latest) fashion *a la (última) moda*, 8
in, by *por*, 4
inexpensive *barato(a)*, 8
intellectual *intelectual*, 2
intelligent *inteligente*, 2
interest *el interés*, 10
interesting *interesante*, 2
to interrupt *interrumpir*, 4
to introduce *presentar*, 9
invitation *la invitación*, 9
to invite *invitar*, 9
island *la isla*, 10
it *lo, la*, 6
It seems unfair to me. *Me parece injusto.*, 5
it snows *nieva*, 3
It's (a little) salty. *Está (un poco) salado*, 6
It's a rip-off! *¡Es un robo!*, 8
It's all right with me. *Me parece bien.*, 5
It's all the same to me. *Me da igual.*, 2
It's awful. *Es pésimo.*, 2
It's cold. *Hace frío.*, 3
It's cool. *Hace fresco.*, 3
It's delicious. *Es delicioso.*, 2
It's hot. *Hace calor.*, 3
It's kind of fun. *Es algo divertido.*, 2
It's not a big deal. *No es gran cosa*, 5
It's okay. *Está bien.*, 3

It's quite good/bad. *Es bastante bueno(a)/malo(a).*, 2
It's sunny. *Hace sol.*, 3
It's windy. *Hace viento.*, 3

jacket *la chaqueta*, 8; *el saco*, 8
January *enero*, 1
jeans *los vaqueros*, 8
jewelry store *la joyería*, 8
job *el trabajo*, 3
joke *el chiste*, 9; **to tell jokes** *contar (ue) chistes*, 9
juice *el jugo*, 6
July *julio*, 1
June *junio*, 1
to just (have done something) *acabar de*, 7

kitchen *la cocina*, 5
knife *el cuchillo*, 6
to know (facts) *saber*, 4; **I don't know.** *No sé.*, 4; **to know people** *conocer*, 9

lake *el lago*, 10
large *grande*, 6
last *pasado(a)*, 8; **last night** *anoche*, 9
late *tarde*, 4; **later** *más tarde*, 8; **latest** *último(a)*, 8
lazy *perezoso(a)*, 2
to leave *irse*, 10; *dejar*, 10; *salir*, 3; **leave** *sal*, 6; **to leave a message** *dejar un recado*, 8; **don't leave** *no salgas*, 10
leg *la pierna*, 7
letter *la carta*, 3
library *la biblioteca*, 4
lift *levantar*, 7; **to lift weights** *levantar pesas*, 7
to like *gustar*, 2; **I (you, . . .) like** *Me (te, . . .) gusta(n)*, 2; **I would like . . . ,** *Me gustaría . . .*, 10; **He (She) likes . . .** *Le gusta . . .*, 3; **My friends and I like . . .** *A mis amigos y a mí nos gusta . . .*, 3; **They like . . .** *A ellos/ellas les gusta . . .*, 3
Likewise. *Igualmente.*, 1
line *la cola*, 10; **to wait in line** *hacer cola*, 10
to listen *escuchar*, 3; **to listen to music** *escuchar música*, 3
little (adv.) *poco*, 2; **a little** *un poco*, 2
live *vivir*, 5
living room *la sala*, 5
long *largo(a)*, 5; **Long time no see.** *¡Tanto tiempo sin verte!*, 9

to look *mirar*, 8
to look for *buscar*, 7
to lose weight *bajar de peso*, 7
to lose *perder (ie)*, 10
luck *la suerte*, 10
luggage *el equipaje*, 10
lunch *el almuerzo*, 4; *la comida*, 6; **to have lunch** *almorzar (ue)*, 5

ma'am; Mrs. *la señora*, 1
magazine *la revista*, 3
mail *el correo*, 7
to make *hacer*, 4; **make** *haz*, 6; **to make the bed** *hacer la cama*, 5
makeup *el maquillaje*, 7
mall *el centro comercial*, 3
man *el hombre*, 6; **for men** *para hombres*, 8
many *muchos (as)*, 4
map *el mapa*, 10
March *marzo*, 1
Mass *la misa*, 9
mathematics *las matemáticas*, 4
May *mayo*, 1
me *mí*, 5; *me*, 9
meat *la carne*, 6
to meet *encontrarse (ue)*, 10
meeting *la reunión*, 3
Merry . . . *¡Feliz . . . !*, 9
message *el recado*, 8
microwave *el microondas*, 6
midday, noon *el mediodía*, 1
midnight *la medianoche*, 1
milk *la leche*, 6
milkshake *el batido*, 8
million *un millón de*, 8
mischievous *travieso(a)*, 5
Miss *la señorita*, 1
to miss *perder (ie)*, 10
mix *mezclar*, 6
mom *la mamá*, 5
moment *un momento*, 8
Monday *lunes*, 3; **on Mondays** *los lunes*, 3
money *el dinero*, 8
money exchange *la oficina de cambio*, 10
monitor, screen *la pantalla*, 10
months of the year *los meses del año*, 1
month *mes*, 1
more *más*, 2; **more than** *más que*, 8; **more . . . than** *más . . . que*, 8
morning *la mañana*, 1; **in the morning**, A.M. *de la mañana*, 1; *por la mañana*, 4
mother *la madre*, 5; **Mother's Day** *El Día de la Madre*, 9
motorboat *la lancha*, 10; **to go out**

in a motorboat *pasear en lancha*, 10
mountain *la montaña*, 10
mouth *la boca*, 7
movie *la película*, 2
movie theater *el cine*, 3
museum *el museo*, 10
music *la música*, 2; **music by . . .** *la música de*, 2
my *mi(s)*, 1; **my best friend** *mi mejor amigo(a)*, 1; **my favorite subject** *mi materia preferida*, 4; **my teacher** *mi profesor(-a)*, 1
mystery *el misterio*, 2

napkin *la servilleta*, 6
neck *el cuello*, 7
to need *necesitar*, 4
neither, not either *tampoco*, 5; *ni*, 7
nephew *el sobrino*, 5
nervous *nervioso(a)*, 7; **to be nervous** *estar nervioso(a)*, 7
never *nunca*, 5; **almost never** *casi nunca*, 3
New Year's Eve *la Nochevieja*, 9
next *próximo(a)*, 4; **next to** *al lado de*, 5
nice *simpático(a)*, 2; **Nice to meet you.** *Encantado(a)*, 1; *Mucho gusto.*, 1
niece *la sobrina*, 5
night *la noche*, 1; **at night**, P.M. *de la noche*, 1; *por la noche*, 4
nine *nueve*, 1
nine hundred *novecientos*, 8
nineteen *diecinueve*, 1
ninety *noventa*, 2
no *no*, 3
nobody, not anybody *nadie*, 5
noon *mediodía*, 1
nor *ni*, 7
nose *la nariz*, 7
not yet *todavía no*, 10
notebook *el cuaderno*, 4
nothing *nada*, 4
novel *la novela*, 2
November *noviembre*, 1
now *ahora*, 9
nowhere *ninguna parte*, 3
number *el número*, 1

October *octubre*, 1
Of course! *¡Claro que sí!*, 4
of the *del, de la, de las, de los*, 2
of *de*, 1
office: post office *oficina de correos*, 10
often *a menudo*, 5

Oh, no! *¡Ay, no!,* 6
Okay. *Vale.,* 9
old *viejo(a),* 5
older *mayor(es),* 5
on the dot *en punto,* 1
on time *a tiempo,* 4
on top of, above *encima de,* 5
one *uno,* 1
one hundred *cien,* 2
one hundred one *ciento uno,* 8
one million *millón (de),* 8
one thousand *mil,* 8
only *sólo,* 7; *nada más,* 8
to open *abrir,* 4; **to open gifts** *abrir regalos,* 9
or *o,* 2
orange *la naranja,* 6; *anaranjado(a),* 8
to order *pedir (i),* 6
to organize *organizar,* 10
our *nuestro(a)(s),* 5
out of style *pasado(a) de moda,* 8
outgoing *extrovertido(a),* 2
oven *el horno,* 6
overcoat *el abrigo,* 8

to pack your suitcase *hacer la maleta,* 10
pain: What a pain! *¡Que lata!,* 5
pair *el par,* 8
pajamas *el piyama,* 7
pants (jeans) *los pantalones,* 7
paper *el papel,* 4
parents *los padres,* 5
park *el parque,* 3; **amusement park** *el parque de diversiones,* 10
party, to have a *hacer una fiesta,* 9; **surprise party** *la fiesta sorpresa,* 9
pass: boarding pass *la tarjeta de embarque,* 10
passenger *el pasajero, la pasajera,* 10
passport *el pasaporte,* 10
pastry *el pan dulce,* 6
patio *el patio,* 5
to pay *pagar,* 8
peach *el durazno,* 6
pen *el bolígrafo,* 4
pencil *el lápiz (pl. los lápices),* 4
person *la persona,* 2
photo *la foto,* 9; **to show photos** *enseñar fotos,* 9; **to take photos** *sacar fotos,* 10
physical education *la educación física,* 4
to pick up *recoger,* 10
picnic *el picnic,* 9
piñata *la piñata,* 9
pizza *la pizza,* 2
place *el lugar,* 10

to plan *pensar + infinitive,* 9
plane ticket *el boleto de avión,* 10
plans *los planes,* 9
plants *las plantas,* 5
plate *el plato,* 6
to play an instrument *tocar,* 3; **to play the piano** *tocar el piano,* 3
to play a game or sport *jugar (ue),* 3
to play sports *practicar deportes,* 3
please *por favor,* 6
Pleased to meet you. *Encantado(a).,* 1; *Mucho gusto.,* 1
pool *la piscina,* 3
porch *el patio,* 5
post office *la oficina de correos,* 10
potato *la papa,* 6; **potato chips** *las papitas,* 9
practice *el entrenamiento,* 3
to prefer *preferir (ie),* 6
preparations *los preparativos,* 9
to prepare *preparar,* 6
pretty *bonito(a),* 2
pretty + adjective *bastante + adjective,* 2
punch *el ponche,* 9
purple *morado(a),* 8
purse *la bolsa,* 8
to put *poner,* 4; **put** *pon,* 6; **don't put** *no pongas,* 10; **to put on makeup** *maquillarse,* 7; **to put on** *ponerse,* 7
pyramid *la pirámide,* 10

quarter past (the hour) *y cuarto,* 1
quarter to (the hour) *menos cuarto,* 4
quiet *callado(a),* 5
quite + adjective *bastante + adjective,* 2

to rain *llover (ue),* 3; **It rains a lot.** *Llueve mucho.,* 3
rather *bastante + adjective,* 2
razor *la navaja,* 7
to read *leer,* 3; **to read magazines and novels** *leer revistas y novelas,* 3
ready *listo(a),* 7; **to be ready** *estar listo(a),* 7
to receive *recibir,* 9; **to receive gifts** *recibir regalos,* 9
red *rojo(a),* 8
red-headed *pelirrojo(a),* 2
refrigerator *el refrigerador,* 6
rehearsal *el ensayo,* 3
to relax *relajarse,* 7
to rent *alquilar,* 3; **to rent videos** *alquilar videos,* 3
to rest *descansar,* 3

restaurant *el restaurante,* 6
restroom *el baño,* 5; *el servicio,* 10
to return, to go back *regresar,* 4; *volver (ue),* 5
rice *el arroz,* 6
to ride a bike *montar en bicicleta,* 3
right? *¿no?,* 4; *¿verdad?,* 4; **to be right** *tener (ie) razón,* 8
ring *el anillo,* 8
rip off *el robo,* 8
romance book *el libro de amor,* 2
romantic *romántico(a),* 2
room *el cuarto,* 5
ruins *las ruinas,* 10
rule *la regla,* 4
to run *correr,* 3

sad *triste,* 7; **to be sad** *estar triste,* 7
sailboat *el bote de vela,* 10; **to go out in a sailboat** *pasear en bote de vela,* 10
salad *la ensalada,* 6
salesclerk *el dependiente, la dependienta,* 8
salty *salado(a),* 6; **It's (a little) salty.** *Está (un poco) salado(a).,* 6
same as usual *lo de siempre,* 9
sandals *las sandalias,* 8
sandwich *el sándwich,* 6
Saturday *el sábado,* 1; **on Saturdays** *los sábados,* 3
sauce, gravy *la salsa,* 6; **hot sauce** *la salsa picante,* 6
to save: to save money *ahorrar dinero,* 8
school *el colegio,* 3
school supplies *los útiles escolares,* 4
science *las ciencias,* 4; **science fiction** *la ciencia ficción,* 2; **computer science** *la computación,* 4
security checkpoint *el control de seguridad,* 10
to see *ver,* 4; **See you tomorrow.** *Hasta mañana.,* 1; **See you.** *Nos vemos.,* 1
to seem *parecer,* 5
to sell *vender,* 8
to send *mandar,* 9
September *septiembre,* 1
serious *serio(a),* 2
to serve *servir (i),* 6
to set *poner (-go),* 6; **to set the table** *poner la mesa,* 6
seven *siete,* 1
seven hundred *setecientos,* 8
seventeen *diecisiete,* 1
seventy *setenta,* 2
to shave *afeitarse,* 7

shirt *la camisa*, 8
shoe store *la zapatería*, 8
shoes *los zapatos*, 4; **tennis shoes** *los zapatos de tenis*, 8
shop window *la vitrina*, 8; **to window-shop** *mirar las vitrinas*, 8; **to go shopping** *ir de compras*, 2
short (height) *bajo(a)*, 2; (length) *corto(a)*, 5
shorts *los pantalones cortos*, 8
should *deber*, 6
shoulder *el hombro*, 7
to show *enseñar*, 4; **to show photos** *enseñar fotos*, 9
shy *tímido(a)*, 2
sick: to be sick *estar enfermo(a)*, 7
silk *la seda*, 8
silly *tonto(a)*, 2
to sing *cantar*, 3
sir, Mr. *el señor*, 1
sister *la hermana*, 5
to sit down *sentarse (ie)*, 10
six *seis*, 1
six hundred *seiscientos*, 8
sixteen *dieciséis*, 1
sixty *sesenta*, 2
size (clothing), *la talla*, 8; **shoe size**, *el número*, 8
to skate *patinar*, 3
to ski *esquiar*, 10; **to water-ski** *esquiar en el agua*, 10
skirt *la falda*, 8
to sleep *dormir (ue)*, 5; **to get enough sleep** *dormir lo suficiente*, 7
small *pequeño(a)*, 5; **pretty small** *bastante pequeño*, 5
to smoke *fumar*, 7; **to stop smoking** *dejar de fumar*, 7
to snack *merendar (ie)*, 5
to snow *nevar (ie)*, 3
so-so *más o menos*, 1
so much *tanto*, 7
soap *el jabón*, 7
soccer *el fútbol*, 3
socks *los calcetines*, 8; **a pair of socks** *un par de calcetines*, 8
sofa *el sofá*, 5
soft drink *el refresco*, 6
some *unos(as)*, 4
some day *algún día*, 10
something *algo*, 4
sometimes *a veces*, 3
son *el hijo*, 5
soup *la sopa*, 6; **vegetable soup** *la sopa de verduras*, 6
Spanish *el español*, 1
to speak *hablar*, 3
to spend time alone *pasar el rato solo(a)*, 3
to spend (money) *gastar*, 8; (time) *pasar*, 9
spicy *picante*, 6
spinach *las espinacas*, 6
spoon *la cuchara*, 6
sports *los deportes*, 2

spring *la primavera*, 3
stadium *el estadio*, 4
to start *empezar (ie)*, 5; *comenzar (ie)*, 10; **to start a trip** *comenzar un viaje*, 10
to stay in a hotel *quedarse en un hotel*, 10; **to stay in shape** *mantenerse (-go, ie) en forma*, 7
stomach *el estómago*, 7
to stop doing something *dejar de + infinitive*, 7
store *la tienda de...*, 8
story *el piso*, 5; **... story building** *el edificio de ...pisos*, 5
street *la calle*, 5
to stretch *estirarse*, 7
student *el estudiante, la estudiante*, 1
to study *estudiar*, 3
style *la moda*, 8; **in the latest style** *a la última moda* 8; **out of style** *pasado de moda*, 8
subject *la materia*, 4
suburbs *las afueras*, 5
subway *el metro*, 10
suitcase *la maleta*, 10
summer *el verano*, 3
to sunbathe *tomar el sol*, 10
Sunday *el domingo*, 1; **on Sundays** *los domingos*, 3
supplies: school supplies *los materiales escolares*, 4
to surf the Internet *navegar por Internet*, 7
surprise party *la fiesta sorpresa*, 9
sweater *el suéter*, 8
sweet *dulce*, 7
to swim *nadar*, 3
swimsuit *el traje de baño*, 8
synagogue *la sinagoga*, 9

table *la mesa*, 5
to take care of *cuidar*, 5; **to take care of oneself** *cuidarse*, 7; **Take care.** *Cuídate.*, 9
to take off *quitarse*, 7
to take out *sacar*, 6; **to take out the trash** *sacar la basura*, 5
to take *tomar*, 9; **to take a nap** *dormir (ue) la siesta*, 7; **to take photos** *sacar photos*, 10; **to take a test** *presentar un examen*, 4
to talk *hablar*, 3; *charlar*, 9
tall *alto(a)*, 2
tamales *los tamales*, 9
to taste *probar (ue)*, 6
taxi *el taxi*, 10
teacher *la profesora* (**female**), *el profesor* (**male**), 1
teeth *los dientes*, 7
telephone number *el teléfono*, 1
television *la televisión*, 3; **to watch**

TV *ver la televisión*, 3
to tell jokes *contar (ue) chistes*, 9
temple *el templo*, 9
ten *diez*, 1
tennis *el tenis*, 3; **tennis shoes** *los zapatos de tenis*, 8
test *el examen*, 4; **to take a ... test** *presentar el examen de...*, 4
Thanksgiving Day *el Día de Acción de Gracias*, 9
thank you *gracias*, 1
that *ese(a)*, 8
the *el, la, los, las*, 2
theater *el teatro*, 8
their *su(s)*, 5
them *los, las*, 6
then *luego*, 4
there *allí*, 10
there is, there are *hay*, 4
these *estos, estas*, 8
they *ellas, ellos*, 1
They like to ... *A ...les gusta...*, 3
thin *delgado(a)*, 5
thing *la cosa*, 4
to think *pensar (ie)*, 8
thirst *la sed*, 4
thirteen *trece*, 1
thirty *treinta*, 1
this *ésta, éste*, 1; **this** *este(a)*, 8; **this weekend** *este fin de semana*, 4
those *esos, esas*, 8
three *tres*, 1
three hundred *trescientos*, 8
throat *la garganta*, 7
Thursday *el jueves*, 1; **on Thursdays** *los jueves*, 3
ticket *el boleto*, 10; **plane ticket** *el boleto de avión*, 10
time *el rato*, 3
tired *cansado(a)*, 7; **to be tired** *estar cansado*, 7
to/for me *me*, 2; **you** *te*, 2; **us** *nos*, 2; **him, her, you, them** *le(s)*, 2
toast *el pan tostado*, 6
today *hoy*, 1
tomato *el tomate*, 6
tomorrow *mañana*, 4
ton: a ton of *un montón de*, 4
too much *demasiado(a)*, 7
toothbrush *el cepillo de dientes*, 7
toothpaste *la pasta de dientes*, 7
to tour *recorrer*, 10
towel *la toalla*, 7
town *el pueblo*, 5
toy *el juguete*, 8
toy store *la juguetería*, 8
train *el tren*, 10
trash *la basura*, 5
to travel *viajar*, 10
trip *el viaje*, 10
to try, taste *probar (ue)*, 6
T-shirt *la camiseta*, 8
Tuesday *el martes*, 1; **on Tuesdays** *los martes*, 3

tuna   *el atún*, 6
turnover-like pastry   *la empanada*, 9
twelve   *doce*, 1
twenty   *veinte*, 1
two   *dos*, 1
two hundred   *doscientos*, 8
two thousand   *dos mil*, 8

ugly   *feo(a)*, 2
uncle   *el tío*, 5
under, underneath   *debajo (de)*, 5
to understand   *entender*, 5
unfair   *injusto*, 5
unfriendly   *antipático(a)*, 2
until   *hasta*, 5; **See you later.**   *Hasta luego.*, 1; **See you tomorrow.** *Hasta mañana.*, 1; **See you soon.** *Hasta pronto.*, 1
up to   *hasta*, 5
us   *nos*, 2; *nosotros(as)*, 3
usual: the usual   *lo de siempre*, 9

vacation   *las vacaciones*, 10
to vacuum   *pasar la aspiradora*, 5
vacuum cleaner   *la aspiradora*, 4
Valentine's Day   *el Día de los Enamorados*, 9
vegetables   *las verduras*, 2
very   *muy + adjective*, 2
very bad   *pésimo(a)*, 2
video   *el video*, 3
video games   *los videojuegos*, 2
village   *el pueblo*, 5
volleyball   *el volibol*, 3

to wait   *esperar*, 8
waiting room   *la sala de espera*, 10
to wake   *despertarse (ie)*, 7
to walk   *caminar*, 7; **to go for a walk** *pasear*, 3
wallet   *la billetera*, 10
to want   *querer (ie)*, 3
to wash   *lavar*, 5; *lavarse*, 7
watch, clock   *el reloj*, 4
to watch   *ver*, 4; **to watch television** *ver televisión*, 3
water   *el agua (f.)*, 6; **to water ski** *esquiar en el agua*, 10
we   *nosotros(as)*, 1
to wear   *llevar*, 8; **to wear glasses** *usar lentes*, 5

weather   *el tiempo*, 3; **The weather is nice (bad).**   *Hace buen (mal) tiempo.*, 3
wedding   *la boda*, 9
Wednesday   *el miércoles*, 1; **on Wednesdays**   *los miércoles*, 3
week   *la semana*, 4
weekend   *el fin de semana*, 3; **weekends**   *los fines de semana*, 3
weight   *el peso*, 7; **to gain weight** *subir de peso*, 7; **to lose weight** *bajar de peso*, 7
weights   *las pesas*, 7; **to lift weights** *levantar pesas*, 7
What?   *¿Cómo?, ¿Qué?*, 1; **What a pain!**   *¡Qué lata!*, 5; **What a shame!**   *¡Qué lástima!*, 10; **What are you going to do?**   *¿Qué vas a hacer?*, 7; **What bad luck!**   *¡Qué mala suerte!*, 10; **What fun!**   *¡Qué divertido!*, 10; **What are you like?** *¿Cómo eres?*, 2; **What day is today?** *¿Qué día es hoy?*, 1; **What did you do?**   *¿Qué hiciste?*, 8; **What do you do to help out at home?**   *¿Qué haces para ayudar en casa?*, 5; **What do you do to relax?**   *¿Qué haces para relajarte?*, 7; **What do you have to do?**   *¿Qué tienes que hacer?*, 7; **What do you like to do?** *¿Qué te gusta hacer?*, 3; **What do you still have to do?**   *¿Qué te falta hacer?*, 7; **What do you want to do?**   *¿Qué quieres hacer?*, 3; **What does ... do?**   *¿Qué hace...?*, 3; **What is ... like?**   *¿Cómo es...?*, 2; **What plans do you have for ...?** *¿Qué planes tienen para...?*, 9; **What time are you going to...?** *¿A qué hora vas a...?*, 4; **What time is it?**   *¿Qué hora es?*, 3; **What is ...'s e-mail address?**   *¿Cuál es el correo electrónico de...?*, 1; **What's ... telephone number?**   *¿Cuál es el teléfono de...?*, 1; **what?, which?** *¿cuál?*, 4; **What's his (her, your) name?**   *¿Cómo se llama?*, 1; **What's new?**   *¿Qué hay de nuevo?*, 9; **What's the matter with ...?** *¿Qué tiene...?*, 7; **What's the weather like?**   *¿Qué tiempo hace?*, 3; **What's today's date?**   *¿Qué fecha es hoy?*, 1; **What's wrong with you?**   *¿Qué te pasa?*, 7; **What's your name?**   *¿Cómo te llamas?*, 1
wheelchair   *la silla de ruedas*, 5; **to be in a wheelchair**   *estar en una silla de ruedas*, 5
when   *cuando*, 3
when?   *¿cuándo?*, 2
Where did you go?   *¿Adónde fuiste?*, 8

where?   *¿dónde?*, 5; **Where can I ...?** *¿Dónde se puede...?*, 10; **Where do you go?**   *¿Adónde vas?*, 3; **Where did you go?**   *¿Adónde fuiste?*, 8; **from where**   *de dónde*, 1
white   *blanco(a)*, 8
whole   *todo(a)*, 9
Who's calling?   *¿De parte de quién?*, 8
Who is ...?   *¿Quién es...?*, 1
why   *¿por que?*, 2
window   *la ventana*, 5; **to window-shop**   *mirar las vitrinas*, 8
winter   *el invierno*, 3
to wish for   *desear*, 6
with   *con*, 3
with me   *conmigo*, 3
with you   *contigo*, 3
witty   *gracioso(a)*, 2
woman   *la mujer*, 5
wool   *la lana*, 8; **made of wool**   *de lana*, 8
work   *trabajar*, 3; *el trabajo*, 4
to work out   *entrenar(se)*, 7
workshop   *el taller*, 4
to worry   *preocuparse*, 10; **Don't worry.**   *No te preocupes.*, 10
worse   *peor(es)*, 8
to write   *escribir*, 1; **How do you spell ...?**   *¿Cómo se escribe...?*, 1; **It's spelled ...**   *Se escribe*, 1

yard   *el patio*, 5
year   *el año*, 2; **New Year**   *el Año Nuevo*, 9; **last year** *el año pasado*, 9
yellow   *amarillo(a)*, 8
yes   *sí*, 4; **Yes, I need a lot of things.** *Sí, necesito muchas cosas.*, 4; **Yes, I have a ton of them.**   *Sí, tengo un montón.*, 4
yesterday   *ayer*, 8
yoga: to do yoga   *hacer yoga*, 7
you   *usted, ustedes* (formal), 1; *tú, vosotros(as)* (informal), 1; **You were lucky!**   *Ah, ¡tuviste suerte!*, 10
young   *joven*, 5
young people   *los jóvenes*, 9
younger   *menor(es)*, 5
your   *tu(s), su(s), vuestro(a)(s)*, 5

zero   *cero*, 1
zoo   *el zoológico*, 10

Índice gramatical

Page numbers in boldface type refer to the first presentation of the topic. Other page numbers refer to grammar structures presented in the **¡Exprésate!** features, subsequent references to the topic, or reviewed in **Repaso de Gramática.** Page numbers beginning with R refer to the **Síntesis gramatical** in this Reference Section (pages R15–R22).

a: for clarification **70,** 102; with pronouns **102,** 130; after **ir** or **jugar 116;** combined with **el** to form **al 116;** with time **150,** 176; with **empezar: 196;** with infinitives **160,** 176, 196
abrir: 162
accent marks: **26,** 38
adjectives: function of **54,** 84; agreement with nouns–masculine and feminine **56,** 84, R16; singular and plural **56,** 84, R16; placement **146;** possessive adjectives all forms **192,** 222, R16
adónde: 116, R18; see also question words
adverbs: adverbs of frequency **112,** R18; adverbs of sequence **144;** adverbs of time **20**
agreement: nouns and adjectives **56,** 84, 192, R16; nouns and definite articles **68,** 84, R16; nouns and indefinite articles **146,** R15; nouns and possessive adjectives **192,** R16; see also adjectives
al: 116
almorzar: 194, R24; all present tense forms **222**
-ar verbs: regular present tense **114,** 130, 194, R18; see also verbs
articles: definite **el, la, los, las 68,** 70, 160; indefinite **un, una, unos, unas 146,** 176
asistir: 162

beber: 162

calendar expressions: dates, days of the week, months **21**
comer: 100, 114; all present tense forms **162,** 176, 194
cómo: 58, 84, R17; see also question words
con: with pronouns **102,** 130; see also prepositions
conjunctions: **porque 70**
conmigo, contigo: 102
contractions: **al 116,** R15; **del 72,** 116, R15
correr: 162
cuál: 19, 23, 58, R17; see also question words
cuándo: 58, 84, R17; see also question words
cuánto: agreement with nouns **146,** 176, R17; see also question words

dates (calendar): **21**

days of the week: **21,** 160
de: used in showing possession or ownership **72,** 84, 192; to indicate a type of thing **72,** 143; to say where someone is from 12, **72;** with **el 72;** with pronouns **102;** used as a preposition 102, 130, **164;** with **salir** and **saber 164; de +** person **192;** see also prepositions
definite articles: **el, la, los, las 68,** 70, 84, 160
del: contraction of **de + el 72,** 116, R15
dormir: all present tense forms **194**

el: 68, 70; with weekdays **160;** see also definite articles
empezar: 196, 222; **empezar a +** infinitive **196;** see also verbs
en: with pronouns **102,** 130
-er verbs: regular **-er** and **-ir** all present tense forms **162,** R18; affirmative and negative command forms R21; see also verbs
escribir: all present tense forms **162,** 176, 194
estar: all present tense forms **206,** 222; to ask how someone is and say how you are 8, **58,** 206; to tell where people and things are located **206;** with prepositions **206,** 222

frequency: adverbs of frequency **siempre 112; nunca, todos los días 112; casi nunca 112; a veces 112,** R18
future plans: expressions in the present tense **ir a +** infinitive **160,** 176

gender: adjectives: **56,** 84, R16; nouns: **56,** 68, 84, R15
gustar: likes and dislikes **70,** 84, 208, 210, R20; all present tense forms **70;** with infinitives **100,** 130; with **a +** pronouns **102**

hablar: 114; all present tense forms 130, **194**
hacer: all present tense forms **164;** with weather **118,** 130, R22
hasta: 194
hay: 158, 187

subjects in sentences: **12,** 38
subject pronouns: 12, **14,** 38, 102, 114, 150, R16; see also
   pronouns

tag questions: **¿no?, ¿verdad? 158,** 162, 176
tampoco: 208
te: indirect object pronoun 63, 70, 102, 210, R16; see also
   pronouns
tener: present tense all forms **148,** 176, 196; with age 52,
   148; idioms: **tener ganas de, tener prisa, tener hambre,**
   tener sed, tener que + infinitive **148;** see also verbs
tilde (~): 26
time: adverbs of, **de la mañana, de la tarde, de la noche 20;**
   at what time **150;** telling time **20,** R22; see also adverbs
tocar: all present tense forms **210,** 222
traer: all present tense forms **164**
tú and **usted** contrasted **14,** 38; see also subject pronouns

u→ue stem-changing verbs: **jugar 116,** 194, R19
una, un, unos, unas: 146, 176, R15
ustedes and **vosotros** contrasted **14,** 38; see also subject
   pronouns

venir: all present tense forms **150,** 176, R18; see also verbs
ver: all present tense forms **164,** R18; see also verbs
verbs: in sentences **12,** 38; irregular verb **ser** 6, 10, 11, 12, **24,**
   38, 49, 54, 84, R21; regular **-ar** present tense forms 114,
   130, 194, R18; irregular verb **ir** all present tense forms
   116, 130, R19; **ir a** + infinitive **160,** 176; regular **-er** and **-ir**
   all present tense forms **162,** 194, R18; irregular verb **ver** all
   present tense forms **164,** R18; **e→ie** stem-changing verbs:
   196; querer 104, 130, 196, R19; **nevar 118; tener 148,** 176,
   196; **venir 150,** 176; **empezar 196; merendar 196; u→ue**
   stem-changing verbs: R19; **jugar 116,** 130, 194; **o→ue**
   stem-changing verbs: R19; **llover 118,** 194; **almorzar,**
   volver 194; dormir 194; tener 148, 176, 196; **venir 150,**
   176; **hacer 164,** 176; **poner 164,** 176; **salir 164,** 176; **traer**
   164, 176; **ver 164,** 176; **saber 164,** 176; irregular verb **estar**
   8, 58, **206,** R21; **e→i** stem-changing verbs R19; verbs
   followed by infinitives; **gustar** 100, 104, 130; **querer** 104,
   130; **empezar 196; tocar** 210

weather: with **hacer 118,** R22; see also **hacer**

Agradecimientos

STAFF CREDITS

Editorial
Priscilla Blanton, Barbara Kristof, Amber P. Nichols, Douglas Ward

Editorial Development Team
Marion Bermondy, Konstanze Alex Brown, Lynda Cortez, Janet Welsh Crossley, Jean Miller, Beatriz Malo Pojman, Paul Provence, Jaishree Venkatesan, J. Elisabeth Wright

Editorial Staff
Sara Anbari, Hubert W. Bays, Yamilé Dewailly, Milagros Escamilla, Rebecca Jordan, Rita Ricardo, Glenna Scott, Géraldine Touzeau-Patrick

Editorial Permissions
Ann B. Farrar, Yuri Muñoz

Design
Book Design
Kay Selke, Marta Kimball, José Garza, Sally Bess, Liann Lech, Lana Cox

Image Acquisitions
Curtis Riker, Jeannie Taylor, Cindy Verheyden, Michelle Dike, Sam Dudgeon, Victoria Smith

Media Design
Richard Metzger, Chris Smith

Cover Design
Marc Cooper, Kay Selke

eMedia
Edwin Blake, Kimberly Cammerata, Grant Davidson, Nina Degollado, Lydia Doty, Cathy Kuhles, Jamie Lane, Sean McCormick, Robert Moorhead, Beth Sample, Annette Saunders, Dakota Smith, Kenneth Whiteside

Production, Manufacturing, and Inventory
Marleis Roberts, Rose Degollado, Jevara Jackson, Rhonda Fariss

ACKNOWLEDGMENTS

For permission to reprint copyrighted material, grateful acknowledgment is made to the following sources:

Agencia Literaria Carmen Balcells: From "Una antigua casa encantada" from *Mi país inventado* by Isabel Allende. Copyright © 2003 by Isabel Allende.

Children's Book Press, San Francisco, CA: "Baile en el jardín" from *In My Family/En mi familia* by Carmen Lomas Garza, translated into Spanish by Francisco X. Alarcón. Text copyright © 1996 by Carmen Lomas Garza. "Tamalada" from *Family Pictures/Cuadros de familia* by Carmen Lomas Garza, translated into Spanish by Rosalma Zubizarreta. Text copyright © 1990 by Carmen Lomas Garza.

Dover Publications, Inc.: From "El fracaso matemático de Pepito" from First Spanish Reader: *A Beginner's Dual-Language Book,* edited by Ángel Flores. Copyright © 1988 by Ángel Flores.

Editorial Fundación Ross: "Dos buenas piernas tenemos..." and "Siempre quietas,..." from *Adivinanzas para mirar en el espejo* by Carlos Silveyra. Copyright © 1985 by Editorial Fundación Ross.

Editorial Sudamericana S.A.: "2" and "16" from *Los rimaqué* by Ruth Kaufman. Copyright © 2002 by Editorial Sudamericana S.A.

Museum of New Mexico Press: "Los cuatro elementos" from Cuentos: *Tales from the Hispanic Southwest,* selected and adapted in Spanish by José Griego y Maestas. Copyright © 1980 by Museum of New Mexico Press.

PHOTOGRAPHY CREDITS

Abbreviations used: c-center, b-bottom, t-top, l-left, r-right, bkgd-background. Others indicate image label.

FRONT COVER: (tl) ©Royalty-Free/CORBIS; (tr) © Kelly-Mooney Photography/CORBIS; (bl) © Erwin and Peggy Bauer; (br) Don Couch/HRW. BACK COVER: Gary Russ/HRW photo.

AUTHORS: Page iii (Humbach) courtesy Nancy Humbach; (Madrigal Velasco) courtesy Sylvia Madrigal; (Chiquito) courtesy Ana B. Chiquito; (Smith) Courtney Baker, courtesy Stuart Smith; (McMinn) Courtney Baker, courtesy John McMinn.

TABLE OF CONTENTS: Page v (br) vi (bl) Don Couch/HRW; (tr) ©Guido Alberto Rossi/Getty Images/The Image Bank; vii (br) John Langford/HRW; (cr) ©Dennis Degnan/CORBIS; viii (bl) Gary Russ/HRW; (cl) Photo Researchers; ix (br) Don Couch/HRW; (cr) ©Buddy Mays/CORBIS; x (bl) Don Couch/HRW; (cl) John Langford/HRW; xi (bl) ©Dennis Degnan/CORBIS; (br) ©Buddy Mays/CORBIS.

WHY STUDY SPANISH: Page xii (Argentina) ©Jeremy Woodhouse, Digital Vision; (Chile, Perú) Don Couch/HRW; (Costa Rica) ©Buddy Mays/CORBIS; (España, México) Corbis Images; (República Dominicana) John Langford/HRW; xiii (bl) Alvaro Ortiz/HRW; (br) Don Couch/HRW; (cl) Don Couch/HRW; (tc) John Langford/HRW; (tr) Alvaro Ortiz/HRW; xiv (b) Sam Dudgeon/HRW; (cl) ©Royalty Free/CORBIS; (cr) Edward M. Pio Roda® ©2003 CNN, an AOL Time Warner Co., All Rights Reserved; xv (br) ©Image 100 Ltd; (c) Alvaro Ortiz/HRW.

IN SPANISH CLASS: Page xvi (cr) ©Brand X Pictures; COMMON NAMES: Page xvii (bkgd) Alvaro Ortiz/HRW. DIRECTIONS: Page xviii (b) Digital Image ©2006 PhotoDisc; xix (bl) Michael Newman/PhotoEdit; (br) Digital Image ©2006 Artville; (tc) Gabe Palmer/CORBIS; (tr) Sam Dudgeon/HRW. TIPS: Page xx (bc) Alvaro Ortiz/HRW; (cl) ©John Burwell/FoodPix; (tr) ©Brand X Pictures; xxi (b) Digital Image ©2006 PhotoDisc; (cl) ©Royalty Free/CORBIS; (cr) Digital Image ©2006 PhotoDisc; (tl) Don Couch/HRW; (tr) John Langford/HRW.

CHAPTER 1 All photos by Don Couch/HRW except: Page xxii (bc) Steve Vidler/SuperStock; (c) ©Guido Alberto Rossi/Getty Images/The Image Bank; (tr) ©Robert Frerck/Getty Images; 1 (bc) ©Nik Wheeler/CORBIS; (cr) ©Larry Lee Photography/CORBIS; (tr) ©Stephen Saks/Lonely Planet

Images; 2 (bl) ©Brand X Pictures; (br) Alvaro Ortiz/HRW; (cr) ©Chip & Rosa María de la Cueva Peterson; (tl) ©Robert Frerck/Odyssey Productions; (tr) Digital Image ©2006 PhotoDisc; 3 (bl) ©Christie's Images/CORBIS; (br) ©James A. Sugar/CORBIS; (cl) ©Robert Frerck/Getty Images/Stone; (cr) ©Chip & Rosa María de la Cueva Peterson; (tl) Zefa Visual Media - Germany/Index Stock Imagery; 4–5 (spread) Alvaro Ortiz/HRW; 6 (icon) HRW Photo; (l) Alvaro Ortiz/HRW; 7, 8, 10 (All) Alvaro Ortiz/HRW; 11 (1) Christine Galida/HRW; (2) ©David H. Wells/CORBIS; (3, 4, Carolina) Marty Granger/Edge Video Productions/HRW; (5) Peter Van Steen/HRW; 12 (tr) Alvaro Ortiz/HRW; 13 (1, 4) Digital Image ©2006 PhotoDisc; (2) ©Digital Vision; (3) Marty Granger/Edge Video Productions/HRW; 14 (bl) ©Pixtal; 15 (A, F) Victoria Smith/HRW; (B) Peter Van Steen/HRW; (C) ©Comstock; (D) ©Digital Vision; (E) ©BananaStock; 17 (br) Martha Granger/Edge Video Productions/HRW; 18 (all numbers) Victoria Smith/HRW; 22 (a, b, e, h, m, p, q, z) Corbis Images; (c, ch, f, i, k, l, ll, n, o, r, rr, t, u, w) Digital Image ©2006 PhotoDisc; (g, ñ, s, v) Sam Dudgeon/HRW; (j) ©Royalty Free/CORBIS; (x, y) Victoria Smith/HRW; 24 (bl) Victoria Smith/HRW; 25 (Ana) ©Alison Wright/CORBIS; (Juan) Mark Antman/HRW; (Lupe, Ricardo) Marty Granger/Edge Video Productions/HRW; 28 (br) ©Robert Frerck/Odyssey/Chicago; 32 (2) ©A. Parada/Alamy Photos; (3) Sam Dudgeon/HRW; 34 (bc) Victoria Smith/HRW; (br) Corbis Images; (cr) Digital Image ©2006 PhotoDisc; 36 (1) ©Jimmy Dorantes/Latin Focus; 40 (tc - boy, tr) Victoria Smith/HRW; (tc - girl, tl) Dennis Fagan/HRW.

CHAPTER 2 All photos by John Langford/HRW except: Page 42 (c) ©Andrea Pistolesi/Getty Images/The Image Bank; (tr) ©Mark Bacon-Latin Focus; 43 (bl) ©Mark Bacon/Alamy Photos; (cr) ©Kevin Schafer/CORBIS; (tl) ©Steve Fitzpatrick/Latin Focus; (tr) ©Steve Bly/Getty Images/The Image Bank; 44 (bl) ©Christie's Images Inc., 1999; (cr) Victoria Smith/HRW; 45 (bc) Ricardo Alcaraz; (bl) ©Dennis Degnan/CORBIS; (cr) ©Michael Friang/Alamy Photos; (tl) Tony Arruza; (tr) ©Robert Fried/Robert Fried Photography; 49 (alta, atlética, baja) Victoria Smith/HRW; 50 (1, 2, 4) Victoria Smith/HRW; (3) Sam Dudgeon/HRW; (tl) Randal Alhadeff/HRW; 55 (cl) ©John Kelly/Getty Images/The Image Bank; (cr, l, r) Victoria Smith/HRW; 58 (bl) Victoria Smith/HRW; 61 (br) Martha Granger/Edge Video Productions/HRW; (tl) Don Couch/HRW; 62 (ajedrez) Digital Image ©2006 PhotoDisc; (CD, mexicana, pizza) Victoria Smith/HRW; (china) Sam Dudgeon/HRW; (helado, italiana) Corbis Images; (icon) Don Couch/HRW; 63 (animales) Digital Image ©2006 PhotoDisc; (carros, deportes, fiestas, frutas, hamburguesas, verduras, videojuegos) Victoria Smith/HRW; 64 (A, B) Sam Dudgeon/HRW; (C) Victoria Smith/HRW; (D) Scott Vallance/VIP Photo/HRW; 69 (1–6) Victoria Smith/HRW; (7, 8) Digital Image ©2006 PhotoDisc; (frutas) ©Brand X Pictures; 70 (bl) Mari Biasco Photography; 71 (burritos, zebras) Corbis Images; (cake, deportes, pizza) Victoria Smith/HRW; (guitar) Digital Image ©2006 PhotoDisc; (marquee) Scott Vallance/VIP Photo/HRW; 72 (1) Corbis Images; (2, 3, 5) Victoria Smith/HRW; (4) ©Lisa Anne Auerbach/CORBIS; (6) Sam Dudgeon/HRW; (animales) Digital Image ©2006 PhotoDisc; 75 (All) Martha Granger/Edge Video Productions/HRW; 80 (All) Victoria Smith/HRW; 82 (1, 4, Ana, Eva, Luz) Victoria Smith/HRW; (2) Digital Image ©2006 PhotoDisc; (3) Corbis Images; 86 (A, C) Victoria Smith/HRW.

CHAPTER 3 All photos by Gary Russ/HRW except: Page 88 (c) ©George H. H. Huey/CORBIS; (icon) Don Couch/HRW; (tr) Sam Dudgeon/HRW; 89 (bc) ©David Muench/CORBIS; (br) Courtesy of Houston Chamber of Commerce; (tc) Corbis Images; (tr) ©D. Donne Bryant Photography; 90 (bl) ©Carmen Lomas Garza, Collection of Paula Maciel-Benecke and Norbert Benecke Aptos, California, photo credit: M. Lee Fatherree; (tl) Courtesy of the San Antonio Public Library; Photographer: Clem Spalding; 91 (bl) ©Jimmy Dorantes/Latin Focus; (br) ©Scott Teven/Photo Houston; (c) Victoria Smith/HRW; (tl) ©Dave G. Houser/CORBIS; 94 (All) Dennis Fagan/HRW; (icon) HRW Photo; 95 (básquetbol, béisbol, fútbol, fútbol americano, volibol) Peter Van Steen/HRW; (juegos) Victoria Smith/HRW; (tenis) ©Getty Images/Stone; 96 (1,) Victoria Smith/HRW; (2) 3 ©Digital Vision; (5) ©Corbis Images/PictureQuest; (6, 8) Dennis Fagan/HRW; (tr) Peter Van Steen/HRW; 99 (c) Sam Dudgeon/HRW; 101 (cl) Digital Image ©2006 PhotoDisc; (cr) ©Peter M. Fisher/CORBIS; (l) CORBIS Images; (r) Dennis Fagan/HRW; 102 (bl) Alvaro Ortiz/HRW; 103 (1-ball, 4) Digital Image ©2006 PhotoDisc; (1-racquet) Digital Image ©2006 Artville; (2) Sam Dudgeon/HRW; (3, 5, tr) Victoria Smith/HRW; 104 (tl) Marty Granger/Edge Video Productions/HRW; 105 (A, B) Corbis Images; (C) Victoria Smith/HRW; (D) Painet; (E) ©Nik Wheeler/CORBIS; 106 (tl) Scott Vallance/VIP Photo/HRW; 107 (br) David Young-Wolff/PhotoEdit; (tl) Don Couch/HRW; 108 (bailar, descansar boy, estudiar, hablar, practicar, tocar - boy, trabajar) Dennis Fagan/HRW; (descansar - lemonade) Victoria Smith/HRW; (icon) HRW Photo; (tocar - piano) Corbis Images; 109 (c, tc) ©Jimmy Dorantes/Latin Focus; (cr) ©Kevin Barry; (tl) Peter Van Steen/HRW; (tr) ©William Boyce/CORBIS; 111 (c) ©BananaStock Ltd.; (tc) ©Stockbyte; 113 (1) Spencer Grant/Photo Edit; (2) David R. Frazier Photolibrary; (3, 4, 5) Michelle Bridwell/Frontera Fotos; (6) Peter Van Steen/HRW; 114 (bl) Bob Daemmrich/The Image Works; 116 (bl) Victoria Smith/HRW; 117 (1) Sam Dudgeon/HRW; (2, 4) Victoria Smith/HRW; (3, 5, Sonia-ball) Digital Image ©2006 PhotoDisc; (Sonia-racquet) Digital Image ©2006 Artville; 118 (bl) AP Photo/The Paris News, Bill Ridder; 119 (A) Henry Bargas/AP/Wide World Photos; (B) Corbis Images; 120 (el arco) /Latin Focus; (el charango) Sam Dudgeon/HRW; (el güiro) Suzanne Murphy-Larronde; (flauta) ©Paul Rodriguez/Latin Focus; (músicos) David Simson/Stock Boston; 121 (br) ©Index Stock Imagery; (tr) Jack Kurtz; 128 (A, F) Digital Image ©2006 PhotoDisc; (B, C, D) Dennis Fagan/HRW; (E) Corbis Images; 132 (A, C) Peter Van Steen/HRW; (D) Digital Image ©2006 Artville.

CHAPTER 4 All photos by Don Couch/HRW except: Page 134 (c) ©Jimmy Dorantes/Latin Focus; (tr) ©Buddy Mays/CORBIS; 135 (bl, cr) Robin Karpan/D. Donne Bryant Photography; (cl) ©Jimmy Dorantes/Latin Focus; (tr) ©Buddy Mays/CORBIS; 136 (br) ©Dave G. Houser/CORBIS; 137 (bl, br) ©Kevin Schafer; 140 (All) Victoria Smith/HRW; (icon) HRW Photo; 142 (All Victoria Smith/HRW; 143 (r) Christine Galida/HRW; 144 (r) Marty Granger/Edge Video Productions/HRW; 147 (cr) Sam Dudgeon/HRW; 149 (bailar) ©Chuck Savage/CORBIS; (descansar) Peter Van Steen/HRW; (pesas) Victoria Smith/HRW; (tarea) ©Stockbyte; (televisión) ©Digital Vision; (trabajar) ©Royalty Free/CORBIS; 153 (br)

Sam Dudgeon/HRW; 154 (icon) HRW photo; 156 (1, 3) Digital Image ©2006 EyeWire; (10) Rubberball Productions®; (2) Corbis Images; (4, 5, 7, 8) Digital Image ©2006 PhotoDisc; (6) Peter Van Steen/HRW; (9) ©Royalty Free/CORBIS; 159 (A) ©Stockbyte; (B) ©Royalty Free/CORBIS; (C) ©Comstock; (r) Sam Dudgeon/HRW; (tr) ©Danny Lehman/CORBIS; 160 (bl) John Langford/HRW; 161 (1) Digital Image ©2006 PhotoDisc; (2, 3, 4, tc) Peter Van Steen/HRW; 174 (A) ©Chuck Savage/CORBIS; (B) Corbis Images; (C) Reuters/CORBIS; (D) Victoria Smith/HRW.

CHAPTER 5 All photos by Don Couch/HRW except: Page 180 (cl) ©Fernando Paste/Latin Focus; (tr) ©Daniel Rivadamar/Odyssey/Chicago; 181 (bl) ©Wolfgang Kaehler/CORBIS; (br) D. Donne Bryant/D. Donne Bryant Photography; (c) ©Graham Neden/Ecoscene/CORBIS; (tr) David Ryan/D. Donne Bryant Photography; 182 (bl) David Phillips/Words & Images; (tl) D. Donne Bryant Photography; 183 (bc) ©Bettmann/CORBIS; (bl) ©Conde Nast Archive/CORBIS; (br) Fundación de Santiago by Pedro Lira; (c) ©Reuters New Media Inc./CORBIS; (tl) Roberto Candia/AP/Wide World Photos; 186 (gato) John Langford/HRW; 187 (azules) ©Royalty Free/CORBIS; (café) Digital Image ©2006 PhotoDisc; (canoso) ©Image Source Ltd./Alamy Photos; (castaño) ©Rubberball Productions; (corto) Sam Dudgeon/HRW; (largo) Peter Van Steen/HRW; (negro) ©Stockbyte; (negros) ©RubberBall/Alamy Photos; (verdes) ©CORBIS; 188 (1) ©John Foxx/Alamy Photos; (2) Mark Richards/PhotoEdit; (3) ©Comstock; (4) ©plainpicture/Alamy Photos; 191 (1) Michelle Bridwell/Frontera Fotos; (2) Martha Granger/Edge Video Productions/HRW; (3) David Young-Wolff/PhotoEdit; (4) ©Comstock; 193 (tl) Victoria Smith/HRW; (tr) Peter Van Steen/HRW; 194 (bl) John Langford/HRW; 195 (a.) ©Comstock; (c.) ©Digital Vision; (cr) Digital Image ©2006 PhotoDisc; (d.) Peter Van Steen/HRW; 196 (bl) Victoria Smith/HRW; 197 (6:30) Sam Dudgeon/HRW; (8:10, 11:45, 3:00, 4:20, 7:00, 8:30) Dennis Fagan/HRW; 199 (br) The Granger Collection, New York; 203 (All) Digital Image ©2006 PhotoDisc; 206 (bl) Chris Sharp/D. Donne Bryant Photography; 208 (bc, bl, br) Victoria Smith/HRW; (cl) Alvaro Ortiz/HRW; 209 (tr) David Phillips/HRW; 210 (hermana) ©Comstock; (hermano) Dennis Fagan/HRW; (mamá y yo) Peter Van Steen/HRW; (papá) Digital Image ©2006 EyeWire; 212 (br) The Museum of Modern Art; (tr) ©Archivo Iconográfico, S.A./CORBIS; 220 (1) Victoria Smith/HRW; (2) Digital Image ©2006 PhotoDisc; (3) Dennis Fagan/HRW; (4) ©Corel; 224 (All) Dennis Fagan/HRW.

LITERATURA Y VARIEDADES: Page 228 (c, l) ©Museo Nacional Del Prado; (cr) Don Couch/HRW; 229 (bl, tr) Museo del Prado, Madrid, Spain; Erich Lessing/Art Resource, NY; (tl) Noortman, Maastricht, Netherlands/Bridgeman Art Library; 230–231 (bkgd) Digital Image 2006 PhotoDisc; 230 (bl) Wolfgang Kaehler/CORBIS; (cl) Kevin Schafer/CORBIS; 231 (cr) Doug Wechsler; (t) Michael and Patricia Fogden/CORBIS; 232 (br) Carmen Lomas Garza, Collection of Paula Maciel-Benecke and Norbert Benecke Aptos, California, photo credit: M. Lee Fatherree; 233 (t) 1995 Carmen Lomas Garza, photo credit: Adam Reich, Collection of Aaron & Marion Borenstein, Coral Gables, Florida; 234, 235 (All) Jorge Alban/HRW; 236–237 (bkgd) ©Jeremy Woodhouse, Digital Vision; 236 (cl) Book cover (Spanish edition) from La casa de los espíritus by Isabel Allende. Reprinted by permission of HarperCollins Publishers, Inc.; (cr) Book cover (Spanish edition) from Paula by Isabel Allende and trans. by Margaret Sayers Peden. 1994 by Isabel Allende. Translation 1995 by HarperCollins Publishers. Reprinted by permission of HarperCollins Publishers Inc.; 237 (tr) Marcia Lieberman Photography.

VOCABULARIO ADICIONAL: Page R7 (bc) Digital Image ©2006 PhotoDisc; (c) Sam Dudgeon/HRW; R8 (cl) Alvaro Ortiz/HRW; (cr) Don Couch/HRW; (tc) Digital Image ©2006 PhotoDisc; R9 (bl) Don Couch/HRW; (br) Alvaro Ortiz/HRW; (cr) Gary Russ/HRW; (tl) Sam Dudgeon/HRW; (tr) Gary Russ/HRW; R10 (bc) Corbis Images; (cl) ©RubberBall/Alamy Photos; (cr) Digital Image ©2006 PhotoDisc; (tl) ©Digital Vision; R11 (bl) Alvaro Ortiz/HRW; (br) ©Dennis Degnan/CORBIS; (tl) ©Buddy Mays/CORBIS.

ICONS: (Cultura) Don Couch/HRW; (Vocabulario 1) John Langford/HRW; (Vocabulario 2) Don Couch/HRW; Communicación Icon (l, c) Steve Ewert/HRW; (r) PhotoDisc/gettyimages; Conexión Icons: (Arte, Geografía, Economía doméstica, Música) PhotoDisc/gettyimages; (Ciencias naturales, Historia) ©Royalty Free/CORBIS; (Ciencias sociales) Wolfgang Kaehler Photography.

NOVELA STILL PHOTOS and GEOVISIÓN ICONS: Spain - Don Couch/HRW; Puerto Rico - John Langford/HRW; Mexico, Costa Rica, Peru, Chile - Don Couch/HRW.